GOOD GOVERNANCE
Never on India's Radar

GOOD GOVERNANCE
Never on India's Radar

MADHAV GODBOLE

RUPA

Published by
Rupa Publications India Pvt. Ltd 2014
7/16, Ansari Road, Daryaganj
New Delhi 110002

Sales centres:
Allahabad Bengaluru Chennai
Hyderabad Jaipur Kathmandu
Kolkata Mumbai

ISBN: 978-81-291-3104-1

First impression 2014

10 9 8 7 6 5 4 3 2 1

The moral right of the author has been asserted.

Typeset by RECTO Graphics, Delhi.

Printed at Replika Press Pvt. Ltd., India

For my grandchildren
ADITI, MANAN, GAAYATRI AND TAARINI
who have filled my cup of joy to the brim

CONTENTS

PREFACE

Sudhir Tailang published a devastating cartoon in *The Hindustan Times* in which Mahatma Gandhi was shown saying dejectedly, 'I hereby resign as Father of the Nation taking moral responsibility for the state of the nation.'

Since Independence 66 years ago, the Nehru-Gandhi family has held the reins of the country for over 45 years if we count the United Progressive Alliance (UPA) I and II era when Sonia Gandhi exercised all authority. It is indisputable that there has been sharp deterioration in the governance of the country in recent years. Some people believe that the UPA government is the most corrupt government since independence. While this is partly true and is partly political rhetoric, in reality it has to be accepted that India could never have passed the test of good governance at any time since Independence, even during the era of Jawaharlal Nehru's Prime Ministership. Nehru, no doubt, gave us the two most precious gifts of democracy and secularism by which the country is held together, but he did not leave behind a legacy of good governance.

There are some who believe that corruption is a recent affliction and signifies India's experiment with liberalization, economic reforms and globalization. But in reality this is far from true. Corruption had become a subject of intense debate in the Congress Party's forums and in Parliament soon after Independence. In 1963 the Committee on Prevention of Corruption was appointed under the chairmanship of K. Santhanam. The committee was given wide ranging and comprehensive terms of reference. But most of the recommendations of the committee remained on paper. A series of commissions of inquiry were appointed to probe corruption in high places. These included an inquiry against K. Karunanidhi, Chief Minister of Tamil Nadu, and Pratapsingh Kairon, Chief Minister of Punjab, Mundhra Commission of Inquiry by Justice M. C. Chagla against union Finance Minister T. T. Krishnamachari, Grover Commission of Inquiry against Devraj Urs, Chief Minister of Karnataka, Justice P. Jaganmohan Reddy Commission of Inquiry in the Nagarwala case, the Justice P. Jaganmohan Reddy Commission of Inquiry against Bansi Lal, Chief Minister of Haryana, to mention a few. These inquiries, however, did not contribute to increasing the confidence of the people in the government's commitment to eradicate corruption.

Good governance was never the proclaimed objective of any of the governments, irrespective of which political party was in power. Clearly, it was never on their radar. During the emergency, the Indira Gandhi government introduced in the

Rajya Sabha on 9 August 1975, the Constitution (Forty-First Amendment) Bill, 1975 which sought to amend Article 361 of the Constitution. According to the objects of the bill, the Prime Minister, the President of India and the governors of states would have enjoyed legal immunity for the exercise and performance of powers and duties of his/her office and for acts done or purported to be done thereby. Also, it would have extended the duration of such protection to all of them even after they quit office, with retrospective effect. The Bill was passed by the Rajya Sabha on the same day but, fortunately, it could not be taken up for consideration by the Lok Sabha and lapsed on the dissolution of the Fifth Lok Sabha.[1] Since the President of India and the governors do not enjoy any day-to-day executive powers, the amendment was, in reality, meant to give unfettered powers to the Prime Minister to make her a constitutional dictator. If the bill had been enacted, it would have meant the demise of good governance forever and would have given a free hand to the holders of these exalted offices to play havoc. There would have also been a demand to extend the same protection to chief ministers and others.

Coverage and Chapter Scheme

The subject covers a very wide canvas. Ideally, the word governance must be defined in the widest sense of the term to cover not just governance by the government and the public sector, but equally importantly also the private sector, corporate sector, cooperatives, media, NGOs and so on.[2] As a society, we must lay down the golden rule that whosoever exercises power must be accountable. Looked at from this perspective, the deterioration in governance in India is more pronounced in sectors other than the government. This is amply brought out by the numerous scandals in the corporate world, the education sector, cooperatives, media, sports, banks, financial institutions, professional bodies and so on. Public life in this country has been sullied and dirtied by all these much more than the government, which is so much in the news. I had dealt with some of these aspects in my book, *Public Accountability and Transparency: The Imperatives of Good Governance* published in 2003.[3] The sharp deterioration in economic and financial governance in the country, which is equally worrisome, has also been kept out of the purview of this book as it is vast enough to merit a separate book.

In this book, I focus attention on issues which I believe are significant for furtherance of the goal of good governance in the government and the public sector. They bring out how changes in policies could have made a marked difference to governance in the country. The book comprises six chapters. The first chapter is an introduction, which gives an overview. The second chapter, 'The Core of Good Governance', discusses the concept of good governance as understood universally. It also takes note of additional criteria which are relevant for conditions in India. The third chapter, 'The Ever Increasing Governance Deficit', brings out the sharp deterioration in governance in selected fields. The fourth chapter, 'Is There Any Evidence of Good Governance Here?', discusses six highly problematic areas of governance. Having thus stated the nature and gravity of the problems, the next two chapters deal with their possible solutions. The fifth chapter, 'If There Is a Political Will, There Is a Way Ahead', invites attention to remedial action on some major issues. The sixth chapter, 'The Strength of a Democracy Lies in Its Institutions', deals with the seven crucial areas which call for urgent action.

Some portions of the text have been italicized to invite pointed attention to contentions and issues.

Acknowledgments

I am thankful to Dev Raj and Sarabjeet Singh for their help during my research for the book in Delhi. Though it may sound too formal, I would like to express how deeply grateful I am to my wife Sujata for her constant encouragement and forbearance. But for her support and patience, it would have been impossible to complete this book. I am also beholden to my daughter Meera Godbole Krishnamurthy for going through the draft and making helpful and insightful suggestions. I am grateful to my editor, Punam Thakur, for giving a finer editorial touch to the draft and going over the manuscript with a toothcomb. I am also thankful to Ritu Vajpeyi-Mohan for her leadership in expediting the publication of the book. Finally, I am indebted to Shri R. K. Mehra and Shri Kapish Mehra of Rupa and Co. for bringing out the book so expeditiously and elegantly. Needless to say, I alone am responsible for any mistakes and deficiencies which may have remained.

Madhav Godbole
August 2013

Notes

1. Kashyap Subhash C., *History of the Parliament of India*, vol. IV, Shipra Publications, Delhi, 1997, pp. 104–05.
2. For example, the major fire in the Advanced Medicare and Research Institute (AMRI) hospital in Kolkata, owned by a leading industrial group, in December 2011 in which 87 patients and four staff members died, is a case in point. The Institute had violated several rules and overlooked the warnings by the authorities.
3. Godbole Madhav, *Public Accountability and Transparency: The Imperatives of Good Governance*, Orient Longman, New Delhi, 2003.

1

INTRODUCTION

> After attaining *Swaraj* (self rule), we need to have *Su-raj*
> (good governance)
> Mahatma Gandhi

Introduction

When Dr Rajendra Prasad, President of the Constituent Assembly, rose to move the motion for adopting the Constitution, in 1949, with great foresight, he said:

> Whatever the Constitution may or may not provide, the welfare of the country will depend upon the way in which the country is administered. That will depend upon the men who administer it. It is trite saying that a country can have only the government it deserves...If the people who are elected are capable and men of character and integrity, they would be able to make the best even of a defective Constitution. If they are lacking in these, the Constitution cannot help the country. After all, a Constitution like a machine is a lifeless thing. It acquires life because of the men who control it and operate it, and India needs today nothing more than a set of honest men who will have the interest of the country before them (Lok Sabha Secretariat 1985: 5).

Similar sentiments were expressed by B. R. Ambedkar, Chairman of the Drafting Committee of the Constitution, in his closing speech in the Constituent Assembly in November 1949:

> However good a Constitution may be, it is sure to turn out bad because those who are called to work it, happen to be a bad lot. However bad a Constitution may be, it may turn out to be good if those who are called to work it, happen to be a good lot. The working of the Constitution does not depend wholly upon the nature of the Constitution. The Constitution can provide only the organs of state such as the legislature, the executive and the judiciary. The factors on which the working of those organs of the state depend are the people and the political parties they will set up as their instruments to carry out their wishes and their politics. Who can say how the people of India and their parties will

behave?...It is, therefore, futile to pass any judgment upon the Constitution without reference to the part which the people and their parties are likely to play (Mukherjee 2007: 211).

Rhetoric and Reality

The last six decades have borne out how true these apprehensions of the founding fathers of the Constitution were. This was also amply highlighted in the Golden Jubilee Session of Parliament held in August-September 1997. The Lok Sabha created history with its longest ever sitting of about 22 hours debating issues of national importance. The Lok Sabha, which assembled at 11 am on Saturday, continued the sitting till 8.24 am on Sunday. A total of 225 members participated in the marathon debate.[1] As many as 91 members spoke during the debate, while 11 members submitted written speeches which were taken as read (*TOI*, 1 September 1997). One of the most prominent speeches was that of Speaker, P. A. Sangma, who gave a rousing call to wage a 'second freedom struggle' against corruption, poverty, disease and deprivation. Sangma was joined by leaders and members of all political parties in addressing the issues at hand firmly and with a new resolve to help change the face of the country.

In his eloquent speech on the occasion of the centenary celebrations of the Indian National Congress in Mumbai, Rajiv Gandhi, 'Mr Clean', openly and ferociously came down on the 'brokers of power and influence' within his own party. 'Riding on the backs of ordinary Congress workers, they had converted a mass movement into a feudal oligarchy,' he said. He vowed not only to eliminate these 'self-perpetuating cliques' but also to break the 'nexus' between political parties and 'vested interests'. He also brought out that corruption was not only tolerated but considered a hallmark of leadership. As Inder Malhotra wrote, 'Had these promises been kept, Rajiv would almost certainly have been remembered as perhaps the greatest political reformer. But, alas, not a single one was honoured or even mentioned again' (Malhotra 1991: 46). The same noises are being made by Rahul Gandhi, the 'prime minister in waiting'.

Needless to say, all this rhetoric and bravado remained on paper and there has been no change in the functioning of the country, except in two striking matters. First, mobile (phone service), categorized by the central government as 'lifeline infrastructure', has come to be added to the three basic necessities of life—*roti* (food), *kapada* (clothing) and *makan* (shelter). The others are the magnificent strides made by India in space and missile technology and sending a satellite to the moon. It is now working on sending a manned mission to the moon. India is also a member of the exclusive club of countries with long range ballistic missile (LRBM) capability. The spread of mobile telephony is due to the opening up of the telecommunications sector to the private sector, in spite of the Sukh Ram and

2G scams which have rocked the country. Notable advances in space and missile technology are due to the encouragement given by the government to science and technology and the initiative and dedication of scientists.

But in a large number of other areas the situation is pathetic. India continues to be described as a 'functional anarchy' and a nation of 'organized chaos'. As Soli J. Sorabjee said, 'No political term has been abused so promiscuously as "democracy"' (Sorabjee 2006: 11). G. K. Reddy, former editor of *The Hindu*, wrote that a well-known Oxford don, while participating in a discussion on BBC on the role of democracy in the newly independent countries, had 'put across the fantastic theory that democracy cannot thrive in a hot climate which is not conducive to cool thinking and calm debate on the intricacies of a parliamentary system of government' (Bhagyalaxmi 1992: 3). If this logic is to be accepted, India will have to welcome climate change!

A London School of Economics study (2012) reached the conclusion that India may never become a superpower since its achievements 'are nullified by its structural weaknesses, widespread corruption, poor leadership, extreme social divisions, religious extremism and internal security threats.' Institutional sclerosis was mostly blamed for this situation. This is not surprising since a popular website listed 93 'scams' since the United Progressive Alliance (UPA) came to power in 2004 (Balachandran 2013).

Cabinet Form of Government Only in Name

The basic requirement of any democracy is its robust Cabinet system and the observance of the principle of collective responsibility. It is pertinent to invite attention to what Jawaharlal Nehru, the then Prime Minister, had written to Balakrishna Kaul, a minister in the government of Ajmer, on 1 August 1952:

> ...The manner of work in Ajmer thus far appears to me that each minister does what he likes with his department. This is completely wrong anywhere...A ministry is a unit, not a set of individuals. Therefore, there should be full consultation at every stage in regard to every important matter. Each minister is responsible for what the other ministers do. This is what is called joint responsibility (Jawaharlal Nehru Memorial Fund 1996: 474–75).

The Government of India (Transaction of Business) Rules, 1961 lay down the cases which 'shall be brought to the Cabinet'. Rule 12 states that, 'The Prime Minister may, in any case or class of cases, permit or condone a departure from these rules to the extent he deems necessary.' It would be pertinent to cite a few important cases in which the Cabinet's approval was not taken. A permanent seat on the United Nations Security Council was offered to India in 1955 jointly by the then USSR and USA but, as stated in the *Selected Works of Jawaharlal Nehru* (Volume 29), Nehru declined the offer and said that China should have first claim on the seat. As is well known, India has been trying hard for a permanent seat on the Security Council for the last several years.[2] This decision to decline the seat, therefore, comes as a shock. It is not known if it was taken by the Cabinet or whether it was Nehru's own, out of his love for China; it is more likely to be the latter. During the periods of Indira Gandhi and Rajiv Gandhi, the Cabinet was only in name and there was hardly any discussion in the Cabinet, even on important issues. It may sound sexist but during Indira Gandhi's regime, it used to be said that she was the only man in the Cabinet. Even her senior ministers hardly ever expressed any independent opinions. As is well known, even the most serious decision to impose the emergency was taken without the approval of the Cabinet. In fact, in her letter dated 25 June 1975, to the President, she wrote, 'I shall *mention* (not seek approval) the matter to the Cabinet first thing tomorrow morning.' (Government of India 1978: 25). (I have used italics here and other places hereafter for emphasis.) And that is precisely what she did. And the 'rubber-stamp' President of India, Fakhruddin Ali Ahmed, also did not have the courage to question this major lacuna, before signing on the proclamation. During Rajiv Gandhi's term as Prime Minister, the decision to withhold the Thakkar Commission report on Indira Gandhi's assassination was taken without discussion in the Cabinet. The same was true of the notorious Defamation Bill (Limaye 1989: 166–67). I have referred elsewhere to how the approval of the Cabinet was not obtained before the Muslim Women (Protection of Rights on Divorce) Bill, 1986 was introduced in Parliament. During the tumultuous Babri Masjid agitation in the 1990s, the matter was never brought before the *full* Cabinet till after the Masjid was wantonly demolished.

All major scams during the UPA regime, namely the 2G, Commonwealth Games, Coalgate, and others seem to have happened because the concerned matters never went before the Cabinet for approval. It is not known if senior civil servants such as the Cabinet Secretary, Finance Secretary and secretaries in the concerned ministries brought this major requirement to the notice of the ministers and the Prime Minister, as the case may be.

But experience has shown that there is no certainty that issues referred to the Cabinet or Cabinet committees are decided rationally. The most outstanding example of this is the way decisions were taken on the report of the Fifth Pay Commission. The United Front Government under I. K. Gujral was in power at the time and a Cabinet committee was appointed to hold discussions with the Central Government employees' federations and associations to avert the strike which they had threatened. The Cabinet sub-committee not only agreed to all the demands of the employees but at the end of the meeting, the employees were asked whether there were any further demands which they would like to be considered! The employees were so satisfied with the bonanza which they had got, that they thanked the ministers and said that they had no further demands! This was the time when not only the very high pay-scales recommended by the Pay Commission were agreed to but in some cases they were further increased. While doing so, all the other important recommendations of the commission to progressively reduce government staff by 30 per cent and to increase the productivity of government employees were shelved! This irresponsible decision led to an increase in expenditure on salaries and pensions from rupees 48,323 crore per year in 1991–94 to rupees 1,33,381 crore in 1999–2000. The revenue deficit increased from 4.3 per cent of gross domestic product to 6.3 per cent, and the fiscal deficit from 8.3 per cent to 9.5 per cent. But the sting is in the tail! As T. S. R. Subramanian, the then Cabinet Secretary, has stated, P. Chidambaram neither objected in person to these give aways, nor participated in the deliberations in protest against the approach of the Cabinet sub-committee (Subramanian 2004: 316–20). Chidambaram, who is the Finance Minister in UPA II, did not have the courage either to speak out or to resign!

Prime Ministerial Form of Government

Jawaharlal Nehru had a small personal secretariat. The expansion of the Prime Minister's Office (PMO) and combining the post of Cabinet Secretary with Secretary to the Prime Minister had come in for considerable resistance during Lal Bahadur Shastri's time and the move had to finally be given up. But as in everything else, Indira Gandhi was more powerful. One manifestation of this was the powerful PMO and the Prime Minister's House (PMH) with its 'palace guards' which became more visible and assertive, thereby undermining the role of the Cabinet Secretariat, ministries and the line bureaucracy. In fact, the PMO functioned as a government within a government and completely overshadowed the Cabinet Secretariat and performed many of its functions. According to B. K. Nehru, 'From LK's [Jha] time started the movement towards the centralization of power in the Prime Minister, whose office, in effect, tended to become a super-government' (B. K. Nehru 1997: 421). This inevitably led to the politicization of decision-making processes, favouritism, assertion of whims and fancies, adhocism and so on, as shown by B. N. Tandon in his book *PMO Diary*. B. G. Deshmukh has pointed out that during the Prime Ministership of Rajiv Gandhi, the PMO played an influential part, often overshadowing the Cabinet Secretary. Arun Singh, as Minister of State, was an important figure for some time before he was shifted to the Defence Ministry. The Prime Minister's House was also very active; M. L. Fotedar and Captain Satish Sharma constituted a powerful PMH. Arun Nehru, though a Minister of State in the Home Ministry, wielded considerable influence (Deshmukh 2004: 142). As brought out later, these dubious traditions have continued to this day. K. Subrahmanyam has correctly said that centralization of authority in the hands of the Prime Minister through the PMO has been the bane of healthy Cabinet governance in India. It has been causing a thrombosis in decision-making and impairing the efficiency of overall governance. It was perfected as an effective instrument to convert a constitutional Cabinet government into a virtual presidential system (Subrahmanyam 1994).

Some Bitter Truths

Margaret Thatcher, Britain's ex-Prime Minister, once pointed out that, 'Countries are not rich in proportion to their natural resources. If that were so, Russia would be the richest country in the world...Japan, Switzerland, Hong Kong, Taiwan, Singapore and so on have no natural resources but are now among the most prosperous countries in the world' (Thatcher 1995). It is time we introspect over this stark reality and ask ourselves some difficult and inconvenient questions.

The courts have time and again held that ministers have to work as trustees and all decisions have to be transparent. Any number of instances can be cited to show how ministers and law givers have taken the law into their own hands to serve their own interests. It will be recalled that way back in 1993, the then Environment Minister Kamal Nath had not only sanctioned forest land in the Kulu-Manali valley in Himachal Pradesh for his Span Motels but had also brazenly diverted the flow of Bias River to protect the land from floods. The Supreme Court had castigated him on this account. In 1997, the Delhi High Court had struck down the allotment of 78 petrol pumps by the then Petroleum Minister Satish Sharma. Among the beneficiaries were the daughter-in-law of former Chief Minister of Karnataka and Prime Minister, H. D. Deve Gowda, controversial god man Chandraswamy's brother and the union Law Secretary's wife. The court had directed that the petrol pumps be taken back from the allottees and sold by auction. The allotment of 3,760 petrol pumps and gas agencies by Petroleum Minister Ram Naik during the NDA regime in 2002 had also become highly controversial. It was in 2006 that the Supreme Court had convicted Swaroop Singh Naik, Forest Minister, and Ashok Khot, Forest Secretary in the Government of Maharashtra, to one month's simple imprisonment for flouting the court's orders and permitting saw and veneer mills in the Tansa reserve forest.

There is no realization either among the law givers or the ruling elite that every law must be rigorously and faithfully implemented, if respect for it is to be maintained. India has a surfeit of laws. The British Government in India passed only a little over 400 laws in the 90 years of their rule between 1857 and 1947. The National Police Commission highlighted in its second report (1979) that in the three decades of 1947–57, 1957–67 and 1967–77, the number of laws enacted by Parliament were 692, 597 and 672 respectively (Government of India

1979: 6). The Parliament has, in the 66 years since Independence, passed almost 5,000 acts *in the Centre alone*. Only a few of them are actually implemented. This is a crucial area of governance which has remained neglected.

Government expenditure, both at the central level and at the level of the states and local bodies, accounts for nearly 33 per cent of India's gross domestic product. The government also needs to step in, in a number of social and economic spheres, to bring about inclusive growth. Therefore, the efficiency and effectiveness of government spending is of crucial importance. It is imperative that we speak in terms of outcomes of such expenditures, rather than just outlays in the government budget. And that is where the efficiency and productivity of the government bureaucracy lies.

During the freedom struggle, Nehru had developed a deep dislike for the Indian Civil Service (ICS) which was effectively ruling India at the time. Referring to it as arrogant and over-bearing and contemptuous of public opinion, Nehru felt that so long as the spirit of the ICS—the spirit of authoritarianism—pervaded Indian administration and its public services, no new order could be built. In April 1940, Nehru went so far as to declare that the first and foremost task of the nationalist government would be to abolish the ICS (Kashyap 2003: 189). However, after Independence, Nehru's views underwent a change and the ICS, Indian Police (IP) and successive all-India services, became the main advisors and instruments of his regime.

S. S. Gill has emphasized that Nehru adopted the colonial system of administration in its entirety. The Constitution of India cannibalized the much maligned Government of India Act, 1935 to the extent of incorporating 235 of its sections. The entire judicial and administrative framework of old rules, regulations and procedures was also adopted wholesale. No wonder then that this mode of transfer of power did not bring about the sort of radical transformation that the national leaders had been talking about (Gill 1996: 30).

Three years before his death, the then Prime Minister Jawaharlal Nehru was asked by Tarzie Vittachi, a foreign correspondent, what he thought his biggest failure was. After reflecting for a long minute, Nehru said very gently, 'I failed to change this administration. It is still a colonial administration' (Kapoor 2005: 119). Nehru admitted that he often felt lost in the 'administrative jungle' in Delhi. He tried his best to have issues pertaining to administrative reforms examined by ministries. In his note to the Home Minister, with a copy to the Cabinet Secretary, dated 24 August 1955, he commented on anomalies and absurdities in service rules. He said, '*These old rules perpetuate a caste system in our services, which is highly undesirable. The least we can do is to set our face against this and try to put an end to it. Unfortunately, our Constitution has given some guarantees*' (Jawaharlal Nehru Memorial Fund 2001: 158–59). His frustration is evident from what he wrote in his note to the Cabinet Secretary on 18 September 1955:

I have, on repeated occasions, drawn the attention of the Cabinet as well as of the Home Ministry to what I considered patent absurdities in certain rules governing the higher services. The question of services has been, in some form or other, under consideration for years past. I write notes and sometimes the matter is referred to the Cabinet also. On every occasion it is said that the matter is under consideration. It is extraordinary how this consideration goes on and on without producing any results (Jawaharlal Nehru Memorial Fund: 2002: 295).

In his address to the civil services of the Government of Andhra Pradesh on 9 December 1955, Nehru elaborated on his ideas of a new role for the services (Jawaharlal Nehru Memorial Fund: 2002: 255). In his letter to G. B. Pant, Home Minister, dated 26 February 1956, he suggested the appointment of a high level commission to consider the question of the reorganization of the administration and the services, with S. Radhakrishnan as its chairman (Jawaharlal Nehru Memorial Fund: 2003: 143–46). Nehru thus cannot be blamed beyond a point for the administration continuing to have its colonial structure and mindset. The fault clearly lies with the lethargy and disinterest of the ministers and senior civil servants.

At the time of Independence, the Government of India was rated as one of the most advanced governments by Paul Appleby, a well-known management expert in the United States, who was asked by the Government of India to study its system and to suggest ways of making it more efficient. In his report submitted in 1953, Appleby stated, 'I have come gradually to a general judgment that *now* would rate the government of India among the dozen or so most advanced governments of the world' (Government of India 1953: 8). Appleby rightly stressed the word 'now' for 'obvious reasons of concern for a future still unfolding and even more dependent on political leadership than on administration.' As is evident, Appleby's concerns about the future have turned out to be true. In his further report submitted in 1959, Appleby had observed that 'India is extremely fortunate in having high ability of this sort [institutional leadership] in its prime minister and in good many of the other ministers and having a corps of civil servants who, at the top level at least, are equal to any in the world' (Government of India 1959: 41).

The fall in the standards of governance since then has been precipitous. This process was particularly hastened by the deplorable and short-sighted policies followed during the internal emergency in 1975–77 when the objectives of 'committed' judiciary and 'committed' bureaucracy were ruthlessly pursued, and relentless efforts made to amend the 'basic structure' of the Constitution, thereby causing permanent damage to the structure, morale and ethos of the instruments of governance. For example, 'the congratulatory message sent by Justice P. N. Bhagwati [sitting judge of the Supreme Court] to Indira Gandhi when she was re-elected in 1980 as also the activism of a section of the bench came in for a serious indictment by Justice Tulzapurkar'. (Desai 1986: 174).

A reference must also be made to the sharp differences which arose between the then President of India, Zail Singh, and the then Prime Minister Rajiv Gandhi, which illustrate the state of governance in the country. The President bitterly complained that the government chose to withhold the reports of the commissions of inquiry from him. He wrote:

> I drew the Prime Minister's attention to the fact that lately certain reports of commissions of inquiry received by the government had not been furnished to me even though my secretariat had written to the Home Ministry on three occasions to convey my desire for perusal of the reports...I often thought that if they could treat the President in such a manner, what would be the fate of a common citizen. It caused me hurt when the PM said that my request was being examined...[As regards stoppage of Intelligence Bureau reports and Ambassadors' reports] I told the PM that in spite of the fact that important information had been denied to me, I was trying to discharge my functions without a 'crisis' situation and the wheels of the Constitution were moving... Rajiv Gandhi's observation about the Thakkar Commission's report were quite upsetting. Even the Cabinet had not seen the report of Justice Thakkar, he claimed, and thus it was not necessary to show it to the President (Singh 1997: 230, 233, 250).

This was in sharp contrast to a situation which arose during the days of Rajendra Prasad as President of India when Jawaharlal Nehru was the Prime Minister. Nehru had graciously conveyed his apology to the President and there the matter ended.

Crony Capitalism

The nexus between the higher civil services, politicians, corporate leaders and criminals has taken such deep roots that questions are being raised about whether India is fast becoming a Banana Republic.[3] Crony capitalism has become a byword in governance. Prime Minister-designate Deve Gowda had no qualms about using Reliance group's airplane to travel from Delhi to Bangalore and back in the company of liquor baron Vijay Mallya of the United Breweries group. Deve Gowda's example was followed by his successor, the Chief Minister of Karnataka, J. H. Patel and his deputy, Siddaramaiah, who travelled by Essar group's plane from Bangalore to Delhi, when there were, in those days at least, seven daily flights between the two cities. It was also reported that Prime Minister Deve Gowda and Finance Minister P. Chidambaram had dinner with Prakash Hinduja, who was an accused in the Bofors case, in a hotel in Davos where he had gone for the annual meeting of the World Economic Forum (*Loksatta*, 3 February 1997). The National Democratic Alliance (NDA) was no exception with Atal Bihari Vajpayee's PMO labelled RH (Reliance and Hinduja) positive. The crony capitalism assiduously promoted by the likes of Pramod Mahajan, the then Minister for Telecommunications, was not new either. It had continued from the hoary past. It is interesting to note that a PIL had to be filed in the Delhi High Court by a vigilant citizen seeking recovery of rupees 13.57 crore from former prime ministers Rajiv Gandhi, Chandra Shekhar, P. V. Narasimha Rao and Deve Gowda for private use of Indian Air Force planes! The striking phenomenon of judicial activism, which is discussed later, is proof of abdication of responsibility by the executive and the legislature, leaving no choice to the common man but to approach the courts.

Particularly distressing is the permissive approach to the harmful culture for the social mores in the country. It was shocking to read that Harshad Mehta, prime accused in the bank scam, was appointed a visiting professor in one of the colleges in Mumbai. Lalu Prasad Yadav of fodder scam fame was taken in procession on an elephant from Patna jail to the Chief Minister's residence (where his wife lived), when he was released by the court on bail. It was unbelievable to read the affidavit filed by the central government in the Supreme Court stating that it would not be possible to terminate the membership of MPs who have been convicted by courts but whose appeals are pending in the higher courts as this would destabilize the government! Fortunately, as discussed later, the Supreme Court has declared the amendment of RPA unconstitutional.

Darkness at Noon

Power sector reforms have been avowedly one of the major planks of development of successive governments for years. But the results are highly disappointing. Electricity boards earlier, and power distribution companies after restructuring of the boards, have continued to incur heavy losses. The World Bank model of trifurcating the electricity boards into separate entities of generation, major transmission and distribution and privatizing them has created more problems. All these complex issues are briefly mentioned only to invite attention to the failure of governance in this crucial sector.

Attention must be invited in this context to the two major inter-state grid failures in 2012 which became big news the world over. Several major newspapers commented on the event editorially underlining governance failure. Below are the extracts from a few (2 August 2012):

The New York Times: 'All the makings of a disaster movie on blackout Tuesday: More than half a billion people without power. Trains motionless on the tracks.

Miners trapped underground. Subway lines paralyzed. Traffic snarled in much of the national capital. For a country considered a rising economic power, Blackout Tuesday—*which came only a day after another major power failure*—was an embarrassing reminder of the intractable problems still plaguing India: inadequate infrastructure, a crippling power shortage and, many critics say, a yawning absence of governmental action and leadership.'

The Guardian: 'Free elections excuse political class from providing basics—To leave one in 20 people on the globe's surface without electricity, that lifeblood of modern society, in the hairdryer heat of the Indian summer is unfortunate. To do it again to one in 12 of the world's population a day later is unpardonable carelessness....Power, so vital to India's growth, is India's biggest bottleneck. It is a paradox that in China unelected leaders are careful to provide the masses with material benefits such as electricity, water and roads because they legitimise dictatorship. Whereas in India, democracy allows just the opposite: free elections excuse the political class from providing the basics of life to the masses who have elected them.'

The Wall Street Journal: 'Capping a surreal day, PM gave an effective promotion to power minister: For a nation that sees itself as an emerging global power, the event was a huge embarrassment. It put on vivid display, for Indians and the world, how rickety the country's basic infrastructure is. And it could further tarnish the perceptions of India among foreign companies who have long viewed the country's outdated roads, ports and power networks as major drawbacks of doing business here...Capping the surreal day when the power outage dominated cable news channels—which continued to broadcast for the benefit of those who still had power—Prime Minister Manmohan Singh gave an effective promotion to power minister Sushil Kumar Shinde, on whose watch the blackouts have occurred. Mr Shinde was named the next home minister...'

The Washington Post: 'Destroyed any hope of a brighter future without improvement in governance. The crisis sharpened fears about India's failure to invest in the infrastructure needed to support its rapidly growing economy, in sharp contrast to neighbouring China. It also destroyed any lingering hope that the nation's entrepreneurial spirit and vibrant private sector could somehow deliver a significantly brighter future without a dramatic improvement in the way the country is governed....Along with a lack of investment in infrastructure, the crisis also had roots in many of India's familiar failings: the populist tone of much of its politics, rampant corruption and poor management in its government and public sector, weak law enforcement, and a maze of regulations that restrict many industries.'

The Financial Times of London: 'Power shortages on a gargantuan scale have crippled the country this week, disrupting economic activity...No wonder India's state power utilities have debts of Rs 3 trillion. And they are expected to treble their losses over the next three years....A functioning electricity supply is essential for any economy, especially one with *India's growth pretensions*. Without far-reaching reforms, Indians will continue to work in the dark.'

Immediately after the massive grid failures, Power Minister Sushil Kumar Shinde was promoted to union Home Minister. This showed how little the UPA cared for good governance in the country.

Equally scandalous is the implementation of the Ganga Action Plan on which literally thousands of crores of rupees have been spent over the years. The position is no different with respect to the Yamuna Action Plan. The tardy implementation of the plans has been adversely commented on by the Supreme Court more than once. But these rivers continue to be as polluted as ever. The Supreme Court had rightly asked, 'What is the point in setting up nodal bodies under the chairmanship of the Prime Minister, who has little time to spare, as no effective monitoring takes place?'

Yet another area of concern pertains to the rapidly deteriorating governance in urban areas. The problem is confined not only to large cities and metropolitan areas but is equally serious in small towns. Lack of even basic infrastructure, unauthorized construction, deteriorating quality of life, the nexus between the builders, politicians, criminals and the staff of the local bodies and ineffective local bodies are some of the common woes of all urban areas. In several states, laws have been passed to regularize unauthorized constructions, thereby encouraging others to follow suit. Delhi, Thane, Ulhasnagar and Bhiwandi are only a few examples where unauthorized and irregular constructions have been regularized in this manner. A committee of senior officers appointed by the Government of Maharashtra under the chairmanship of Swadheen Kshatriya, Additional Chief Secretary, has blatantly recommended that all unauthorized constructions made in all municipal areas till the end of February 2013 should be regularized by imposing penalties!

M. J. Antony has, in his article 'Mushrooming Illegalities', discussed three judgments of the Supreme Court. They pertain to three different parts of the country but the circumstances are the same. The Supreme Court, in dealing with the problem of illegal buildings in Maharashtra's Bhiwandi town, in *Mahendra Mahadik v. Subhash Kanitkar*, made two emphatic points. It asserted that such buildings could not be authorized by devious methods like 'regularisation' and 'compounding'. It also reiterated the right of aggrieved citizens to examine documents in official records that allowed such constructions in the first place. As in several other fields, the judiciary has advanced the [cause of] right to information, while the law makers and the executive are hesitating in granting this valuable power to the citizens. In another case, *Friends Colony v. State of Orissa*, the Supreme Court roundly condemned the municipal authorities who permitted deviations by regularization and compounding. Such procedures should be allowed only in exceptional cases, the court said. The court regretted that this had become the rule now. In a third case, *MI Builders Ltd. v. Radhey Shyam*, upholding the decision of the Allahabad High Court order, the Supreme Court said, 'This court, in numerous decisions, has held that no consideration should be shown to the builder or any other person where construction is unauthorised. This diktat is now almost bordering on the rule of law...Unauthorised construction, if it is illegal and cannot be compounded, has to be demolished. There is no way out...Judicial discretion cannot be guided by expediency' (Antony 2005). The Bombay High Court ordered the removal of 1.25 lakh unauthorized constructions in Pimpri Chinchwad Municipal Corporation area. With concerted efforts, the corporation was able to remove only 350 structures in 2012. The corporation is at a loss on how to comply with the court orders (*Loksatta*, 11 August 2013).

Delhi, the nation's capital, has become increasingly notorious for the manner in which illegal constructions and encroachments have been permitted. Over the years, politicians have colluded with the building mafia and carved out over 1,200 unauthorized colonies around 364 villages. Over 55 per cent of Delhi's population (over a crore) is estimated to be living in 1,218 unauthorized colonies, 45 JJ colonies and 685 slums. The Delhi government has regularized 895 unauthorized colonies and given ownership rights to the residents of 45 resettlement colonies (*gfiles* 2013: 37–38). The Delhi High Court had issued directions to the municipal corporation for removing illegal constructions, encroachments on public lands and commercial establishments from residential areas. The matter was later elevated to the Apex Court which too had directed that strong action should be taken in all such cases. However, there was such an uproar and protests that the government decided to revise the Delhi Master Plan to effectively regularize the encroachments and violations in the Master Plan. The Supreme Court pulled up the Delhi government for frustrating the efforts to remove the encroachments in this manner. Thereafter, the Parliament passed a law to delay action by local authorities. The Supreme Court strongly criticized this action as well (see Godbole 2008: 296–97). It is a classic case of how the provisions of law and the Master Plan were blatantly violated by direct support from all political parties.

These cases are illustrative of a larger picture. Similar problems are seen in many other sectors. It will be impossible to find a lasting solution to these complex problems unless there is strong political will. But since this is lacking, the administrative will is also eroding rapidly.

The Curse of Corruption

Elimination of corruption is recognized as an integral part of good governance. The eradication of corruption has become the most visible rallying point in the country today. Widespread public support for mass movements against corruption organized by Anna Hazare, Baba Ramdev and Sri Sri Ravi Shankar and by lesser known NGOs have driven home the point that political parties can neglect these concerns at their own peril. At least outwardly they are making efforts to show their sympathy and support for the eradication of corruption. Time alone will tell how genuine their commitment is.

Eradication of corruption has become a matter of concern not only in India but the world over in recent years. By the end of 2007, across the world, 104 governments had ratified or acceded to the United Nations Convention Against Corruption. The Convention came into force on 14 December 2005 after 38 countries ratified it. India was one of the last countries to ratify it in May 2011. The United Nations Development Programme (UNDP) highlighted in its report that 'today genuinely combating corruption makes more political sense than ever before' (UNDP 2008: 149–50). In the past, the rich countries generally turned a blind eye when corporations in their countries bribed officials in developing countries. But the Foreign Corrupt Practices Act prohibits firms operating in the United States from bribing government officials around the world to win business. The Organisation for Economic Cooperation and Development (OECD) countries have set standards which their companies have to follow anywhere in the world. Companies found to be paying bribes overseas are now liable to be prosecuted at home. The case study of the clean up at Siemens, the German engineering major, after it admitted to several bribery charges and paid US$1.6 billion in fines makes an absorbing read. The bribery trail went across the globe to Venezuela, Argentina, Iraq, China, Bangladesh and Vietnam. Its clean-up operation has lessons for India: redrawing the organization map, informing everyone, setting the tone from the top, top priority for compliance, building structures and creating partnerships. Clearly, 'Siemens was moving from structures to values' (*ET*, 19 April 2012). According to the World Bank, the war on corporate bribery has intensified in the US. As many as 78 corporations were under investigation in the US for alleged payoffs to win business deals in other countries. In the past four years, a total of 58 companies paid a combined US$3.74 billion to settle bribery charges (*ET*, 12 March 2012). The UNDP report identified three areas for concerted action—the police, social services and natural resources. Looking at India's experience it can be seen how relevant these areas are. The report rightly urges that governments should be seeking ways of reducing the forms of corruption that hit the poor the hardest.

The United Nations Convention Against Corruption (UNCAC) is the first legally binding international anti-corruption instrument. It obliges the states to implement a wide and detailed range of anti-corruption measures affecting their laws, institutions and practices. These measures aim to promote prevention, criminalization and law enforcement, international cooperation, asset recovery, technical assistance and information exchange, and mechanisms for implementation (*The Other Side*, May 2011: 41).

In 1996, the Congress Party in its election manifesto promised to set up a high powered independent commission on corruption for suggesting measures to control corruption and the appointment of a Lok Pal having jurisdiction over the Prime Minister and chief ministers. It also promised to eliminate the nexus between criminals and politicians and control organized crime that has vitiated the country's social, political and administrative structure. It was also undertaken that all legislators and members of local bodies would declare their assets at the time of assuming and leaving office (*TOI*, 13 April 1996). The Congress Party has been in power again since 2004 but it has not only not implemented even one of these promises made way back in 1996, but is itself seeped in corruption.

In May 1997, a Chief Ministers' Conference on efficient and responsive administration debated the varied facets of corruption at great length and agreed to take time-bound action to curtail corruption at all levels. A nine-point programme was adopted by the conference which included making changes in laws and rules to enable the government to dispense with the services of corrupt officers expeditiously. A sub-committee of chief ministers was appointed to suggest the requisite changes in the laws within a period of six months at the latest. A newspaper had editorially commented (*Loksatta*, 26 May 1997) that it was comic relief to see Lalu Prasad Yadav, the then Chief Minister of Bihar, who was implicated in the Rs 1,000 crore fodder scam, expressing his concern over corruption. Needless to say, this resolve too has remained on paper.

Corruption in the judiciary is even at the highest level. Shanti Bhushan, senior advocate and former union Law Minister, filed an affidavit in the Supreme Court alleging that eight of the past chief justices of India (CJIs) had given questionable and highly flawed judgments (*Outlook*, 4 October 2010: 30–33). In recent years, serious allegations have also been made against at least two former chief justices of India, Y. K. Sabharwal and K. G. Balakrishnan. In the first, highly respected former judges of the Supreme Court like V. R. Krishna Iyer, P. B. Sawant and Late CJI, J. S. Verma, called for a thorough investigation into Sabharwal's judicial misconduct and so did a number of well-known lawyers, social activists and civil servants (*EPW*, 13 October 2007: 4099). Former CJI, J. C. Verma and V. R. Krishna Iyer, former judge of the Supreme Court, demanded that Justice K. G. Balakrishnan, Chairman of NHRC, be asked to resign from his post due to amassing of wealth under suspicious circumstances by his son-in-law and daughter. In the Ghaziabad provident fund scam, one Supreme Court judge and 13 High Court judges, among others, are reported to be involved (*Outlook*, 10 November 2008). S. P. Bharucha, the then Chief Justice of India, had publicly bemoaned that at least 20 per cent of the judges were corrupt and they should be identified and dismissed. The day that Justice G. B. Pattnaik took over as CJI, he said that corruption had dented the image of the judiciary to some extent. V. N. Khare, former CJI, bluntly stated, 'corruption is rampant in lower courts' (*Outlook*, 9 July 2012: 16). In another interview he added that the CJI does not have the powers to curb the rampant corruption in lower judiciary, 'Give some powers to the CJI. What powers does he have? How do I control the situation?' (*TOI*, 24 February 2004). Similar sentiments were expressed by CJIs thereafter but the scourge continues, though action has been taken against some judges. The main cause for corruption in the lower judiciary, however, is the huge pendency of cases which, at various levels together, is estimated to be about 3 crore, as compared to just 1.64 lakh in 1957.[4] The Bar Council of India has drawn up a list of 131 High Court judges in whose courts relatives are appearing as lawyers. If this is the state of affairs in High Courts, imagine what the situation must be in the lower courts (*ET*, 30 July 2003). At least two judges of the Bombay High Court, B. A. Masodkar and B. G. Kolse Patil, jumped straight from the High Court bench into electoral politics to contest elections. Another judge of the Nagpur Bench of the Bombay High Court, Bhausaheb Wahane, publicly declared that he would be prepared to fight Lok Sabha elections if the Third Front unanimously decided to give him a ticket (*Loksatta*, 6 April 1996). Unfortunately for him and fortunately for us he was not given a ticket! Flirting with politics in this manner while occupying the chair of a High Court judge can show what will happen if the concept of 'committed judiciary' is not nipped in the bud. Against this background, it is distressing to see that the proposals for setting up a National Judicial Commission and a mechanism for ensuring judicial accountability have been pending for over two decades. Clearly, there is no political will to evolve a consensus on the subject.

Even prestigious religious places have not escaped the blot of corruption scandals. These include the Lord Venkateshwara temple in Tirupati, Siddhivinayak temple in Mumbai, Satya Sai Baba trust in Puttaparthy, Shani Shingnapur temple in Ahmednagar district and the Sai Baba temple in Shirdi. Several Waqf boards and gurudwaras are also in a same situation. Political appointees, office-holders and staff in these temples and trusts have often faced public ire on this account. As an example, the then Chief Minister of Andhra Pradesh, Chandrababu Naidu, had to publicly announce that within a month, Lord Venkateshwara, the richest temple in the country, would be made free of corruption in any sphere (*HT*, 6 January 1997).

The severity of the problem of corruption is borne out by the observations of superior courts, often made in sheer exasperation and disgust, at the fast deteriorating situation. The Supreme Court warned of 'denationalisation' of the banking system if disciplinary measures were not taken to eradicate corruption among bank officials. The court observed that the banking business and services were 'vitally affected by catastrophic corruption' and steps were necessary to eradicate the corrupt proclivity of conduct on the part of employees and officers (*TOI*, 13 March 1997). Expressing deep concern over the alleged covert attempts made to stall the investigation in corruption cases pertaining to the fodder scam, the division bench of the Patna High Court observed that if things continued in this fashion, there was every likelihood of India soon emerging as the number one country as far as corruption was concerned (*TOI*, 24 May 1997). A decade later, during the hearing of the fodder scam appeal, the Supreme Court observed, 'Everyone wants to loot the country; the only panacea to rid the country of corrupt elements was to hang a few of them on the lamp post. The law does not permit us to do it but [given the choice] we would prefer to do it' (*IE*, 8 March 2007). On 5 August 2008, the Supreme Court judge hearing the VIP bungalows case said, 'The whole government machinery is corrupt, whether at the centre or in the states. They (senior officials) don't apply their mind, rather they don't have a mind to apply...Even God will not be able to help this country...Our country's character has gone.' In another case, the Supreme Court Bench said, 'In this case you need huntering (flogging, presumably) to make you work' (Noorani 2008: 62).

It is disheartening to note that in a list of 28 countries which were surveyed, India ranked 19th in the global bribery index 2011 of Transparency International, while China and Russia fared the worst, at twenty-seventh and twenty-eight positions respectively. The index was based on a survey of 3,000 business executives from developed and developing countries. India's score improved to 7.5 points, up by 0.7 points since the last survey in 2008. This was the maximum improvement for any country, but India still remains near the bottom of the table, said Transparency International. India's score was below the global average of 7.8 points. (*IE*, 3 November 2011). India's rank declined perceptibly in 2011 to 95 among 183 countries in the Transparency International's corruption perception index from 72 in 2007 and 87 in 2010 (*IE*, 2 December 2011).

With graft and bribery so common, there is genuine fear that voters may suspect that *all* candidates and *all* political parties are tainted, thereby neutralizing corruption as an election issue. One only hopes that this will not happen in the impending Lok Sabha elections in 2014.

India is increasingly recognized as an emerging regional power. The Planning Commission is aiming at an annual average growth rate of 8 per cent for the Twelfth Five Year Pan (2012–17). The economy has to grow at 9 per cent in the last few years of the Plan period to achieve the 8 per cent average growth rate. With the recent sharp downturn in the economy, this seems most unlikely to happen. However, it will clearly be impossible to achieve any perceptible rate of growth unless some tough decisions are taken and the quality of governance improves noticeably. A new terminology, 'governance deficit', has been added to hitherto prevalent terms such as fiscal deficit, revenue deficit, trust deficit, image deficit, credibility deficit, perception deficit and so on. And an important component of bridging such a deficit will have to be eradication of corruption.

Other Comparators

A report released by Global Financial Integrity shows that India was the 8th largest victim of black money loss of US$123 billion during 2001–10 (*IE*, 19 December 2012).

India was ranked at the bottom of a table on transparency rankings by international property markets. The rankings of property markets have been worked out on the basis of five attributes: presence of public and private performance indices, quality of market fundamentals research, availability of reliable financial statements, alignment of interest among directors, managers and investors/shareholders and taxes and restrictions on cross-border transactions.

The Human Development Report (HDR) 2011 ranked India at 134th among 187 countries, as compared to the ranking of 127 in 2004 and 132 in 2008. With an HDI value of 0.547—where one is the highest and zero the lowest—India fares worse than even the average global value of 0.682. While India's global value and ranking has improved to some extent, India is the lowest among the BRICS nations—Brazil (84), Russia (66), China (101) and South Africa (123). China has registered a faster improvement in HDI value—1.73 per cent annually since 1980—than India (1.51 per cent) (*IE*, 3 November 2011).

According to the 'Doing Business Report' 2009, released by the International Finance Corporation, India is the most difficult country to enforce contracts in a court or otherwise. With its rank of 122, India trails Nepal and Bangladesh.

According to the World Economic Forum Global Competitiveness Report 2008, with its inadequate infrastructure, inefficient bureaucracy and tight labour laws, India at 50th position is no match for China.

As per the Global Corruption Perception Index 2008, India's rank fell from 72 in 2004 to 85, even as China, with which it was on par, maintained its position at 72. The UNIDO report 2009 lists India at 54 (down from 51 in 2000). It trails China by 28 points in the Competitive Industrial Performance Index.

According to the Index of Economic Freedom 2009, with a shackled judicial system, excessive regulation and a 'mostly unfree' reputation, India at 123rd position, trails Gabon.[5] This brings out the enormous challenges facing India in improving its governance to reach global standards.

The World of Have-nots

India is clearly divided into two worlds—the much touted 'shining India' signifying the glossy, superficial, highly westernized sections of society with their extravagant lifestyles, and the 'left-behind India' or Bharat, which consists of the poor, deprived, malnourished, under-fed, neglected and marginalized sections of society, residing largely in rural areas and in slums and hutments in urban areas. There is an ever widening gap between these two Indias.

Concerns for the governance of the 'left-behind India' are becoming more severe each day. To cite an example, the UN Working Group on Human Rights (2012) reported that, as a result of 'development' projects, 60 to 65 million people have got displaced in India since Independence. As the expert group of the Planning Commission has stated, 'Whereas the tribals constitute 8.08 per cent of the country's population, they are 40 per cent of the total displaced/affected persons by the projects. Similarly, at least 20 per cent of the displaced/affected are Dalits and another 20 per cent are OBCs. The resettlement record is also very dismal. Only a third of the displaced persons of planned development have been resettled' (Government of India 2008: 15). Once proud owners of agricultural land, their status has since degenerated to that of daily wage workers leading sub-human lives. As Sarma has highlighted, gross domestic product is therefore anything but inclusive: it is more apt to call it the gross displacement product (Sarma 2013: 4–5).

Another shocking example is the tardy manner in which the farm loan waiver scheme, announced with so much fanfare by the UPA government in 2008, was implemented. It shows that implementation of a scheme through banks is no guarantee of smooth disbursal of funds. The C&AG audit of 100,000 bank accounts showed that documents had been tampered with to provide benefits to ineligible farmers, some eligible beneficiaries got less benefits than their due, others got more than their due, some banks wrongly charged farmers for their services and a large number of farmers did not get loan waiver/debt relief certificates. The union Finance Ministry has admitted that one in ten of the intended 3.45 crore eligible farmers did not get to avail the loan waiver.

India's performance with respect to the eight Millennium Development Goals—eradicating extreme poverty and hunger, achieving universal primary education, promoting gender equality and empowering women, reducing child mortality, improving maternal health, combating HIV/AIDS, malaria and other diseases, ensuring environmental sustainability and developing a global partnership for development—which are to be reached by 2015, is dismal.

The neglect of the dehumanizing practice of manual scavenging in India is a matter of national shame. According to one estimate, around 3 lakh persons are still engaged in this practice. The C&AG report (2003) on the subject is damning. As a last resort, the matter has been raised before the Supreme Court in a PIL. But as in all such cases, there is lack of political will to act.

Unless the existence of a problem is recognized, one cannot find a solution to it. Bonded labour is one such issue. It is shocking to see that most states deny the existence of bonded labour. As a result, a number of PILs have been filed in the high courts and the Supreme Court. Tiwari wrote, 'The judicial interventions provided a fresh lease of life to the problem of bonded labour identification, release and rehabilitation. Several judgments and pronouncements primarily made by the Supreme Court of India also led to a more comprehensive definition of Bonded Labour System (Abolition) Act, 1976' (Tiwari 2011: 99–100).

While submitting the report of the National Commission for Enterprises in the Unorganised Sector, its Chairman, Arjun Sengupta, in his covering letter to the Prime Minister dated 15 May 2005, defined unorganized/informal employment as 'consisting of casual and contributing family workers; self-employed persons in unorganized sector and private households; and other employees in organized and unorganized enterprises not availing any security benefits given by the employers.' Employment covered by this definition is over 91 per cent of the total employment in the economy. The social security problems of unorganized/informal workers arise out of the deficiency or capability deprivation as well as vulnerability to conditions of adversity. These give rise to enormous social costs which are often not appreciated enough (Government of India 2005). Follow-up action, if any, taken on the report must be a classified secret as it is not in the public domain!

Malnutrition remains a 'silent emergency' in India. Children's malnutrition, particularly in tribal areas such as Gadchiroli, Nandurbar and Melghat in Maharashtra and Kalahandi, Bolangir, Nuapara, Koraput, Malkangiri etc in Odisha, is so shocking that the high courts and the Supreme Court had to step in *suo motu* or on being approached by vigilant and concerned citizens by filing writ petitions, to direct the government to take time-bound action. But this has helped only up to a point. According to the "*agenda*, 'half of India's children and a third of all adults are undernourished. In Raichur district in Karnataka, where over 4,500 children face acute malnutrition and 2,689 died of malnutrition in two years, there is a vested interest in maintaining the status quo' (Shahina 2012: 31). During 2005–10, India was at the last-but-one rank among 129 countries in malnutrition. Each year 300,000 new-born babies die in India within 24 hours of their birth. This number is the highest in the world and accounts for 29 per cent of total deaths. In Maharashtra, there has been no perceptible change in child mortality and infant mortality during 2008–09 to 2011–12. In a PIL, the Bombay High Court castigated the government of Maharashtra for the deaths of over 4,000 children due to malnutrition between April 2012 and January 2013. Of these, 3,060 were in the age group of 0–1 year and the remaining 940 between 1–6 years. Of the total deaths, as many as 1,025 were in Nandurbar district (*Loksatta*, 4 May 2013). The basic weakness in terms of lack of political and administrative commitment to addressing the relevant issues has continued, though Prime Minister Manmohan Singh has lamented India's poor performance and called it a national shame. This is starkly brought out once again by mismanagement in the mid day meal scheme in 16 states. It is seen that 106 complaints were received during 2011 to July 2013. One of the worst tragedies was in Chapra, in Bihar in July 2013 in which 23 students lost their lives. The states worst affected by this neglect are Uttar Pradesh, Bihar, Haryana, Madhya Pradesh and West Bengal. This shows the total callousness of the system.

According to the World Bank's World Hunger Index, in 2012 India was at the 65th rank among 79 countries which were surveyed. Even Pakistan and Nepal performed better than India. In 2012, India's hunger index increased to 22.9, as compared to 22.6 in 1996. India dropped to 128th rank among 177 countries on the Human Development Index, not something to be proud about.

William Dalrymple has quoted Amartya Sen and Jean Dreze from their recent book *An Uncertain Glory—India and its Contradictions*, which states, 'While India has climbed rapidly up the ladder of economic growth rates, it has fallen behind Nepal and Bangladesh in the scale of social indicators. Brazil, with much slower economic growth, has a far better record of poverty reduction. India remains an oddity among the BRIC countries. 'India's per capita GDP is less than half of China's, one third of Brazil's and one fourth of Russia's.'

This is the most shocking part of the book. 'Every year, more children die in India than anywhere else in the world: 1.7 million children under the age of 5, largely from easily preventable illnesses such as diarrhoea. Of those who do survive until the age of 5, 48 per cent are stunted as a result of a lack of nutrients: child malnutrition in India is higher than in Eritrea.'

In this respect, write Sen and Drèze, 'South Asia fares distinctly worse than sub-Saharan Africa. More than 40 per cent of South Asian children (and a slightly higher proportion of Indian children) are underweight in terms of WHO norms, compared with 25 per cent in sub-Saharan Africa.'

Likewise, the most basic health measure that any government can provide for its people is immunizing very young children but in India, only 43.5 per cent of children are completely immunized, compared to 73.1 per cent in Bangladesh. 'India is falling behind every other South Asian country, with the exception of Pakistan, in terms of social indicators.' For instance, life expectancy was the same in India and in Bangladesh in 1990 but today it is 'four years higher in Bangladesh than India, 69 and 65 respectively. Similarly, child mortality, a tragic indicator, was estimated to be about 20 per cent higher in Bangladesh than India in 1990, but has fallen rapidly in Bangladesh to now being 25 per cent lower than in India by 2011.'

'In sub-Saharan Africa, only 8 out of 25 countries have immunization figures as bad as India's. India's adult literacy is not quite the lowest in the world but, at 65 per cent, is the same as in Malawi and Sudan. Adult literacy in China, by comparison, is 91 per cent.' So bad is the situation that Sen and Drèze go as far as stating that Indian democracy is 'seriously compromised by the extent and form of social inequality.'

Improving education lies at the heart of solving many of these problems. India's underperformance, they write, can be traced to a failure to learn from the examples of so-called Asian economic development, in which rapid expansion of human capability is both a goal in itself and an integral element in achieving rapid growth. Japan pioneered that approach, starting after the Meiji restoration in 1868, when it resolved to achieve a fully literate society within a few decades. As Kido Takayoshi, one of the leaders of that reform, explained, 'Our people are no different from the Americans or Europeans of today; it is all a matter of education or lack of education.'

Indians hugely value this too, but effective public education remains out of reach of millions. The private sector is often excellent but state schools—all that is available for most ordinary Indians—remain abysmal (Dalrymple 2013).

What Lies Ahead

A study conducted by Professor Adrian White of the University of Leicester on happiness among people across the globe reveals that Indians are among the least happy people in the world, occupying 125th position. According to him, happiness is closely associated with health, wealth and education. Indians lag behind others in all these three key indicators (Mishra, Das, Sahoo 2009: 142). It is difficult to accept these generalizations and findings at face value but the basic thrust has much to commend itself.

In this background, it was shocking to see the representatives of the corporate world rejecting Prime Minister Manmohan Singh's plea of developing a social charter that 'stems the widening rich-poor divide by sharing the benefits of growth with the underprivileged.' He had warned the industry at the annual general meeting of the Confederation of Indian Industry (CII) on 24 May 2007 that rising income and wealth inequalities, if not matched by a corresponding rise of incomes across the nation, can lead to social unrest. But the response was of total smugness and unconcern! The mainstream corporate media immediately pounced upon him, with a leading newspaper editorial accusing him of 'making the rich fearful', and one commentator lamenting that inequality in our society was increasing 'not because of capitalism but because of the limited spread of capitalism' (*EPW*, 9 June 2007: 2131).

The men and women who rule India and will continue to do so in the foreseeable future belong to what Warren Buffet once reportedly called the 'Lucky Sperm Club of India'. The political dynasties in India dot the whole country— the Nehru-Gandhis, the Abdullahs of Kashmir, Karunanidhis of Tamil Nadu, the Thackerays of Mumbai, Lalu and family in Bihar, the Pawars of Baramati in Maharashtra, Karnataka—the Gowdas' own country, Mulayam and Co in Lucknow, the NTR/Chandrababu and YSR families in Andhra Pradesh, Tamil Nadu's Ramdosses, the Badals of Punjab, the Chautalas of Haryana, the Sangmas of Meghalaya, the Pilots of Rajasthan and the Scindias of Madhya Pradesh to cite only a few. What India does or fails to do will mostly depend on their vision, if any.

As George Santayana said, 'Those who cannot remember the past are condemned to repeat it.' I firmly believe that India does not have to plod along this beaten path in the future. I have therefore made an attempt in this book to show the mirror and the way ahead. Fortunately, the concept of good governance has entered the vocabulary of political parties in India in recent years. In fact, it is likely to be the key catch phrase in the forthcoming Lok Sabha elections due in 2014. For the first time since Independence, political parties are trying to woo the voters on the promise of good governance.

The new generation of leaders who have taken over the reigns of power in China, Japan and Latin America have shown how to blaze a new trail. It should not be difficult to do the same in India. As shown in this book, the possibilities are immense.

Notes

1. The only other instance of this kind was the debate in the Lok Sabha on Chinese aggression in 1962 which went on for six days. More than 150 members participated in the debate.
2. B. K. Nehru was also not sponsored for the post of Secretary General of the United Nations due to Krishna Menon's opposition.
3. The term banana republic originally denoted the fictional 'Republic of Anchuria', a 'servile dictatorship' that abetted (or supported for kickbacks) the exploitation of large-scale plantation agriculture, especially banana cultivation. A banana republic is a commercial enterprise for profit by collusion between the state and favoured monopolies, whereby the profits derived from private exploitation of public land is private property, and the debts incurred are public responsibility (see http://en.wikipedia.org/wiki/banana republic).
4. As seen from the speech of Prime Minister Jawaharlal Nehru at a conference of law ministers on 18 September 1957, quoted in Krishna Iyer (1993: 110–12).
5. India Today, 6 April 2009, quoted in Government of India (2009: 4).

2

THE CORE OF GOOD GOVERNANCE

> Laws must apply equally to everybody. And that includes the government
> too, whose actions must be—and to be seen to be—subject to those laws
> Philosopher Hayek

What Is Governance

The term 'governance' has very wide connotations and covers all aspects of
the manner in which authority is exercised and public affairs are conducted.
The Webster's dictionary defines it to mean 'control, direct or strongly influence
the actions and conduct of; authoritative direction or control', while the Oxford
dictionary defines the word to mean 'act, manner, fact or function of governing,
sway, control'.

As Vineeta Rai explains, the word 'governance' is derived from the Greek
Kubernao which means to 'steer' and was used for the first time in a metaphorical
sense by the Greek philosopher Plato. Governance is defined as the exercise of
economic, political and administrative authority to manage a country's affairs at
all levels. It consists of mechanisms, processes and institutions through which
citizens and government articulate their interests, exercise their legal rights, meet
their obligations and mediate their differences (Rai 2011: 156).

The term governance has been conceptualized in various ways (Government
of India: 115). The World Bank defines it as the manner in which power is
exercised in the management of a country's economic and social resources. The
Bank has identified three distinct aspects of governance: (i) the form of political
regime; (ii) the process by which authority is exercised in the management of a
country's economic and social resources for development; and (iii) the capacity
of the government to design, formulate and implement policies and discharge
functions.

UNDP views governance as the exercise of political, economic and
administrative authority in the management of a country's affairs at all levels. It
comprises mechanisms, processes and institutions through which citizens and
groups articulate their interests, exercise their legal rights, meet their obligations
and mediate their differences.

According to OECD, the concept of governance denotes the use of political authority and exercise of control in a society in relation to the management of its resources for social and economic development. This broad definition encompasses the role of public authorities in establishing the environment in which economic operators function and in determining the distribution of benefits, as well as the nature of the relationship between the ruler and the ruled.

The Commission on Global Governance believes that governance is the sum of the many ways in which individuals and institutions, public and private, arrange their common affairs. It is a continuing process through which conflicting or diverse interests may be accommodated and cooperative action may be taken. It includes formal institutions and regimes empowered to enforce compliance, as well as informal arrangements that people and institutions either have agreed to or perceive to be in their interest.

The Mahbub ul Haq Human Development Centre underlines that humane governance is governance dedicated to securing human development. It must enable the state, civil society and the private sector to help build capacities which will meet the basic needs of all people, particularly women, children and the poor. It requires effective participation of people in state, civil society and private sector activities that are conducive to human development.

It is clear that while each one of these definitions has its points of emphasis, broadly speaking the term governance encompasses all processes, institutions, rules and regulations through which human activities take place, whether individually or collectively, and whether in the government, in the private sector or in the cooperative and NGO sectors. They all have a bearing on common good.

Good governance has almost become a *mantra* the world over, in both developed and developing countries. (Italics have been used for connoting emphasis throughout the chapter.) On 28 September 1996, the African governors of the World Bank presented President James D. Wolfensohn with an alarming report which stated:

> If there is one most obvious lesson that can be drawn from the experience of the generation after independence in Africa, it is the crucial importance of establishing good governance...Almost every African country has witnessed a systematic regression of capacity in the last thirty years; the majority had better capacity at Independence than they now possess...In practically every country the civil service was found to be too large in nonessential areas and in critical need of personnel in others. The civil service is also too politicized and lacking in professionalism (Klitgaard 1997: 5.1 and 5.2).

This sounds so familiar to a person acquainted with the Indian scene.

As can be seen, while some elements of good governance are universally recognized, some others have found acceptance only in certain countries. Those in the first category, that is, which have been accepted universally, include corruption-free administration, public accountability, transparency, rule of law— equality before law and equal protection of law, sensitivity to people's grievances, participative governance, predictability in decision-making, responsiveness to people's needs and citizen friendliness. As can be seen, each one of these is an important dimension of good governance and adds value to it in a perceptible manner.[1] The other elements which have been accepted by some, but not all, include respect for human rights, right to information, right to privacy, right to employment, right to education, right to housing and so on. Effectively, these signify elements which enhance the quality of life and impart dignity to human existence.

The indicators of good governance considered relevant by the World Bank include voice and accountability, political stability, government effectiveness, regulatory quality, rule of law and control of corruption. As can be seen, the emphasis here is on some important elements such as political stability and regulatory quality. Christian Roland has stated that India and China's rankings show that 'they are only medium performers at best...The governance indicator score has only slightly improved in India between 1996 and 2005, and even declined in China during the same period' (Roland 2011: 158–59).

D. H. Pai Panandikar has pointed out that the index of economic freedom compiled by the Heritage Foundation and published by the *Wall Street Journal* puts India down at 120 in a group of 150 countries. Our ranking indicates more what we have not done rather than what we have. Panandikar has stated that economic freedom is a composite assessment of freedom in 10 major areas. These include taxation, government intervention, money management, capital flows and foreign investment, banking, wages and prices, property rights and black market activity. A remarkable finding of the study is that countries with the highest levels of economic freedom also have the highest standard of living (Pai Panandikar 1997).

The Second Administrative Reforms Commission (SARC) summarized the core principles of good governance as comprising:

- Rule of law which requires that laws and their implementation be transparent, predictable, equitable and credible;
- Accountability at each level of administration;
- Minimization of unfettered discretion;
- Putting the citizen first;
- Government to be built on a strong ethical foundation; and
- Principle of subsidiarity, which implies both devolution and delegation of authority (Rai 2011: 157).

The ability of the state to provide the institutions that support growth and poverty reduction is often referred to as good governance. Whether we look at it from a restrictive angle or the enlarged definition as given earlier, it will have to be accepted that India is still far from achieving the goal of good governance.

Fortunately, in recent years, good governance is also seen to be politically rewarding in terms of electoral victories for ruling political parties by even reversing the established trend of anti-incumbency. In the recent past, several state governments (Andhra Pradesh, Chhattisgarh, Delhi, Odisha, Madhya Pradesh and Sikkim) have come back to power on their records of good governance.

Though the term 'good governance' does not appear in the Indian Constitution, various provisions of the Constitution taken together underline this concept comprehensively. The Constitution has laid down that the state shall strive to promote the welfare of the people by securing and protecting as effectively as it may, a social order in which justice, social, economic and political, shall inform all institutions of national life. The fundamental rights are: (i) right to equality; (ii) seven freedoms, namely, freedom of speech and expression, to assemble peacefully and without arms, to form associations or unions, to move freely throughout the territory of India, to reside and settle in any part of the territory of India, to acquire, hold and dispose of property, and to practice any profession, or to carry on any occupation, trade or business; (iii) right to life and personal liberty; (iv) right to freedom of religion; (v) right against exploitation; (vi) cultural and educational rights; (vii) right to property; and (viii) right to constitutional remedies. The Constitution has also laid down the directive principles of state policy, which are not legally enforceable in courts, but are nevertheless fundamental to the governance of the country.

The fundamental rights and directive principles of state policy taken together thus encompass all the characteristics of good governance. Article 13 (2) has laid down that all laws and executive orders inconsistent with the fundamental rights would be *ultra virus* and void. It says, 'The State shall not make any law which takes away or abridges the rights conferred by this part and any law made in contravention of this clause shall to the extent of contravention be void.' Apart from the web of democratic and potentially vibrant institutions created by the Constitution, the special powers given to the Supreme Court under Article 32 to oversee the enforcement of fundamental rights is a strong point of the Indian Constitution. It is a unique feature of the Constitution of India that a citizen can directly approach the highest court in the land for any violation of his guaranteed fundamental rights within the terms of the Constitution. It is important to note that this power is itself a fundamental right which has been declared a part of the 'basic structure' of the Constitution. It must be underlined that fundamental rights have become a living reality for the poor, indigent and disadvantaged people due to the intervention of high courts and the Supreme Court.

N. R. Madhava Menon has emphasized:

> Among the radical changes rendered by the [Supreme] Court are the discovery
> of 'basic features' beyond the amending powers of Parliament, the introduction
> of the 'due process clause' in its substantive and procedural aspects in regard to
> the reading of Article 21 and Article 14, and the generation of numerous rights
> and freedoms not expressly given in Part III of the Constitution...We have
> today the world's most powerful judiciary guiding the constitutional destiny of
> 'We, the People of India' (Menon 2006: 59).

It is because of the basic structure doctrine that India will not have the fear
of a completely majoritarian rule again, as happened during the emergency.
Andhyarujina, an eminent Supreme Court advocate, has underlined how
incremental 'interpretations' by the Supreme Court have introduced the far-
reaching concept of 'due process' in the Constitution though the 'framers of the
Indian Constitution had rejected it after deep deliberations' (*The Indian Advocate*
2003: 9). Effectively, whenever the government's action is challenged under
Article 21 of the Constitution, it can be justified only as being 'right, just and fair'
and not arbitrary, fanciful or oppressive.

The state has, however, been dragging its feet in enforcing some of the crucial
rights which accrued to the citizens under the Constitution. Thus, 44 years
after the Constitution was enacted, the Supreme Court stepped in and added its
weight to turn the wheel of education (*Unnikrishnan v. State of Andhra Pradesh*,
AIR 1993 SC 2178). Of the five judges on the Bench, two said that the issue
did not arise for decision. But the three remaining judges held that the right to
education, at least at the primary level, was a fundamental right. The court noted
that the ten year limit, which had been provided under Article 45 for provision
for free and compulsory education for children had long expired. The Supreme
Court directive given in 1993 was however officially recognized by Parliament
only in 2002 when the right to education was inserted as a fundamental right by
amending the Constitution (Pal 2006: 117–18). Mention must also be made of
yet another landmark judgment of the Delhi High Court in 2004 which led to the
Delhi government directing some 1,600 private schools in Delhi to allot 20 per
cent seats for free to poor students.

It is only through judicial creativity or judicial activism that certain freedoms
like freedom of the press, the right to privacy, the right to travel abroad, the right
to education mentioned earlier and freedom from cruel and inhuman punishment
or degrading treatment have acquired the status of fundamental rights (Sorabjee
2007: 7).

'The right conferred by Article 14 (equality before law) is available to citizens
and non-citizens alike. Articles 15 (prohibition of discrimination on grounds of

religion, race, caste, sex or place of birth) and 16 (equality of opportunity in matters of employment) which together constitute a code of equality along with Article 14 are, however, available only to citizens of India...The concept of 'state' has undergone a radical change in recent times and the state can no longer be looked upon simply as a 'coercive machinery wielding the thunderbolt of authority.' By expanding the scope of the expression 'other authorities', judges have made the guarantee of equality meaningful and more effective...What Article 21, which provides that no person shall be deprived of his life and personal liberty except according to procedure established by law, means [the Supreme Court has held] is that the procedure by which life or liberty is taken away or abridged must be reasonable, fair and just' (Chandrachud 1989: 9, 20).

With the onset of economic liberalization, a disconcerting number of pressures for undermining the rule of law have surfaced in recent years. The otherwise progressive and erudite Arun Shourie, who was then Minister for Information Technology and Disinvestment in the NDA government, had gone overboard by declaring that entrepreneurs must exceed the limits of law to grow in a market. He was commending the way Reliance Infocomm had changed the rules of the game in the telecom sector. Shourie had added that there should not have been any restrictions on people like Dhirubhai Ambani. Shourie's open invitation to industrialists to break the law was shocking and was a negation of the concept of good governance. If everyone follows this route, one can well imagine what chaos will ensue. We have enough of crony capitalism as it is.

It may be relevant to give an instance of arbitrary decision-making in the government. In the PIL filed in the Delhi High Court against certain amendments made with respect to the trust deed of the Indira Gandhi National Centre for Arts (IGNCA), the Division Bench expressed its displeasure over Sonia Gandhi being made the president of the trust. The Bench asked, 'how being the widow of a former Prime Minister conferred any qualification of being an expert on art and culture and entitled her to be president of the trust without authority from the government...Merely because some eminent people are involved does not mean that the trust should be given largesse' (*Frontline*, 24 December 1999: 35).

The Government of India in the Ministry of Home Affairs (Inter-State Council Secretariat) had undertaken an exercise in 2004 to prepare a concept paper on good governance. The paper covered familiar ground, that is, the role of civil society, electoral reforms, judicial reforms, civil service reforms, administrative procedure reforms, economic reforms, fiscal reforms, labour market reforms, citizen-centric reforms, rural decentralization, urban sector reforms, e-governance etc. It also suggested adopting a short term action plan for transforming the government into a growth-friendly, citizen-centric and performing government. But like most other initiatives, this is where it appears to have ended!

Inter-Country Comparators and India's Performance

A number of comparators are developed internationally to compare governance among countries. It is a matter of serious concern that based on most of these comparators, India's governance has perceptibly declined over the years. The comparators include, among others, the human development index, freedom index, opacity index, corruption perception index, bribe payers index, transparency and corruption in civil society organizations, budget transparency, wages and corruption, gender and corruption, governance and corruption, governance and growth and so on. Some of these have been referred to in the introduction to this book. Transparency indices have also been developed to look at the performance of sectors such as real estate, capital markets, regulatory mechanisms and so on. The Political and Economic Risk Consultancy in Hong Kong surveyed the bureaucracy in 12 Asian countries in 2009. It found that the Indian bureaucracy was the most slow-moving and that it is a frustrating experience to approach the Indian bureaucracy to get any work done. (*Sakal* 4 June 2009: 9)At the annual meeting of the World Economic Forum in Davos in 2001 Price Water House Cooper unveiled an index that measured the impact on business of economic, legal and ethical transparency on the cost of capital in 35 countries, called the Opacity Index or the O Factor. The index identified the specific incremental borrowing costs imposed by the lack of transparency in areas of legal protection of business; macroeconomic policies; corporate reporting; corruption; and government regulations. Opacity is defined as the lack of clear, accurate, formal and widely accepted practices (*Public Eye* 2001: 5). Based on this too, India's performance leaves a great deal to be desired.

It will be pertinent to consider what the Joint Parliamentary Committee (JPC) on the bank scam (1993) had to say regarding the state of governance in the country:

"There are several dimensions of this entire episode: the functional one concerns the banks, brokers, PSUs [public sector undertakings/units] and ministries, etc. Here accountability was largely absent, punishment for a wrong committed was rare, an ethos of non-implementation prevailed all around. The second aspect about which the committee express its grave concern is the supervisory role and responsibility. That supervision failed from top to bottom is both self-evident and is detailed in subsequent chapters. What is extremely worrisome to the committee, however, is an unhappy side effect. Amongst all witnesses that appeared before the committee in all the many hours of evidence taken, the committee seldom came across an instance where responsibility for wrong was forthrightly accepted. Further, and more worrisomely, the committee found that as of routine, through the entire apparatus of governmental machinery, a very damaging approach seems to pervade, that of transferring responsibility downwards. This distressing lack of fibre in the apparatus of governance can only debilitate the state. This persuades the committee to briefly comment upon the third dimension of the entire matter, which is moral. No system can work through regulations alone, of course, it cannot work if they are flouted; but much more than that, if a system be devoid of the moral quotient, of a common sense appreciation of right from wrong, of a sense of public duty particularly when entrusted with public funds, then it cannot work" (Lok Sabha Secretariat 1993: 8).

I have given this, perhaps not too well-written, long quotation as it shows how a powerful committee of Parliament felt totally helpless where governance failures were concerned. It can be seen from the analysis presented in this book, that the position has deteriorated even more sharply over the 20 years since then.

Martin Jacques has highlighted that:

China is indubitably the outstanding example of a developing country, having grown at around 10 per cent a year for over 30 years and lifted an estimated 600 million out of poverty. These achievements have brought China considerable prestige in the developing world....The strengths of Chinese governance are threefold — its ability to think strategically, its infrastructural prowess and the impressive competence of its government. While the Western tradition emphasizes democracy, the Chinese attach equivalent importance to state competence, which is closely linked to the idea of meritocracy (Jacques 2013).

However, the Chinese system is reported to have been greatly afflicted by the virus of rapidly spreading corruption.

Uma Lele has pointed out that the World Bank's governance indicators empirically rank 210 countries using six criteria. Their methodology has flaws in the representativeness of the responses on which the ranking is based, but the relative positioning of the countries, presented in Table 2.1, offers a start and seems plausible. China ranks 200th among 210 countries on voice and accountability, compared to India's ranking of 86. China ranks 126th, relative to India's ranking of 100, on the rule of law and 149th in the control of corruption as compared to India's 136. China, however, ranks higher than India in political stability, government effectiveness and regulatory quality (Table 2.1). These latter three characteristics of China are critical for why a particular water strategy, which relies on large scale formal infrastructure and command and control, has been effective. These are precisely the areas in which Indian water strategy has gradually become ineffective...We argue that India is falling behind in developing an integrative approach to technology, infrastructure, funds and accountability of institutions. While India cannot adopt China's model, these comparisons do help to throw light on the huge challenge India faces to catch up on water governance.

Table 2.1
Worldwide governance indicators for Brazil, China, India, Indonesia, South Africa and the US

Country	Voice and accountability		Political stability and absence of violence/ terrorism		Government effectiveness		Regulatory quality		Rule of law		Control of corruption	
	Estimate	Rank	Estimate	Rank	Estimate	Rank	Estimate	Rank	Estimate	Rank	Estimate	Rank
Brazil	0.50	76	-0.04	113	-0.01	95	0.17	94	0.01	94	0.17	79
China	-1.64	200	-0.70	157	0.12	84	-0.20	116	-0.46	126	-0.67	149
India	0.41	86	-1.20	183	-0.03	97	-0.34	127	-0.08	100	-0.56	136
Indonesia	-0.08	112	-0.82	165	-0.24	113	-0.33	124	-0.65	146	-0.68	152
South Africa	0.57	72	0.02	109	0.37	75	0.44	73	0.10	87	0.03	86
United States	1.13	30	0.54	76	1.41	25	1.49	18	1.59	20	1.25	31

Source: The World Bank (2011).
Note: Estimate of governance ranges from approximately -2.5 (weak) to 2.5 (strong) governance performance.

This is especially so given its current ground water exploitation crisis and the already low rates of agricultural productivity growth. It calls for attention to policy as if on a war footing' (Lele, Klousia, Goswami 2013: 11–12).

India's poor performance in governance is largely due to the democratic system of governance *as practised in India*. In fact, the democratic system, as opposed to dictatorship, autocracy or any other authoritarian system should help in establishing good governance at all levels. What is wrong with the democratic system as practised in India is the manner in which it has been reduced to a farce. This is evident when one opens any newspaper any day. More than half of it consists of items on the dissatisfaction, complaints and grievances of citizens and their utter helplessness in making the system address issues and concerns effectively. This is all the more troubling since India is a rapidly urbanizing nation. It is estimated that by 2050, over 55 per cent of India's population will be living in urban areas. But the increasingly complex problem of restructuring institutions, policies and programmes has eluded policymakers. For example, the question of unauthorized constructions, referred to in the introduction, in cities such as Mumbai, Delhi, Kolkata, Pune, Thane, Ulhasnagar, Navi Mumbai, Pimpri Chinchwad and Pune Cantonment, to name just a few, is staggering. In the most recent shocking case, which is by no means exceptional, seven high rise buildings were constructed at Worli in Mumbai between 1981 and 1989. The builder had permission to build only six floors. One of the buildings, however, has 20 floors and another 17 floors (*IE*, 3 May 2013). It appears that the persons who had purchased flats on the higher floors were fully aware that the construction was unauthorized but, in keeping with the permissive governance, had hoped that the construction would be regularized! Reportedly, nearly 40 per cent of the buildings in Mumbai do not have an occupancy certificate from the Brihanmumbai Municipal Corporation (BMC) but are occupied (*Sakal*, 4 May 2013). After a lapse of over two decades, the Supreme Court in 2013 directed the demolition of the extra floors! There is no mention of action, if any, taken against the officers who had permitted the construction in the first place. There is no political will to deal with such a humongous problem. Rather, the emphasis is on regularization, thereby encouraging other unscrupulous operators to adopt this easy path.

The delay of more than four years in holding elections to the Chapra Municipal Corporation in Bihar was agitated before the Patna High Court in a PIL. The court was so upset that it asked the people to take to the streets and wage revolution instead of approaching the judiciary to solve their problems. The judges went on to state that if the state government was unable to move forward the vehicle of democracy, then the judiciary could not be expected to give it a push every time (*IE*, 5 August 1999). The decaying conditions of almost all urban areas are so shocking that one wonders what India would be like in 2050 if concerned institutions continue to function in the same manner. Against this background it is highly disappointing that the recommendation of the NCRWC that 'a new national commission on urbanisation should be constituted' has not received any attention. The fate of rural areas is worse with extreme poverty, deprivation, malnutrition, high infant mortality, farmers' suicides and so on, signifying an abject failure of governance.

Attention may be invited to the Seventy-third and Seventy-fourth Amendments to the Constitution which mandated decentralization of powers and functions in rural and urban local bodies respectively. Most of the states have been reluctant to give effect to these amendments. Wherever they have been implemented, it is seen that they have not worked well. The provisions of these amendments are seen to be based more on ideological considerations and political correctness than on ground realities. It is time to take a fresh look at these amendments.

A related question pertains to the highly questionable scheme initiated by the Government of India in the mid-1990s, called the Members of Parliament Local Area Development Scheme (MPLADS) under which currently Rs 5 crore are placed at the disposal of every sitting Member of Parliament (MP) each year for undertaking development work in his or her constituency. This largesse is also available to members of the Rajya Sabha, including to nominated members who do not have any constituency as such. With this 'dubious' example set by the central government, similar schemes have been approved by state governments for members of legislative assemblies (MLAs), members of legislative councils (MLCs), municipal corporators, municipal councillors, and members of the zilla parishads and panchayat samitis. A corporator of the BMC gets an astounding amount of Rs 1.45 crore each year for the development of his municipal ward! Nominated corporators get Rs 35 lakh each year (*Loksatta*, 22 February 2008). In no other western democratic country is such a scheme in operation. Unfortunately, when the scheme was challenged through a number of PILs, the Supreme Court declared it *intra virus*. The scheme can be questioned on a number of very valid grounds. The most important of these is that it militates against providing a level playing field to all contestants in an election. It also militates against the principle of separation of the executive from the legislature. But with the vested interests of elected representatives, these arguments had no impact on the thinking of the government or the legislators. Since even the Apex Court has declined to intervene, public pressure needs to be built to prevail on the government to cancel this scheme, as has been done by the Nitish Kumar government in Bihar. It is pertinent to note that the National Commission to Review the Working of the Constitution (NCRWC) as also the Second Administrative Reforms Commission (SARC) have recommended the abolition of this scheme.

The recent controversy in Maharashtra about the inefficacy of public expenditures, particularly in the irrigation and water supply sectors, should be an eye opener. In spite of huge expenditure incurred on irrigation and water supply schemes, the results and outcomes are negligible. In the report on State Finances of Maharashtra submitted in April 2013, the Comptroller and Auditor General (C&AG) highlighted that the cost of 242 irrigation projects in the state increased by an astronomical amount of Rs 26,617 crore over the years but none of the projects had been completed! (*IE*, 19 April 2013). To give another example, the verification of attendance in primary schools carried out in Maharashtra in 2011 showed that the actual attendance in several schools was less than 40 per cent of what was shown on the registers. This goes to highlight the importance of zero based budgeting. Maharashtra was the pioneer in taking this initiative in 1986 under the leadership of S. B. Chavan as Chief Minister when I was the Principal Finance Secretary. The scheme envisaged examination of all on-going schemes and programmes afresh each year to decide the budgetary allocation which should be given. The objective was to close the unproductive schemes and to divert the outlays thereon to more productive schemes. As a result, in less than two years, saving of over Rs 300 crore was effected by closing of out-dated schemes and the staff thereon redeployed. In spite of these successes, due to political pressures, the successor Sharad Pawar government disbanded zero based budgeting in 1989—the usual fate of such initiatives, giving a body-blow to a major economic reform.

Right to Information

The enactment of the Right to Information (RTI) Act, 2005 must be reckoned as a seminal landmark in the fight for good governance. The act recognizes the citizens' right to information comprehensively. Thus an applicant can ask for information on any subject except those which are specifically excluded from the purview of the act. Any information which cannot be denied to the legislature has to be made available to a citizen. The operation of the Official Secrets Act has also been restricted to some extent. The obligation cast on various offices for *suo motu* periodical publication of information is a step in the right direction. The right to information, which the Supreme Court has declared as a fundamental right, has made a qualitative difference to the fight against corruption by empowering people. Several large scams have been unearthed from the information collected under the act. It is not therefore surprising that so many in the government are opposed to the provisions of the act. The then CJI, K. G. Balakrishnan, had taken a position that he and the judges of the Supreme Court were not public servants 'in the strict sense' but were constitutional authorities and hence were outside RTI Act's ambit. The question is whether or not constitutional functionaries are public servants. But the Supreme Court itself had earlier held a contrary view: a five-judge bench had ruled with a 4:1 majority on 25 July 1991 that a judge of the High Court or Supreme Court is a public servant within the meaning of Section 2 of the Prevention of Corruption Act (*AA*, 25 April 2008).

It is pertinent to note that the President of India, A. P. J. Abdul Kalam, while giving assent to the landmark RTI Act had underlined in his note to the Prime Minister that: (i) communication between him and the Prime Minister should remain confidential; (ii) Rashtrapati Bhavan documents are privileged; and (iii) official notings of senior bureaucrats need to be kept out of the law lest it hampers decision making (*IE*, 25 June 2005). This showed an age-old mentality and the lack of awareness of where the world was headed! As a part of these efforts, attempts are still being made to withhold information in file notings. A campaign was carried out to propagate the view that right to information was obstructing the working of officers and ministers as they were afraid to express their free and frank opinions on files. To me personally, this does not make any sense since the assurance that file notings will eventually become available to the people to see should encourage officers to express their views fearlessly. But obviously a case is being made out for curbing the freedom of information available under the act. No less a person than Prime Minister Manmohan Singh has spoken on the subject and supported the amendment to the act to keep file notings out of its purview. 'The RTI should not affect the deliberative processes in government,' he cautioned. Fortunately, due to the pressure of public opinion, these efforts were given up.

Constant vigil will be necessary to ensure that similar efforts in the future do not succeed. For example, the RTI rules framed by some high courts have not been in keeping with the spirit of the RTI Act. The Allahabad High Court RTI rules 2006, were the most obstructive of all High Court rules and laid down an exorbitant application fee of Rs 500 and imposed an inflated cost of Rs 15 per page of information sought. Delhi based NGO, Common Cause, filed a PIL in the Supreme Court in 2012 asking for relief and to direct the High Court of Allahabad and the subordinate courts within the jurisdiction of the High Court to follow the Right to Information (Regulation of Fee and Cost) rules, 2006 framed by the central government that are also being followed by the Supreme Court.[2]

When I was doing research for my book, *The Judiciary and Governance in India* in 2007, I wrote to all high courts seeking information on a few points. The Andhra Pradesh High Court wanted to treat the request as an application under the RTI Act and wanted the application to be sent by affixing a court fee stamp of Rs 25. Since adhesive court fee stamp of the requisite denomination was not available in Pune, I got the letter franked for the amount of Rs 50, which was the minimum amount prescribed for franking, and requested the High Court once again to furnish the information. However, the High Court conveyed that the information could not be supplied without court fee stamp of Rs 25! I finally gave up in sheer exasperation. The Delhi High Court (Right to Information) rules, 2006, also raise a number of concerns (Godbole 2008: 139, 406). It is thus evident that mere enactment of a law is not enough unless there is a change in the mindset and a desire to implement the law, in letter and spirit.

SARC has rightly recommended that MPs and MLAs be declared 'public authorities' under the RTI Act, except when they are discharging legislative functions (Government of India 2007: 176). This is particularly important in view of the MPLADS executed by MPs and MLAs with large annual provisions from state exchequers.

Constant efforts are also being made to restrict the scope of the RTI Act. Thus, the CBI has been included in the list of exempted institutions for no justifiable reasons. One can understand if information pertaining to cases under investigation is withheld from the public but there is no reason why information pertaining to cases which are closed at the behest of the CBI, ostensibly due to lack of evidence, or the cases which CBI has lost in courts, should not be made public. Examination of such cases can bring out the manner in which the CBI operates, the pressures—political and extraneous—which it faces, how faulty and self-serving legal advice is often given to the CBI and so on. It is only by such public surveillance and scrutiny that the workings of the CBI can be improved.

It is interesting to see that the Supreme Court itself is reported to have observed that public authorities need not be generous in their interpretation of the RTI Act. As a result, the department of personnel issued a circular dated 16 September 2011 to ministries and state governments not to draw an 'inference' or make 'assumptions' or provide 'opinions' or 'advice' in RTI replies. The circular says that the 'information officer is not supposed to create information, or to interpret information or to solve the problems raised by the applicants or to furnish replies to hypothetical questions (*IE*, 4 October 2011). What an eloquent commentary on the government of the people, by the people and for the people!

Particular attention must be invited to the very retrograde stand taken in 2002 by the CVC, which is the highest integrity institution in the country, when due to the allegations of corruption and clamour in Parliament, he was asked by the NDA government to scrutinise defence procurement transactions dating back to 1989. The CVC, N. Vittal, is said to have examined as many as 500 top secret files but recommended to the government that his report should not be made public and should not even be shared with the Public Accounts Committee (PAC). As a result, the government rejected PAC's demand of seeing the report. This made no sense and the whole purpose of entrusting the scrutiny of the files to CVC was lost. It is thus necessary to change the mindset, not just of government functionaries, but also of statutory authorities and to sensitize them about the precepts of public accountability and transparency.

A reference must also be made to a number of progressive and forward looking decisions given by the information commissioners. By one such decision, the Reserve Bank of India and commercial banks have been asked to publish the names of large loan defaulters, which were being kept away from people. By another landmark decision in June 2013, the Central Information Commission declared that six major political parties—Congress, BJP, CPM, CPI, NCP and BSP—were public authorities under the RTI Act and directed these parties to appoint information officers, make voluntary disclosures and provide information sought under the act within six weeks. This decision will go a long way in cleansing political and public life in the country, particularly since there is no law in India on political parties. The Supreme Court has already suggested that early action should be taken to enact a law on political parties. But, as was to be expected, the Congress Party, which takes credit for having introduced the RTI Act for empowering the common man, has opposed the decision saying that 'the CIC order is a rather unusual interpretation of the provisions of the RTI Act' and such an 'adventurist approach' by the CIC will harm democratic institutions! This is not surprising given the background of what used to be said during the very long tenure of Sitaram Kesari as the Congress treasurer, *Na khata na bahi, jo kesari kahe wohi sahi* (there is neither any account book nor an exercise book, Kesari's word alone is the last word). It is, however, surprising to see the CPM and CPI joining the Congress Party in opposing the move as retrograde. It was also surprising to see the otherwise progressive newspaper like the *Indian Express* editorially opposing the CIC's decision. The government has decided to amend the RTI Act to supersede the CIC decision. Since most political parties are likely to support the bill, it will be passed in Parliament. Thereafter, the matter will inevitably be raised by civil society in the Supreme Court. Let us hope that the CIC decision will ultimately be upheld by the court.

Access to several reports of committees appointed by the government was also being denied to the people. These included the Arun Singh Committee Report on defence expenditures which was kept confidential in spite of repeated demands in Parliament. The Central Information Commissioner has directed that this report should be made available to the people. Surprisingly, the Ministry of Defence has now made a statement that the report is not traceable! Considerable information pertaining to the 2G scam came out only because of applications filed under the RTI Act.

I had earlier referred to the tardy investigations by central police agencies such as the CBI and the Enforcement Directorate. An outstanding example of this is the Bofors case in which after spending hundreds of crores of rupees on investigations and undertaking countless foreign trips, the CBI had the temerity to say in court that there was no case against Quattrochi. The CBI also pleaded before the court that Quattrochi's bank accounts in London and elsewhere which were frozen a few years earlier should be defrozen by the court. If this state of affairs is to be remedied it is necessary to bring the CBI in the purview of the RTI Act so that *cases in which investigations have been closed or the accused have been acquitted by the courts*, people have the freedom to see the relevant documents. This will be the most effective countercheck on the working of the CBI and other organizations like the Enforcement Directorate.

The obsession with secrecy continues to prevail in government. For example, it is difficult to understand why the official histories of the three wars with Pakistan and the 1962 war with China should be treated as secret even after so many years. Even former chiefs of the three armed forces have been pressing for the release of these war histories so that lessons can be learnt for the future. The contents of the time capsule which was buried during the regime of Indira Gandhi are also treated as secret. There is no reason why people cannot see the contents, which are meant to be seen by posterity, and decide how realistic the depiction therein is of what India has been through. The Task Force on Border Management appointed by the Government of India, of which I was the Chairman, had recommended that the report should be released to the public for creating greater awareness and public participation in the handling of issues. A similar recommendation was made by the Task Force on Internal Security, of which N. N. Vohra, Governor of Jammu and Kashmir, was the Chairman. But the then NDA government decided not to release either of the reports. Madhav Gadgil, who was Chairman of the Western Ghats Environment Committee, had recommended that the report of the committee should be made available to the people in the concerned states in local languages, and placed before all gram sabhas for their considered feedback. However, the central government first suppressed the report, releasing it only when forced to do so. The Centre and the states also declined to make the report available to people in regional languages (Gadgil 2013: 52–54). The horrendous tragedy in Uttarakhand in 2013 due to the havoc caused by floods, cloud bursts and massive landslides was partly a natural phenomenon, but it was certainly exacerbated by flouting environmental concerns. Unless lessons are learnt from it, the Western Ghats will be at a similar risk.

According to a news item, the PMO has refused to make available the papers pertaining to Robert Vadra, Sonia Gandhi's son-in-law's land deals, called for in a PIL in the Allahabad High Court on the specious plea that it is holding them as a trustee! (*Loksatta*, 13 June 2013). This confirms the worst fears that the PMO is an extension of Sonia Gandhi's office at 10 Janpath.

This brings me to the important question of the continuance of the Official Secrets Act. Certain secrets pertaining to national security and defence will, no doubt, need to be safeguarded but the ambit of their coverage must be carefully restricted. This subject has been debated by a number of committees including SARC and the H. D. Shourie Committee on Right to Information. The Press Council of India has also made some salutary recommendations in the matter. It is time these are taken into account and very early steps taken to repeal the Official Secrets Act, which is of 1923 vintage, and to incorporate a chapter in the National Security Act containing provisions pertaining to official secrets, which may be defined as, 'information which is likely to prejudicially affect the sovereignty and integrity of India, the security of state, friendly relations with foreign states, economic, commercial, scientific and technological matters relating to national security and may include any secret code, password, sketch, plan, model, article, note or document in relation to a prohibited place' (Government of India 2006: 58). This will go a long way in opening the working of the government and improving its efficacy and accountability.

With the experience of the RTI Act so far it can be said that it has served a useful purpose in bringing about greater accountability and transparency in the working of the government. At present, attention to governance issues has been confined to the functioning of the government and its agencies. But, as stated earlier, deterioration in governance in other sectors of society is no less worrying. These include the private sector, cooperatives, political parties, the media, non-governmental organizations, trade unions, sports bodies and so on. For example, the betting and match-fixing scandal has shown how opaque the BCCI's functioning is. It has prominent national leaders of several political parties on its board but none of them has dared to open his mouth on the subject. The same is true of prominent past and present cricketers, except for Rahul Dravid. The disreputable functioning of the Indian Olympic Association, which had led to its derecognition by the international body for some time, was a national shame. The affairs of the Indian Hockey Federation have similarly become controversial. India abolished the privy purses and successfully merged the princely states but the 'princely states' of various organizations have flourished uninterruptedly. It is time that the RTI Act is extended to all sectors of society. Empowering people in this manner will be the surest way of strengthening democracy and its vitality.

Finally, at present, almost all posts of information commissioners and chief information commissioners all over the country are manned by retired civil servants. Persons from outside the bureaucracy occupying these posts are rare (Dhaka 2010: 195). There is no reason why *persons of honesty and integrity* from other walks of life cannot be appointed to these posts. Such a step will certainly increase the credibility, public acceptability and the impact of the act.

The Criminal Justice System and Its Apathy for Human Rights[3]

Justice Sujata Manohar has stated:

> Justice P. N. Bhagwati, one of the founders of human rights jurisprudence in our country, has this to say about human rights. He says, 'Human rights are as old as human society itself, for they derive from every person's needs to realize his essential humanity. They are not ephemeral, not alterable with time, place and circumstances. They are not the product of philosophical whim or political fashion. They have their origin in the fact of the human condition, and because of this origin they are fundamental and inalienable' (Manohar 2013: 62).

However, everyday life in India is marked by serious and constant violations of human rights. Needless to say, human rights' violations will come down only when the law asserts itself. And this is not just rhetoric. It has a great deal to commend itself as a major constituent of public policy. It has to be accepted that respect for law has declined perceptibly over the years. Neither is there a fear of law enforcement agencies. There was a 336 per cent increase in child rape cases between 2001 (2,113 cases) and 2011 (7,112 cases). This included widely prevalent crime against children in remand homes and other correctional institutions.

The common refrain is that with political and monetary clout, one can literally get away with murder. In such a situation, human rights are the first casualty. If supremacy of law is to be re-established, all institutions concerned with upholding the rule of law will have to be strengthened and rejuvenated. As the Supreme Court has laid down, the concept of reasonableness must be projected in the procedure contemplated by Article 21. According to Justice Bhagwati, the procedure 'must be "right and just and fair" and not arbitrary, fanciful or oppressive; otherwise it would be no procedure at all and that requirement of Article 21 would not be satisfied' (Sharma 1995: 99).

The right to a speedy trial has been recognized by the Supreme Court as a part of protection available under Article 21 of the Constitution. Unfortunately, all such pronouncements have remained on paper with pendency of cases reaching a figure of 3 crore. Of these nearly 70 per cent are criminal cases and the balance are civil cases. According to a news item, it took 22 years for the Bombay High Court to give a decision in an appeal in a criminal case involving rioting in the Godrej factory in Mumbai. This is equally true of several major criminal cases which have attracted national attention such as those pertaining to the bank scam and Bofors, discussed in Chapter 3. Unfortunately, the high courts and Supreme Court do not publish any annual administration reports to disseminate periodical information regarding the administration of justice. This major lacuna needs to be rectified. The April 2002 decision of the Constitution Bench of seven judges of the Supreme Court setting aside the earlier decision of that court to close criminal cases which remain pending for over two years needs to be seen against the large pendency of criminal cases. This decision will imply that till the relevant provisions of the legislation are amended, the accused in criminal cases will languish in jails for years together. The late N. A. Palkhivala, one of the most outstanding advocates in the country, had rightly said:

> I am not aware of any country in the world where litigation goes on for as long a period as in India. The law may not be an ass, but in India it is certainly a snail and our cases proceed at a pace which would be regarded as unduly slow in a community of snails. Justice has to be blind but I see no reason why it should also be lame: here it just hobbles along, barely able to walk (Palkhivala 1994: 216).

There are only 10–12 judges for every million people in India, while advanced countries have more than 50 judges per million. And in those countries, hardly 7 to 10 per cent of the cases go to trial. The rest are settled out of court.

A related and important aspect pertains to updating the old and outdated laws. A commission appointed by the central government has pointed out that over 1,200 central laws were outdated and either needed to be repealed altogether or amended suitably. It is a travesty that most state governments have not even started an exercise to identify laws which have outlived their utility. Time and again it is seen that the punishments prescribed under laws are so nominal and paltry as not to have any impact on the crime situation. It is a waste of time to carry out elaborate, costly and time-consuming police investigations and court proceedings which result in a paltry fine of a few hundred rupees or simple imprisonment of a few days. All such penal provisions will have to be amended to provide deterrent punishment. There is also a need for distinguishing between first offenders and habitual offenders.

The most striking feature of the Indian judicial system is the large number of under trials at any given time. The estimated number of under trials in the country is about 200,000. Upendra Baxi has emphasized that, 'The view that prisoners are non-persons, that assured fundamental rights are not available to them by their being incarcerated, received considerable judicial support in the celebrated *Gopalan* case' (Baxi 1982: 209). However, later, *Hussainara Khatoon v. The State of Bihar* made judicial history in many ways. As Dhagamwar has stated, the Supreme Court gave a series of interim orders to give relief to under trials (Dhagamwar 1997: 166–81). These included those who had served more than the maximum sentence that could have been given had they been convicted, were to be discharged and proceedings against them to be quashed; bail on personal recognizance if they fulfilled certain conditions; (this decision was set aside by a Constitution Bench of the Supreme Court in April 2002); releasing all prisoners against whom no charge sheets had been filed for two years; all prisoners who were unable to hire counsel had a right to legal aid; all women and children in protective custody, whether victims or witnesses, to be released on personal bonds; the state cannot avoid its constitutional obligation to provide speedy trials to the accused by pleading financial or administrative inability and so on. However, Dhagamwar found that the Bihar government had no intention of implementing the Supreme Court directives. She rightly underlined, 'On its own the Court cannot do very much more. If the trail blazoned by the Court with so much wisdom, courage and foresight peters out, the fault will rest squarely with us.'

For want of adequate manpower and supervision in jails, and neglected police investigations and follow-ups, the undertrials have to languish in jails for years. In addition, the bail system prevalent in India suffers from a property oriented approach making it difficult for the accused to furnish bail. As NHRC has underlined:

> There was an over-crowding to the extent of 44.2 per cent for the country as a whole in 2006 as compared to 39 per cent on 31 December 2004. Nine states, namely, Jharkhand, Chhattisgarh, Bihar, Gujarat, Delhi, Madhya Pradesh, UP, Sikkim, and Odisha experienced overcrowding ranging from 52 per cent to 216 per cent above the authorised capacity...Jharkhand (216.3 per cent) is maintaining its top position followed by Chhattisgarh (114.9 per cent), Bihar (107.1 per cent), and Gujarat (100.2 per cent)...The proportion of under trial prisoners was more than 80 per cent of the total prison population in seven States/Union Territories (Government of India 2006-07: 195).

According to the National Crime Records Bureau, Uttar Pradesh had the maximum number of under trials (54,062) at the end of 2011. Bihar was next with 23,417, with Madhya Pradesh, Maharashtra and West Bengal making up the top five. Venkatachelliah, the former Chairman of NHRC, rightly described Indian jails as 'penal dustbins'.

A suggestion made in this context by a group of retired police officers in their report needs to be noted. The group suggested decriminalization of certain traditionally recognized crimes such as gambling, drinking and prostitution to relieve the police of looking after these crimes and instead concentrating their attention on other more important crimes. As society advances, the emphasis ought to be on public education and creating greater awareness about these social evils, rather than stretching an already over-burdened criminal justice system by classifying them as crimes.

The Committee on Reforms of the Criminal Justice System (Justice V. S. Malimath Committee), in its report submitted in March 2003, made wide-ranging recommendations to deal with the two problems—huge pendency of cases and poor rate of conviction—which have plagued the Indian criminal justice system (Government of India 2003). According to the committee, two areas which need special attention for improving the quality of justice are prescribing required qualifications for judges and the quality of training being imparted in judicial academies. The committee also dealt with the widely prevalent practice of perjury in criminal cases. Like so many reports of other committees, this report too has been languishing without any perceptible action for a long time.

The creation of the National Human Rights Commission (NHRC) was a major step forward in our drive to establish the supremacy of human rights. Several states have also established such commissions. However, the composition of the human rights commissions requires urgent review. These commissions have become the preserves of retired judges (and police officers). The presumption seems to be that only judges can be entrusted with the responsibility of upholding human rights in the country. It is time eminent and upright persons of standing from different walks of life, including persons working in well-known NGOs and others in the field, are appointed to these commissions to bring in greater public participation and grassroots experience in their deliberations. The same is true of the work of inquiring into complaints by commissions. These inquiries should not be entrusted only to police officers, as at present, but should also be given to NGOs, professionals and persons of integrity and honesty working in various fields. This will inspire greater confidence in the working of the commissions.

Judicial Activism and Good Governance[4]

Judicial activism has been a subject of intense debate within the judiciary, in the government and among members of the public for over two decades. A number of those who were strong proponents of the concept in the beginning have been disenchanted and have become its strong critics. The opposite is equally true. Those who were strong critics of judicial activism have now become its supporters. Let us discuss these pros and cons and analyse the extent to which judicial activism should have a legitimate place in a democratic polity.

The Indian Constitution has recognized the principle of separation of powers between the three wings of the legislature, the judiciary and the executive, though not as water-tight compartments. The founding fathers had not visualized that any one organ of the state would so vigorously interfere in the field of any other organ. But judicial activism should not be confused with judicial review which is a legitimate function of the judiciary. In fact, independence of the judiciary and power of judicial review have been declared by the Supreme Court as parts of the 'basic structure' of the Constitution.

Articles 32 and 226 of the Constitution of India come into play in matters pertaining to judicial activism. The plain reading of these articles brings out how thin the dividing line between the legitimate duties of the high courts and the Supreme Court and the perceived judicial activism of the courts is. From the point of view of a common person, the heart of the Constitution is its chapter on fundamental rights and the related chapter on directive principles of state policy. While the fundamental rights are justiciable, the directive principles are not enforceable by any court. The principles laid down therein are nevertheless declared fundamental in the governance of the country and it has been declared by the Constitution that it shall be the duty of the state to apply these principles in making laws. However, over time the Supreme Court has treated the directive principles on the same footing as fundamental rights.

Article 32 of the Constitution lays down the remedies for enforcing fundamental rights. Article 32 (1) states that 'the right to move the Supreme Court by appropriate proceedings for enforcement of the rights conferred by this Part is guaranteed.' This itself is a fundamental right and the Supreme Court is under duty to grant relief for violation of a fundamental right. Under Article 32 (2), the Supreme Court has powers to issue directions or orders or writs, including writs in the nature of *habeas corpus, mandamus*, prohibition, *quo warranto* and *certiorari*, whichever may be appropriate, for enforcing any of the rights conferred by the chapter on fundamental rights. Article 32 (4) lays down that 'the right guaranteed by this article shall not be suspended except as otherwise provided by this Constitution.' It is important to note that the Supreme Court has declared Article 32 to be part of the basic feature of the Constitution which cannot be taken away even by amending the Constitution.

Article 226, regarding the concurrent powers of high courts, pertains to the issue of certain writs. Article 226 (1) states:

Notwithstanding anything in article 32 every high court shall have power, throughout the territories in relation to which it exercises its jurisdiction, to issue to any person or authority, including in appropriate cases, any government, within those territories directions, orders or writs, including writs in the nature of *habeas corpus, mandamus*, prohibition, *quo warranto* and *certiorari*, or any of them, for the enforcement of any of the rights conferred by Part III [fundamental rights] and for any other purpose.

Against this background, it will be interesting to take a look at the genesis of judicial activism. Indira Gandhi's campaign in the 1970s to malign the judiciary as status quoist, obstructionist, reactionary, against the common man's interests and favouring capitalists was largely responsible for the higher judiciary going on the defensive. The judgments of the Supreme Court in important cases such as *Kesavananda Bharati* and the abolition of privy purses were severely criticized by the ruling Congress Party and its Leftist allies in Parliament. This confrontation led to reactions from the judiciary and several judges felt that it was necessary to refurbish the image of the judiciary (Godbole 2008: 219). The Gujarat High Court was the harbinger in encouraging a PIL which was quickly adopted thereafter by the Supreme Court and other high courts. New and innovative procedures were recognized by the courts for the purpose. The most important of these was the relaxation of the age-old doctrine of *locus standi*. As a result, anyone could approach the court for redressal of grievances of an individual or a group of people. Formal requirements of filing of papers were done away with. The court could even be approached by writing a postcard to the court registry. The applicant could appear in the court himself to plead his own case and did not need to engage a lawyer. Rules regarding producing evidence were relaxed. A PIL was to be a non-adversarial litigation with the court playing a proactive role in finding a solution to the problem at hand.

Decisions of the courts in some PILs have made a substantial difference to public life and governance in India. I illustratively refer to a few of them. One, the decision of the Delhi High Court in *Association of Democratic Reforms v. Union of India* (AIR 2001 del 126), followed by the decision of the Supreme Court in appeal in June 2002, making it compulsory for each candidate to give his criminal background, if any, while contesting elections to the State Legislature or Parliament, has gone a long way in cleansing public life and empowering the voter. It was particularly noteworthy that this decision was enforced by the court through the Election Commission of India in spite of stiff opposition by all political parties in Parliament. As a result, each candidate has to furnish information regarding his or her assets and liabilities and those of his or her dependents, and details of his or her criminal background—convictions by courts, cases in which he or she is charge sheeted etc, if any, while filing the nomination papers. This enables voters to judge the credentials of candidates. Two, the tendency of governments at the national as well as state levels to rule by ordinances, instead of going before the legislatures in time to get necessary laws passed, is a national phenomenon. Bihar was the worst culprit in this regard in terms of reissuing ordinances by which 256 ordinances were kept alive for periods ranging from one to 14 years. The Supreme Court's decision in the *D. C. Wadhwa v. State of Bihar* (AIR 1987 SC 579) finally put a stop to this practice. Three, the rampant misuse of Article 356 of the Constitution by imposition of President's rule and dismissal of state governments, often for purely political objectives, had become a source of friction between the Centre and the states. B. R. Ambedkar had stated in the Constituent Assembly that he hoped that this article would be used so sparingly that it would remain a 'dead letter'. However, till recently, the reality was quite the opposite. For years, the Centre used this power arbitrarily. It was believed that such a decision being a 'political question', was beyond the competence of the court. However, in the case of *S. R. Bommai v. Union of India* (1994, 3 SCC 1) the question of President's 'satisfaction' and powers came to the fore. Earlier, in the case of the *State of Rajasthan v. Union of India* (1977, 3 SCC 592), the court had held that if the satisfaction was *mala fide* or was based on wholly extraneous and irrelevant grounds, the court would have jurisdiction to examine it. Although the adequacy or sufficiency of grounds on which action could be taken under Article 356 (1) was held to be non-justiciable, most of the judges were unwilling to concede to the central government that 'satisfaction' under Article 356 (1) was not open to scrutiny by the court under any circumstances. Two of the judges held that, 'If the satisfaction is *mala fide* or is based wholly on extraneous or irrelevant grounds, the court would have jurisdiction to examine it, because in that case there would be no satisfaction of the President in regard to the matter in which he is required to be satisfied.' The scope of judicial review was further expanded in the *S. R. Bommai* case. The nine-judge Bench unanimously held the presidential powers under Article 356 to be amenable to judicial review. The court also laid down that the power under Article 356 though based on subjective satisfaction is only conditional and not absolute. The President can be satisfied only when a situation as laid down in the article exists. The President was under an obligation to consider the advisability and necessity of the action (The Indian Law Institute 1994, reprint: 127–29). This decision of the court had a significant impact on Centre-state relations and a major irritant in these relations was removed. Article 356, for the first time, became 'dead letter', as was visualized by Ambedkar. The Centre's efforts to impose President's rule in Uttar Pradesh in 2007 did not succeed partly because of the Supreme Court's disapproval of the Centre's action of imposing President's rule in Bihar in 2005, though the court had refrained from reviving the State Legislature. But the Governor who had recommended the imposition of President's rule had to resign. Four, the Supreme Court has expanded its role significantly by putting new interpretations and reading new meaning in constitutional provisions. As a result, it can now be said without any exaggeration that the Indian Constitution is what the Supreme Court says it is. Otherwise, the powers of appointments of judges to higher judiciary would not have been taken over so completely by the collegium of the Supreme Court to itself. Five, the court has expanded the scope of Article 12 of the Constitution. This article defines the 'state' to include the government and the Parliament of India and the government and the legislature of each state and all local or other authorities within the territory of India or under the control of the Government of India. However, over the years, this definition has been expanded to cover a number of entities such as insurance companies, nationalized banks, airline corporations, electricity boards and so on. Once any authority is declared an 'instrumentality' of the government, it becomes subject to discipline of fundamental rights, and its actions and decisions can be challenged with reference to fundamental rights. It also becomes subject to the discipline of administrative law and the writ jurisdiction of the Supreme Court and the high courts. Six, in the path-breaking judgment in *Kesavananda Bharati v. State of Kerala*, (AIR 1973 SC 1461) the court gave a new and innovative interpretation of Article 368 by declaring that the Parliament's powers to amend the Constitution were limited by the basic structure of the Constitution. The court did not spell out the term 'basic structure' comprehensively in that judgment but dilated on only a few of the features such as parliamentary democracy and judicial review. In subsequent cases, the term basic structure was defined to include supremacy of the Constitution; federalism; secularism; separation of powers; free and fair elections; the principle of equality, not every feature of equality, but the quintessence of equal justice; judicial review; rule of law; sovereign, democratic, republican structure; and powers of the Supreme Court under Articles 32, 136, 141 and 142. Looking to the manner in which the Constitution was repeatedly and arbitrarily amended by the Indira Gandhi government, often to suit her political needs, the restrictions put on the powers of the Parliament, though resented by the ruling Congress Party and its Leftist allies, were widely welcomed by the people. Seven, though the Constituent Assembly had consciously decided against the concept of 'due process of law' and had opted for the words 'except according to procedure established by law', the Supreme Court effectively veered round to accepting the 'due process' in a number of cases. As Soli Sorabjee has rightly stressed, it is due to judicial creativity or judicial activism that certain freedoms have acquired the status of fundamental rights (Sorabjee 2007: 7). Eight, the Supreme Court's striking down of the Illegal Migrants Determination by Tribunals Act (*Sarbananda Sonowal v. Union of India and another* [2005, 5 SCC 665]), as unconstitutional on 13 July 2005 and the strictures passed by the court against the central government for neglecting the defence of the country's borders was a tremendous morale booster to those who were agitating against the flood of illegal migration from Bangladesh.

Judicial activism has also led to containing police atrocities, vigorously pursuing investigations in cases of police encounter deaths, effective action against bonded labour, protecting the interests of tribals, laying down the principle of 'polluter must pay', prescribing guidelines against sexual harassment of women at the workplace (*Visakha v. State of Rajasthan*, 1997 [6, SCC 241]) and so on.

But this is only one side of the story. We must now turn to the other side and see whether judicial activism has led to any negative results. The first and foremost area of concern is that judicial activism has compromised the principle of separation of powers between the three organs of the state. A section of the higher judiciary has put such liberal interpretation on its own powers under the Constitution, referred to earlier, that it has not hesitated in interfering in executive decision-making and even legislative functions. Somnath Chatterjee, former Speaker of the Lok Sabha, bluntly stated, 'The responsibility for managing public affairs should be well left to those on whom the Constitution has imposed such obligation and for which they are accountable to the people' (Chatterjee 2007: 9). Only a few instances will suffice to bring home the seriousness of the issues. The Supreme Court had asked that the report of the Parliamentary Standing Committee on reservation of seats for the other backward classes (OBCs) should be placed before it in a sealed cover, even before it was presented to Parliament. This was grossly in violation of parliamentary procedure. The court is expected to take up a constitutional challenge to a legislation only after it is passed by Parliament. As was to be expected, the court's intrusion in parliamentary deliberations, even before they were concluded, was much resented and led to widespread adverse comments. Finally, the court had to withdraw its order and it told the government on 17 October 2006 that the report of the committee should be submitted to the court only after it is submitted to the House.

The Supreme Court is not expected to interfere in any matter which is before Parliament or a State Legislature. However, this norm has been breached more than once with the court asking the speakers of state legislatures (Uttar Pradesh, Jharkhand) when and how meetings of the legislature are to be convened, how they are to be conducted, the observers who will attend the meetings, videographing of the proceedings and so on. This has raised major questions about the independence of the legislatures. Questions have also been raised about a likely scenario if the Speaker refuses to abide by the direction of the Supreme Court and the consequences of such a confrontation. It must be said to the credit of these legislatures that they did not take such a precipitous step and graciously stepped back.

The Supreme Court holding hearings to examine how the power shortages in Delhi were proposed to be redressed by the Delhi government led to considerable controversy. The government's counsel raised questions as to how this could be the legitimate function of the court. Instead of doing self-introspection, the court expressed its unhappiness with the government counsel which led to his being taken off the case. The appointment of forest advisory committees was yet another bone of contention between the government and the Supreme Court. The nominees suggested by the government for appointment on the committees were not found suitable by the court due to the objections raised by civil society. Appointments of such committees fall squarely in the domain of the executive but the court has taken a hand in them. The Supreme Court decision in August 2010 that the government should distribute surplus grain rotting in its storage to poor people free has also been questioned by the government. Prime Minister Manmohan Singh has said that the court should not interfere in policy matters and it is best that these are left to the executive to deal with. By another decision in August 2010, the Supreme Court asked the government to consider appointing a separate pay commission for the armed forces.

Once an act is passed by the legislature, it is the executive which is responsible to the legislature for its implementation. However, in recent years the courts have been taking a hand in supervising the implementation of acts. For this purpose, empowered committees are appointed by the courts which are answerable only to the court and not to the executive or the legislature. This happened in 2006–07 with the Delhi High Court and the Supreme Court taking a hand in the removal of encroachments in Delhi, stopping conversion of residential buildings/areas into commercial areas and ensuring that the Delhi Master Plan was strictly adhered to. For several weeks Delhi was in turmoil, law and order problems arose and the police even had to resort to firing in certain localities. Unable to contain public anger and protests, the government resorted to the subterfuge of redefining certain areas as non-residential and enacted the Delhi Laws (Special Provisions) Act, 2006 to freeze the implementation of the Delhi Master Plan for a period of two years. This was frowned upon by the court and a major war of words ensued, with the government threatening to put the relevant act in the Ninth Schedule of the Constitution to oust the jurisdiction of the courts. This shows the limits to which judicial activism was stretched and the response of the government thereto.

At the same time, it has to be admitted that certain decisions taken by the courts in the interest of public order, improving the quality of life and establishing the rule of law could not have been taken by the elected governments due to their preoccupation with populism. One of these decisions delivered in 1996 pertained to the abatement of noise pollution and restrictions on playing music and use of loud speakers from 10 pm to 6 am. On persistent demand by political parties, the court agreed to relax these restrictions somewhat for up to a maximum of 10 festival days in a year, as may be notified by the state government and local authorities. Another major decision pertains to putting a complete ban on political parties declaring *bandhs* (stoppage of all work and activities) in protest against some decision or the other. In a state like Kerala, such *bandhs* had become a public menace. The Supreme Court had no hesitation in dubbing the Gurjjar agitation in Rajasthan a 'national shame'. The court ordered that any damage and destruction of public property caused during *bandhs* and agitations should be recovered from the concerned political party or organization. Needless to say, these decisions have caused a great deal of resentment among some political parties.

Public interest litigation has at times been misused by some persons to settle individual scores and to harass the opposite party. The courts themselves have described them as publicity interest litigation or *paise* (monetary) interest litigation. The Supreme Court and the high courts have come down heavily in such cases by imposing heavy fines and award of costs. But the size of the problem of PILs is far from clear. No data is available about the number of PILs filed year wise, their disposal, pendency and so on. Some PILs have languished for years. Efforts made by me to compile data by a survey of high courts and the Supreme Court did not yield any results due to the uncooperative attitude of the courts. However, from the number of court decisions reported in newspapers almost every day, it is clear that PILs take a considerable time of the higher courts. In some PILs, dozens of hearings have been held by the courts. This is of particular concern due to the large and increasing pendency of other cases in these courts.

In recent years, decisions of the courts in some PILs have made politicians in general, and the ruling elite in particular, extremely unhappy. This is primarily due to the cases involving prominent leaders, in which the court has ordered investigation of corruption and other serious charges. In some of these cases, the court has also ordered that the investigating agencies should report the progress of the investigation to the court and not to the executive. This has rattled the political leadership. The same is true of cases in which the courts have frowned upon lack of transparency in government decisions on major projects and contracts. Such decisions have been widely welcomed by the people but have created unease in politicians. This has led to demands from time to time to curtail the powers of the courts to entertain PILs. The Supreme Court is disinclined to lay down any guidelines for the purpose, though almost all central governments during the last decade have toyed with this idea. However, since the powers of the courts are derived from constitutional provisions, which are a part of the basic structure of the Constitution, it is not legally feasible to put any restrictions on the powers of the courts. As an alternative, the government has thought of increasing the financial burden on the petitioner by increasing the stamp duty for approaching a court. But this has met with stiff resistance from the media, civil society and activists. It will be interesting to see how far an elected government, irrespective of which political party it belongs to, will be prepared to go to shield its actions from the scrutiny of the courts.

Reference must also be made to a few other aspects of PILs. The actual experience of PILs shows that they are not non-adversarial. In fact, in most cases, the government or the concerned agencies contest them vigorously. The criteria for admission of PILs are far from clear. Not all PILs pertain to the neglected and poor sections of society. Generally, PILs pertain to major public grievances of governance which political parties are not interested in redressing due to vote bank politics or certain vested interests. Civil society and NGOs have therefore nowhere to go except to the courts to get relief. In several cases, the courts have involved civil society groups and NGOs in arriving at decisions. This is welcomed by them as a step towards participatory democracy. In a few cases, however, the government has been successful in stone walling the efforts of civil society and the courts to address issues. One such prominent case was that of the appointment of a Lok Pal (ombudsman) to oversee the actions of elected representatives, ministers, senior bureaucrats and others. Common Cause, an NGO in Delhi, filed a PIL in the Supreme Court in this regard since the proposal was pending in Parliament for over 40 years. The court issued nearly 30 notices to the government asking it to present its say on the matter but since the government was not forthcoming, the court finally dismissed the PIL!

Finally, one must take a close look at the impact of judicial activism on the day to day life of the country. As stated earlier, the impact is visible in a number of areas of public life. But in a large number of cases it is also highly disappointing. For example, the orders issued by the Supreme Court for cleaning Ganga and Yamuna waters have had no impact, though crores of rupees have literally gone down the drain. The court itself has expressed its frustration and disappointment with the results more than once. Another major disappointment is with respect to the follow-up action on the decision of the Supreme Court in the case of police reforms which are long overdue. In spite of the court's unambiguous and time-bound directives issued on 22 September 2006, hardly any action has been taken by the states so far. Finally, the court appointed a committee under the chairmanship of one of its retired judges to visit states, hold discussions with state governments and chalk out a programme for time-bound action. In each state, there are a number of similar other decisions which have remained on paper. The courts may be able to take contempt of court proceedings in a few cases but this cannot be done in a routine manner in dozens of cases. What is at stake is the institutional prestige of the Supreme Court and the high courts. If the courts come to be equated with the executive in public perception in terms of ineffectiveness of governance, a potent instrument will be undermined forever.

This brings us to the question of public accountability and transparency, the two imperatives of good governance. Unless effective steps are taken to put in place a legal and institutional framework for ensuring good governance, judicial activism may prove to be a temporary palliative. The Contempt of Court Act which is the mainstay of judicial power, prestige and authority may not be of much help forever either.

We have seen in this discussion that on a number of burning questions the high courts and the Supreme Court had to be approached by members of the public for redressal of their grievances. The activist role of the courts in some of these cases has come in for criticism from some quarters. But if public authorities and the government were responsive enough, approaching the courts would not have been necessary. Recourse to public interest litigation can be considered the test of good governance. Ideally it should not be necessary to seek the intervention of the courts in such matters. But when members of the public find that all doors are closed and they have nowhere left to go they inevitably turn to the courts. This is a major remedy made available to the people by the Constitution and India has been lucky in having an activist judiciary which has taken a leading role in bringing good governance to the people.

Notes

1. The central government's lack of sensitivity was evident in the affidavit filed by the Archaeological Survey of India in the Supreme Court in the Sethusamudram canal project case that Lord Ram never existed and there was no historical evidence of Ram *setu* (bridge) having been built at his behest. When there was a sharp public reaction and protests, the affidavit was hurriedly withdrawn by the government.
2. *Common Cause*, Writ Petition (Civil) No. 194 of 2012, vol. xxxi, No. 3, July–September 2012, pp. 7–16.
3. Partly based on Godbole (2004: 82–96).
4. Based on Godbole (2010: 8–15).

THE EVER INCREASING GOVERNANCE DEFICIT

Those who cannot remember the past are condemned to repeat it
George Santayana

The National Commission to Review the Working of the Constitution
(NCRWC) observed:

> In the beginning, the constitutional arrangements relating to governance
> worked more or less to general satisfaction...However, as time passed, their
> inadequacies have become evident and government has lost its élan as it has
> failed to live up to the expectations of the Constitution to give real substance
> to the policies designed to promote social well-being. Even the most modest
> expectations have remained unfilled....The present situation is characterised by
> a pervasive disenchantment with the way things have worked out. It is futile
> to debate whether it is the institutions provided by the Constitution that have
> failed or whether the men who work those institutions have failed.[1]

The canvas of this subject is far too large and due to the constraints of space,
I focus attention on some glaring and highly disturbing examples which show the
continuous downward slide in public affairs in the country. They also underline
the aptness of the title of this book.

Communal and Ethnic Violence

In spite of our claim of being a secular polity, the country has been rocked by
horrific communal violence from time to time. During 1968 and 1970, there
were large-scale communal riots in Gujarat, Maharashtra, Uttar Pradesh and
Bihar. Apart from countless communal conflagrations over the years, major riots
in Meerut, Allahabad, Ahmedabad, Jabalpur, Bhagalpur, Malegaon, Bhiwandi,
Jalgaon and Ranchi were marked by their ferocity and the large-scale destruction
of life and property. One of the worst was in Ahmedabad city on 18 September
1969 in which 434 persons were killed. In the arson, 98 shops, 166 houses and
seven religious places were burnt. As the riots spread to other areas in Gujarat,
38 more persons were killed.

But the worst three were the anti-Sikh riots in Delhi in 1984, following Indira Gandhi's assassination, which claimed nearly 3,000 lives; riots in December 1992 and January 1993 as a reaction to the demolition of the Babri Masjid; and the Godhra riots in Gujarat in 2002. They are a blot on India's plural society.

Anti-Sikh Riots in Delhi

Even after 27 commissions and committees of inquiry, hardly anyone of consequence has been held accountable or punished in the 1984 riot cases. Of the three prominent MPs who are widely believed to have been involved, H. K. L. Bhagat is no more. Jagdish Tytler has recently been acquitted and Sajjan Kumar's case is still in the court. The High Power Citizens' Commission comprising respected persons, namely, S. M. Sikri, former Chief Justice of India; Badr-ud-din Tyabji, former Commonwealth Secretary and Vice-Chancellor, Aligarh Muslim University; Rajeshwar Dayal, former Foreign Secretary; Govind Narain, former Governor and Home and Defence Secretary; and T. C. A. Srinivasavaradan, former Home Secretary, submitted its report in January 1985. The commission, *inter alia*, observed:

> Many who came forward...have specifically and repeatedly named certain political leaders belonging to the ruling Congress party. These included several MPs belonging to the ruling party in the outgoing Parliament, members of the Delhi metropolitan council and members of the municipal corporation... They have been accused of having instigated the violence, making arrangements for the supply of kerosene and other inflammable material and of identifying the houses of Sikhs...We have referred to the utter failure and dereliction of duty of the police in Delhi. Some of them have been accused of instigating or even participating in the criminal acts committed during the fateful five days. Wherever such officials are found to have committed crimes, they should be prosecuted according to the law. Negligence or dereliction of duty calls for exemplary punishment after departmental inquiry. Where appropriate, recourse could be had to the proviso to Article 311 of the Constitution (Godbole 1996: 328).

Unlike other communal riots, this time the central government could not blame anyone else as it was in charge of law and order and police in Delhi during that time. During my term as union Home Secretary in 1991–93, all efforts to bring the guilty to book were stymied by political interference. The details of this have been given in my memoirs. The position remains the same ever since. The only saving grace was Prime Minister Manmohan Singh tendering an apology in Parliament on behalf of the government, but it was too little and too meaningless considering the horrific tragedy and loss of life.

Babri Masjid Related Riots

With the rise of both Hindu and Muslim communalism and militancy over the years, the toll of human life has gone up steeply. The *rath yatras* (chariot processions) and *kar seva* (voluntary service) for the construction of a Ram temple organized by the BJP contributed substantially to the escalation of communal tensions. During the *shila pujan* (worship of the foundation stone) in September-November 1989, 79 communal incidents occurred which resulted in 505 persons being killed and 768 being injured. In the *kar seva* in August-November 1990, there were 304 incidents of communal violence which led to 442 deaths and 1,936 people being injured. In the communal disturbances following the demolition of the Babri Masjid, 2,026 persons were killed and 6,957 were injured in various parts of the country, apart from large-scale arson and looting (Godbole 1996: 411–12).

In the post-Babri demolition riots, the worst affected was Mumbai where the state government had clearly been afflicted by a paralysis of will. The Shiv Sena was primarily responsible for the large-scale violence, destruction and terror in Mumbai. The Justice Srikrishna Commission of Inquiry has said:

> Communal riots, the bane of this country, are like incurable epileptic seizures, whose symptoms, though dormant over a period of time, manifest themselves over and over again. Measures of various kinds suggested from time to time dealt with symptoms and acted as palliatives without effecting a permanent cure of the malaise...The voluminous evidence produced before the commission strikingly brings home the stark reality that the beast in man keeps straining at the leash to jump out; frictions, irritations and disputes based on colour, race and religion are but excuses (Government of Maharashtra 1998: 3, 48).

In its action taken report, the then Shiv Sena-BJP government had stated:

> The government has accepted most of the recommendations of the commission relating to police administration and effective controlling of riots. But the government is of the view that some of the conclusions are one-sided, biased and arrived at with a view to indict a particular person or community. Therefore, the government rightly fears that after 5 years, the wounds instead of getting healed will be reopened again and may start festering. The government, therefore, reiterates that on account of the reasons given above, it cannot agree with the conclusions of the commission (Government of Maharashtra 1998: 23).

Gujarat Riots in 2002

On 27 February 2002, the Sabarmati Express coming from Ayodhya was carrying *kar sevaks* (volunteers). Their bogey S-6 was allegedly attacked at Godhra by a

Muslim mob. There is a controversy on this point. According to one version, the train bogey was set on fire by Muslims, while according to another, Muslims had nothing to do with it and either one of the passengers was carrying inflammable material or that there was an electrical short-circuit which caused the fire. But the fact remains that the riots spread quickly, not only in Godhra but also some other cities and led to the death of over 2,000 persons, apart from large-scale atrocities against Muslim women and the looting and plundering of property.

The reason why Godhra is unique is because of the alleged instigation, if not connivance, by Chief Minister Narendra Modi and the state administration. These allegations have not been proved so far in spite of several writ petitions in the High Court and the Supreme Court. The commissions of inquiry have come to diametrically opposite conclusions, depending on whether the commission was appointed by the Gujarat government or by the central government, or if it was a concerned citizens' tribunal.

The last-named tribunal, comprising Justice V. R. Krishna Iyer and Justice P. B. Sawant, retired judges of the Supreme Court, Justice Hosbet Suresh, retired judge of the Bombay High Court, and others, submitted its report on 21 November 2002. In its strongly worded report, the tribunal, *inter alia*, recommended:

> The centre must bring in a new legislation to implement the Genocide Convention, which India has signed and ratified, and must use these measures to prosecute and punish all those who participated in the planning and the execution of murder, sexual violence, theft and destruction in...the communal carnage. The tribunal finds that the state-sponsored crimes committed...are nothing short of genocide and crimes against humanity. Hence the need to have a suitable legislative measure as required by the Genocide Convention (Concerned Citizens Tribunal 2002: 169).

As compared to this report of the tribunal which was completed within a few months of the monumental tragedy, the term of the two-member Nanawati-Mehta Commission, appointed by the Gujarat government, has been extended for the 20th time up to 31 December 2013 (*Sakal*, 3 July 2013). There was so much furore in the country over the Godhra riots but the then Prime Minister Atal Bihari Vajpayee remained satisfied by only reminding Modi of his *raj dharma* (responsibilities of the ruler). The Supreme Court, however, was not satisfied with such mere utterances. Justice V. N. Khare, the then CJI, stated in an interview, 'I have no faith left in the prosecution and the Gujarat Government. I am not saying [use] Article 356. You have to protect people and punish the guilty. What else is *raj dharma*? You quit if you cannot prosecute the guilty...We will not be silent spectators. We will do it if the state keeps silent in its prayers before the high court' (*TOI*, 14 March 2004).

The then Chairman of NHRC, Justice J. S. Verma, recommended that the Centre should use Article 355 in Gujarat which casts the duty on the Centre to protect states against external aggression and internal disturbance so as to ensure that governance in every state is carried on in accordance with the provisions of the Constitution:

I was told 'we are examining it' and nothing was done...I am shocked that [Justice] Nanawati should say the NHRC got the Gujarat government's co-operation. His absolving it of failure to implement the NHRC recommendations goes against public records...Please see my letter of January 3, 2003, to the Prime Minister, within a fortnight of when I demitted office. In the letter, I expressed my deep anguish that a lot remained to be done to give justice to the victims of Gujarat which required reparation and also identifying perpetrators and punishing them' (*Outlook*, 13 October 2008: 14,16).

With Modi chosen to head the BJP's 2014 election campaign committee and possibly being declared the Prime Ministerial candidate, the ghost of Godhra continues to haunt Modi and the BJP. Many people expected Modi to at least apologize for his government's lapses in controlling the riots but he has brazenly decided not to do so. This too is a sad reflection on the office of the Chief Minister.

The Big Picture

I have cited only a few cases here to highlight the gravity of the problem. An analysis of the common causes and administrative failures in these riots brings out some disturbing aspects. **First,** it cannot be denied that there is communalism of both the Hindus and Muslims. But, the communalism of Hindus is more worrisome as they, with their overwhelming majority, have to bear the main responsibility of protecting the minorities. **Second,** exemplary punishment must be imposed on all those who are guilty of disturbing peace and tranquillity. As seen again and again, the ground reality is quite the opposite. **Third,** large-scale and grave communal riots leading to widespread atrocities and large loss of life and property should be considered adequate justification for dismissal of a state government and the imposition of President's rule. This has not been done in a single case. The dismissal of the three BJP-ruled state governments in Madhya Pradesh, Himachal Pradesh and Rajasthan, soon after the demolition of the Babri Masjid in December 1992, were ostensibly for neglecting their law and order duties, but the Maharashtra government, in spite of the worst riots, was spared because it was a Congress government. This sort of partisan treatment sends a very wrong political message. **Fourth,** reports of the commissions and committees appointed to inquire into the riots, have largely remained unimplemented. In the case of the Justice B. N. Srikrishna Commission pertaining to riots in Mumbai, the Shiv Sena-BJP government made its best efforts not to publish the report till the Bombay High Court directed it to do so, leave aside taking any action thereon. The commission had examined over 500 witnesses but most of the criminal cases lodged during the communal riots were abruptly closed, pending the commission's report. **Fifth,** reference must be made in this context to communalism in the police to which reference has also been made by the Srikrishna Commission. The commission named 31 police officers for 'actively participating in riots, communal incidents or incidents of looting, arson and so on' (Government of Maharashtra 1998: 54–55). As I have stated in my memoirs:

> The UP police in general and the UP Police Armed Constabulary (UPPAC), in particular, had the reputation of being communal and biased...There were repeated complaints about the partisan behaviour of the UPPAC towards the majority community. The Home Minister [S.B. Chavan] had, during his visit to UP, publicly talked about the need for disbanding the UPPAC, but there had been such a strong protest that he hurriedly withdrew the statement, as was his wont in other similar situations. Disbanding of the UPPAC would not have been easy but its composition certainly required to be changed radically so as to make it multi-religious, on the pattern of the Rapid Action Force under the CRPF. The men of the UPPAC also needed to be re-trained to change their psychological orientation (Godbole 1996: 361–62).

Similar traits of communalism in the police had come to light before the demolition of the Babri Masjid and riots in Delhi, Mumbai, Bhiwandi, Malegaon, Godhra, Ahmedabad and so on. No remedial action has been taken on this. **Sixth,** eruption of communal riots, or for that matter any riots, whatever the provocation, is clearly a failure of governance and on this test too India fails miserably.

Ethnic Violence

Ethnic violence is yet another curse which has been afflicting India. Some of these cases are so appalling that they ought never to be forgotten. For, only when there is collective memory can lasting solutions be found for the deep gangrenous problems which political leaders are prone to push under the carpet till there is yet another volcanic eruption.

On 18 February 1983, 14 villages of Bengali-speaking Muslims in Nellie in Assam were surrounded, thousands of villagers were hacked to death and their homes set on fire in the worst massacre in independent India. More than 3,000 Bengali Muslims perished. The number of people rendered homeless was 2,25,951. A signboard put up by the refugees read, 'Save Us, We Have Become Insecure and Homeless in Our Own Land'. While 668 FIRs were registered, many cases were summarily closed. Following a government plea after the Assam Accord in 1985, all cases under section 321 Cr.P.C. were withdrawn from the trial court! In the context of the widespread clashes in 2012, the Chief Minister of Assam, Tarun Gogoi, said, 'You don't know what happens where. Clashes keeping (sic) occurring in the State, whether in Kokrajhar, Karbi Anglong or Dima Hasao' (*IE*, 8 August 2012: 9).

Periodic violence in Bodo areas has continued over the years. The original agreement entered into with the Bodos in 1993, purely for self-aggrandisement by Rajesh Pilot, who was then the Minister of State for Internal Security, without Cabinet approval, was flawed and he rushed into it against the advice of the Home Ministry. The non-tribal groups in Assam and the Assam government were also not in favour of the accord. As I have written in my memoirs, 'As was to be expected, the agreement came unstuck even before the ink on it was dry and all the earlier elaborate and painstaking work was wasted. The Bodo Security Force...had again become active, creating a reign of terror in the region. The Plains Tribals Council of Assam had abstained from the function held for signing of the accord and from the celebrations on 7 March 1993.' The *Indian Express*, in its editorial on 31 May 1994, wrote, 'From the start, the Bodo accord, providing for the formation of a Bodoland autonomous region and council, was heavily flawed and in view of many experts virtually un-implementable given the demography of the area' (Godbole 1996: 28). Further amendments to the accord were still more disastrous. The spurt of violence in 2012 left 4,00,000 people homeless. The 1,80,000 who were rendered homeless in earlier violence had already been living in the relief camps for nearly five years. According to the Chief Minister of Assam, Tarun Gogoi, economic development is the key to all problems. But, this is stating the obvious and skirting the main issues.

There is a deliberate effort to underplay the severity of the problem of illegal migration from Bangladesh. The non-Bodos in the Bodo Tribal Council areas have a feeling of discrimination and neglect. There is an urgent need to bridge the widening divide between the Bodos and non-Bodos. Wisdom does seem to be dawning on the Congress leadership. Congress General Secretary, Digvijaya Singh, was candid enough to say, 'The Bodo Accord should be revisited. Non-Bodos should be given a fair share of power in the Bodo tribal area. We need to bridge the ethnic divide between them and the Muslims which appears to be almost total in some areas. Our first challenge is to resettle and rehabilitate 3,00,000 refugees' (*IE*, 5 August 2012: 6). As can be seen, the figure of refugees is grossly understated but at least there is recognition of the problem. However, there has been no further progress in resolving the issues. The policy of *thanda karke khao* (let the things cool down) ascribed to Govind Vallabh Pant, who was Chief Minister of Uttar Pradesh and union Home Minister in the early years after independence, still seems to hold sway.

Centre-State Relations

The repeated misuse of Article 356 of the Constitution to dismiss state governments belonging to opposition parties has been a source of major friction between the states and the Centre. A. G. Noorani has stated, 'Article 356 is based on the notorious section 93 of the Government of India Act, 1935, which provided for "Governor's rule" in the Provinces just as section 45 provided for the Governor-General's rule at the Centre...In India, Article 356 is a weapon of first resort [rather than being the last]' (Noorani 2000: 260–61). Even in the Constituent Assembly, fears were expressed that the article may be misused. Replying to the debate on 4 August 1949, B. R. Ambedkar, *inter alia*, said,

> I do not altogether deny that there is a possibility of these Articles [pertaining to emergency powers] being misused or employed for political purposes. But that objection applies to every part of the Constitution which gives power to the Centre to over-ride the provinces.[and the Centre has in fact done so, as brought out in this book]...*The proper thing we ought to expect is that such Articles will never be called into operation and that they would remain a dead letter.* (Italics are used here and in other places to bring out the emphasis)

The Commission on Centre-State Relations (1988) had unambiguously recommended, 'Article 356 should be used very sparingly, in extreme cases, as a measure of last resort, when all available alternatives fail to prevent or rectify a breakdown of constitutional machinery in the State. All attempts should be made to resolve the crisis at the State level before taking recourse to the provisions of Article 356' (Government of India 1988: 15).

The following examples illustrate the gross misuse of the article over the years, starting with the very first year after the adoption of the Constitution. Granville Austin wrote:

> the first use of President's Rule was a far cry from the Constituent Assembly's intentions, growing as it did from an internal Congress dispute. The Government of Punjab in 1951 held a majority in the legislature, and the Governor's report to President Rajendra Prasad that the constitutional machinery had broken down was an *official fiction*. Additionally, the Centre, and not the Governor, had initiated the letter to the President. Leading the Congress Parliamentary Board, Prime Minister Nehru, against Prasad's remonstrances, ordered Chief Minister Gopichand Bhargava to resign despite his having a majority. Nehru claimed that the law and order situation was worsening, but his arguments to Prasad that Bhargava was not acting 'straight' and that it was inevitable for parties to give directions to their members told a different story...The office of Governor for the first, but hardly the last, time had been mangled between

the Congress Party and the Constitution to the detriment of even limited federalism and of representative democracy. It was widely acknowledged that Nehru had set the country a bad example (Granville1999: 606–7).

The other instance of the use of Article 356 in the Nehru era is when the duly elected Communist government in Kerala was dismissed by the Centre. D. R. SarDesai underlines that:

It is indeed sad that the Congress Party, in keeping with its historically derived 'catch-all' character, ended up sacrificing the federal rules of the game for the purpose of maintaining its hegemony in the political system. The net result of this was that *no non-congress chief minister lasted his full term in office in the Nehru era*…Nehru did use Presidential Rule, although for a limited number (six) of times and under pressure from within his own party. In fact, the party initiated the process of 'politics of defection', thrived on it under the very watchful eyes of its 'god-father' and legitimized the process by accommodating defectors with political prizes (SarDesai and Mohan 1992: 234–35).

These 'glorious' traditions were carried forward by subsequent governments, whether belonging to the Congress or other political parties, by dismissing duly elected state governments on about 100 occasions. The invocation of Article 356 became particularly contentious on a few occasions such as the dismissal of the S. R. Bommai government in Karnataka in 1988, which led to the famous judgment of the Supreme Court cited earlier restricting the use of the article; dismissal of the Kalyan Singh government in Uttar Pradesh in 1997 but due to public protests, the order had to be taken back; and dismissal of the Rabri Devi government in Bihar in 1999 but the resolution could not be passed in the Rajya Sabha and hence the order imposing President's rule was revoked. But, on two occasions when its use could have not only been fully justified, but even welcomed, Article 356 was forgotten. The first was in Uttar Pradesh *before* the demolition of the Babri Masjid in December 1992, and the second in Gujarat *after* the Godhra pogrom in February 2002. On both occasions, for the narrow political ends of the Congress and the BJP respectively, the Centre turned a blind eye. For the 1984 Sikh riots, the Centre, being in charge of law and order in Delhi, itself was responsible but there is no provision in the Constitution to impose President's rule in the Centre!

Nehru must not have visualized that his short-sighted policy in this matter would set in motion forces which would undercut the very foundations of the federal structure in the country. Permanent distrust about the Centre created in state governments, not just those belonging to opposition parties but also the UPA constituents, is seen in their opposition to enlarging the jurisdiction of the central government in any field, whether it be the Central Bureau of Investigation

(CBI), the Railway Protection Force, the National Counter-Terrorism Centre (NCTC), enactment of a law to deal with terrorism and communal violence, or enactment of a central law on Lok Ayukta. Another manifestation of this is the inordinate delay by the Centre in giving President's assent to the laws passed by state legislatures.

As Austin has stated, after Kerala was placed under President's rule in 1959, well-known constitutional expert B. Shiva Rao, had suggested to the then Congress President, Indira Gandhi, that a 'board of advisors' might be constituted to 'greatly strengthen the President's position so that there should not be any impression in the public mind that in matters like this the President is guided by the Party Cabinet in power at the Centre (Granville 1999: 607). As was to be expected, this advice fell on deaf ears. In any case, Indira Gandhi, who misused this provision blatantly in her long tenure as Prime Minister, would have been the last person to heed to such sane advice.

Former CJI, K. Subba Rao, wrote, 'It is said that in issuing the said proclamations [for imposition of President's Rule] the Governors and the President acted as the agents of the Central ministry...and...the Congress Party... manipulated the said proclamations in a bid to regain power in those States where it was defeated' (Granville 1999: 607). The data in this regard is illuminating. Of the 57 instances of President's rule from 1951 to 1987 (excluding the mass dissolutions of state governments ordered by the Janata and Congress [Indira] governments in 1977 and 1980 respectively), the Sarkaria Commission thought 23 had been inevitable, 15 had been without allowing other claimants to test their strength and 13 had taken place when the ministry commanded a majority (Sarkaria Commission 1988: 186–89). This means nearly 50 per cent cases of President's rule were due to the wishes of the central government.

Fortunately, the Supreme Court, in S. R. Bommai v. Union of India unanimously held that a presidential proclamation issued under Article 356 of the Constitution is not completely beyond judicial review. It was held that the President's satisfaction has to be based on objective material and further that the objective material available either from the Governor's report or from other information or both must indicate that governance in the state cannot be carried on in accordance with the provisions of the Constitution. Consequently, the validity of the proclamation issued by the President under Article 356 (1) is judicially reviewable to the extent of examining whether it was issued on the basis of any material or whether the material was relevant or whether the proclamation was issued in the mala fide exercise of power (Laxminath 2002: 294–95).

In spite of this clear warning by the Supreme Court, the UPA government brazenly dissolved the Bihar Assembly in 2006. The decision was taken at a Cabinet meeting at midnight and sanction for the move was obtained from the President from Moscow, over fax. The Supreme Court made a scathing attack on

THE EVER INCREASING GOVERNANCE DEFICIT •63

the Governor, Buta Singh, for manufacturing a 'perverse' and 'malafide' report, and said, 'the Council of Ministers should have verified the report before accepting it as gospel truth.' The Supreme Court made it clear that it would intervene to stop gubernatorial misdemeanours and violation of constitutional norms, and the decision to dissolve the Assembly was clearly taken to prevent Nitish Kumar from becoming the Chief Minister (*ET*, 25 January 2006). As a result, Governor Buta Singh had to resign in disgrace. Earlier, President K. R. Narayanan, who was called a textbook President, had, on 21 October 1997, rejected the advice of the Council of Ministers to impose President's rule in Uttar Pradesh. In contrast, R. Venkataraman earned a deserved stricture from the Supreme Court in 1994 in the *Bommai* case in relation to the proclamation of 21 April 1989 imposing President's rule in Karnataka. Two other proclamations which Venkataraman had signed were also struck down: one with respect to Nagaland (1988) and another for Meghalaya (1991) (Noorani 2000: 269). This underlines the importance of checks and balances in a democracy and the crucial role played by the Supreme Court in upholding the Constitution and contributing to good governance in the country cannot be emphasised enough.

Abolition of Privy Purses

At the time of Independence of India, there were some 540 princely states which accounted for 47 per cent of the total area of the country and 28 per cent of its population. Both Nehru and Vallabhbhai Patel had given solemn assurances to the rulers of these states that they would safeguard their position in the Constitution and accordingly four articles, namely, 291, 362, 366 (22) and 363 about the privy purses and privileges were incorporated in the Constitution. Patel, with the support of V. P. Menon, was eminently successful in the merger of states and unifying the country for the first time. There was no need thereafter to insist on the abolition of privy purses in the name of doing away with the 'anachronisms of purses and privileges'. As M. V. Kamath has pointed out:

> Out of the 554 states that surrendered to the Indian Union, over 450 had annual revenues of less than Rs 15 lakh. The privy purse of the Nizam of Hyderabad, though amounting to Rs 50 lakh annually, represented no more than 2 per cent of the State's revenue. The Nizam, moreover, was made to surrender his personal estate yielding an annual revenue of Rs 1.24 crore in return for a compensation of Rs 25 lakh per annum. The original agreement had laid down that the privy purses should be reduced with each succession to the title. As result, by 1967 [when the issue of abolition of purses came to the fore], the list of beneficiaries had been reduced from the original 600 to 200. Similarly the amount given to them had come down from Pounds 2.3 million a year in 1948 to the third of that figure (Kamath 2007: 143).

As G. K. Reddy (1970) has stated, the princes became the 'principal victims of the political vagaries of Congress Socialism...The princes themselves had played a patriotic role during the critical aftermath of Partition in the consolidation of India's newly won freedom...Even in these days of soapbox socialism, they still symbolise to the outside world the romance and magic of India, if not its mystique' (Bhagyalakshmi 1992: 11–12).

Going back on the solemn constitutional guarantees given to the rulers without any provocation, was totally unjustified except as a pretence of socialism (Godbole 2008: 220–29). In fact, the fascination for the Maharaja was evident when it was adopted as the logo of the national carrier Air India. The position has become much more ludicrous over the years, with an X, Y, Z category of security becoming a status symbol for every MLA, MP, and self-proclaimed leaders of political parties at all levels. There was a demand by the then 'Young Turks' to do away with special car number plates and so on. In 2012, a Parliamentary Standing Committee made a recommendation that MPs' vehicles should be provided with a red light on top. Once this is conceded, similar demands will come up from MLAs, municipal councillors, zilla parishad office-bearers and others. In reality, we have abolished the princely states, privy purses and their privileges, which were negligible by any standards, but have created thousands of self-proclaimed maharajas who flaunt themselves every day. Reportedly, in West Delhi there is a house with a nameplate declaring 'Relatives of the President' of India [Pratibha Patil] (*Outlook*, 7 May 2012: 9). Thus, a giant hypocrisy is all that remains of this great socialist hoax.

Declaration of Internal Emergency

On 12 June 1974 Indira Gandhi's election as a Member of Parliament from Rae Bareilly was set aside as a result of Raj Narain's election petition. Soon after, on 25 June 1975, came the declaration of emergency which came as a rude shock not just to the people in India but to the whole democratic world. The Constitution, in the opinion of the Shah Commission, 'does not contemplate the proclamation of an Emergency upon an Emergency already existing [from the time of Bangladesh war]'. According to the testimony of Sidharth Shankar Ray, Chief Minister of West Bengal before the Shah Commission, Indira Gandhi had told him on two or three occasions prior to the declaration of emergency that 'India required a shock treatment' (Government of India 1978: 23). Some 676 leading opponents of Indira Gandhi were detained in prisons.

In the emergency session of Parliament which began on 21 July 1975, the government moved a motion in both Houses on the very first day for the suspension of the rules of procedure, including Question Hour and Private

Members' Business, so that only government business could be transacted during the session.

B. K. Nehru was at the time canvassing for India to change over to the presidential form of government. When he tried to ascertain the reactions of senior Congress leaders, the responses which he received were unbelievable. The responses of Jagjivan Ram, Swaran Singh and Y. B. Chavan, though put in different words, were in essence that if the Prime Minister wanted these changes to be made, they would support them. As Nehru aptly stated, 'What they were really interested in was to find out whether the Emperor thought it was high noon or midnight.' The response of Giani Zail Singh, then Chief Minister of Punjab, and later the President of India, was that whatever 'Bibiji wanted was alright with him'. Bansi Lal, the Chief Minister of Haryana's response was typical: 'Are Nehru Saheb, ye sub election phe lection ka jhagra khatam kariye. Main to kahta hoo ki Behenji ko President for life bana dijiye baki kucch karne ki jarrorat nahin hai' (Nehru Sahib, get rid of all this election nonsense. If you ask me, just make our sister President for life and there is no need to do anything else) (Nehru 1997: 558–59). Congress President D. K. Barua came up with the slogan, 'India is Indira and Indira is India'. A. R. Antulay, former Chief Minister of Maharashtra, floated a paper on the need to adopt the presidential form of government. P. N. Dhar, who was then the Secretary to Prime Minister, has stated, 'The worst part of the Antulay exercise was that his document gave ideas to Sanjay Gandhi, whose minions hijacked the idea of constitutional reform and organized a campaign for convening a new Constituent Assembly. They had no thoughts on what the Constituent Assembly should do beyond a single point programme of continuing the Emergency in one form or another. Things were now getting out of control' (Dhar 2002: 337).

It would be worth recalling some of the striking observations of B. K. Nehru, who was related to the Nehru family and was close to Indira Gandhi, on what was happening during the emergency. They throw light on the real state of governance at the time, whatever drum beating of the achievements of the emergency may have been done by the blind followers of Indira Gandhi and her son Sanjay:

What was highly dangerous and highly objectionable was that the rule of law was being replaced by the rule of Sanjay Gandhi...The sole basis of his absolute authority was that he was his mother's darling boy. The horror stories that I heard were not only about the incredibly childish, ham-handed and tyrannical way in which he had decided to solve the Indian population problem. They were also about the manner in which money was extorted from all kinds of businessmen for the grant of all permissions...It was no great advertisement for the character of the political leadership of the country that these orders, sometimes verging on criminality, were obeyed without question. Not one of them had the guts to resign or even to protest...She [Indira] was absolutely blind as far as that boy was concerned...the tyranny that a wayward, uneducated and inexperienced boy inflicted on the people of India for the whole of next year... so damaged all the institutions of democratic government and civilized progress which his grandfather had built up with such infinite care, as to make it almost impossible to restore them...The cult of corruption, which had begun to affect our public life since the Congress split in 1969 [in fact, as shown in this book, since Independence], gathered so much momentum that by now it has become a way of life throughout the country and seems impossible to eradicate...The rule of law was totally destroyed as the group around Sanjay, whose characteristics were similar to his, attained absolute power (Nehru 1997: 560–61).

Writing about Sanjay's death, B. K. Nehru bluntly stated:

It was decided that the cremation would take place in Shantivan near the spot where his grandfather was cremated. Rajiv [Gandhi] voiced the objection felt by many others to this course on the ground that, Sanjay, having no official position, should not be given the honour of cremation on the hallowed ground. Shantivan was not a private family cremation vault. However, the end result was that except for lying in state in Teen Murti House and the use of gun-carriage, the ritual of funeral was almost identical to that followed in the case of Jawaharlal, Indira and Rajiv. *The day after the funeral, I asked Rajiv whether the money Sanjay had collected allegedly for the Congress was safe. He said all that they found in the almirahs of the Congress office was Rs 20 lacs. I asked how much Sanjay had. He held his head in his hands and said, 'crores and uncounted crores'* (Nehru 1997: 582).

During the period of the Fifth Lok Sabha (1971–76), as many as 19 Constitution amendment bills were passed. This was by far the largest number of such bills passed by any Lok Sabha. These included some of the most important and controversial bills in the constitutional history of India and sparked serious debates (Kashyap 1997: 63).

The emergency years were witness to several atrocities unknown to India till then. S. S. Gill has written:

The All India Railwaymen's Federation led by the firebrand Socialist, George Fernandes, served a strike notice in April 1974 demanding hike in pay and dearness allowance, grant of bonus, etc. The strike, coming as it did on the heels of Gujarat and Bihar agitations, would have disrupted the movement of foodgrains and other essential commodities and created a chaos in the country. Mrs Gandhi acted with speed and fury and declared the strike illegal under the Defence of India Rules. Never before had workers been dealt with so harshly.

Thousands of them were arrested, severely beaten, thrown out of their quarters, and hundreds of them dismissed. As a result of these repressive measures the strike was withdrawn after three weeks. Not a single demand of the strikers was conceded (Gill 1996: 270).

The Turkman Gate tragedy in Delhi signified the worst features of the emergency. The large-scale demolition of structures and dislocation of a population which had lived there for centuries covered the oldest part of the city—Ajmeri Gate, Jama Masjid and Turkman Gate. They were not squatters, nor were the buildings unauthorized. Sanjay Gandhi wanted to beautify Delhi by removing the pock-marks of congested colonies and dirty slums. According to Shah Commission's estimates, nearly 1,50,000 houses and shops were demolished and 7,00,000 people rendered homeless. They were all carted 15–20 kilometres away to new settlement colonies. An even worse fate was to befall Varanasi but, somehow it was brought to the notice of Indira Gandhi by her close friend Pupul Jayakar and it was averted. But many other cities saw similar beautification drives and large-scale demolitions of properties and dislocation of residents.

However, the worst calamity was the forced sterilizations carried out as a part of Sanjay Gandhi's programme of population control and the race to achieve the laid down targets. It covered the whole of north India and villages were the main targets. Even widows, young unmarried girls and boys and old persons were not spared. As public anger rose, there were riots in several places. Forty people were killed in police firing in Muzzafarpur and a dozen in Sultanpur district in Uttar Pradesh. Hundreds died owing to faulty sterilization operations (Gill 1996: 283–85).

A Boeing plane was hijacked by a Youth Congress worker as part of the protests against Indira Gandhi's imprisonment in the contempt of Lok Sabha case. Indira Gandhi rewarded the hijacker later by making him an MLA (*HT*, 20, 21, 22 December 1978). Seven commissions of inquiry were appointed by the Janata government during 1977–79 on various aspects of emergency rule:

- Justice J. C. Shah Commission to inquire into emergency excesses;
- Justice A. C. Gupta Commission to inquire into the affairs of Maruti Automobiles Limited controlled by Sanjay Gandhi;
- Justice P. Jaganmohan Reddy Commission to inquire into the circumstances leading to the death of Nagarwala who had taken out Rs 60 lakh from the State Bank of India by using Indira Gandhi's name;
- Justice Vimadalal Commission to inquire into allegations of corruption against the then Chief Minister Vengal Rao and other ministers of Andhra Pradesh;

- Justice A. N. Grover Commission to inquire into allegations of corruption against the then Chief Minister Devraj Urs and other ministers of Karnataka;
- Justice Jaganmohan Reddy Commission to inquire into allegations of corruption against Bansi Lal, former Chief Minister of Haryana and union Defence Minister; and
- Justice C. A. Vaidialingam Commission to inquire into allegations against Morarji Desai and Charan Singh's family members.

The Congress Party labelled these inquiries as a witch-hunt. The most important of these inquiries was the Shah Commission of Inquiry. Indira Gandhi questioned the authority of the commission, did not cooperate with it and refused to answer any questions put to her by the commission. In fact, she went out of her way to deride it and bring it down in public esteem. As Pupul Jayakar has written, 'The Janata leadership failed to realize that in their decision to force Indira to appear before the Shah Commission, they had provided Indira with a stage. She was adept at political theatre and now fighting for the survival of her son and herself, she assumed the role of a Joan of Arc on trial, refusing to recant or retrace a step' (Jayakar 1988: 352).

At the outset, it is necessary to refer briefly to the notorious Maintenance of Internal Security Act (MISA), which, with its widespread misuse, became the flagship of the emergency. The seeds of MISA are to be found in the Preventive Detention Act which was passed by Parliament on 25 February 1950. A. K. Gopalan, CPI(M) leader, was detained by the Madras government in February 1950 under the Preventive Detention Act. He was released on 22 February 1951 on his questioning the legality of the detention order, but was rearrested immediately under a new Preventive Detention Act which had received the President's assent that very day (Jawaharlal Nehru Memorial Fund 1993: 156).

It is shocking to see that the same Congress Party, which had strongly denounced the British for the use of preventive detention during the freedom struggle, had no qualms in continuing the act and taking action under it such as of detaining Gopalan after the transfer of power. J. B. Kripalani likened the proposed detention law to the Rowlatt Act, resistance to which led to the freedom movement under Gandhi. Rebutting the argument that those acts were passed by a foreign government and this act was being passed by our own government, Kripalani said, 'foreign rule lasts for a short time, but the tyranny of our own people is with us always' (Kripalani 2004: 754). By the approval of Parliament given in early 1951, an amended form of the act remained in force until 1952. The bill for further extension of the act up to 31 December 1954 was brought before Parliament in 1952. In his lengthy and rambling speech dated 2 August 1952, Prime Minister Jawaharlal Nehru strongly defended the bill saying 'the main approach of this Bill is not only right but is fully democratic'. Opposition members questioned the necessity for the extension of the act when the subversive or anti-national acts were not of such magnitude that the normal process of the law could not suffice. They saw in it an 'authoritarian tendency' and denounced it as 'vicious', 'brutal', 'a stinking piece of legislation' and a 'black Act'. A section of the opposition walked out when the bill was introduced. Opposing the motion for extension, S. P. Mookerjee said on 9 July 1952 that the principle of detention without trial was inconsistent with and repugnant to the principle of democracy (Jawaharlal Nehru Memorial Fund 1996: 453–66).

MISA was introduced in 1971 by promulgating an ordinance and gave power of preventive detention to the government to ostensibly deal effectively with threats to the defence of India and to its security, especially from external sources and espionage activities of foreign agents. The ordinance was issued in the context of the happenings in Bangladesh, though all opposition parties had expressed deep concerns about the government assuming such wide powers. For example, Atal Bihari Vajpayee had prophetically said in the Lok Sabha on 16 June 1971, 'This is the beginning of a police state and a blot on democracy. It is the first step towards dictatorship...These powers will not be used against foreign spies but against political opponents.' Similar sentiments were expressed by stalwarts such as L. K. Advani, Jyotirmoy Basu, Amrit Nahata, Krishna Menon, Piloo Modi, Frank Anthony and Somnath Chatterjee, among others.

On 27 June 1975, President of India F. A. Ahmed issued an order forbidding the detainees from invoking their constitutional rights to equal protection of the laws, protection of life and personal liberty and protection against unwarranted arrest and detention, in order to obtain their release. On 29 June 1975, MISA was amended to remove the requirement that a detainee must be informed of the reasons for his detention within a specified period. Diabolically, MISA was put in the Ninth Schedule by the Constitution (Thirty-ninth amendment) Bill, 1975, introduced in the Lok Sabha on 7 August 1975, to protect it from challenge in the court. Defending the inclusion of MISA in the Ninth Schedule, Law Minister H. R. Gokhale brazenly stated, 'its mere inclusion in the Constitution did not make it a permanent feature. It did not preclude Parliament from amending or even repealing the internal security law at any appropriate time' (Kashyap 1997: 85–86). The Shah Commission report shows how true were the fears expressed by opposition parties.

Shah Commission of Inquiry

It would be useful to make a brief mention of some of the important findings of the Shah Commission as they throw a spotlight on the state of governance in the country. In its interim report I, the Commission stated:

- Orders had been passed to lock up the high courts and to cut off the electricity connections to all newspapers. When told, Smt Gandhi immediately said this [action] should be stopped.
- The watch on a senior minister of the Cabinet and tapping of the telephone of Jagjivan Ram could not be justified.
- Appropriate safeguards are necessary and should be devised by the government so as to protect the activities of IB being used as an instrument of political spying either by the government or by someone in the government. This issue has been raised to concentrate attention and, if considered appropriate, to generate public opinion on the question.
- A large number of arrests/detentions followed under MISA in which the safeguards guaranteed against the misuse of the act were ignored and grounds of detentions were not furnished in a large number of cases and in many cases grounds of detentions were prepared and even pre-dated and sent many days after the person concerned had been arrested/detained in jail. In a number of cases grounds of detentions had no relevance to the factual positions and in a few cases grounds were fabricated by the police and the magistrates did not hesitate to sign them. An era of collusion between the police and the magistracy ensued (Government of India 1978: 31).

In its interim report II, the Commission, *inter alia*, stated:

- With the press gagged and a resultant blackout of authentic information, arbitrary arrests and detentions went on apace. Effective dissent was smothered, followed by a general erosion of democratic values. Highhanded and arbitrary actions were carried out with impunity. The nation was initially in a state of shock, and then of stupor, unable to realise the directions and the full implications of the actions of the government and its functionaries. Tyrants sprouted at all levels overnight—tyrants whose claim to authority was largely based on their proximity to the seats of power...Desire for self-preservation as admitted by a number of public servants at various levels became the sole motivation for their official actions and behaviour. Anxiety to survive at any cost formed the key-note of approach of the problems that came before many of them. The fear generated by the mere threat and without even the actual use of the weapon of detention under MISA became so pervasive that the general run of public servants acted as willing tools of tyranny.
- A calculated effort was made to place persons in vital positions who were willing to further the interests of the centre of power in gross violation of the established administrative norms and practices.

- The commission invites the government's attention pointedly to the manner in which the police was used and allowed themselves to be used for purposes, some of which were, to say the least, questionable. Some police officers behaved as though they are not accountable at all to any public authority...The government must seriously consider the feasibility and the desirability of insulating the police from the politics of the country and employing it scrupulously on duties for which alone it is by law intended.
- In the final analysis, this country will be governed well or ill by the competence and character of the government officers. If they are content to be mere tools and willing to lend themselves to questionable objectives, there will never be a dearth of unscrupulous operators. There is no substitute for a vigilant, enquiring and enlightened public opinion which keeps a close watch on the doings of the public servants.
- The commission has viewed with concern some of the secret operations of the Intelligence Bureau and the complete absence of in-built constraints subject to which it functions (Government of India 1978: 140, 142, 144).

The Shah Commission, in its final report, highlighted some important observations (Government of India 1978: 39, 228, 229, 230, 232, 238).

- Political detention is to be basically preventive in character and not punitive. This aspect seems to have been conveniently ignored during the emergency.
- Among the abuses and misuse of authority by the administration, the one single item which had affected the people most over the entire country, was the manner in which the powers assumed by the government to detain persons under the amended MISA were misused by the officials at various levels.
- A large number of officers—District Magistrates and Commissioners of Police, who exercised the powers of District Magistrates ex-officio, obediently carried out the instructions emanating from politicians and administrative heads issued on personal or political considerations.
- The political system that our Constitution has given to our country is such that it contemplates parties with different ideologies administering the affairs of the centre and the state governments. It is necessary in the interest of the territorial, political and economic integrity of the nation to ensure that the factors which contribute to such integrity are forever and continuously strengthened and not impaired. It is necessary to face the situation squarely that not all the excesses and improprieties committed during the emergency originated at the political level. In a large number of cases it appears that unscrupulous and over-ambitious officers were

prepared to curry favour with the seats of power and position by doing what they thought the people in authority desired.

- Unless the services work for and establish a reputation of political neutrality, the citizens will have no confidence in the impartiality and fairness of the services.

- The commission has viewed with concern the evidence relating to the enormous power that was wielded by the lower functionaries like Shri R. K. Dhawan, Shri R. C. Mehtani, Shri Navin Chawla and some others.

- Parliament and court proceedings were also subject to censorship. Not merely publication of court judgments were censored, but directions were also given as to how judgments should be published.

Particular attention may be invited to the following concluding observations of the Shah Commission:

The commission has had occasion to peruse the findings of the earlier commissions appointed by the government at the centre and in the states to probe into the conduct of the ministers of the state governments—particularly the reports of Shri S. R. Das who inquired into the conduct of late Shri Pratap Singh Kairon, Chief Minister of Punjab (1963–64), Shri Rajgopal Iyengar who inquired into the conduct of late Shri Bakshi Ghulam Mohammed, ex-Chief Minister of J&K (1965–67), Shri Venkatrama Iyer who inquired into the conduct of certain ministers of Bihar (1967–70), Shri Mudholkar who looked into the affairs of the ministry of Mahamaya Prasad Sinha, Chief Minister of Bihar and other ministers (1968–69), Shri A. N. Mulla who looked into the affairs of the ministers of Kerala—Govindan Nair and T. V. Thomas (1969–71), and Shri G. K. Mitter who looked into the Tendu leaves purchases in Orissa (1973–74). The commission is not aware of the action taken, if any, in response to these reports submitted from time to time in regard to the minister-civil servant relationship. The fact, however, remains that the refrain in all these reports in so far as this concerns the relationship of the ministers with the civil servants, is the same. *One cannot but be struck by the near unanimity in the observations of the several commissions on the unhealthy factors governing the relationship between the ministers and the civil servants. Yet nothing seems to have been done, at any rate effectively, to set right such of the aspects of these relationships which, prior to the emergency, had contributed to the several developments which came in for indictments by the commission. In the light of this, it may be easy to conclude that what happened during the emergency is merely a tragic culmination of the particular trend that had been identified and condemned from time to time by the commissions of the past.* The commission owes it to the citizens of India to emphasise that appointments of commissions by themselves are not enough if the governments concerned do not follow up and implement at least such of the recommendations as are avowedly accepted by the government. *Unless the government is prepared to apply the corrective principles in the minister-civil servant relationship effectively and with a determination to produce the desired results at different levels and within the several components of the government, the agonising impact of this unfortunate malaise would be felt by the common man in the streets, in the villages, in the factories and in the far distant corners of this vast country.*

Nothing has changed over the last 35 years from the time these eternal truths were propounded! If by some misfortune another emergency were to be proclaimed today, another commission of inquiry will come to similar conclusions. The only saving grace is that due to the Forty-fourth Constitution Amendment Act 1978, the fundamental rights to life and liberty guaranteed by Article 21 can never be suspended even during the emergency, as they are now a part of the basic structure of the Constitution.

The Shah Commission report was withdrawn from the ministries as soon as Indira Gandhi came back to power in 1980. The famous 'time capsule', buried for future generations to know about India, obviously will not contain any mention of the Shah Commission reports or any other commission reports of this inglorious period, which should never be forgotten if democracy is to remain alive in India.

Fali S. Nariman has stated: 'Few people realize that if Article 31C [Saving of laws giving effect to certain directive principles], introduced in its extended form during the 1975 Emergency by the Forty-second Amendment Act (and at that time lauded by some of the country's eminent jurists and lawyers), in its plenitude had remained a part of our Constitution, and had not been struck down by the majority in a Bench of five judges in the *Minerva Mills* case (1980), not only Parliament, but more realistically any State Legislature, could have by ordinary law effectively censored the press, and also prohibited public speaking on any topic without a police permit on the specious and vague plea that it was implementing some particular directive principle of state policy. This is the personal liberty that the Supreme Court of India (or a perceptive majority of its judges) has helped us save, and for this we lawyers and we citizens must be forever grateful and beholden to the Court' (Nariman 1999–2000: 19–20).

The Short-lived Janata Government

The short-lived Janata government failed to pursue any follow up action on the inquiry reports. Madhu Limaye has rightly lamented:

The whole gigantic effort made by the Janata government to investigate the dark area of corruption, nepotism, abuse of power and negligence of duty on the part of those in authority, in the end, produced no positive result…The reports meticulously composed are left to gather dust on the shelves of government departments and libraries. When Indira Gandhi returned to power [in 1980] her government decided to bury hastily all the Janata Inquiry Commission reports (Limaye 1994: 509).

A similar conclusion is arrived at by Arun Shourie, 'Thus law takes its own course and one more device we had for reforming our public life—that of commissions of inquiry—is bled to death' (Shourie 1980: 24, 51).

Arun Shourie has in the fascinating account of Indira Gandhi's second reign, described how the higher judiciary was sought to be brought under government control through appointments of High Court judges, not extending the term of additional High Court judges, manipulating IB reports regarding the antecedents of candidates for judgeships, making the Chief Justice of India just an advisor to the government in matters of appointment of judges, their transfers, promotions, and supersession of judges for appointment as Chief Justice of India and so on. The account also throws light on how the Special Courts Act was made into a dead letter by the tactics employed by Indira Gandhi and her followers. The original question referred to the special courts was about the emergency and its excesses; that had been reduced to 21 FIRs; these in turn had been reduced to four cases. Now, if truth be told, the courts never really got around to examining the substance of even these paltry cases (Shourie 1983: 243–50, 266–67, 384).

Nexus between Criminals, Bureaucrats and Politicians

The hawala case, dealt with in the following section, underlined the issues which were highlighted by the N. N. Vohra Committee report (Government of India 1993). *It is interesting to note that some members of this high-level top secret committee appeared to have some hesitation in openly expressing their views and also seemed unconvinced that the government actually intended to pursue such matters.* Only on being reassured by Vohra, Chairman of the committee and union Home Secretary, they came forward to give their views on the subject.

The committee's deliberations showed that '*the network of the mafia is virtually running a parallel government, pushing the state apparatus into irrelevance. There were extensive linkages of the underworld in the various government agencies, political circles, business sector and the film world. The crime syndicates have become a law unto themselves.* In cases where a crime syndicate has graduated to big business, it would be necessary to conduct detailed investigations into its assets, both movable and immovable.'

It came to light that '*a report on the nexus between the Bombay city police and the Bombay underworld was prepared by the CBI in 1986.*' It was suggested that it would be useful to institute a fresh study by the CBI, on the basis of which

THE EVER INCREASING GOVERNANCE DEFICIT • 75

appropriate administrative measures could be initiated. 'Creation of a nodal agency to collect information regarding the activities of mafia organizations is very essential. In the bigger cities, the main source of income of the crime syndicates and the mafia relates to real estate—forcibly occupying lands/buildings, procuring such properties at cheap rates by forcing out the existing occupants/ tenants etc. Suitable amendments need to be introduced in the existing laws to more effectively deal with the activities of mafia organizations, etc; this would also include review of the existing laws. A detailed case study of 10–15 cases would provide useful information regarding the administrative/legal measures which would be required to be taken to effectively tackle the functioning of mafia organizations. It was assured that the CBI can do this within a short time. For example, if Mirchi [mafia] is investigated, the entire patronage enjoyed by him and his linkages will come to light. The assistance of banks is an essential input.[2] Bank managers can be placed under obligation to render reports on all heavy transactions and suspicious accounts to the enforcement agencies. Such a practice exists in UK.'

'At present each concerned organization/agency is anxious to protect its sources and is apprehensive that a full sharing of all information might jeopardize its operations on account of premature leakage of information. It was therefore suggested that it is necessary to immediately have an institutional system which, while giving total freedom to various agencies to pursue their charter of work, would simultaneously cast on them the onus of sharing such inputs with a nodal outfit whose job will be to process this information for attention of a single designated authority. This will enable the nodal group to provide useful leads to the various agencies and, over time, a progressive database will get generated to facilitate periodic reviews and analysis which could then be passed to a designated body.'

The utter inadequacy of the criminal justice system was also highlighted by the committee. 'The existing system, which was essentially designed to deal with individual offences/crimes, is unable to deal with the activities of the mafia; the provisions of law with regard to economic offences are weak; there are insurmountable difficulties in attaching/confiscating property acquired through mafia activities. Cases are not heard in a timely manner. Functioning of the government lawyers is grossly inadequate. This results in a low percentage of convictions and mild punishments.'

'Field officers in various agencies of the Revenue Department are often pressurized by senior government functionaries/political leaders, apparently at the behest of crime syndicates/mafia elements. Unless field level officers are offered effective protection, they cannot be expected to maintain an interest in vigorously pursuing action against the activities of such elements. A possible approach to effectively liquidating the linkages developed by crime syndicates will be to mercilessly prosecute the offenders without succumbing to any pressure. The narcotics trade has a worldwide network of smugglers who also have close links with terrorists. Terrorists indulge in narcotics trade to amass huge funds, in various foreign currencies, from which they source their procurement of weapons etc. Finally, it was underlined that the problem of this nexus has an enormous impact on national security and is indeed highly political in nature.'

The move to have these issues examined was no doubt bold, but that is where it ended. The government developed cold feet when it realized how politically sensitive and uphill the task was. The Parliament also failed to create pressure of public opinion to force the government to take action. Finally, as in all such cases, the matter had to be raised before the Supreme Court. The relevant case—the hawala scandal—has been discussed in the following section. The court, by its decision dated 18 December 1997, *inter alia*, passed the following orders:

> A Nodal Agency headed by the Home Secretary with Member (Investigation), Central Board of Direct Taxes, Director General, Revenue Intelligence, Director, Enforcement, and Director, CBI, as members shall be constituted for coordinated action in cases having politico-bureaucrat-criminal nexus. *The Nodal Agency shall meet at least once every month.* Working and efficacy should be watched for about one year so as to improve it upon the basis of the experience gained within that period.[3]

This decision was published in December 1997. It is not clear what follow-up action has been taken by the government in the last 16 years since the decision of the Apex Court.

According to news reports published in 1997, the government had set up a committee comprising N. N. Vohra, who was then the Principal Secretary to the Prime Minister, S. V. Giri, then the CVC, and B. G. Deshmukh, former Principal Secretary to the Prime Minister, to follow up on such cases. In my article published in The Hindu on 30 September 1997, I had, *inter alia*, emphasized:

> It is doubtful whether serving bureaucrats, that too working so closely with the highest chief executive of the country, will have the requisite freedom to deal with these highly sensitive and often politically explosive cases. Mr Deshmukh is an employee of the Tatas as its Director. He is also reported to be the Chairman of the Times Bank. The Tatas too have come to adverse notice in some cases. It is a moot point whether a person in the full-time employment of a large industrial house should be a member of such a high level committee dealing with the nexus between the politicians, bureaucrats and criminals. Ideally, the institution which is to follow up such cases must have a constitutional status and its members must work on a full-time basis (Godbole 2000: 73–74).

I still hold the same view. The problem of this unholy nexus has become much more acute in recent years, with dozens of scams coming to light. At the same time, the government has become more impervious and has no political will to address it. This will continue to be the same unless the pressure of public opinion forces a change.

The Hawala Scandal

In early 1991 the story of the Jain diary broke out which contained information about pay-offs to 115 prominent politicians and bureaucrats—a veritable Who's Who. Its full implications became clearer five years later in Sanjay Kapoor's book, *Bad Money, Bad Politics: The Untold Hawala Story* (*Sunday*, 21–27 April 1996). The money involved in pay-offs had clandestinely come from foreign sources through the hawala route. At least two politicians, Sharad Yadav and Devi Lal, had admitted that they had got the money, albeit only for 'political purposes'. Payments of at least Rs 65 crore, mainly to public servants—some 67 politicians and bureaucrats—were made in two years (*Frontline*, 27 June 1997). The Santhanam Committee on Prevention of Corruption, in its report submitted in 1963, had also invited attention to the diaries confiscated in the Sirajuddin case in which too large payments made to ministers and officers had been recorded. These cases are shining examples of the nexus brought out by the Vohra Committee referred to earlier. It also showed how impossible it was to punish the guilty.

It is well-known that the matter was taken up in a PIL in the Supreme Court and its judgment made waves for quite some time.[4] It was aptly described as pertaining to the criminalization of politics. Reference may be made to some important findings and directions of the court, which have remained on paper: The court had observed that 'the law does not classify offenders differently for treatment there under including investigation of offences and prosecution of offences, according to their status in life.' The court effectively underlined that howsoever high one may be, the law is above you and it does not distinguish between persons on the basis of their status in life.

The question of the independence and autonomy of the CBI and other investigating agencies was gone into by the court fully. The court's significant observations were that:

> There can be no quarrel with the Minister's ultimate responsibility to the Parliament for the functioning of these agencies and he being the final disciplinary authority in respect of the officers of the agency with power to refer complaints against them to the appropriate authority...However, all the powers of the Minister are subject to the condition that none of them would extend to permit the minister to interfere with the course of investigation and prosecution in any individual case and in that respect

the concerned officers are to be governed entirely by the mandate of law and the statutory duty cast upon them.

The Supreme Court had also quoted the caution administered by Lord Denning in a case which read:

I have no hesitation, however, in holding that, like every constable in the land, he [Commissioner of Police] should be, and is, independent of the executive. He is not subject to the orders of the Secretary of State...I hold it to be the duty of the Commissioner of Police, as it is of every chief constable, to enforce the law of the land....but in all these things he is not the servant of anyone, save of the law itself...He is answerable to the law and to the law alone.

It is well known that nothing came of this injunction of the Supreme Court. It may be recalled that the Supreme Court itself called the CBI a 'caged parrot' with too many masters in the coalgate scam case in 2013.

The other significant direction of the Supreme Court was that the CVC should be responsible for the efficient functioning of the CBI and the CVC should be entrusted with the responsibility of superintendence over the CBI's functioning. The court further directed that the CBI should report to the CVC about cases taken up by it for investigation; progress of investigations; and cases in which charge sheets are filed and their progress. However, the government was reluctant to give such powers to the CVC. The CBI too did not want to have the CVC supervising its work. As a result, the CBI has continued to plod along, with the government interfering in its work as it sees fit.

Another important directive pertained to the follow-up action on the N. N. Vohra Committee report referred to earlier. Evidently, this critical, highly worrisome and sensitive aspect of the functioning of the politico-bureaucratic system has been brushed under the carpet once again.

In Chapter 5 I refer to the importance of having an independent and competent prosecution agency if the rule of law is not to suffer. Unfortunately, in the hawala case, the Supreme Court did not accept the suggestion of the *amicus curiae* for the appointment of an authority akin to the Special or Independent Counsel as in the United States for the investigation of charges in politically sensitive matters and for the prosecution of those cases. The court observed:

We are of the view that the time for these drastic steps has not come. It is our hope that it never will, for we entertain the belief that the investigative agencies shall function far better now, having regard to all that has happened since these writ petitions were admitted and to the directions which are contained in this judgment. The personnel of the enforcement agencies should not now lack the courage and independence to go about their task as they should, even where those to be investigated are prominent and powerful persons.

These fond hopes were belied even before the ink on the judgment was dry. In almost all politically sensitive cases since then, the investigating agencies and the prosecution wings have totally failed in fulfilling their duties. One cannot cite a single major case in which the law has been permitted to take its course.

The Supreme Court had also struck down the Single Directive under which prior approval of the government is required before initiating action against senior officers of the rank of Joint Secretary and above. This too was nullified by the then NDA government by a suitable amendment to the relevant act.

It can thus be seen that the only purpose that the much celebrated hawala case served was in creating public opinion on the subject, for whatever it was worth. But, as in the case of most other PILs, in terms of bringing about institutional and policy changes, its impact was nil.

Finally nothing came out of the hawala case either as the diaries were not considered admissible evidence by the court. Ironically, special judge V. B. Gupta, while dismissing the case, stressed, 'corruption has eaten into the nation's moral fibre and rectifying this should be top priority' (*TOI*, 17 May 1997). The usual peroration! On 8 April 1997, Delhi High Court judge Mohammad Shamim acquitted L. K. Advani and the Jain brothers, 18 months after being first implicated in the case. Also cleared was V. C. Shukla (*Sunday*, 4–10 May 1997). 'Harshad [Mehta] se bada ghotala, CBI ne dabaa dalaa' (CBI has hushed up even a bigger scandal than that of Harshad Mehta) was the refrain of news reports. J. S. Verma, Chief Justice of the Supreme Court who had presided over the Hawala Bench, publicly castigated the investigating agencies for a sloppy investigation. Verma said giving autonomy to CBI was not enough. It did not have the will to conduct a proper investigation. The then joint director of CBI, B. R. Lall, in his statement before the Central Administrative Tribunal, stated that due to the interference by the then director CBI, K. Vijaya Rama Rao and involvement of Rajiv Gandhi and Narasimha Rao which had come up in the depositions of the Jain brothers, could not be pursued and this delayed the investigation (*Sakal*, 14 October 1997). In the raids on the Jain brothers, Rs 58 lakh in cash, Rs 10 lakh worth of small savings certificates, $20,000 in cash and other important documents were seized by the authorities (*Sakal*, 21 August 1995). But, like several other cases this case too was given a (in)decent burial. No appeals were filed in higher courts. Neither was any departmental action taken by the government against any of the bureaucrats.

Bofors—Innumerable Questions, No Answers

The Bofors scandal broke out following the Swedish Radio broadcast on 16 April 1987 that bribes had been paid by AB Bofors to some Indian politicians, bureaucrats and middlemen in the Rs 1,437 crore Howitzer gun deal. Later in January 1997, Michel-Andre Fels, Swiss Justice Ministry official, stated that the material handed over to India contained ample evidence that bribes were paid in connection with the 1986 Bofors Howitzer deal (*HT*, 24 January 1997). Former Swedish Police Chief, Sten Lindstrom, who leaked the Bofors papers in 1987, candidly stated, 'Can you imagine...no one from India met the real investigators of the Bofors deal' (*Outlook*, 7 May 2012: 9). Martin Ardbo, the man who negotiated the contract for Bofors, has never spoken out. The CBI has made no attempt to contact him or for that matter, anyone else in the company (*IE*, 3 September 1995). Chitra Subramaniam Duella has written that:

> My Swedish source—'Sting'—now identified as Sten Lindstrom, chief of Swedish police who led the investigation into the India deal, gave me documents and information that nailed the lies put out by the Indian authorities....The Swedish government assisted India in the cover-up...Twenty-five years later, whichever way you roll the dice, the same question pops up: what services did Quattrochi, as a part of AE Services, render so as to be paid 47.5 million in a Swiss bank in 1986? The AE Services contract has no terms of reference and performance status (Duella 2012: 26–27).

In his interview with Seema Mustafa in Stockholm, Sten Lindstrom raised six questions which are all relevant today: Who introduced Quattrochi to Bofors officials? What was his value proposition that led him to assure Bofors contractually that he need not be paid if the howitzer deal was not closed in their favour? Why did Bofors pay him? What services did his company AE Services offer? What are the links between Quattrochi and Sonia Gandhi? Who is the Gandhi trustee lawyer Martin Ardbo (Bofors chief) met in Geneva? (Mustafa 2011: 14).

Over the years, Bofors has become a metaphor for corruption even in the remote rural areas in the country. *Isme kuch bofors hai*, is a popular retake on the traditional, *dal me kuch kala hai* (there is something suspicious in the curry) adage.

The unbelievable 'exploits' of central ministers during this period would take anyone's breath away. 'All the Prime Minister's men' were vying with each other to prove their loyalty. In the first case of its kind, even in the shady world of diplomacy, during his visit to Switzerland, Madhavsinh Solanki, External Affairs Minister in the Narasimha Rao government, passed on an unofficial note to his counterpart that investigations in Bofors case be stopped! Narasimha Rao, the senior-most minister in Rajiv Gandhi's Cabinet and also then Minister for External Affairs, pleaded before the court that all his actions such as alleged fabrication of evidence against V. P. Singh in the St Kitt's case were because of directions of the former Prime Minister, Rajiv Gandhi and/or his office. B. Shankaranand, Chairman of Bofors JPC, was instrumental in white washing the scandal. The culture of sycophancy was all-pervading. There was a joke doing the rounds in Mumbai during the Shiv Sena-BJP regime in Maharashtra, when

Balasaheb Thackeray was the 'remote control'. Someone asked the chief minister of Maharashtra, 'What is two plus two?'. He replied, 'It is four but let me ask Balasaheb'. In the Delhi version, the punch line was, 'Who wants to know?' (Godbole 2000: 105–08). As is well known, some bureaucrats who openly covered up the government's lies were later rewarded with governorships or were sent out of the country on important, high-profile postings.

The 28-year journey of the Bofors case is like the eighth wonder of the world. The Bofors probe is described as the longest and costliest probe in recent times. Arun Jaitley, the Additional Solicitor General of India during the short-lived V. P. Singh government, has stated that:

> ...for the first two-and-a-half years, the effort of the Indian government and its agencies was only to hush up the whole matter...I think that the 11 months from December 1989 to November 1990 was the only period when a serious investigation was carried out. The pre-condition for conducting an inquiry about the Bofors accounts in Switzerland, according to international treaties and principles of dual criminality, was that a criminal case must be registered in India and it should not merely pertain to income tax, revenue loss or FERA [Foreign Exchange Regulation Act] violation. It must relate to something which is considered an offence both in India and Switzerland. During Rajiv Gandhi's Prime Ministership, the CBI failed to file an FIR. They would simply send letters to Switzerland saying: please co-operate with us, we are investigating income tax and FERA violations. So the Swiss would write back: you are asking the wrong questions; since there is no criminal case, we cannot cooperate. The first thing the new government did in December 1989 was to register an FIR in which bribing public servants was mentioned as the principal offence...the day the Swiss formally informed India that Quattrochi was one of the appellants [in a case in Switzerland], he left the country in a very suspicious manner and without the CBI interrogating him (*TOI*, 10 February 1997).

Crores of rupees were spent on a make-believe investigation and countless jaunts abroad by CBI and law ministry officials. At one stage, K. Madhavan, former deputy inspector general in the CBI who played a key role in preparing the FIR, was confident that it would lead to the conviction of the accused. Asked why it took nine years to file the chargesheet—the FIR was filed in 1990 in which the name Rajiv Gandhi figured, for the first and last time, as an accused—Madhavan blamed successive governments for putting hurdles in the path of the CBI probe, including 'succumbing to the pressures from extra-constitutional authorities' (*TOI*, 30 October 1999).

The CBI's conduct during the entire investigation was suspicious. Even though an inquiry against him was in progress, instead of arresting him, Ottavio Quattrochi was permitted to leave India. Later, the CBI took its own time in announcing the detention of Quattrochi by Interpol in the Argentinean province of Misiones while on the way to capital Buenos Aires on 6 February 2007. His extradition from Argentina, as also Malaysia earlier, was handled by the CBI so sloppily that it could not have succeeded. In January 2006, Additional Solicitor General, B. Dutta, obviously with the approval of the CBI and the Ministry of Law, conveyed to the British authorities India's no objection to the defreezing of two London bank accounts in the name of Quattrochi and his wife. Quattrochi's son Massimo was in India for several months and was permitted to conduct business here. Earlier, on 4 February 2004, the Delhi High Court struck down charges of bribery and corruption against all the accused, including Quattrochi. Interestingly, neither the NDA nor the UPA governments filed any appeal! (*Tehelka*, 10 March 2007). Not surprisingly it was rumoured that there was a tacit understanding at the highest level not to pursue the matter. I have stated elsewhere how the PMO during Vajpayee's Prime Ministership was considered to be Hinduja positive.

The last hope of fixing accountability in this monstrous scandal was demolished when the Joint Parliamentary Committee (JPC) did a complete whitewash of the episode and gave a clean chit to all those who were involved in it. The JPC held 50 sittings—30 for recording evidence, seven to study classified documents and 13 for in-house deliberations—spread over 142 hours and 25 minutes and submitted its report in April 1988. The Lok Sabha discussed the report for 60 hours. In the 12 years up to February 1997, the Parliament had spent 202 hours and 25 minutes discussing the Bofors scandal but it remains as much of an enigma now as ever.

Several suggestions were made by the opposition parties when the motion to appoint a JPC was moved by the government in Parliament, including there was no need to appoint a JPC as the requisite information on who had received the payments, what the amounts were and at what point of time the payments were received could be obtained by the government of India directly from A. B. Bofors; Swiss banks should be approached to ascertain the payments made; the inquiry should be referred to an independent tribunal to be presided over by a judge of the Supreme Court; Bofors should be asked to disclose the names of recipients forthwith, failing which the agreement should be cancelled; more representation should be given to the opposition parties and groups on the committee; the chairman of the committee should be appointed from amongst the members of the opposition; the committee should have powers to examine the ministers; and the Official Secrets Act should not be allowed to come in the way of the committee. Several of these suggestions were rejected by the government. As a result, most of the opposition parties boycotted the JPC which made the task of whitewashing that much easier.

It is necessary to underline that the JPC on the bank scam, appointed in August 1992, was permitted to call ministers for tendering evidence. The JPC report states, 'Hon. Speaker, Lok Sabha,...while granting approval, stated that this was being done in view of the uncommon nature of the case and the views expressed by the leaders of all parties at the time of constituting the committee and also later.' The JPC wrote to a number of persons, including several serving and former ministers, to furnish information on certain points. These included Manmohan Singh, B. Shankaranand, V. P. Singh, Yashwant Sinha, S. P. Malaviya, Madhu Dandavate, Madhavrao Scindia, N. D. Tiwari and P. Chidambaram. The committee also took evidence of: (i) Manmohan Singh, Finance Minister, (ii) B. Shankaranand, Minister for Health and Family Welfare and former Minister of Petroleum and Natural Gas and (iii) Madhu Dandavate, ex-Minister of Finance (Lok Sabha Secretariat 1993: 5). It can thus be seen that a similar approach could have been adopted in the case of the Bofors JPC but then the purpose of a political cover-up would not have been served.

And the JPC report did do a thorough job of a cover-up. The committee, *inter alia*, concluded:

- The committee are firmly convinced that the procedure followed for the selection of the Bofors gun system was sound and objective, and the technical evaluation of the various gun systems considered was thorough, flawless and meticulous.
- The committee have noted with satisfaction that the price of the Bofors gun system in the Indian contract was the lowest compared with prices in contracts with other customers.
- No extraneous influence or consideration such as kickbacks or bribes as alleged in the media affected at any stage the selection and evaluation of the gun systems or the commercial negotiations with the competing suppliers. The committee have not come across any action or decision of any officer or member of the government which could be viewed with slightest suspicion at any stage of the Bofors contract. The evidence before the committee conclusively establishes that the decision to award the contract to Bofors was purely on merits.
- Bofors paid SEK 319.4 million to the three companies, not domiciled in India, as winding-up charges for terminating agreements for consultancy and marketing services etc.
- The fact that the investigation initiated in this case by the public prosecutor in Sweden was closed after examining Bofors' officials and the relevant records of the company, suggest that no offence could be made out under the Swedish law. In other words, the public prosecutor who had access to all

the records in Sweden has not been able to establish any charges involving bribes and kickbacks in Bofors' Indian contract.

- There is no evidence to show that any middleman was involved in the process of acquisition of the Bofors gun. There is also no evidence to substantiate the allegation of commissions or bribes having been paid to anyone.
- There is no evidence of any other payment having been made by Bofors for winning the Indian contract (Lok Sabha Secretariat 1988: 189–92).

The Bofors case was formally judicially (but not judiciously) buried when on 4 March 2011, the Delhi High Court allowed the CBI's plea to withdraw the case against Quattrochi. Quattrochi died on 13 July 2013. He must have literally laughed his way to the grave! But the ghost of Bofors refuses to go away. The Delhi Bench of the Income Tax Appellate Tribunal (ITAT) has pulled up the Income Tax Department for not penalizing Quattrochi for the undeclared income he had earned out of the Bofors gun deal in 1986. ITAT has reportedly held that Quattrochi and his wife Maria controlled the two Swiss bank accounts held in the name of Colbar Investments Limited and Wetelsen Overseas, in which Bofors paid the commission money (*The Sunday Guardian*, 9 January 2011).

Thus, a potentially powerful instrument of ensuring public accountability in a parliamentary democracy was rendered toothless and effectively brought into ridicule. It is noteworthy that the other JPCs—the stock market scam, the Harshad Mehta scandal and the safety standards for soft drinks and juices—have met with the same fate.

The JPC on the bank scam, for example, merely noted, 'The committee have come across various instances of close nexus between prominent industrial houses, banks and brokers.' Further, the JPC remained satisfied only by stating, 'Considering the nature of the case and the complexity of the transactions, the committee recommends that the matter should be enquired thoroughly by a joint team consisting of CBI, CBDT [Central Board of Direct Taxes], SEBI, Department of Company Affairs, and RBI [Reserve Bank of India]' (Lok Sabha Secretariat 1993: 322–44). Someone may well ask, 'Did we require a high power, high profile JPC to tell us this?' It is another matter that nothing came out of further inquiries, except for some criminal cases and the matter was shelved for all practical purposes! The committee's report did, however, have several detailed notes appended by its members stating how the report of the committee had failed to look into a number of important issues! R. C. Murthy stated, 'A major failure was the JPC's inability to bring out fully the nexus between industrial houses, politicians, brokers and bankers. Brokers by themselves could not have digested all the money they hijacked. Businessmen entered the fray, used the brokers for their own ends' (Murthy 1995: 216). The Supreme Court is reported to have slammed the central government for its 'duplicity' and 'absolute indifference' in unravelling the truth behind the 1990s securities scam. The court said, 'the professed purpose of the Special Courts Act, [set up] in the backdrop of the scandal that shook the nation, and the manner in which the litigation was conducted coupled with absolute indifference of government to get at the truth only demonstrates the duplicity with which the government can act' (*IE*, 1 August 2013). Strong words indeed but the government is so impervious, impersonal and indifferent that no one is bothered in the least by these scathing observations of the court.

The report of the Committee to Inquire into the Complaint Made by Some Members Regarding Alleged Offer of Money to Them in Connection with the Voting on the Motion of Confidence (Fourteenth Lok Sabha) (hold your breath, this is the *actual* name of the committee!) also shows that the joint committee of the two Houses was a futile exercise as the committee ended by merely suggesting, 'this matter may be probed further by an appropriate investigating agency' (Lok Sabha Secretariat 2008: 57). This raises a pertinent question whether we require such inquiries by parliamentary committees which serve no purpose.

Jharkhand Mukti Morcha Case—The Depths to Which We Fell

P. V. Narasimha Rao, the so-called Chanakya of Indian politics, will be remembered by history as the only Prime Minister of India who faced a series of criminal cases—bribing MPs to save his government in a vote of no-confidence, the St. Kitts forgery, and cheating of Lakhubhai Pathak pickle manufacturer—to name a few, but like a proverbial cat with nine lives, was let off in all these and other cases. The most glaring of these was the Jharkhand Mukti Morcha (JMM) case involving the bribing of MPs which brought the institution of Parliament into shame. The 'galaxy' of leaders who figured in the charge sheet filed by the CBI included, apart from P. V. Narasimha Rao, former Haryana Chief Minister Bhajan Lal, former and the present union Minister Ajit Singh, Rao's former Cabinet colleagues Buta Singh and Satish Sharma, and five former MPs of the Jharkhand Mukti Morcha (JMM). In July 1993, four MPs belonging to JMM, along with seven members of a breakaway faction of the Janata Dal (A) were allegedly paid Rs 8.7 crore to ensure the survival of the P. V. Narasimha Rao government in a no-confidence motion. The Special Court presided over by Ajit Bharihoke on 29 September 2000 found Narasimha Rao and Buta Singh guilty and sentenced them to three years of rigorous imprisonment and a fine of Rs 200,000 each (*The Indian Advocate*, vol. 29, 1999–2000: 81). The case went in final appeal to the Supreme Court. But the majority decision of the court, based on hair-splitting of the laudable constitutional provision pertaining to the immunity provided to law givers for anything said or done in the House, shocked the conscience of the country.[5] The Supreme Court, which had taken pride in the past on making 'complete justice' in every case which came before it, made a distinction between bribe-giver and bribe-taker and upheld the immunity of the bribe-taker! Professor N. R. Madhava Menon has rightly said, 'The ingenious ways in which politicians seek to evade accountability explain why the "law is an ass."'[6]

According to the majority decision of the Constitution Bench:

> the alleged bribe-takers were entitled to immunity under article 105(2), the alleged conspiracy and acceptance of bribe being 'in respect of' or having nexus with the vote against no-confidence motion. However, the MP, who despite having received the bribe pursuant to the conspiracy, had abstained from voting, would not be entitled to such immunity since protection under article 105(2) must relate to the vote actually given or speech actually made in Parliament by an MP and therefore prosecution against such MP must proceed. As regards bribe-givers, the charge against them of conspiracy with the bribe-taking MPs, who abstained from voting, must proceed. However, *Parliament may proceed against both bribe-takers and bribe-givers for breach of privileges and contempt.*

It is important to note that the Parliament has refused to codify its privileges, even though over six decades have elapsed since the adoption of the Constitution. The Committee on Privileges, in its report given in 1995, stated:

> With the strength of statistics as mentioned, the committee feel no hesitation in holding that the ground reality is entirely opposite to the picture projected in so far as allegations of misuse are concerned. These facts and figures explode once and for all the myth of misuse [or even non-use as in the JMM case] and abuse of privileges. The committee are of the view that the legislature's powers to punish for contempt is more or less akin and analogous to the power given to the court. Even the Contempt of Court Act, 1971 does not specify the matters which constitute contempt...The committee recommend that it is not advisable to codify parliamentary privileges (Lok Sabha Secretariat 1995: 35).

There has been no change in the position since then. Parliament, the highest institution of democratic governance, does not consider itself answerable to anyone. There is no rule of law so far as the Parliament is concerned.

However, as per the minority judgment, 'the words "in respect of" mean "arising out of" and therefore immunity under Article 105(2) is available only to give protection against liability for an act that follows or succeeds as a consequence of the making of a speech or giving of a vote by an MP and not for an act that precedes the speech or vote and that gives rise to liability which arises independently of the speech or vote—offence of criminal conspiracy under Section 120-A of IPC is made out on conclusion of the agreement to commit the offence of bribery and performance of the act pursuant to the agreement is immaterial. Act of acceptance of a bribe for speaking or giving a vote against the motion arose independently of making the speech or giving of vote by the MPs—hence the liability for the offence cannot be treated "in respect of anything or any vote given in Parliament" and neither the bribe takers nor the bribe-givers entitled to any immunity under article 105(2).'

The majority decision inevitably prevailed. A number of important points arise from this unfortunate decision. **First**, the government should have quickly filed a review petition in the Supreme Court for reconsideration of the majority decision of the court. Though the decision of the court was dated 17 April 1998, the government was not serious in the matter and took its own time and filed the petition only in November 1998 (*TOI*, 13 November 1998). The court could have condoned the delay in filing the petition but it did not do so and the petition was rejected. **Second**, the Supreme Court had suggested that Article 105(2) and Article 194(2) of the Constitution be amended to clarify that the privilege therein will not apply to any act of corruption. This was way back in 1998. A similar recommendation was made by the NCRWC in 2001. Murlidhar Bhandare wrote:

> In the US, Canada, Australia and most commonwealth countries a legislator can be prosecuted for accepting bribes intended to influence his vote or decision on any question brought before him in his official capacity. The position is crystal clear as observed by the Chief Justice of the US Supreme Court in Brewster's case: Taking a bribe is no part of the legislative act. It is not by any conceivable interpretation an act performed as a part of or even incidental to the role of a legislator (Bhandare 1998).

Though more than a decade and a half has elapsed, no action has been taken to amend the Constitution by the NDA government or the successor UPA government. **Third**, earlier, the Bombay and the Orissa high courts had held that MLAs and MPs are not public servants. Fortunately, the Supreme Court held in the JMM case that an MP (and, by the same logic also an MLA) is a 'public servant' and that he holds an 'office' and performs 'public duty'. The court, however, found that there was no authority competent to remove him from office. While the majority had held that merely because there is no authority to remove an MP from his office, he does not cease to be a public servant for the purpose of the Prevention of Corruption Act, 1988. The court had directed that till provision is made by Parliament in that regard by a suitable amendment in the law, the prosecuting agency should obtain the permission of the Chairman of the Rajya Sabha and the Speaker of the Lok Sabha, as the case may be. However, the remaining two judges had held that prosecution would be possible only with respect to a public servant who is removable from his office by a competent authority. This issue has remained unsettled for want of the requisite amendment of the relevant provisions of law, once again underlining how farcical the rhetoric of 'zero tolerance for corruption' mouthed by our rulers is. **Fourth**, as stated earlier, the Supreme Court had stated that Parliament could proceed against persons concerned for breach of privilege and contempt of the House. It is interesting to note that Parliament, which is so very vigilant about its rights and privileges, has conveniently turned a blind eye to this atrocious behaviour of the government and its own members. The notices of question of privilege given by Jaswant Singh, Indrajit Gupta and Jagmeet Singh Brar were disallowed by the Speaker on 12 March 1996 in view of his ruling in the House on 11 March 1996 in which he had observed:

> The matter is before the court which may take a proper decision on the basis of evidence that may be produced before it. Three years back some allegations were voiced about the illegal payments. At that time itself, the House could have been asked to look into it. On the basis of other kinds of inducements, the matter could have been asked to be looked into the House (sic). In view of these facts and the available evidence, I find it difficult to give the consent (Lok Sabha Secretariat 1996: 187).

No one questioned this ruling. This shows that no political party wanted to pursue the matter and embarrass the government.

Enron Project—Failure of Governance

The Enron project was a high profile failure of governance which led to the sullying of India's image abroad. The Enron power project of Dabhol Power Company (DPC), with a proposed installed capacity of 2,184 MW, involving an investment of over Rs 12,000 crore, was undertaken in 1993 as a showpiece of economic liberalization. When it was approved, it was the single largest foreign direct investment (FDI) in India. But, in reality, the project was badly conceived and should not have been approved as it was economically and commercially unviable. The power purchase agreement (PPA) was so one-sided and inequitable that it brought the State Electricity Board (SEB) to financial ruin. Enron power was exorbitantly expensive and under the agreement for power purchase, the electricity board had to purchase it even by backing down its own cheaper hydro and thermal power stations. The Shiv Sena and BJP severely criticized the project while in the opposition and had promised that the project 'will be dumped in the Arabian Sea' if they were elected, but on coming to power they fell prey to the charms of Enron and approved the project once again with a much larger installed capacity! While dismissing the writ petition against this decision, the Bombay High Court had made some scathing observations:

> Even after 50 years of Independence, political considerations outweigh the public interest...[A multinational] should behave like an investor or an industrial

house, and not as a government...We are distressed to note the extent to which political compulsions or motivations could get priority over public interest...As was said by the Chief Minister [Manohar Joshi] in the context of the original PPA, (one might say) Enron revisited, Enron saw and Enron conquered—much more than what it did earlier...In any event, one thing is obvious that at every stage, it is the common man who has been taken for ride during elections by the Shiv Sena-BJP alliance by making Enron an election issue.

Finally, the state government appointed a high level Energy Review Committee (ERC) under the chairmanship of this author, with Deepak Parekh, R. K. Pachauri, E. A. S. Sarma and Power Secretary in the state government as members, to review the project and to suggest a way out. The committee's report submitted in April 2001 made for disturbing reading (Government of Maharashtra 2001: 83–84). Enron is an outstanding example of arbitrary and opaque decision-making by the government. The committee has brought out the serious flaws in the project, how it was intrinsically unviable, how the statutory sanctions were given without application of mind, and why the project ought not to have been approved. It also brings out how the state and the central government, their several agencies and organizations, and the all-India financial institutions failed in their responsibilities to scrutinize the project. The committee observed that it:

is concerned that there are numerous infirmities in the process of approvals granted in the project, which bring into question the propriety of the decisions... *The committee is troubled with the failure of governance that seems to have characterised almost every step of the decision-making process on matters relating to DPC. The failure of governance has been broad, across different governments at different points of time, at both the state and the central level, and across different agencies associated with examining the project, and at both the administrative and political levels. It strains belief to accept that such widespread and consistent failure to execute assigned responsibilities is purely coincidental.*

The mothballed power project (now renamed the Ratnagiri power project) in which investments of over Rs 10,000 crore had been made had to be revived by the central government in the interest of rehabilitating its own image! But this was at tremendous cost, the hidden and explicit subsidies amounting to nearly Rs 10,000 crore, to the unsuspecting Indian taxpayer (Godbole and Sarma 2006: 3640–642). It was unfortunate that the central government failed to give wide publicity abroad to the wrong-doings of Enron in India.

Phyllis Dininio has stated in the *Global Corruption Report 2003*, 'Since 1989, the energy giant Enron had contributed soft money totalling US$5.95 million (with 74 per cent going to Republicans) and it enjoyed a close connection with policy-makers in the Bush administration. In his book *The Buying of the President*

2000, Charles Lewis identifies Enron as president Bush's top career patron and the Enron CEO, Kenneth Lay, as a close personal friend...Indeed there are already accusations of bribery by Enron in India and Ghana' (Transparency International 2003: 79–80). The United States senate governmental affairs committee had subpoenaed the White House records of its interactions with Enron. The material revealed many links with Lay, who was a major Bush campaign contributor and served on a transition committee that searched for people to fill energy-related positions in the administration. Of the 21 individuals recommended for appointment in the administration, three ultimately received appointments (*ET*, 24 May 2002).

If such mistakes are to be avoided in the future and history is not to repeat itself, every endeavour must be made to learn lessons from the past. It is not enough that the project is merely restructured and revived. It is equally, if not more necessary, to make sure that there will not be more Enrons and Dabhols to haunt us in the future. It is with this intention that though the three other members of the ERC were opposed to the suggestion, this author and E. A. S. Sarma had recommended that a judicial commission of inquiry should be set up under the Commissions of Inquiry Act, 1952, under the chairmanship of a serving or a retired judge of the Supreme Court for fixing both administrative and political accountability for the lapses, if any.

Though ERC's report was submitted to the state government on 10 April 2001, it was only on 7 November 2001 that the state government finally set up a commission of inquiry under the Commissions of Inquiry Act, 1952, under the chairmanship of Justice S. P. Kurdukar, retired Judge of the Supreme Court. The commission was asked to examine and make a report on: (i) the validity of all the agreements, clearances, concurrences, licences, permits or sanctions under the relevant laws relating to electricity and the failure of governance, if any; (ii) the correctness of all and any representations made by Enron and/or the DPC including, but not limited to, costs, project costs, financing and any or all projections that affect the PPA tariff or the tariff determined in accordance with the norms under section 43A of the Electricity (Supply) Act, 1948 (54 of 1948), the technical and operating parameters of the plant and all aspects of the plant and its tariff; (iii) the circumstances in which the PPA was negotiated, cancelled and renegotiated; the role played by persons associated with the decision-making process and the circumstances in which the phase II contract or contracts were made binding and whether the decisions taken were in the interest of the state of Maharashtra; (iv) the compliance with statutory clearances, licences, permits and approvals or sanctions; and (v) to make recommendations arising out of the findings on these points. The state government was further directed by the same order that, having regard to the nature of the inquiry to be made by the said commission of inquiry and other circumstances of the case, the provisions of sub-section (2) of section 5 of the Commissions of Inquiry Act, 1952, shall also apply to the said commission. The commission was asked to submit its report to the state government within a period of six months from the date of publication of the notification in the official gazette.

Even after two and a half years had elapsed since the appointment of the commission, there was no progress in its work. This was mainly because of the objections raised by some affected persons—Sharad Pawar, former Chief Minister, and N. Raghunathan, former Chief Secretary in Maharashtra, among others, and the Government of India (GoI) (this was during the NDA regime) that the commission had no jurisdiction to inquire into GoI's actions and/or that the issues had already been earlier looked into by the High Court and the Supreme Court. Justice Kurdukar, however, is reported to have ruled that the commission did have the jurisdiction to probe the decisions taken or approvals given by the Centre and its authorities. At the same time the commission observed that it cannot decide on the challenge to the constitutional validity of the state government notification with regard to the terms of reference. The commission said that whosoever wanted to challenge the constitutional validity of the notification could approach the appropriate forum (*FE*, 25 March 2003). This led to the central government filing a petition in the Supreme Court under Article 131 of the Constitution. On 9 April 2003 the Supreme Court gave an *ex parte* stay restraining the Kurdukar Commission from proceeding further with the inquiry when the Attorney General made a mention of the petition by the Centre (*FE*, 10 April 2003). Even a year after the grant of stay, the inquiry was still in cold storage. Though it was amply clear that GoI would approach the Supreme Court in the matter, it was not known why the GoM could not file a caveat requesting the court not to grant a stay before giving it a hearing. Even otherwise, one would have normally expected the court to issue notices to the concerned parties and giving them a hearing in such a matter involving public interest before granting a stay but this was not to be. Even the hope that the stay would not continue indefinitely in this manner and that the court would decide the matter one way or the other in a reasonable time too was belied. It is also not known if any effort was made by the Government of Maharashtra to get the stay vacated.

This brings us to the provisions of the Commissions of Inquiry Act, 1952, under which the inquiry was ordered by the state government. This legislation was enacted by Parliament after the central government had gone through the process of due consultation with the state governments to facilitate the setting up of commissions with requisite powers to inquire into and report on any matter of public importance. The Law Commission of India in its report on the act in question referred to the observations of the Lord Chancellor, Viscount Kilmuir, in his reply to the debate in the House of Lords in the *Waters* case made in defence of a similar act in that country:

> Let me state quite shortly the arguments for some such procedure as the present. The sanction of the public inquiry is necessary on occasions for the purpose of maintaining a high standard of public administration and, indeed, of public life...After the true facts have been found and stated, it may be necessary to stigmatise conduct which, although not a criminal offence or a civil wrong, falls short of the requisite standards of our public life...These ends may well be of such importance to the life of the nation as to justify means which inflict hardship on individuals (Government of India 1962: 6).

Chandrachud, J., as he then was, had in his judgment in *State of Karnataka v. Union of India* (1977, 4 SCC 608) referred to what Sir Cyril Salmon, Lord Justice of Appeals, had said in a lecture on 'tribunals of inquiry' and summarized the position in the following word:

> It is clear from the provisions and the general scheme of the act that a commission of inquiry appointed under the act is a purely fact-finding body which has no power to pronounce a binding or definitive judgment. It has to collect facts through the evidence led before it and on a consideration thereof it is required to submit its report which the appointing authority may or may not accept. There are sensitive matters of public importance which, if left to the normal investigational agencies, can create needless controversies and generate an atmosphere of suspicion. The larger interests of the community require that such matters should be inquired into by high-powered commissions consisting of persons whose findings can command the confidence of the people (Malik 1995: 12).

Section 2 of the act defines, *inter alia*, appropriate government for the purpose of setting up a commission of inquiry to mean the central government in relation to any matter relatable to any of the entries in List I or List II or List III in the Seventh Schedule of the Constitution, and the state government in relation to any matter relatable to any of the entries in List II or List III in that Schedule. Since electricity is in the Concurrent List (List III), a plain reading of the act shows that the state government was competent to order an inquiry in this case. Further, as required by Section 3 of the act, the state government had already declared that the inquiry pertained to a 'definite matter of public importance'. Proviso (a) to Section 3 states that, 'Provided that where any such commission has been appointed to inquire into any matter by the central government, no state government shall, except with the approval of the central government, appoint another commission to enquire into the same matter for so long as the commission appointed by the central government is functioning.' This also was not applicable in this case as no commission of inquiry had been set up by the central government. In such a situation, the question of the federal structure getting adversely affected due to the setting up of the commission of inquiry by the state government was not germane. Also, the argument of the field having been occupied by the central government was not relevant. Further, the Dabhol power project had been approved by both the state government and the central government so far as their own respective spheres of responsibilities were concerned. Any inquiry, to be meaningful, would therefore, have to cover the actions and decisions of both these governments. It is also necessary to appreciate that, as opposed to a litigation in the High Court or the Supreme Court in which the decision of the court is binding on the parties, any commission appointed under the Commissions of Inquiry Act, 1952, is only a fact-finding commission. It can only make recommendations to the government. These are not binding on the government and it is upto the government to disregard or reject the recommendations altogether, as several state governments and the central government have done in a number of instances in the past. But the commissions of inquiry have an important role to play in a democracy in which, in the final analysis, it is the court of civil society and the common man which matters the most. The commissions of inquiry are meant to help them form informed and unbiased opinions in crucial and complex matters pertaining to the governance of the country. In a sense, it is therefore, inexplicable that elected governments and public functionaries should refuse to submit themselves to an open, impartial and transparent judicial inquiry presided over by a retired judge of the highest court in the country.

It is indeed unfortunate that the work of some important inquiry commissions has been unduly delayed in recent years due to stays granted by courts. While the powers of the high courts and the Supreme Court embodied in the Constitution cannot and should not be curtailed in any manner, it is time for the courts themselves to lay down guidelines for their working so that no *ex parte* stays are granted and stays are for a period not exceeding three months at the most, particularly in matters pertaining to commissions of inquiry. Otherwise, the very purpose of setting up of a commission of inquiry is frustrated, thereby holding to public ridicule yet another statutory institutional mechanism created by Parliament to instil confidence in the functioning of the government.

Against this background, the worries of civil society and common persons relate to whether the higher judiciary can be counted on to safeguard their interests in these highly adversarial litigations where large industrial houses, multinationals, foreign investors and the government make common cause and are on the same side, and are represented by reputed, well-established and highly paid senior advocates. Just as the Supreme Court relaxed several of the rigours, rules and procedures to develop the innovative instrument of a PIL, why should it not be possible for the courts to adopt a similar approach where public interest is perceived to be adversely affected? Why should it not be possible for the courts to take up such cases for hearing on priority and to pronounce judgments without undue delay? Looked at from this point of view, the picture does not appear to be encouraging because it is unlikely to happen.

All efforts to get the courts to look into these issues have been unsuccessful. Taking advantage of the stay, which continued indefinitely, the state government promptly decided to wind up the commission of inquiry when its term expired at the end of 2005. A case study of the DPC litigation might reveal whether the claims made by the then Chief Justice of India, Y. K. Sabharwal, are justified. In another controversial power project, Cogentrix in Karnataka, the judgment was delivered by the Supreme Court after a long gap of several months after the conclusion of hearing of the case. All one can say is that inspiring confidence in civil society and people at large in the country should be as important as inspiring confidence among foreign investors, which Chief Justice Sabharwal had rightly talked about.[7]

Demolition of Babri Masjid—A National Shame

India's secular credentials were severely questioned worldwide when the central government failed to stop the wanton demolition of the Babri Masjid in Ayodhya on 6 December 1992 by frenzied Hindu mobs assiduously incited by the BJP over the previous two-three years. The account of this shameful chapter in India's history cannot be lost sight of while discussing the state of governance in the country. This author was the Home Secretary in the Government of India at the relevant time. The full account of the efforts made by the Ministry of Home Affairs to persuade the government to dismiss the Uttar Pradesh government headed by Kalyan Singh of the BJP and to impose President's rule so as to be able to protect the monument were unsuccessful due to the indecision of Prime Minister P.V. Narasimha Rao. A full account of the developments throughout this critical period has been given in this author's memoirs published in 1996 (Godbole 1996: 332–418).

A reference must be made to the Places of Worship (Special Provisions) Act, 1991, which was gazetted on 18 September 1991. Section 3 of the act states, 'No person shall convert any place of worship of any religious denomination or any section thereof into a place of worship of a different section of the same religious denomination or of a different denomination or any sect thereof.' This section was meant to protect Muslim shrines which the VHP and the BJP were threatening to take over and convert to temples. However, care was taken to ensure that the Babri Masjid dispute did not get covered by the provisions of this act. A proviso to Section 4 made clear that any suit, appeal or other proceedings which may be pending on the commencement of the act 'shall not so abate and every suit, appeal or other proceedings shall be disposed of...'. Further, Section 5 clearly states that the act shall not apply to Ram Janma Bhumi Babri Masjid.

After World War I, a French general is said to have written a glowing account of how well the French troops had fought and won in a battle in which the French forces had actually suffered an ignominious defeat. The general gave the account to his second-in-command and asked him to dispatch it to army headquarters. The next day the general asked him whether he had done so. The officer said, 'Sir, I have not sent it since the account which you have written is quite the opposite of what actually happened.' The general coolly told him, 'Ami, c'est pour l' histoire' (Friend, it is for history). The same can be said of Rao's book, *Ayodhya 6 December 1992*, (2006). In the following paragraphs, the relevant page numbers of Rao's book are given in brackets.

It is important to try and understand the underlying issues that led to the demolition of the Babri Masjid (Godbole 2006: 2076). Rao, absolving himself in his book states, 'They [Congress leaders] had already made up their minds that one person was to be made historically responsible...in case the issue ended in tragedy.'

Rao states that 'from millions of people has come the inevitable and irresistible question: Why did the President of India not impose President's rule under Article 356 of the Constitution of India and save the structure in time? The central government certainly owes a full explanation to the people. It has been given several times, but it would be proper to consolidate the reply to the question in all its relevant aspects, to stand witness to history and throw light on the future' (p. 166). The book has miserably failed to achieve this avowed objective. In fact, Rao has been economical with the truth. Incidentally, President's rule is not imposed by the President of India but by the central Cabinet with the approval of the President.

The book was published 14 years after the event. According to the publisher's note, Rao wrote this account after he stepped down as PM in 1996 and made revisions to the manuscript till a few days before his death in December 2004. It is not therefore surprising that it is a totally sanitized account of events. Since Rao has so little to add to what is already contained in the central government's *White Paper on Ayodhya* (1993), it is not clear why he wanted to have it published only after his death. Was he afraid of people questioning him closely and joining issues with him?

The title of the book *Ayodhya 6 December 1992* itself is significant and essentially follows the title of the government's white paper. It characteristically brings out Rao's penchant for adopting the 'middle path'. The entire *Mahabharata* on that day was due to the demolition of the Babri Masjid but if prominence had been given in the title to the Masjid, Hindus would have been angry, and if prominence had been given to the *Ram Janmabhoomi* (birth place of Ram) Muslims would have been upset. Hence the middle path choice of the title: 'Ayodhya'.

The book refers to the contingency plan prepared by the central government for dealing with the situation in more than one place (pp. 125,151) but says that it was only to assist UP government in dealing with the situation effectively and 'ensuring compliance with the orders of the Court'. This is far from true. In fact, it is a travesty of truth. Rao himself states that 'As a measure of abundant caution, however, the central government had stationed 195 companies of central paramilitary forces (CPMFs) near Ayodhya in November 1992 so that these could be made available at short notice if and when required by the state government *or for any other contingent purpose*' (p. 125). He prefers not to talk about the other contingent purpose of dismissal of the state government and imposition of President's rule in UP as it would have raised embarrassing questions regarding his leadership during this critical period. Rao makes much of the fact that 'the central government did not have even a toe-hold anywhere in UP at the time. In the absence of such a hold, the centre could not have found it feasible to take an extremely crucial step like the imposition of president's rule in the teeth of determined resistance by an entrenched state government' (p. 173). But it must be emphasized that the comprehensive contingency plan prepared by the Ministry of Home Affairs was meant to deal with any such eventuality effectively and to ensure protection of the Babri Masjid by swift action of commandos and paramilitary forces. In fact, the union Home Minister, in his reply to a marathon debate in the Lok Sabha on 3 December 1992 had clearly stated that 'the Centre could easily resort to Article 355 of the Constitution pertaining to the duty of the union to protect states against external aggression and internal disturbances' (p. 136). This was in accordance with the contingency plan which the Ministry of Home Affairs had prepared. Since Prime Minister Rao did not want to take action under Article 356 coupled with pre-emptive action under Article 355, the contingency plan in fact became infructuous in so far as the original objective was concerned. The statement in the book that 'it was not the position of the state government that they would not use the CPMFs even if it became necessary to do so' (p. 141) is factually incorrect and misleading. The resolve of the state government not to use CPMFs was amply brought out by its disinclination to deploy these forces near the Masjid even though they were stationed in Faizabad and other nearby locations from 24 November 1992, the deliberate delay on the part of the state government in calling for the CPMFs on 6 December after the demolition of the structure began, and the refusal of the state government to provide magistrates to escort the CPMFs which led to their going back to the barracks. And since the government of UP had all along declared its intentions of not using force to deal with the *kar sevaks* and not deploying the central paramilitary forces in and around the vicinity of the disputed structure, the paramilitary force was not useful even as a show of force, far from it being deployed by the state government to deal with the situation effectively. The procurement of rubber bullets, action-ready commando units, dog squads, bomb disposal squads, hundreds of requisitioned vehicles, water cannons, tonnes of concertina wires and such other elaborate preparations remained unutilized. The huge paramilitary force assembled from all over the country and stationed just a few kilometers away from Ayodhya ended up watching helplessly as the Masjid was wantonly demolished. Rao prefers to keep this shocking reality away from the reader.

When a Prime Minister writes an account of a seminal historical event such as the demolition of the Babri Masjid was, it is not unreasonable to expect that he will elucidate on the discussions which took place on the pros and cons of the issues in the government and the considerations which weighed with him in taking the decisions that he did. The book sheds no light on this aspect whatsoever. Rao blames his ministerial colleagues for making him a scapegoat but never says what were the points that they were urging and why they were not accepted. Rao makes no mention of the advice which he got from officers closely connected with and responsible for the relevant subjects. It is amazing to read his observation that 'the officers told me again and again that whatever was being done for queering the pitch was for political reasons and not based on what obtained on the field. They said they had studied the field and were quite clear that the *kar seva* would be peaceful. This was the situation' (p. 185). This is untrue. His assertion that 'today's hindsight was not available to anyone in the Government of India on those dates...The formidable snag is that no one at that crucial time knew *how it was going to happen*' (emphasis in the original) (p. 171) is also far from true. While none could have categorically known 'how it was going to happen', there were serious apprehensions about the forthcoming calamity among at least some of Rao's advisors, including this author, which were voiced to him. A full account of this has been given in my memoirs *Unfinished Innings: Recollections and Reflections of a Civil Servant* (1996).

In fact, generally, it is the Prime Minister who makes an effort to find a scapegoat for each of the failures of his government, and particularly when it is as monumental as the demolition of the Babri Masjid. A Prime Minister must be prepared to take moral responsibility for every major decision, even if he is not directly involved in it. In this particular case, since he had himself taken all decisions (or was disinclined to take any decisive action) he must be prepared to take the blame himself and must not try to palm it off to his Cabinet colleagues.

Rao's arguments for non-invocation of Article 356 are curious and hardly convincing. The assertion that 'it was not possible to identify the stage, event or moment that could fit in the above description (i. e. when it could be said that the government of the state could not be carried out according to the provisions of the

Constitution) had not arisen' (p. 169) is preposterous. This is amply borne out by the central government's repeated pleadings before the Supreme Court, as brought out in Rao's book itself. For example, the Solicitor General told the Supreme Court on 24 November 1992 that 'the situation on the ground is escalating day by day' (p. 111), the Attorney General told the court on 25 November 1992 that 'the situation in Ayodhya had reached a boiling point' and warning the court that 'even one day of adjournment could prove costly'. The Attorney General had also told the court that the state government had clearly stated that 'use of force to prevent *kar seva* will not be appropriate' (p. 113). In its order the court had taken note of the serious situation pointed out by the Attorney General. 'The deficiencies in the existing security arrangements [made by GoUP to safeguard the Masjid] which were pointed out by the central government were taken note of by the court' (p. 124). Rao admits that 'the law and order implications of the RJB-BM dispute had always been serious' (p. 124). He further admits that 'Based on past experience and the continuing undercurrent of communal tension on account of the RJB-BM dispute, serious apprehensions existed about the outbreak of fresh violence in various parts of the country, particularly if any untoward incident took place in Ayodhya during the proposed *kar seva*' (p. 125). All this was more than enough to come to the conclusion that this was a fit case for the dismissal of the state government. Every time President's rule is imposed in any state, it involves use of discretion by the Governor, the central Cabinet and finally the President. This has not stopped the Centre from taking recourse to Article 356 on nearly 100 occasions, as discussed in the previous chapter. If there was one occasion on which the imposition of President's rule was fully justified, it was in November 1992, *before* the *kar sevaks* started congregating in Ayodhya in droves. And this is what the Home Ministry was repeatedly urging. The Law Ministry too had concurred in the Cabinet note prepared by MHA for the dismissal of the state government. Rao's assertion that 'any prudent President or Prime Minister would not have gone ahead and clamped Article 356 under these circumstances' (p. 180) will not have many takers.

Rao claims that he could not have taken action to impose President's rule in UP when the Supreme Court was holding hearings on the UP situation practically on a day-to-day basis during the last few days preceding the demolition of the Masjid. However, the court itself had clearly pointed out on 25 November 1992 that 'the central government is, of course, at liberty to make its own assessment of the matter and take such action on its own as may appear to it proper and permissible' (p. 115). As the book itself brings out, this matter had come up again during a further hearing in the court, 'Declining to direct the central government to withdraw paramilitary forces [as urged by GoUP] from Ayodhya, the judges said that neither of the court's [previous] orders had prevented any constitutionally elected government from performing its duty in accordance with the law' (p. 130).

It is amazing to see that in spite of this clear enunciation of the position by the Supreme Court, Rao maintains that since the matter was before the Supreme Court he could not have imposed President's rule in UP. Rao's argument that 'the Supreme Court's refusal even to make the central government a receiver for the limited and specific purpose of giving adequate protection to the disputed structure at Ayodhya is also a meaningful pointer; it only translates into a 'hands off the state' directive to the centre' (p. 180) is breathtaking and preposterous. Clearly, the fact that the central government did not have even a 'toe-hold in UP' (the words used by Rao himself on p. 173) must have weighed with the Supreme Court in not involving the Centre with such a responsibility. The convenient but untenable interpretation of the Supreme Court position given by Rao shows his desperate attempt to justify his indecision and inaction at one of the most critical moments in the history of India.

Rao makes much of the advice given by Governor of UP against imposition of President's rule on the most untenable plea that 'the Governor is in charge of the State' (p. 170). Needless to say, the Governor is in charge of a state only when the state is under President's rule. In other cases, he is just the constitutional head of a state. In the situation which was developing in UP and was detailed day after day by IB reports to which Rao was privy, apart from newspaper reports (on which Rao has, in this book, relied a great deal), it was clear that the Governor had not kept himself fully briefed about what was happening in the state. Nowhere is it laid down that the Centre must necessarily go by a Governor's report. This was particularly so in this present case when the situation in Ayodhya was so explosive. It must be stated that after the Masjid was demolished, the central Cabinet took the decision to dismiss the state governments, not just in UP, but also the other three BJP governments in Madhya Pradesh, Himachal Pradesh and Rajasthan. After taking such a decision, the governors of these states were told orally to send suitable reports for the purpose. So much for Rao's touching faith in and show of adherence to constitutional proprieties!

Rao states, 'I held a large number of meetings with individual and groups directly concerned with the dispute, as well as journalists, political, religious and social leaders' (p. 95). These discussions are only stated to have 'facilitated a better understanding of the position of the parties concerned and enabled various sections of them to put forward their own insights into the various facets of the problem (p. 96). As Rao states, 'No specific proposal or suggestion for a solution was put forward on behalf of the government.' There is no indication as to what transpired in these meetings and the outcomes, if any, of these meetings in which no official or anyone other than Rao was present. This point was also raised earlier by a number of people with regard to the government's white paper.

To conclude, let me refer to Rao's own observation that 'Constitutional pundits, administrators and others understand that in some critical situations, time is of the essence in taking a decision' (p. 181). Ironically, Rao's handling of the RJB-BM dispute and its disastrous outcome bear this out fully.

Foot-dragging by Prime Minister Rao, which was the hallmark of the handling of the Ayodhya imbroglio, was faithfully followed by the Liberhan Commission of Inquiry in submitting a totally inconsequential report, after scores of extensions and 17 long years, the longest time ever taken by any commission of inquiry in Independent India!

Higher Civil Services—Nothing to Be Proud Of[8]

There are widespread misconceptions and myths about the civil services in the pre-Independence period. The so-called 'steel frame' which the civil services signified was such only when there were no elected governments in power. Repeated complaints were made by the leaders of the Congress Party and the Muslim League regarding the ineffectiveness of the administration in dealing with communal violence and its partisan attitude. The main reason for the overall deterioration in administration, which started during this period, was the uncertainty as to the future of these premier civil services and this undermined the confidence and the morale of their members. It was claimed by the British that the watershed event was the advent of the elected governments taking over power in the provinces. By his letter dated 6 January 1947, Pethick-Lawrence, Secretary of State for India and Burma, asked the governors for their views as to how the two premier 'security services', the Indian Civil Service (ICS) and the Indian Police (IP), were standing up to the strain of the transition period and how far they were getting on with the popular ministry. The replies received from the governors were startling. In his reply, Nye, Governor of Madras, *inter alia*, lamented that:

> *There is a section of these officers who, with an eye to the future, are unduly subservient to the ministers and some, I fear, are prepared to curry favour with the ministers at the expense of their duty*...There is no doubt that, with the changes which are contemplated there will be a great loss of efficiency in the administration which will persist for many years, and unless active steps are taken to recruit and train officers of very good type for the future, it will have a permanent effect on the efficiency of the government in this province (Godbole 2006: 92–93).

The views of Burrows, Governor of Bengal, were contained in his letter dated 25 January. He attributed the running down of the administrative machine to a course of events over which the services had no control, 'In almost every department in public life there is ample evidence of very serious degree of demoralisation of services. *There is no longer any feeling that any disgrace attaches to inefficiency or even to dishonesty (the only sin is being found out); it is comparatively rare nowadays to find officers who value doing good work for its own sake.'* He bluntly stated that *'The steel frame is admittedly and avowedly on the way out and is rapidly becoming "Lath and Plaster"*...There is more insidious canker of what I may call "administrative trimming", so as to secure favour or at all events to avoid offending the rising power' (Godbole 2006: 93).

Wylie, Governor of United Provinces, enclosed with his letter a copy of the letter which he had received from an English collector, which observed:

> The change [in the transition period] may not be so apparent in the secretariat appointments; it is grimly clear here [in the field]. We are working in conditions which our predecessors would have found intolerable and we watch what we consider the elementary principles of administration disregarded. *We have no guarantee that we would be supported or, which is more important, that we will be able to support our own officers or that there is any authority capable of supporting us.* You have only to read the evidence before the Calcutta inquiry committee [on Calcutta riots] *to realize that and the meaning of 'appeasement' applied to law and order.*

The note prepared by the Joint Planning Committee stated that the administration in the Provinces had continued to run down. It referred to the case of the Inspector General of Police (IGP) in the United Provinces, where the Home Minister belonging to the Congress Party was corresponding directly with police officers in the field, instead of through the head of department. The IGP issued instructions to his officers to disregard such directions. The Home Minister was offended and insisted that the IGP should leave. In spite of the intervention of the Chief Minister and the Governor, the IGP had to leave when Nehru threatened that the Congress members in the interim Government in Delhi would resign if the police officer was permitted to continue on the post. As a result, the officer had to go on leave preparatory to retirement.

These instances and observations read as if they are of the present state of civil services in the country. Thus, a new and corroding administrative ethos had set in even before Independence. The so-called impregnable bastion of the ICS and IP, which represented the 'steel frame' of administration, had started crumbling with the very first in-roads of political interference (Godbole 2006: 94–95). Over the years, of course, this position has further deteriorated rapidly.

Not just public perceptions, but self-introspection by the services too will reveal the reality of a precipitous and calamitous fall in the standards of personal behaviour and work performance, ethics and image of the civil services. It is not therefore surprising that all civil servants from a lowly clerk to the highest echelons are derogatorily referred to as mere *babus* (clerks) in public discourse and in the media, which I find most offensive. But, the only remedy against this onslaught will be taking steps to improve the working of the services.

It may be appropriate to recall a few shocking examples which bring this out fully. The then Information and Broadcasting Minister, K. P. Singh Deo reportedly laid down certain ground rules for the functioning of civil servants in his ministry, 'Servants should not speak till the master permits' and 'You are not to apply your mind, you are just to do what you are told.' There was also the unsavoury controversy with regard to the sugar scam when former Food Minister, Kalpanath Rai, lashed out at the Secretary in the Ministry. The then Chief Election Commissioner and a former civil servant himself, T. N. Seshan, colourfully described civil servants as 'call girls' and 'backboneless wonders'. Interestingly, there was no organized protest by civil servants or their associations in any of these instances. The master-servant relationship between the minister and the civil servant was sanctified by the intemperate observations of Justice M. P. Thakkar during the course of a hearing on a writ petition in 1998 on the opaque selection procedures for appointment as Secretary to the Government of India. The judge observed, 'Even when a person appoints a cook or a watchman he looks for a person in whom he has faith. How can the Government of India appoint any person as Secretary in whom it has no faith?' A cartoon pithily showed a civil servant addressing his colleague, 'I belong to the V. P. Singh batch. You must be of Rajiv's' (Godbole 2000: 176–77). Once loyalty and servility was established to the Gandhi-Nehru family, for example, an officer has nothing to worry about and can look forward to an illustrious career and cosy after-retirement assignments. This undermines the basic concept of a non-political and neutral civil service which the then Home Minister, Vallabhbhai Patel had advocated so strongly in the Constituent Assembly.

This is borne out time and again by the way the All India Service (AIS) officers have been treated by the Centre and the states. Wholesale transfers of officers with every change in the government have become common practice. Transfer *bazaars* are held in all states to give plum postings to those who are close to the political bosses and to sideline those who are not inclined to fall in line. Suspension is yet another instrument which is used ruthlessly to assert the importance of the political executive and to put the bureaucracy in its place. The arbitrary use of the power of suspension has led to serious demoralization of the services in the states. The most recent case of this kind is the suspension of young IAS officer, Durga Shakti Nagpal, Sub-Divisional Magistrate of Noida in UP, for taking action against the unauthorized construction of a mosque and the sand mafia. It has made no difference to the time-worn governance practices in UP even after the young Chief Minister, Akhilesh Yadav, took over the reins. Looking to the blatant misuse of powers by the states, it is high time the powers of suspension are taken over by the central government if the protection given by the Constitution to the AIS is not to become meaningless.

In this context it is relevant to refer to the observations of eminent civil servant B. K. Nehru:

> I also studied that organization of the home civil service and how it was that in spite of vigorous democracy the civil service had retained its independence in that it was guided by the rules and the law and not by the whims and wishes of transient ministers. The answer was simple. *All the three powers which are exercised by the ministers in India to bend the civil servant to his will, namely, appointments, transfers and suspensions, are not exercised by them at all in the United Kingdom. They are exercised by a small group of senior secretaries presided over by the secretary of the civil service department who reports to the prime minister direct. It is they who appoint people, transfer them and punish them, not ministers.* Their proposals are, of course, approved by the Prime Minister but when I asked the head of the civil service department what would happen if the Prime Minister refused to sign, he was shocked out of wits. He said, 'But that can't happen.' Such is the power of the conventions of the British Constitution, which, if broken, would lead to furore in Parliament (Nehru 1997: 556).

A politician in India would be aghast and shocked to read this. Mayawati, the then Chief Minister of UP, had issued instructions that district office-bearers of her party would submit annual evaluation reports on the work of the District Magistrates and the District Superintendents of Police, thereby totally undercutting their independence and self-respect.

What ails the civil services is already well known. As stated earlier, since Independence reportedly more than 600 committees and commissions have gone into the relevant issues at the behest of state governments and the Government of India. But, what is wanting is action thereon. There is neither administrative nor political will to deal with the issues firmly and decisively. The same fate has befallen SARC. Its reports are also languishing though over three years have elapsed since their submission. A new 'cold storage device' seems to be in place of referring any matter to a group of ministers. This is what has been done with the SARC reports as well.

A question is often raised about whether we require politically neutral and permanent civil services patterned on the British model. My answer, looking at the fractious polity, is a categorical yes but only if the services are provided enough protection and not left to their own devices as at present. There are those who suggest that the civil services should be restructured in such a way that for higher levels of Joint Secretary and above, there is lateral entry, particularly from academics and the corporate sector. But, who will enter the civil services if the higher jobs are to be given away to 'outsiders'? This debate is often joined by people who have little experience of how the government functions in reality, the checks and balances which operate or are expected to operate in government and the compulsions under which the higher civil services have to function. Just as it is not easy to transplant a person from the civil service into the corporate world, except to undertake lobbying and liaison assignments, an executive from the private sector cannot easily be placed at policymaking levels in the government, except in a few advisory assignments. Further, we cannot have a halfway house. If one is so enamoured by the American system of governance, it is best that it is adopted fully and not in a piecemeal manner to accommodate the nominees of the high and mighty in senior posts in the government.

A move in this direction has already started with the induction of some corporate heavyweights in senior positions in the government. There is no evidence to show that it has led to any improvement in the functioning of the concerned organizations. They are reported to have written to Prime Minister Manmohan Singh to rein in the bureaucracy if they are expected to deliver results. They have pressed that the government should apply the concept of 'agencification'—the process of agencies being carved out of government departments to carry out specific executive functions within a mandate and framework of policy provided by the relevant ministry—to improve delivery performance (*IE*, 30 March 2012). If this concept is to be followed on the lines of UK, it must be done as a conscious policy, after considering its pros and cons, and not on an ad hoc basis just for a few appointees from the corporate sector.

It is also necessary to remember that the assertion of lateral entry for outsiders can be relevant only at the secretariat level and not in thankless assignments such as in the urban local bodies and panchayat raj institutions, where dealing with elected representatives on the one hand and the dissatisfaction of the general public on the other, is a delicate and risky tightrope walk. There may not be any lateral candidates for these field level jobs. In these circumstances, civil services will continue to grow and expand in India in the foreseeable future, particularly in the social sectors. The challenge is to make them honest, productive, accountable, transparent, sensitive and responsive in their functioning. And this is where India has failed miserably both at the political and senior administrative levels. In fairness it is wrong to lay the blame only with the political class.

According to B. K. Nehru, an outstanding civil servant, diplomat and a former governor of three states, 'the reason why India was increasingly becoming a lawless country was that those to whom the law had been entrusted for enforcement were not allowed to exercise their powers. The autonomy of the services was therefore vital for the establishment of rule of law' (Dhar 2002: 335). He suggested that the position of civil servants should be specifically and clearly defined in the Constitution. The Late K. Subrahmanyam, a reputed civil servant and defence analyst, had also expressed a similar view, 'Parliamentary democracy elsewhere in the world is anchored on a totally apolitical civil service in which political parties do not interfere. That ensures good governance. It is a major challenge in India whether with politicising civil services it is at all possible to have good governance with levels of prevailing political corruption' (Subrahmanyam: 11). As mentioned later, E. A. S. Sarma and I had made precisely this submission in our PIL in 2004 before the Supreme Court but the court declined to even admit it! (Godbole, Sarma 2004: 1)

It is well accepted that with globalization and the economic reforms set in motion since the early 1990s, administration has to inevitably change. It is fashionable to say that the change has to be from regulatory to promotional. But this is only partly true. Globalization and doing away with the 'licence-permit raj' should not be construed as 'free for all' functioning, and an opaque, non-transparent and ad hoc decision-making processes. The root causes of dozens of major scams which have tarnished the image of the country are to be found in such non-accountable and feudalistic functioning. If India is to be an attractive destination for foreign investment and has to be globally competitive, it must endeavour to provide a level playing field to all players, whether domestic or foreign. Public-private partnerships for funding and implementing projects should not mean compromising public interest and subserving the interests of private partners. For example, the concept of recovery of costs of infrastructure projects through levy of tolls has been accepted by the people but it is being misused in some projects with the active connivance of public authorities who are turning a blind eye to the gold-plating of costs of the projects or tardy audits of the accounts of private partners in the projects. Blindly following the examples of advanced countries, without taking note of the parliamentary ethos and public expectations in this country can lead to immense problems and misunderstandings. Another example is the decision taken by the Rajiv Gandhi government to permit senior officers in government to go on deputation to private companies for a period of up to five years. Already in Delhi, officers are categorized as AB+ and AB-(Ambani positive or Ambani negative), or RH+ (Reliance and Hinduja positive) and RH-(Reliance and Hinduja negative) and so on. The insidious influences which large industrial houses exert in postings and transfers of officers are common knowledge in Delhi and in all state capitals. Creating vested interests among officers and making them obliged to particular business houses is hazardous and has brought a bad name to the civil services.

T. S. R. Subramanian, who was Cabinet Secretary during the United Front government, has written:

No one can now aspire to a posting in any ministry in Delhi, unless his or her name is vigorously sponsored...The merest wish of an official of the PMO becomes a command to the system. The personnel department at the centre has become helpless in enforcing the existing regulations. Even the cabinet secretariat has been overwhelmed, unable to stem the rot in recent years.

The system has sent strong messages to entire cadres of aspiring civil servants that hard work and performance are irrelevant: the path is to gain effective access to one or more in power. Of course, there is a price to pay for the short-cut. The carefully built-up structure for identifying suitable officers for posting in Delhi has now been demolished (Subramanian 2004: 157–58).

The RTI Act was passed with a lot of fanfare in 2005 but it must be admitted that it is mainly the senior bureaucracy which has been responsible for making its provisions redundant in a number of cases. It must be noted that most decisions on implementing the act and supplying information there under are taken at the level of officers. Only a few matters involving politically sensitive information have to go to ministers for decisions. It is unfortunate that the bureaucracy has turned out to be the biggest hurdle. The Supreme Court has recognized the right to information as a fundamental right. It is therefore binding on every functionary in the government to supply all information to the public, except that which has been specifically barred under the act. However, one reads of dozens of cases in which secretaries in the government have taken a negative view. If such is the mindset at the highest level, how can the lower bureaucracy be expected to change its ways? A recent proposal, strongly supported by the Committee of Secretaries was on withholding file notings from people. I have been strongly arguing against this for several years. Once a decision is taken on a file, all notings on the file, including the Cabinet note, must be made available to the people to see. If those who handle the file know that what they advice on the file will be subjected to public scrutiny later, it will be the best way to prevent misuse of power. Another recent case was the proposal of the CBI to exclude it from the purview of the RTI Act. In this case too, the Committee of Secretaries is reported to have recommended this to the Prime Minister. This came very handy to the government and it has approved the proposal! It is a travesty that while the higher judiciary is endeavouring to make CBI's working more credible and to improve its image, the bureaucracy is bending backwards to help the CBI in continuing with its much discredited and highly politicized functioning. No one is asking for CBI records to be thrown open to the people when an investigation of a case is in progress. But once the case is closed or decided by the court or is withdrawn by the CBI, people must have a right to see how it was handled by the CBI, what its law officers advised and so on. But this is precisely what the CBI does not want! It is said that sunlight is the best disinfectant but the higher bureaucracy does not seem to believe in this universal truth.

A related question is of the continuance of the archaic Officials Secret Act (OSA), 1923. England, from where the legislation had been copied, has already recast it completely. Some major political parties had announced their intention to abolish the act if they came to power. But once they assumed charge in the

North Block, the seat of power of the Ministry of Home Affairs in Delhi, their views changed completely. OSA will have to continue but in a very restricted form by recasting it completely. Several proposals on this behalf, including the one framed by the Press Council of India, have been with the government for quite some time. But there is a fear of the unknown among politicians and senior administrators. They apprehend that their closely guarded citadel of power will be invaded if OSA is recast. It is high time pressure is brought on policymakers to see reason.

There was a time when, but for some rare exceptions, the higher civil services were known for their honesty, integrity and probity. Now the position is reported to have reversed. Honest civil servants are the exceptions. A majority may not be personally dishonest but they will not go out of their way to keep the system under them clean and would prefer to go along with the current. Recent cases such as the 2G scam, the Commonwealth games scam, the Adarsh Cooperative Housing Society and so on are a mere tip of the iceberg. As a result, in common public perception, all government servants are corrupt, unless proved to the contrary. In such an environment, it is demoralizing for an honest civil servant to function effectively. Some time back, the Uttar Pradesh IAS Association had taken a bold initiative to identify two most corrupt officers in their cadre by a secret ballot. It is difficult to believe but the same officers were later appointed as chief secretaries by the government. The astounding story of corruption of a husband and wife in Madhya Pradesh was numbing, but there are such cases in all states.

The question is where do we go from here? Is there a way out? In Andhra Pradesh, AIS offices had been kept out of the purview of the Lok Ayukta on the basis of a misconceived judgment of a single member Bench of the Andhra Pradesh High Court. Fortunately, the decision was reversed by the High Court in appeal. It is not surprising that the people at large believe that the higher civil services in the state have a vested interest in perpetuating the present position. Needless to say that the fight against corruption will be futile unless the higher civil services have a commitment to making it a success. To argue, as some people do, that the civil services are drawn from society at large and are bound to have all the weaknesses and drawbacks of society is one thing but to accept this argument would mean the AISs are not the cream of society and are no better or worse than the common so-called babudom.

It needs to be noted that as compared to earlier years, present recruits in the civil services are more qualified, particularly in professional streams. The competition for getting into the top services is intense. Against this background one wonders why there is such all-pervasive corruption and debasement of standards in the higher services. One reason could be the lack of a value system and inadequate emphasis on the inculcation of appropriate values in the initial training as also refresher and higher in-service training. Role models of proper behavioural standards need to be placed before the officers during these training programmes. Most importantly, officers whose integrity is doubtful and who do not come up to the desired standards of probity and behaviour must not be seen to be rewarded and recognized by way of foreign training or foreign or coveted postings. The age of recruitment also needs to be lowered if proper values are to be ingrained in the officers at the induction stage itself.

With the politicization of civil services, the *esprit de core* which used to be the hallmark and the strength of the services is no more. Each officer is now left to his own 'devices', in every sense of the term. This is evident from the manner in which scores of officers have been given post-retirement assignments, or extensions in service or have been appointed in constitutional positions. One other cause is mass transfers of officers every time there is a change of government so as to reward those who are supporters of the party coming to power and to teach a lesson to those who were sympathetic to the outgoing government. Repeated efforts made to stop the 'transfer bazaars' had failed. The high courts and the Supreme Court too have refused to intervene, except when an injustice was caused to an individual officer. Even in such cases, it was difficult for an officer to establish before the court that the government's action was biased and taken with prejudice. A PIL filed by Common Cause, an NGO in Delhi, failed in eliciting any response from the government or remedial action by the Supreme Court. At the same time the issues continue to be important and therefore require to be pursued.

Finally, a reference may be made to the recommendations of the Sarkaria Commission which, *inter alia*, stated:

- The All India Services are as much necessary today as they were when the Constitution was framed and continue to be one of the premier institutions for maintaining the unity of the country.
- Any move to disband the All India Services or to permit a state government to opt out of the scheme must be regarded as retrograde and harmful to the larger interest of the country. Such a step is sure to encourage parochial tendencies and undermine the integrity, cohesion, efficiency and co-ordination in administration of the country as a whole.
- The All India Services should be further strengthened and greater emphasis given to the role expected to be played by them (Government of India 1988: 229).

The main challenge is how to ensure that these services are not politicized and that they are given the freedom, autonomy and independence to uphold the rule of law in the country. Unfortunately, no political party is interested in accepting this challenge.

Road and Rail Safety—Increasing Concerns

With one death every four minutes—most in the four states of UP, Punjab, Maharashtra and Gujarat—India's highways can hardly be called world-class. Rail safety has been totally neglected over the years. There are 17,000 unmanned railway crossings in the country and these primarily account for the accidents. The C&AG has made scathing comments on the performance of the railways in ensuring passenger safety.

The problem of railway safety is not new. A number of committees have studied it. One of the earliest was a committee appointed in 1962 under the chairmanship of H. N. Kunzru. The committee's report contained 243 recommendations which comprehensively dealt with all aspects of the problem (Government of India 1963: 237–73). The wide-ranging recommendations covered, among others, collisions, derailments, accidents at level crossings, fires in trains, the human factor, signalling, tracks and so on. However, it was felt necessary to 'reinvent the wheel' once again after two successive accidents occurred involving heavy casualties and damage to railway property in 1968. There was also a demand in Parliament that some radical measures were required to ensure a reasonable measure of safety in rail travel. C. M. Poonacha, the then Railway Minister, announced a committee under the chairmanship of K. N. Wanchoo, retired CJI. The committee made 221 recommendations pertaining to all aspects of the problem, which included among others, statistical appreciation of important categories of train accidents, accidents at level crossings, fires in trains, accidents on narrow gauge lines, breach of block rules, disregard of signals by drivers, averted collisions, serious accidents from 1963–64 to 1967–68—causes and consequences, an appreciation of the recommendations made by the Kunzru Committee and of action taken thereon, etc. (Government of India 1968: 138–63). It is not known what follow-up action, if any, was taken by the Railway Ministry on these reports.

Accidents have continued to occur periodically. There were, for example, four major accidents in 2011, leaving 125 dead and over 430 injured. An internal assessment report presented before the high level committee headed by Anil Kakodkar, former Chairman of the Atomic Energy Commission, highlighted poor training of and attention to work by drivers (*Outlook*, 12 December 2011: 20) Yet another panel headed by Sam Pitroda, Advisor to the Prime Minister, has been appointed to suggest financial strengthening and modernization of the railways.

While all this is welcome, some basic concerns remain. Is it necessary to have a separate budget for railways? Why should the Railway Ministry not be one of the dozens of other ministries and function accordingly? In view of its unwieldy character, why not hive off some of the ministry's functions to autonomous agencies and the private sector? Why should there not be an independent tariff commission to decide railway fares, both for passengers and goods? Why not have statutory services boards to decide all staff matters? Why should the minister continue to be in charge as in the colonial days? These are only a few of the issues which need to be addressed on priority. Mere tinkering with the problem and to show action where there is none, will not take us far. But as would be seen from the analysis in this book, this is what is holding India back.

The Increasing Clout of the Corporate World

During the early years after Independence, the interaction of the government with industry and business was largely confined to the annual meetings of their apex bodies which were addressed by the Prime Minister and other senior ministers. This has perceptibly increased over the years, but not necessarily for the larger public good. Industry and business representatives are no longer coy about taking a hand in influencing policies, bargaining for large concessions for themselves at the cost of the exchequer, ensuring that their competitors are denied fair and equitable treatment and so on. It is evident that the apex bodies of industry and trade are taking an active part in influencing public opinion in the selection of not just a political party's candidates but also the top leaders of political parties. I have referred elsewhere to how certain business houses have been closely associated with the PMO from time to time.

The sale of Indian Petrochemicals Corporation (IPCL) to Reliance Industries in May 2002 was one of the more controversial decisions of the NDA regime. Public sector oil companies had shown keen interest in acquiring IPCL but the government preferred to sell it to Reliance though in the process Reliance became a virtual monopoly in petrochemicals with an average market share of 67 per cent in most petrochemical products and 98 per cent in paraxyline. The consumer had every reason to view Reliance's buyout of IPCL with mixed feelings. Another highly questionable disinvestment decision of the NDA pertained to the sale of Centaur Hotel in the exclusive Juhu Beach area in Mumbai—six acre, 371-room Five-Star hotel—for just Rs 153 crore.

Crony capitalism is evident wherever one looks. Virendra Kapoor has written about how the price of Jet Airways' shares was artificially jacked up when it was on the verge of signing a deal with Etihad:

> Honestly, the UPA government produces so many scams that a number of them go unreported and unnoticed. For instance, take the recent Jet Airways-Etihad deal. Thanks to the largesse of Civil Aviation Minister Ajit Singh, Air India, the national carrier, has again been short-changed. The Abu Dhabi-based airline paid an unusually high price for the 24 per cent stake in the Naresh Goyal-owned Jet only after the Ministry of Civil Aviation granted it 40,000 additional seats per week on the India-Abu Dhabi sector. In other words, Ajit Singh's Ministry sweetened the deal for Goyal (Kapoor 2013: 11).

After public uproar and the Parliamentary Standing Committee raised a number of questions and seriously criticized the government's actions, the PMO developed cold feet and has embarked on a re-examination of the issues. Once again, Manmohan Singh has said that he was misguided!

The doubling of natural gas producer price to $8.2 per mmBtu from April 2014 has become highly contentious. The proposals made by various ministries varied widely, with the Power Ministry and Fertiliser Ministry, two of the largest users of gas, suggesting a price which was to be much lower than others such as the Petroleum Ministry. The expert committee's recommendation too is highly questionable. Large vested interests are at play. It is important to note that RIL had ostensibly incurred a huge cost, disproportionate to the production of gas, and wants to recover it from consumers before profits are shared with the government. The actual production of gas is only about 14 mscmd as compared to the initial projection of 80 mscmd. Asking for an exorbitantly high gas price for lower gas production is a clever devise to recoup dwindling profits. Fixing the price in dollar terms will introduce significant further in-built periodical increases, as the rupee depreciates. We have obviously not learnt any lessons from the Enron power purchase agreement which brought the Maharashtra Electricity Board to financial ruin. To argue that a higher gas price will lead to larger investment in the sector does not hold water as the investment will be dependent on *reliable* (and not artificially inflated, as in the case of Reliance) gas discoveries. It is therefore necessary to declare the price in a transparent manner, which will not give rise to suspicions of crony capitalism at work and burden the consumer beyond sustainable levels. The price charged by several countries from domestic gas consumers is only about 2–4 dollars per mmBtu, and nowhere near the exorbitant price agreed to by the central government. The UPA government is unlikely to relent and it will be a major test of good governance for whichever government comes to power after the impending elections in 2014.

T. N. R. Rao, former Petroleum and Natural Gas Secretary, has rightly asked, 'Why did our market-friendly policymakers revert to the much maligned administered price only for gas, batting for market prices for all else [other oil products]? In a classic case of policy capture by a corporate...The grounds adduced [by government] are specious. [Domestic] Crude oil gets international prices since the '90s but production has stagnated. The gas story won't be any different' (Rao 2013: 36).

E. A. S. Sarma, former Power and Economic Affairs Secretary, in an article in *EPW*, emphasized:

by the earlier decision in 2009 [to increase the price by $1.86 mmBtu] and once again in 2013, the government has compromised economic reasoning at the altar of crony capitalism and political expediency. In the absence of a homogeneous gas market, the only alternative open to the government is to allow an independent, professional, quasi-judicial regulator to compute efficiency-based costs and determine the price on the basis of a reasonable return. It is improper to entrust this task to a GoM [group of ministers] which is merely a political entity (Sarma 2013: 15).

Surya P. Sethi, another well known energy expert, has also stressed that the presently approved formula for KG Basin gas violated international practices, 'Under prevailing market conditions, the KG Basin gas receives a price well beyond the price at which the same gas was bid out under an international tender or its cost of service. Despite the C&AG's report, the full extent of the KG basin scam is far from being completely exposed.' Sethi has underlined that the Rangarajan Committee formula is based on numbers from foreign markets even though these do not reflect the supply, demand or cost of production in India (Sethi 2013).

As the world enters, what the International Energy Agency has called, the 'golden age of gas', it is expected that there will be vastly increased supply, competition and diversified sources of supply in the LNG field. With the golden age on the horizon, to agree to an unduly high domestic administered price for natural gas, is suicidal for India. The timing of this decision is also significant with impending elections to the Lok Sabha. Such an important decision should have been appropriately left to the next government. In spite of weighty arguments and well placed criticisms, the Petroleum and Natural Gas Minister, M. Veerappa Moily, has staunchly defended the government's stand and has stated that there will be no reconsideration of the decision. At least, the suggestion of the Ministry of Finance that Reliance be paid the current price of $4.2 per mmBtu till it delivers on the committed gas, needs to be accepted. The deafening silence of all major political parties, except the Communists and AIADMK, on a matter which is of such vital concern for the people at large, is unbelievable. The conspiracy of silence of the media, particularly the electronic media and the chambers and federations of commerce and industries is striking and is resounding proof of the might of the corporate world.

A reference must be made to what Debashis Basu has called, Unit [Mis]Trust of India. He exposed the 'benumbing story' of how the UTI 'continuously raised public funds by exploiting its brand image of stability and security and frittered away that money through incompetence and nexus with companies, brokers and market operators' (Basu 2003: 34, 43). Basu has highlighted that the committee under the chairmanship of S. S. Tarapore, former Deputy Governor of RBI, had come out with absolutely scandalous facts that pointed to the key problem in UTI: corruption. The Deepak Parekh Committee set up earlier in late 1998 had pointed out how untrustworthy UTI had become. However, the committee attempted a valiant whitewash job of the key processes in running the US-64 Scheme. Basu competently exploded the common myths put out by the Parekh Committee: (i) US-64 was doing fine until 1995 after which the economy went downhill and the market turned bearish; (ii) US-64 invited trouble by changing its investment mix; (iii) US-64 suffered because it was forced to buy government stocks as part of the disinvestment programme; and (iv) US-64 did not have the money to buy growth stocks. Basu has underlined the real facts for the collapse: imprudent practices—it invested in risk (equities) but offered almost guaranteed returns (debt); incompetence; lack of accountability; and absence of regulation.

Until 1992, UTI was being used as an arm of the Ministry of Finance:

> If the market needed to be supported, the ministry would call UTI's boss...UTI mulishly refused to be regulated by SEBI, citing arcane laws and structures. In fact, S. A. Dave [Chairman, UTI] went on to claim that UTI disclosed much more than other funds and that there was strong internal accountability... The real issue was a corrupt nexus of politicians, brokers and UTI officials.... Unfortunately, the collective "wisdom" of the then Finance Secretary (Montek Singh Ahluwalia), the Economic Advisor (Ashok Desai) and the Finance Minister (Manmohan Singh) killed the first and last chance to get UTI to be transparent before it could inflict further damage. A victorious UTI bottled up the problem of poor returns and collected more money from the public—to lose more.

When the two bailouts proved unsuccessful, the US-64 Scheme had to be wound up, inflicting huge losses on millions of its unsuspecting small investors. No responsibility was ever fixed for this horrific man-made calamity, except for the sacking of its Chairman P. S. Subrahmanyam. The criminal case filed against him was presumably just forgotten.

But industrial and commercial houses are no longer happy at just paying their contributions to political parties or getting doles out of largesses. They are now increasingly interested in entering Parliament and are willing to spend crores of rupees for the purpose. Members of Parliament who have been jailed or are facing serious criminal charges in courts continue to be members of standing committees of Parliament and even its prestigious committees such as the Public Accounts Committee and the Joint Parliamentary Committee. Members who have their business interests in particular sectors are made members of the standing committees of the concerned ministries. Clearly, conflict of interest is of no concern to anyone, least of all to the power elite.

One powerful instrument for increasing leverage is by taking over the print and electronic media. It is therefore not surprising that currently there are as many as 825 private satellite television channels in India. A bar owner in Mumbai started a new TV channel, *Jai Maharashtra*, in April 2013. Sharad Pawar and

Sushil Kumar Shinde, ministers in the UPA government, and Prithviraj Chavan, Chief Minister of Maharashtra attended the inaugural function! According to Arundhati Roy, 'RIL, for example, owns controlling shares in 27 TV channels. Logically, RIL's political candidates are going to be promoted on these channels' (Roy 2013: 29). Equity holdings of corporate houses in media companies influence their stand and postures on all major issues. This has been borne out in the phenomenon of 'paid news' and the opinion and exit polls carried out by newspapers and television channels. If the sanctity of democratic processes is to be ensured, it is necessary that all information with regard to holdings in media companies be in the public domain and be periodically updated and made available to the people at large. It is only after the close involvement of the Saradha Group chit fund companies in media houses came to light that the central government woke up from its slumber and asked all television channels— general entertainment as well as news and current affairs—to furnish details of their shareholding patterns and their equity structures (*IE*, 29 April 2013).

It may be recalled that the involvement of large industrial and commercial houses in the print media and their nefarious influence had come for close scrutiny during the period of internal emergency (1975–77).[9] In keeping with Indira and Sanjay Gandhi's mindset, efforts were made to increase the government's hold on these companies. But this remedy was worse than the disease. The steps taken by the government during the emergency to control the media through measures such as censorship and the *Kissa Kursi Ka* kind of tactics left their long shadows for quite a while. Even established and well-known media elite could not withstand the pressures and fell prey. India should never have to go through such a harrowing experience again at any time. At the same time, concerns about the media exerting motivated and self-serving influence on democratic functioning must be reckoned with. An independent ombudsman and statutory regulatory mechanisms must be put in place if the present free for all, unregulated functioning of the media is to be curbed.

Regulatory Bodies

Economic liberalization and free markets do not mean that unrestricted freedom has to be given to everyone to do as he pleases. The rules of the game have to be clearly spelt out and observed by everyone equally and scrupulously. Ideally, this task has to be entrusted to independent, autonomous and statutory bodies which enjoy credibility. Such bodies have been created in some sectors.

In western democracies globalization has meant a strong regulatory framework to oversee the activities of dominant players in the sector. Wherever such regulatory mechanisms were weak or ineffective the system received rude shocks and led to wiping out of shareholder value and even liquidation of dominant conglomerates such as Enron, WorldCom and so on. The more disturbing development was the failure of major financial institutions and banks. India will have to ensure that in our quest for globalization and economic reforms we do not land ourselves in similar situations.

In India, regulatory mechanisms are currently in operation only in some sectors and their experience generally has been far from happy. The JPC on the bank scam regretted to note that the Ministry of Finance took three-and-a-half years to give the needed statutory backing to SEBI. We have already discussed how UTI was kept out of SEBI's purview for quite some time, leading to its continued malpractices and large bailouts from the government. Experience shows that it is unable to effectively deal with malpractices such as insider trading by major corporates. D. R. Mehta, former Chairman of SEBI, in an interview after demitting office, observed:

> One of the important lessons I have learnt is that corporates don't want a strong regulator. They are working overtime to attack SEBI and even resort to personal attacks on senior officials. The moment you try to take action against any powerful corporates then you should see how they try to browbeat you through various means. I have faced this from the very beginning. When I took action against HLL [Hindustan Levers Limited, as it then was] in the insider trading case, they tried to put all kinds of pressure. Now the industry associations and chambers are openly attacking the regulator...Will anybody dare to attack the Securities and Exchange Commission (SEC) in the US? Here people don't want to comply with the law and make any disclosures... What powers do we have? (*ET*, 19 February 2002).

SEBI's inquiries into irregularities by the Sahara Group, for example, show how deep the rot in the system is. According to one news report, 'SEBI has been able to find just 68 genuine investors from among the details of lakhs of investors which Sahara group had sent to its office. A government source said that based on the present trend, the percentage of genuine investors turned out to be less than one per cent of the total of 3 crore claimed by the group in their depositions to SEBI' (*IE*, 13 March 2013). SEBI's role has also come into question regarding the large-scale defalcations in the Ponzi schemes. The SEBI Act must be amended extensively to give it all powers of an investigating agency so as to deal effectively with multifarious malpractices and crimes such as duping the investors, benami transactions, insider trading, money-laundering, manipulation of accounts and so on indulged in by companies.

The regulator in the telecom sector, namely, the Telecom Regulatory Authority of India (TRAI) has come in for adverse comments by the Supreme Court in the 2G spectrum scam and the then Chairman of TRAI is facing prosecution. Alam Srinivas has stated, 'When TRAI came into existence as an independent regulator, it faced two problems. One, it was created under a "toothless" Act, which gave it limited powers to force Department of Telecommunications (DOT) to act on its recommendations. Two, DOT tried every trick to tarnish TRAI's and its members' images' (Alam 2012: 37). The first Chairman of TRAI, Justice S. S. Sodhi, stated, 'The government in its wisdom, decided to keep us out of this process [change over to the revenue sharing regime]. We would have followed a completely transparent and consultative process' (IE, 9 August 1999). In January 2000, the Vajpayee government decided that TRAI was too independent for its comfort. It sacked all senior members of the telecom regulator. Its powers were whittled down to advisory functions.

The actions of the regulator in the hydrocarbon sector in the Krishna Godavari Gas field (D6) of Reliance Industries have also been highly controversial. C&AG has held the Ministry of Petroleum and the regulator, Directorate General of Hydrocarbon, responsible for lapses in the monitoring of the exploration and production activities of Reliance.

The Electricity Regulatory Commissions (ERCs) are functioning in several states but in most cases their work has come in for public criticism and led to disenchantment. Prayas, a Pune-based NGO, undertook a study of resources, transparency and public participation in ERCs in India. This author, along with E. A. S. Sarma and S. L. Rao were on the expert panel to guide the study. The report clearly brought out the need to address the following issues relating to the functioning of ERCs: independence and autonomy of ERCs; empowerment of ERCs; accountability of ERCs; transparency and public participation in ERC proceedings; need to enhance the quality of professional inputs for the ERCs; and ensuring that ERCs remain sensitive to important social issues. Commenting on the empowerment of the ERCs, the expert panel underlined that the ERCs cannot effectively discharge the responsibilities envisaged in the ERC Act, 1998, unless all the regulatory, licensing and other related powers listed under the sub-section are incorporated as inherent powers of the ERCs. Otherwise, the functioning of ERCs will remain confined to that of mere tariff-setting with no say whatsoever in deciding on the capacity additions and fuel choices and the terms of PPAs. The empowerment of ERCs is necessary for safeguarding the interests of consumers. On all major initiatives for restructuring the electricity industry at the Centre or in the states, as the case may be, the concerned ERC should be consulted and this should be mandated statutorily. It is also necessary to mention here that many state governments have been brazen in defying the orders and directives of the ERCs, year after year. Even the basic requirement of submitting full data in support of tariff increase proposals is not being met by the utilities. This does not augur well for the ERCs and suitable safeguards need to be incorporated in the law (Prayas 2003: 3–5). The Prayas survey found that many state governments and utilities have not responded to the commissions

THE EVER INCREASING GOVERNANCE DEFICIT •117

in a positive manner; in fact, at times, they have attempted to either 'manage' the process, or curtail the commission's authority and independence. A key conclusion of the report is that civil society institutions need to participate more actively and effectively in the regulatory process and put pressure on governments and utilities (as well as ERCs) to ensure that this new mechanism is used to protect and further public interest. The ERCs also need to respond positively and proactively to these efforts.

These concerns were further elaborately discussed in my D. T. Lakdawala Memorial Lecture. I said that:

> If any proof is required that India is one country, all one has to do is to read the reports of various ERCs. The grievances of consumers as also the ills afflicting the power utilities are the same in all states. The situation is as deplorable and beyond redemption from one end of the country to the other... Mere privatisation does not seem to be an answer to the problems either...It is now imperative that the ERCs take a strong position and refuse to entertain the submissions of SEBs and licensees for tariff revisions till their reasonable directives are complied with. It is time the ERCs made full use of their penal powers available under the concerned legislations. For what is at stake is not only the viability and the future of the power sector but also the credibility of the ERCs. The jury is still out and has yet to pronounce whether the ERCs have adequately fulfilled the responsibilities entrusted to them (Godbole 2002: 19–20).

The position has not changed much since the time I delivered this lecture in 2002.

There is a move now to set up a regulator for the coal sector and it is to be seen to what extent it will be empowered and how effectively it will be permitted to function. According to news reports, the regulator is not to have a role in allocation or de-allocation of coal blocks or price determination for the fuel (*IE*, 28 June 2013). This hardly makes any sense, when compared with the powers given to ERCs. The primary prerequisites for the success of a regulator is the independence in the process of selection of the regulator, autonomy in his functioning and non-interference by the government so as to inspire public confidence in his working. We have a long way to go in ensuring that each one of these requirements is met.

Another regulator under the Ministry of Finance has been similarly sidelined. When the insurance sector was opened up, it was decided that there will be a level playing field as far as regulation of all players was concerned. However, in recent years, the Finance Ministry has been prevailing on the Life Insurance Corporation of India to invest in equities of PSUs from which the government has been reducing its stake, so as to meet the targets for disinvestments announced by the government. This has serious implications for the interests of policy holders. The government has undermined both the authority and the autonomy of the insurance regulator.

P. Chidambaram, union Finance Minister, had in his 2013–14 Budget speech, announced a move to set up a regulator for the road sector saying it will be important 'as the road construction sector is facing unusual challenges including financial stress, enhanced construction risks and contract management issues that are best addressed by an independent authority.' Accordingly, the government had set up a task force for suggesting the framework for a regulatory mechanism. However, Montek Singh Ahluwalia, Deputy Chairman of the Planning Commission, is reported to have objected to the proposal saying, 'I am not persuaded that there is a case for a road regulator as I am not sure that it will solve the problem. The principle reason why the system is not working is that people have bid aggressively. The economy was facing headwinds and clearances were being delayed. None of these issues can be solved by a road regulator' (*IE*, 12 July 2013). Negating a Budget announcement in this manner due to internal differences in the government is a sad reflection on the state of governance in the country. Second, none of the points mentioned by Ahluwalia can lead one to the conclusion that a road regulator is not necessary. In fact, looking at the shambles in which the flagship programme of construction of highways finds itself, setting up a road regulator is long overdue. Third, the mechanism of charging, or rather overcharging, toll, and that too for an unduly long period, has become highly controversial in several parts of the country and a number of PILs have been filed by people to seek redress from the courts. It is time the quantum and duration of toll in each case is left to be decided by an independent regulator in a transparent manner. Finally, the objections raised by Ahluwalia, who is supposed to be one of the foremost proponents of liberalization, is all the more surprising. Instead of suggesting how the proposed regulatory mechanism can be strengthened by the government by withdrawing itself from its decision-making role in number of areas, the Planning Commission has objected to the setting up of a regulator itself. This once again brings out how important it is to ensure that public good is not sacrificed at the altar of economic liberalization.

As compared to this kind of foot-dragging, it is gratifying to note that the government has decided to set up a Civil Aviation Authority (CAA) to take over the responsibilities of the Directorate General of Civil Aviation (DGCA), which was for a long time handicapped by limited powers, inadequate staff, lack of financial autonomy and so on. India was also faced with a threatened safety downgrade by international aviation agencies like the US's Federal Aviation Administration. The UN's International Civil Aviation Organization (ICAO) was also getting ready to audit DGCA's oversight record. The fake pilot licences scandal in 2011, which brought senior DGCA officials under the scanner for corruption, had severely dented DGCA's image and had undermined the confidence of passengers. But this by itself will not be enough. The ministry must give up its tendency to micro-manage the aviation sector (*IE*, 12 July 2013).

The proposal of setting up a CAA was pending with the government for over three years. The CAA is to be established in accordance with standards laid down by ICAO. The regulator is expected to be empowered to provide a transparent system of policing airlines that will include pricing of seats, ensuring safety, managing standards of air service navigation operators and other civil aviation facilities. It is to be seen how much power the Ministry of Civil Aviation actually cedes. The success of the regulator will also depend on how the CAA is manned.

And a final example. As a part of the conditionality laid down by the World Bank for a $350 million loan given for the Maharashtra Water Sector Improvement Project in 2005, the Maharashtra Water Resources Regulatory Authority (MWRRA) was to be set up. The authority was to look into equitable distribution of water and implement the water policy. It was also to fix the rates for use of water. Accordingly, an act was passed in 2005. Since then, the authority has mostly remained dormant. The post of Chairman and Member (Economy) were lying vacant for a long time and were finally filled up only after the direction of the Bombay High Court in a PIL filed to press for release of water to drought-affected areas. The court observed that in the absence of a functional MWRRA, the court was left with no option other than ordering the release of water from the Ujani dam to Solapur. The MWRRA experiment has failed primarily due to the apathy and negligence of the state government. The irrigation sector in Maharashtra has suffered a great deal due to the alleged horrendous corruption in the sector. It is unfortunate that due to lack of political and administrative will, yet another potentially crucial regulatory institution has been brought to a standstill.

Notes

1. Government of India (2001: paras 6.2 and 6.2.2). NCRWC's monumental report has been consigned to the archives by the UPA government mainly because the commission was set up by the NDA government. As a result, important issues have been brushed under the carpet. The way politics is brought in, in everything, is unbelievable.
2. Mirchi is reported to have died recently in London. This was the only way India could have got rid of him!
3. Vineet Narain & Others v. Union of India & Another, judgment dated 18 December 1997 in writ petition (Cr) Nos. 340–343 of 1993, *1997(7) SCALE.*
4. Vineet Narain & Others v. Union of India & Another, 1997 (7) *SCALE.*
5. *P.V. Narasimha Rao v. State* (CBI/SPE), (1998) 4 SC *Cases 626,* decided on 17 April 1998.

6. Post- SC judgment in JMM case: Is bribery legal now? (*ET*, 28 April 1998: 11).

7. In his wide-ranging interview after demitting office as the Chief Justice of India, Y. K. Sabharwal stated, 'Any cases related to [economic] reform should be on the fast track...I have said as the Chief Justice that if in the present economy, a foreigner or foreign investment has to come, he must have confidence. Disputes are bound to arise, but those disputes must be resolved in a reasonable time. They must not be pending for years...But, even on speed, many of these decisions which have taken place right up to the Supreme Court were decided within a reasonable time. We have to keep pace with the changing time. Can we say, sorry, we cannot give any priority to these cases? The entire development process will come to a standstill' (*IE*, 23 January 2007: 9).

8. Largely based on this writer's article in *Dialogue Quarterly* (2011: 125–33).

9. Electronic media was a government monopoly and hence only the print media was a matter of concern.

4

IS THERE ANY EVIDENCE OF GOOD GOVERNANCE HERE?

> The legal sovereignty in this country vests with the Constitution and
> the political sovereignty is with the people of this country.
> The executive possesses no sovereignty.
> K. S. Hegde, former judge of the Supreme Court

Corruption—India's Ugly Face

The 1999 Report on Human Development in South Asia emphasized that corruption in the region is widespread and far more dangerous than in other regions and had the following characteristics:

- Corruption occurs at the top, not the bottom, distorting decisions on development programmes and priorities;
- Corruption money 'has wings, not wheels' and is smuggled abroad to safe havens, not ploughed back into the domestic economy; and
- Corruption often leads to promotion, not prison, and 'the big fish—unless they belong to the opposition—rarely fry' (*TOI*, 3 November 1999).

So far as India is concerned, this is only partly true. The ground reality is much worse. We have widespread corruption not only at the top but also at the bottom, which deeply hurts the common people. Rampant corruption, though much in the news now, is also not a recent phenomenon. It has taken deep roots right since Independence and has in fact been nurtured by the political system, irrespective of which political party was in power. The examples cited throughout this book bear this out fully.

Nehru's Approach to Corruption

J. B. Kripalani has, in his autobiography, written, 'In the administrative field, the authorities had admitted that corruption had increased. The higher services were not free from it and it had crept into the political field.' He also mentions his speech which:

> ...raised an uproar [in the Congress] during the Budget Session in 1951 on a discussion of what was alleged the sugar muddle. The price of sugar had risen very high, of course not as high as afterwards. The facsimile of a letter from a minister in U.P. to the sugar mill owners, asking them to contribute so much per bag of sugar for Congress Party funds, had appeared in one of the English dailies. I drew the attention of the House to this and gave this as the main reason for the inordinate rise in the price of sugar. I further said that not only sugar but other articles of general consumption were being sold in the black market. I concluded my speech by saying 'govern or get out'. This created a furore among the ministers and their supporters. A meeting of the Parliamentary Party was called to consider the question of taking disciplinary action against me for what I had ventured to say...This irritated the Sardar [Patel]. He wanted to take action against me. Jawaharlal was usually against taking any extreme action. He realised that it would create an awkward situation if action was taken against an ex-President of the Congress in a matter in which public resentment had been roused against the authorities. The matter was, therefore, talked out. Jawaharlal asked the party members to be more careful in future of what they said in Parliament about their own party. Whatever complaint they had to make must be made in party meetings. This ban on a member speaking against the party continued almost throughout the Congress rule (Kripalani 2004: 825, 730–31).

I have given this somewhat extensive quotation to show how the highest leadership of the Congress Party approached the issue of corruption.

Shiv Raj Singh has talked about how Nehru, who had denounced corruption so angrily earlier, had become more tolerant towards such cases and more sceptical about allegations in later years. He frequently expressed annoyance at the widespread talk of corruption. For example, commenting on the Gorwala report, he stated that the constant talk of 'scandals' in government, at least a great deal of it, 'is completely without foundation.' Throughout his days in power, he was reluctant to put into practice his earlier idea that every important charge of corruption must be fully enquired into (Shiv Raj Singh 2005: 117). This is borne out by his note to Home Secretary, H. V. R. Iengar, dated 4 October 1951. Nehru wrote:

> For a considerable time past, numerous charges have been made against the ex-ministers of the Punjab government and enquiries have been demanded...At the public meeting at Ludhiana recently, I referred to these charges and said that it was not possible or proper for us to hold roving and general inquiries into an

administration. Therefore, we did not propose to have any such inquiry. But whenever any specific case of alleged corruption was brought to our notice and prima facie there appeared some substance in it, it was government's duty to have further investigation, whoever the person concerned might be (Jawaharlal Nehru Memorial Fund 1994: 741).

Nehru often asked the IB to carry out secret inquiries to ascertain whether there was any substance in the allegations. At other times, he asked Supreme Court judges to make informal inquiries and submit their reports. These reports were never made public. Thus, for example, the report of inquiry done by Justice S. K. Das, former judge of the Supreme Court, into allegations against K. D. Malaviya, which was devoid of any legal sanction, was never made public. In fact, it was not even made available to the Sarjoo Prasad Commission of Inquiry which was appointed to inquire into allegations against Mahtab. Initially, the commission was told that the report was a secret document. Later, when the commission pressed for getting a copy, it was told that it was not possible to trace it (Noorani 1973: 190–91).

B. N. Mullik, the then Director of IB, has written in his memoirs:

One day [when I went to meet Prime Minister Nehru], he named a Cabinet colleague of his and said that he had heard allegations of his contacts with certain business houses and wanted me to find out the facts. I demurred and said that the SPE [Special Police Establishment] and not the IB was the right body to do this enquiry and that all Cabinet ministers were well known to me and so I would find it very embarrassing to do this work. The Prime Minister said that it was essential that his Cabinet colleagues should be men of unquestionable rectitude and honesty in their private and official lives...He did not want a formal enquiry as it would get tied down by various procedures. Moreover, such enquiry could not be kept secret and there would be unnecessary publicity...Probably, if the Prime Minister had been well I would have still refused to do this enquiry; but I did not want to disappoint him on his sick-bed (Mullik 1972: 19).

The Chagla Commission of Inquiry into the Mundhra deal is considered a feather in the cap of the Nehru government and proof of its commitment to rooting out corruption. But, in reality, Nehru was very unhappy with the inquiry and lost no opportunity to say how unfair and uncalled for it was. A one-man commission, consisting of M. C. Chagla, the Chief Justice of the Bombay High Court, was appointed on 7 January 1958 to enquire into the investments made by the Life Insurance Corporation (LIC) in the six companies controlled by Haridas Mundhra. These investments were made in contravention of LIC's policy of investing money only in blue-chip companies on the advice of its investment committee. Moreover, the value of the shares of these companies was going down when LIC made the investment. Chagla submitted his report on 10 February 1958, the shortest time taken by any commission of inquiry so far. Nehru was greatly troubled with the report. He was critical of the fact that loudspeakers were installed during the inquiry and publicly spoke against it. Chagla wrote to Nehru that the crowds outside Council Hall, the venue of the inquiry, were uncontrollable and the police insisted on loudspeakers being installed to satisfy the people. Nehru then wrote to Chagla that his 'remarks in Bombay [about the loudspeakers] were directed to the people'. Nehru was also critical of the part played by M. C. Setalvad, Attorney General, in the inquiry. Nehru raised the matter in the Cabinet, whose minutes read:

> The Attorney General's line of argument struck the Cabinet as most extraordinary. He had not consulted government with regard to their point of view, although he was supposed to appear on behalf of government and, strangely enough, had proceeded to make insinuations of malafides without adequate justification...It was considered too late to take any action. The Cabinet, however, decided that with regard to future inquiries of this kind, care should be taken not only for evolving a correct procedure but for briefing of government counsel.

Chagla wrote in his autobiography, *Roses in December*: 'I did not want him [Setalvad] to appear for government as though it were a party to a dispute, but as government was as much interested as I would be in arriving at the truth, his primary function would be to assist me in arriving at a proper decision.' In his letter dated 9 February 1958 (that is, even before receipt of the Chagla Commission report) to Vijaya Lakshmi Pandit, Indian High Commissioner to the UK, Nehru wrote:

> This whole business has been a wretched affair. It is quite wrong, I think, to say that the Life Insurance Corporation has suffered any material loss by this investment...Our Finance Minister, T. T. Krishnamachari, as minister, has to shoulder responsibility to some extent, though I do not think that he was to blame except in so far as he allowed others to go ahead without further enquiry...The way Setalvad conducted this case was rather extraordinary. He is a member of government and yet he functioned as a prosecuting counsel. Chagla appeared to encourage him though we have to wait for his report to see what he says.

There can be two views on whether Setalvad committed any impropriety. According to one view, the Attorney General is also an officer of the court and is obliged to assist the court in ensuring that justice is done in a case. Some people give credit to Setalvad for what he did and note that he was the only law officer of the government to have taken such a principled stand in the matter. I am also of the same view. But obviously this larger view did not appeal to Nehru. In his letter dated 12 February 1958, to T. T. Krishnamachari, Nehru reiterated, 'In effect, there was rather a one-sided presentation of facts...I have still a feeling that all the relevant facts connected with this unhappy matter have not been brought out [in the inquiry]' (Jawaharlal Nehru Memorial Fund 2010: 343–46, 350–51). Finally, under considerable public pressure, Nehru reluctantly accepted Krishnamachari's resignation.

Commissions of Inquiry With Respect to States

A number of commissions of inquiry were appointed against chief ministers and other important functionaries in the states in the 1960s, which show the extent of corruption and maladministration during the period. A. G. Noorani has, in his book, analysed these inquiries extensively in eight chapters—the early warnings, the Kairon raj, the Bakshi era, dynamic men of Orissa, Bihar's misfortunes, resourceful Mehtab and so on (Noorani 1973). Some of his significant observations, illustratively cited later, bring out how the general approach to corruption and maladministration was permissive. The page numbers in Noorani's book are given in brackets:

- The judgment of the Supreme Court gave a shot in the arm to the agitation for a judicial inquiry against Sardar Partap Singh Kairon. Nehru could hardly ignore the Supreme Court's judgment and he sent a note to the President on 25 October 1963, in which he made a vain effort to minimise the gravity of the charges against Sardar Partap Singh Kairon. The note all but exonerated Kairon. But, it had, however grudgingly, to concede the demand for an inquiry...Sardar Partap Singh Kairon continued to remain Chief Minister of the state while the inquiry against him went on. The memorialists demanded that the least he could do was to resign pending the inquiry, but this demand was turned down...Mr Justice S. R. Das submitted his report on 11 June 1964, just three days after Lal Bahadur Shastri was sworn in as Prime Minister. Shastri at first decided not to publish the commission's report. But Kairon's wilfulness had got the better of his political judgment. He refused to resign, the report notwithstanding. Shastri had no option but to publish the report. The resignation followed. From then till his assassination in February 1965, Kairon spent his time writing and speaking in denigration of the Prime Minister and the Home Minister Gulzari Lal Nanda (pp. 52,53,62).
- Despite the fact that the commission of inquiry against Bakshi Ghulam Mohammed had, in its report submitted on 30 June 1967, found Bakshi guilty of corruption and abuse of power, he was given the Congress

Party's ticket to contest the Lok Sabha elections in 1971 from Srinagar constituency (p. 63).

- Both Mahtab and Biju Patnaik earned notoriety as chief ministers but they were shielded by the Centre until matters went out of hand and a hostile state administration launched an inquiry. The public owes a lot to Justice Khanna and Sarjoo Prasad [former Chief Justice of Rajasthan and Assam high courts and a practicing senior advocate of the Supreme Court] who executed their assignments so impartially and thoroughly. Their reports reveal the rot that had overcome the public life of Orissa (p. 91).

- Bihar's politics revolved around caste...Charges of corruption, nepotism and plain abuse of power were freely bandied about. The Centre, true to form, ignored the charges....The report T. L. Venkatarama Aiyar [former Judge of the Supreme Court] gave on the charges against the Congress Chief Minister and five of his colleagues exposes the sub-committee's report to be what it was—a cynical whitewash of the black deeds of the Bihar ministers...The commission of inquiry which inquired into the charges against the United Front ministers consisted of J. R. Mudholkar, also a former Judge of the Supreme Court. The Aiyar and Mudholkar reports make sorry reading (pp. 121–23).

Interestingly, in all inquiries pertaining to corruption and crony capitalism in the states, it made no difference to their outcome which political party—Congress, National Conference, United Front, Jana Congress, Ganatantra Parishad, Soshit Dal, Samyukta Vidhayak Dal, Swatantra Party—was in power. Finally, it is necessary to note an important point made by Noorani: 'All the commissions have insisted on "a high standard of proof, that is, proof beyond reasonable doubt, (as in criminal trial) than on preponderance of probability as in a civil action,"' as S. Velu Pillai put it. This affects the finding a commission should finally give, not the approach it should adopt during the inquiry. That approach should be "inquisitional" throughout. If the commissions of inquiry had followed this approach...many more misdeeds on the part of ministers would have come to light than they have been able to run to earth' (pp. 332–33).

Justice Jaganmohan Reddy Commission

It is pertinent to refer here to the observations of some important commissions of inquiry. The Justice P. Jaganmohan Reddy Commission of Inquiry report relating to Bansi Lal, had, *inter alia*, underlined the need to have a strong, independent, fearless and dedicated bureaucracy or administrative service imbued with public spirit, which will not succumb to pressures of political heads...The way in which civil servants are allowed to function is very important. They must function in a manner that is expected of them as persons of high integrity, impartiality and in the efficient discharge of their functions in the best public interest. This vital requirement and expectation of the functioning of the public servant must exercise the mind of every responsible member of the government because in the larger public interest the survival of a strong and independent civil service apparatus is a *sine qua non* for the proper functioning of the democratic government... Shri Bansi Lal evolved a style of administration designed to maintain a direct control over the administration whether as Chief Minister or as Union Defence Minister with the object of subordinating and controlling them as well as even the institutional structures and to reduce the civil service from an advisory asset to a pliant instrument for carrying out his will. He adopted methods which created fear and helplessness in those who worked under him by humiliating them, by suspending them and even by transferring them so that others may... pliantly comply with his will and wishes...The way in which Shri Bansi Lal acted as Chief Minister leads one to examine how the whole elaborate machinery of administration can be subverted to the personal whims and objectives of a single person (Government of India 1978: 304–05, 308).

Justice Gupta Commission on Maruti Affairs

Justice A. C. Gupta, in his report dated 31 May 1978 on Maruti affairs, *inter alia*, stated: 'The affairs of the Maruti concerns...appear to have brought about a decline in the integrity of public life and sullied the purity of administration... Threat of detention under MISA or a CBI inquiry or other forms of harassment made it hazardous for officers to insist on the rules...They could not enforce the laws against those who appeared to be the law's masters' (Government of India 1979: 141).

Justice Khanna Commission in Orissa

Concluding his report against three former chief ministers and some ministers of Orissa in 1968, H. R. Khanna, a Judge of the Delhi High Court, observed, 'No codification of rules of conduct or declarations of assets can ensure rectitude among ministers and other men in public life. What is needed is a climate of strong public opinion wherein none may dare to deviate from the path of rectitude. The ramparts of a clean and healthy administration are in the hearts of people; laws can punish only occasional lapses' (Khanna 1986: 59).

Justice Grover Commission in Karnataka

The observations of the Grover Commission of Inquiry against Devraj Urs, Chief Minister, and some ministers in the Karnataka government may also be cited:

> If administrative standards have to be kept at a high level of propriety and efficiency, the services must maintain an attitude of strict political neutrality. Legally and constitutionally they have to carry out the policy laid down by the government in power but that does not mean, nor does it require that impartiality and fairness should not receive dominant and paramount consideration. That can only be done if the members of the services do not get personally involved in various matters on which a decision is to be given by them or advice has to be tendered. There should also be adequate protection for the civil servants if they express their views frankly and in a forthright manner (Government of India 1979: 377).

Justice Sarkaria Commission in Tamil Nadu

The Sarkaria Commission of Inquiry against M. Karunanidhi, Chief Minister, and some other ministers in Tamil Nadu in 1978 showed the depths to which the state administration had fallen. The commission observed:

> Several distressing cases have come to the notice of the commission in this inquiry, where even senior officers of the I. A. S.—some of them otherwise having a clean record—have committed deliberate dereliction of duty, knowing fully well that they were acting wrongly. *They have pleaded that they had no alternative but to carry out the verbal orders of the minister. They went to the extent of allowing themselves to be used as negotiators and even collectors of bribes for the minister....*When this rule [of requesting orders of the minister in writing] was specifically brought to the notice of some of the civil servants who appeared as witnesses before the commission, they pleaded that it was not possible to insist on having orders in writing or getting confirmation in writing from the minister in such cases without incurring the risk of losing their job or grievous injury to their service career. In support of this plea, they cited the examples of a Chief Secretary and an Inspector General of Police who, they said, were victimised by the erstwhile DMK government simply because they refused to deflect from the path of administrative rectitude, to toe the line of the minister concerned (Government of India 1978: 134–35). *Italics are mine and have been added to invite special attention, also at other relevant places below.*

Madhu Limaye has stated:

> When the Morarji Desai government came to power in 1977, it took no action on the Sarkaria report as the DMK and the Janata Party had an alliance in 1977

Lok Sabha elections. In 1980, it was Indira Gandhi's turn to ally with the DMK and there was no question of proceeding against Karunanidhi. In Orissa also the same thing happened to the charges against Biju Patnaik and his colleagues. Those who were the loudest in demanding a probe into allegations against him ended up by accepting him as their leader or as a colleague (Limaye 1994: 510).

Justice Lentin Commission in Maharashtra

The Justice B. Lentin Commission of Inquiry was appointed by the Government of Maharashtra to inquire into deaths of patients in Bombay's J. J. Hospital in January-February 1986 due to an alleged reaction to drugs. The much-anticipated Lentin Commission report was submitted in November 1987. In a hard-hitting report, Lentin wrote, 'If I could have my way, several would be candidates for instantaneous dismissal from service and certain others for permanent cancellation of their licences. However, the rule of law must prevail' (Government of Maharashtra 1987). Hence, the commission suggested departmental and other actions against several persons, including the Dean and the Superintendent of the hospital, professors, pharmacists, the officers of the Director of Industries who dealt with the procurement of medicines and the officers of the Food and Drug Administration. Criminal prosecution of drug manufacturers and drug-testing laboratories was recommended. The Health Minister, Bhai Sawant, former Health Minister, Baliram Hiray, and some doctors were held liable to be proceeded against on charges of corruption. The commission also recommended a number of measures to ensure that there was no recurrence of such cases in the future. The report thus presented the sorry state of governance in the so-called progressive state of Maharashtra. As was to be expected, the action taken report submitted by the government to the State Legislature was more an action not taken report!

Prelude to the Santhanam Committee

In July 1959, C. D. Deshmukh, the then Chairman of the University Grants Commission and former Finance Minister, said at a lecture in Madras that if a standing judicial tribunal was set up to inquire into corruption, 'I shall be happy to make a beginning by lodging half a dozen reports myself' (Rajya Sabha Secretariat 1996: 26). Nehru found the suggestion 'unworkable' and said, 'we cannot make progress in this country if everybody suspects the other of lack of integrity'. However, on 14 June 1960 the Congress President, N. Sanjeeva Reddy, announced that the Congress Working Committee had authorized him to set up a 'permanent machinery to examine the merits' of complaints of corruption against ministers and other responsible Congressmen. By another resolution, the

Working Committee authorized the Congress President to 'require the Congress ministers of central and state governments and Congress MPs and MLAs to submit to him annual statements of their assets, income and expenditure.' On 28 June 1960, the Congress President announced the formation of a panel of five eminent jurists. Corruption in public life was thus taken serious note of but nothing tangible came out of it.

The Santhanam Committee on Prevention of Corruption

In June 1962 a committee of a few MPs under the chairmanship of K. Santhanam, MP, was appointed 'to consider the important aspects of the evil of corruption'. The committee held 87 sittings. It made interim reports on the setting up of a central vigilance commission, modification of the government servants' conduct rules, changes in rules relating to disciplinary proceedings and the question of government servants accepting commercial employment after retirement. The committee defined the problem of corruption, in its widest connotation, to include 'improper or selfish exercise of power and influence attached to a public office or to the special position one occupies in public life.' Some of the salient observations of the committee, which are as relevant today, may be recapitulated:

> Two of the major contributory factors for the growth of corruption are, firstly, the partially acknowledged unwillingness to deal drastically with corrupt and inefficient public servants and secondly, *the protection given to the Services in India, which is greater than that available in more advanced countries...*Article 311 of the Constitution as interpreted by our courts has made it very difficult to deal effectively with corrupt public servants. *When the question of amendment of Article 311 came up before Parliament, the issue of corruption was altogether ignored and overwhelming stress was laid upon protection of the individual government servant. This is an important issue which deserves to be urgently reconsidered by Parliament.* The committee had noted with regret that the Federation of Indian Chambers of Commerce which could have given powerful support to the fight against corruption would not even accept its invitation to meet the committee. It was represented to the committee that corruption has increased to such an extent that people have started losing faith in the integrity of public administration. We heard from all sides that corruption has, in recent years, spread to those levels of administration from which it was conspicuously absent in the past... The public belief in the prevalence of corruption at high political levels has been strengthened by the manner in which funds are collected by political parties, especially at the time of elections (Government of India 1963: 1,3,5,10–12,104).

This enunciation was way back in early 1964 but is as much, if not more, true today.

Unfortunately, most of the major recommendations of the Santhanam Committee were not implemented by the government. To name a few: **First,** the committee had recommended that whenever a specific allegation of corruption on the part of a minister was received, it should be promptly investigated. If a formal allegation was made by any 10 Members of Parliament or a legislature in writing addressed to the Prime Minister or the Chief Minister, it should be referred to a committee for investigation. In other cases, the minister concerned should, as a rule, institute legal proceedings by filing a complaint of criminal defamation. If the minister was unwilling to take legal action, he should be asked to resign or be dismissed from the Cabinet. If these recommendations had been followed, India would have seen a cleaner public life. **Second,** the committee said that there was no justification to treat income tax returns and assessments as secret. Publication of such returns and assessments would have a salutary effect on those persons in business and professions who were inclined to take advantage of secrecy provisions to evade income tax. Equally importantly, though the committee did not mention it, making income tax returns and assessments public would also be a check on widespread corruption. It was only after the RTI Act was enacted that access to these documents became available. **Third,** to buy and sell properties at prices much greater than those recorded in the conveyance deeds had become a common method of cheating the central government of income tax and other taxes etc. Such properties could be acquired at the stated value, or even at a small premium when it was considered that the properties had been deliberately undervalued. This would strike a blow against black money. **Fourth,** the committee was of the opinion that Article 311 of the Constitution needed to be amended. Regarding clause (c) of the proviso to sub-clause (2), in particular, the committee was of the view that after the words 'in the interest of security' the words 'or integrity' should be added.[1] **Fifth,** the committee recommended the setting up of a Central Vigilance Commission (CVC) and entrusting it with powers similar to those under Sections 4 and 5 of the Commissions of Inquiry Act, 1952. The commission was to be independent of the government and was not to be answerable to any minister, even though administratively placed under the Ministry of Home Affairs. The committee felt that the CVC should comprehensively deal with two of the major problems of administration, namely, prevention of corruption and maintaining integrity and ensuring just and fair exercise of administrative powers vested in various authorities by statutory rules or by non-statutory executive orders. It also recommended that the powers and responsibilities in disciplinary matters which were at present decentralized should in the main be centralized in the commission, the only exception being the powers given to the Delhi Special Police Establishment to make preliminary inquiries and to institute and investigate a regular case whenever they considered it necessary to do so. The members of the committee also expressed concern that in a matter like the Sirajjuddin affair, it had been possible for a number of high ranking officials to be involved in the alleged malpractices over a period of time without their involvement being detected.[2] The committee therefore made a supplementary recommendation that the CVC should be given, by suitable legislation, the powers that would be exercised by a commission of inquiry appointed under the Commissions of Inquiry Act, 1952, so that he may undertake any inquiry relating to transactions in which public servants are suspected to have acted improperly or in a corrupt manner.

The government, however, decided to take action only on the recommendations of the committee relating to prevention of corruption and maintaining integrity of the public services. Accordingly, the commission was not to have a Directorate of General Complaints and Redress. The question of evolving a machinery for dealing with the grievances of citizens against the administration was to be examined separately. The government also felt that complete centralization of powers and responsibilities with regard to inquiry and investigation into complaints and all subsequent action thereon would not only undermine the initiative and sense of responsibility of the ministries/departments/undertakings, but would also lead to practical and legal difficulties. The government also felt that the minister's responsibilities, and his accountability to Parliament, should remain unaffected. *Most importantly, the government decided that in the constitutional and legal sense, the CVC's function should be advisory. The CVC was therefore set up not by an act but by executive order.* Thus, the government had watered down the recommendations of the committee drastically and as a result, the cause of putting down corruption with a heavy hand was considerably diluted.

In September 1972, the Congress Parliamentary Board decided that Congressmen may not make their charges of corruption publicly but may pass on the relevant information to the Prime Minister and Congress President. If the two of them found reasonable grounds for suspecting the integrity of any minister, he may be asked to resign. With respect to charges against a Chief Minister, he was expected to send his comments to the Prime Minister to enable him to decide whether to appoint a commission of inquiry.

The Indira Gandhi Regime

Arun Shourie has written at length how Balram Jakhar, the then Speaker of the Lok Sabha and M. Hidayatullah, the then Chairman of the Rajya Sabha, by their partisan rulings in the two Houses prevented the members from discussing the Kuo Oil deal (Shourie 1983: 182–92). On 22 February 1980 the then Petroleum Secretary B. B. Vohra was told to send a written directive to the Indian Oil Corporation asking it to award the contract to Hindustan Monark, the bicycle parts firm, and through it, to Kuo Oil for the supply of 5 lakh tonnes of diesel and 3 lakh tonnes of kerosene. The deal was worth $175 million, the largest oil contract ever handed over to a private party in India till then. According to the records of the Registrar of Companies in Hong Kong, the paid up capital of Kuo Oil was only about 50 US dollars! Available and published forecasts suggested that the prices of the product were likely to fall in the coming months so that entering into a fixed-price contract would inflict a grave loss to the country. The minister overruled the advice of every single expert and disregarded what was common knowledge about market prospects. An elaborate effort was made to cover up everything about this deal; the anxiety of the PMO to ensure the cover-up was evident. All that Shiv Shankar, the then Petroleum Minister, had to say in the Lok Sabha was that the Kuo Oil deal was 'an error of judgment'.

Opposition members on the Committee On Public Undertakings were agitated that Bansi Lal, the chairman of the committee, had prevented them from expressing their views on the Kuo Oil deal in the committee. They had even charged that minutes of committee meetings were doctored. Shourie states, 'Given the role of the PM's office in the matter, given the fact that two-thirds of the 22 members of the committee were from the ruling party, given the absolute prohibition against filing minutes of dissent, where was the scope for members to register the complaint that the Speaker said he could not find in the report?' (Shourie 1983: 188).

Another case of a blatant cover-up was that of the Tulmohan Ram licensing scandal which rocked Parliament during Indira Gandhi's time. According to Noorani, the provocation for the clamour in the House was grave. On 9 September 1974, union Home Minister, Uma Shankar Dixit, solemnly promised the Lok Sabha that he would report to it 'after the investigation is over'. A couple of hours before Parliament's winter session began on 11 November, a charge sheet was filed in the court so that the government could argue in the House that since the licence scandal was now subjudice, the Parliament could not discuss it... Interestingly, during the interval, the Home portfolio was transferred from Mr Dixit to Mr Brahmananda Reddy in order to save the former from embarrassment (Noorani 2000: 147). This shows the extent to which the government was prepared to go to keep its dirty business away from Parliament. Finally, the government had to agree to permit the opposition to study the official records.

B. N. Tandon, the then Joint Secretary to Prime Minister Indira Gandhi, has written, 'Some time ago I had talked to the PM about a case. The Orissa government wants that Hare Krushna Mehtab [former Chief Minister] should be prosecuted on the basis of a CBI inquiry...PM had desired that K. D. Malaviya should be consulted...Politics should have no place in tackling corruption but these days decisions are being taken mainly on the basis whether a decision will harm the Congress Party, particularly the supporters of the PM. I have seen this in countless instances (Tandon 2003: 151).

The Committee on Privileges opined that 'Shrimati Indira Gandhi, former Prime Minister, had committed a breach of privilege and contempt of the House by causing obstruction, intimidation, harassment and institution of false cases against the concerned officers...who were collecting information for preparing an answer and a note for supplementaries for a starred question' (Limaye 1984: 277).

The attitude of the government in these cases was in sharp contrast to the healthy traditions established by Jawaharlal Nehru to treat Parliament as the highest temple of democracy and 'the grand inquest of the nation'.

It is worth noting the observations of B. G. Deshmukh, who was Cabinet Secretary and Principal Secretary to prime ministers Rajiv Gandhi, V. P. Singh and Chandra Shekhar, and thus had a ring-side view of the happenings in Delhi at the highest levels of government:

> The genesis of Bofors lies in the practice initiated by Indira Gandhi and further refined by her son Sanjay for collecting funds for the Congress party. No doubt the Congress party and other political parties in India have needed funds mostly to fight elections from 1947 when the country became independent. Till the middle of 1960s, during the regime of Jawaharlal Nehru, collection of funds for the party was a more transparent business and business houses were also permitted to make open donations. Collection of funds for one's party was then not a highly competitive and corrosive practice corrupting the whole social, economic and political fabric as happened later. Indira Gandhi at the very beginning of her tenure as prime minister found that she was in dire need of funds to fight elections to establish herself as the undisputed leader of the Congress party. As I was then in Maharashtra I know that in that state she depended heavily on her loyal supporters Rajni Patel [President of Bombay Pradesh Congress Committee] and Vasantrao Naik [Chief Minister of Maharashtra] to raise funds and they did this by literally selling sheets of sea water in the Nariman Point area [which was being reclaimed].[3] Later, when she had established her supremacy in Indian politics, she decided that a far better way to collect funds for the party was through claiming cuts from foreign deals. Sanjay Gandhi perfected and refined this still further from 1972 onwards...I might also add that the practice of getting kickbacks earned us notoriety in foreign countries. In the HDW submarine case I was told that the West German Defence Ministry had intimated to the German defence supplier the amount of commission that would be required to be paid in selling defence equipment. The Latin American and African countries were in the bracket of 10 per cent and above whereas we were placed in the bracket of 5 to 10 per cent (Deshmukh 2004: 217–18).

Deshmukh has also quoted R. Venkataraman, former President of India, who has written in his autobiography (p. 40), 'J. R. D. Tata made a courtesy call on me...commenting on Rajiv's statement on Bofors...it would be difficult to deny the receipt of commission by the Congress Party. He felt that since 1980 industrialists had not been approached for political contributions and the general feeling among them was that the party was financed by commission on deals' (Deshmukh 2004: 218). I have previously quoted a similar assessment by B. K. Nehru.

P.V. Narasimha Rao's Reign—More of the Same

One of the worst cases of its kind was that of Sukh Ram, the then Minister of State for Communications in P.V. Narasimha Rao's government. When his residence was raided by the CBI on 16 August 1996, it discovered Rs 3.66 crore in cash. 'It is worth noting that the CBI did not enter Sukh Ram's house looking for bundles of cash. The raid was actually in connection with an unrelated and somewhat trivial equipment contract in which the minister is alleged to have cost the exchequer Rs 1.68 crore by placing order for an inferior variety of equipment when a superior variety was available' (Visvanathan and Sethi 1998: 195). The saga of the Sukh Ram cases has dragged on in the courts for over 15 years. Sukh Ram has been convicted in two of these cases so far. His appeal in one of them is still pending and is quite unlikely to be decided in his lifetime since he is already 86 years old.

The sugar scandal in Prime Minister P. V. Narasimha Rao's regime rocked Parliament for days. Finally, the government relented and appointed a one-man committee under the chairmanship of a former C&AG, Gian Prakash. The report fixed responsibility for the delay in imports on the Food Minister. However, the government refused to place the report in Parliament on the specious plea that such administrative reports are not placed in Parliament. There was no basis for such an excuse which goes against all canons of transparency and accountability in the system. However, finally Kalpnath Rai, Food Minister, had to resign from the Cabinet. Kuldip Nayar states, 'In a democracy, it is not only necessary for the government to be honest, it should also be seen to be so. *The Rao government, whose 16 ministers had to resign under a cloud, has a question mark against it*' (IE, 15 April 1996). P. V. Narasimha Rao being charge sheeted for forgery, cheating and bribery and criminal conspiracy exemplified the unimaginable depths to which the Indian political system had fallen.

United Front and After

The brief United Front government tenure was marked by a number of dubious decisions. This included the arbitrary allotment of government quarters, petrol pumps, gas agencies and kerosene outlet dealerships. When the matter regarding arbitrary allotment of government quarters was raised in a PIL in the Supreme

Court, the court stated in no uncertain terms that 'what was found was a scam, and a big scam at that.' This period was also marked by Prime Minister H. D. Deve Gowda's visit to the residence of the then Chief Justice of India, A. M. Ahmadi. It was widely believed that it was to intercede on behalf of his predecessor P. V. Narasimha Rao, who was involved in a number of criminal cases (*Frontline*, 1 November 1996: 33).

Bangaru Laxman, former President of BJP when it was in power, was caught on camera allegedly accepting cash in a sting operation conducted by *Tehelka.com* journalists on 5 January 2001. He was convicted by the CBI court only in April 2012, 11 years after the crime was detected. His appeal will take several more years to be decided.

The allotment of agencies for LPG, kerosene and diesel, and distribution of petrol pumps has always been considered to be a lucrative business. It was not, therefore, surprising that there were scams during the Congress and also the NDA regimes. Three ministers for petroleum and natural gas—Satish Sharma, B. Shankaranand and Ram Naik—came in for severe criticism and indictment. It made no difference which political configuration was in power.

The CBI inquiry into the disproportionate assets case against Mayawati, former Chief Minister of UP, is still languishing, with the Supreme Court itself saying that it had never asked the CBI to investigate the case. This contention is being questioned by some senior advocates. There are allegations that the case of disproportionate assets against Mulayam Singh is being cleverly used by the Congress Party to ensure his continued support to the government.

Reference may be made to another celebrated case which has several firsts to its credit.[4] This was the first-ever privately filed case of alleged corruption against a powerful politician, A. R. Antulay, the then Chief Minister of Maharashtra, pertaining to the Indira Prathishthan (trust) case. This is also the case which was finally closed not because there was no case against him but because his fundamental right to speedy trial was adversely affected due to the long drawn out court trial, which was his own doing! Madhu Limaye has written, 'Ten years have passed and even the trial of Antulay's offences has not yet commenced... Now Antulay's counsel is demanding that the proceedings be terminated on grounds of inordinate delay. He argued that in order to make speedy trial meaningful, enforceable and effective, there had to be an outer limit beyond which the continuance of a criminal trial should be held violative of Article 21 of the Constitution' (*The Statesman*, 31 October 1991).

Upendra Baxi has written a monograph on this case which 'is based on the premise that the judicial discourse in the Antulay case (and the issues it raises) is next in importance only to *Kesavananda*.' Baxi has listed what, according to the majority decision of the Supreme Court in 1988, were the seven deadly sins in the decision of the same court in 1984. The trial, said the majority, must now proceed 'in accordance with the law' all over again, after seven long years. Baxi asks:

> How could the distinguished Justices of the Supreme Court (including Justice Pathak who in the meantime was elevated to the exalted position of the Chief Justice of India) have gone so comprehensively wrong? How come they did not know the elementary principles of the law like the rules of natural justice? The basic provisions of the act of 1952? The scope of constitutional guarantees of due process and equality? The luminous precedent of *Anwar Ali Sarkar* and the immortal words of Justice Vivian Bose? How is it that they came to lack abundantly plain constitutional sense in 1984? These questions have to be asked this way and no other, given the uninhibited criticism of the 1984 decision by the majority in 1988. If on closer examination of the dissenting opinions of Venkatachaliah and Ranganathan, and of the 1984 decision, we come to an opposed conclusion, very similar questions may arise concerning the juristic competence of Justices who formed the majority opinion in 1988! Obviously, there is something wrong in the state of Denmark, as Prince Hamlet would have ruefully remarked (Baxi 1989: i, 127–28).

Nalini Gera, Jethmalani's authorized biographer, has pointed out how Ram Jethmalani fought valiantly and pursued vigorously the case against Antulay to have him convicted (Gera 2002: 349–51). The final blow came when the Supreme Court, by a majority decision, held that a Special Court, rather than the Bombay High Court, should have heard the case and that the trial should start afresh, after all the years. Thus, all the evidence which had been presented in the High Court would have to be presented in the court of the special judge once again. The account does not inspire any faith in the Indian judicial system. Jethmalani calls it one of the *'darkest chapters in the history of the Supreme Court'*. As J. K. Jain has stated:

> This is a case in which the Supreme Court, in 1986, heard arguments at length on the question whether certain charges against the accused were properly dropped by the Bombay high Court. Now, the function of framing charges, in our system, properly belongs to the sessions judge or the district judge. It is not the function of the Supreme Court. Moreover, the Supreme Court had decided to transfer the case from a special court under the Prevention of Corruption Act, to the Bombay High Court in 1984. But in 1986 a writ petition challenging the 1984 order was allowed, and two Justices raised questions as to whether this was a proper procedure. And then in 1988, the Supreme Court decided, by a seven-judge Bench, that its own order can be challenged by a writ petition. This was momentous indeed, because it meant that *no decision of the Bench of the Supreme Court can be final by this reasoning'* (Jain 1992: 134–35).

A. Lakshaminath has also invited attention to how the transfer of the case from the Special Court to the High Court was not an issue before the Constitution Bench as neither side had argued or pleaded or prayed for the said direction. Apparently, the court had failed to notice the special provisions of the Criminal Laws Amendment Act, 1952, which barred the transfer of the case to the High Court. On appeal by the accused, a Bench of seven judges was constituted to examine the correctness of the transfer order passed by the Constitution Bench four years earlier. The majority judgment of the five judges held that the transfer of the case to the Bombay High Court was without jurisdiction and bad in law being vitiated on *per in curium* grounds. In conclusion, Lakshaminath states, 'One may ask whether the majority judgment does not strike at the very root of finality and does not impair the much wanted certitude in criminal law which are persuasive reasons for not recalling even an erroneous order especially at a later stage in the same case which has not yet finally closed?' (Lakshaminath1991: 2, 3, 7).

The observations of the Chief Justice of India, P. B. Gajendragadkar, are relevant in this context:

> In actual practice, however, where civil and criminal matters tended to attract the provisions of Articles 133 and 134, the tendency was to take to Article 136 [special leave to appeal]. Article 136 was no doubt intended to confer, upon the highest court, wide powers, but they were to be exercised sparingly in the interest of justice. It was not intended to grant leave to the petitioner to give him a chance to argue that the judgment of the high court may be erroneous. All errors committed by the High Court are not intended to be corrected under Article 136. Otherwise, Articles 133 and 134 may be pointless (Gajendragadkar 1982: 138–39).

But the court battles are only one part of the story. The other is the murky world of Indian politics, which never ceases to shock a common person. Gera has written that Jethmalani:

> ...subsequently discovered that BJP leaders Murli Manohar Joshi and Pramod Mahajan were instrumental in getting the complainant to withdraw the case. Nayak [the complainant] said, 'I am a loyal soldier of the BJP'. The party bosses had taken the decision to let Antulay go. When Ram questioned Mahajan about it, he admitted, 'Yes, it is true.' The explanation he offered was that the party wanted to build up a force against Sharad Pawar in Maharashtra and, therefore, wanted to build bridges against [sic] Antulay. No one had spent any money on the case and so it made no difference to them that Ram had spent several years, not to mention a substantial amount of money, on the legal battle. Ram had a vitriolic correspondence with Advani on the matter (Gera 2002: 350–51).

B. K. Nehru has written about his experience as Governor of Assam and Nagaland, who was concurrently appointed as Governor of Meghalaya, Manipur and Tripura:

> The next difference I had with my ministers [in Manipur] was when it was reported that they were selling for cash every single job within their gift, starting from the inspector general of police to the foot constable and the office peon. In return, the beneficiaries were permitted of course not only to recoup the expenditure but make as much profit on their investment as they could....On my upbraiding a couple of ministers, they told the chief secretary, 'Ask your governor what his own [central] government in Delhi is doing. We have no licences, no permits, no quotas to sell. The only thing we can sell is appointments. We also have to live as much as the people in Delhi. The argument was irrefutable. Mr Lalit Narayan Mishra, the [union]Commerce Minister, was quite openly selling for hard cash across the table, licences, permits and quotas to the highest bidder. This is the manner in which the Congress Party funds were collected after the party had decided that to show their purity and freedom from the pressure of capitalists, they would make illegal all contributions from companies to political parties...My recriminations naturally had no effect. All jobs continued to be sold: the fixed rate for these jobs was not lowered. The general public got used to the new charges. What I learnt was that the practice of selling appointments in Manipur pre-dated the introduction of democracy; it was the accepted practice during the Maharaja's days, though the rates were then lower (Nehru 1997: 532–33).

As stated elsewhere in the book, we abolished the princely states and privy purses and privileges, but the practices and the mindsets of that period have not only continued but have taken firm roots in the soil of Indian polity.

The hearings of the Commission of Inquiry into the Adarsh Housing Society scam in Mumbai were marked by the three former chief ministers of Maharashtra—Sushil Kumar Shinde, Vilasrao Deshmukh and Ashok Chavan—trying to wriggle out by shifting the blame to the other chief ministers. Taking a cue from Prime Minister Manmohan Singh, each one of them took the position that he was misguided by the bureaucracy and had relied on the advice and notings of the officers.

How the World Looks at Us

India's reputation for corruption has travelled far and wide. It is therefore not surprising that in major international economic and trade negotiations, India is asked for assurances on this score. One such occasion was the visit of American businessmen led by the US Commerce Secretary, Ronald Brown, to India in

1995 when Narasimha Rao was the Prime Minister. In fact, some US CEOs had pulled out of the negotiations because of worry over bribes (*FE*, 19 January 1995).

The New Zealand High Commissioner made an earnest plea that bureaucrats in India be made more accountable to hasten the process of economic reforms. He underlined that New Zealand could boast of fast development by having 60 per cent fewer bureaucrats. Speaking at a function on economic reforms in Pune, he vented his ire at the Indian bureaucrats who proved to be a stumbling block in the economic reform process and without mincing words urged, 'get those wretched bureaucrats and ministers off the back of the private sector' (*IE*, 11 October 1995).

The then US Ambassador to India, Frank Wisner, stated that a regulatory framework of independent and transparent regulatory bodies was imperative for protecting an efficient market economy and India needed to ensure that market participants were comfortable with the integrity of the market... Hundreds of billions of dollars will flow to India only as long as this country offers an environment that is attractive to investors, a playing field that is level, and rules that are equally applied and transparent (*TOI*, 16 February 1995).

The President of the Board of Trade in UK, Michael Heseltine, during his visit to Delhi, emphasized that 'transparency of procedures was in everybody's interest because it would remove the opportunities for corruption' (*FE*, 16 February 1995).

The Prime Minister of Singapore, Goh Chok Tong, said, 'many rules were not transparent...Commitment to reforms from the central government alone will not be enough. State governments play a critical role. They can facilitate the implementation of a project or stymie it with innumerable hurdles' (*IE*, 7 January 1995).

At a conference on emerging markets organized by the US Department of Commerce in Washington in July 1995, the Americans wanted the Indian government to cut red tape, simplify procedures and enhance transparency in the government decision-making process (*IE*, 27 July 1995).

All these quotations are from 1995, nearly two decades ago. The tone of foreign dignitaries remained the same in 1997. Addressing the Partnership Summit organized by the CII in Delhi, British Prime Minister John Major said, 'bureaucratic inertia and lack of transparency in the award of contracts continue to discourage foreign investors.' The then Prime Minister H. D. Deve Gowda laid stress on transparency in decision-making. He said he would ensure that 'middlemen' were completely eliminated in government deals with other countries. 'Henceforth no industrialist, big or small, will have to take help from middlemen to approach me or the government.' Deve Gowda said the country had suffered a lot at the hands of middlemen (Chaudhuri and Krishnaswamy 1997: 101).

Vinod Gupta, a well known IT industrialist, in his interview to TOI stated, 'The biggest complaint about doing business in India was bureaucracy and corruption....You have too many restrictions, which are not being dismantled because the bureaucrats don't want to give up control. Otherwise, who will give them bribes?' (*TOI*, 1 January 1998).

Has anything changed since then? If at all, more the things change, more they remain the same. It is important to note that several countries have *publicly* and repeatedly spoken about their frustrating experiences of and exasperation in dealing with India, without regard to diplomatic niceties.

The observations described in the previous section are borne out by how decisions were taken over the years in the telecommunications sector. Minister Sukh Ram changed the rules of the game after bids for mobile phone services were floated in 1991. By the time the eight licences were awarded in 1994, several businessmen, especially those unable to get a licence or who had not bid, put pressure on Sukh Ram to further open up the sector. The next year, the minister floated tenders for the entry of more mobile players in other cities and new ones in basic landline telephony, which was controlled by state-owned entities. When he found that one of the units—HFCL—had to be bailed out, the rules were changed after the bids had been opened. It was decided that the winners could only have licences for a maximum of three circles (Alam 2012: 36–37).

Later, in Atal Bihari Vajpayee's term as Prime Minister, the government agreed to switch over from the fixed licence fee regime stipulated in the contractual obligations to a revenue sharing regime. Since the then Minister for Telecommunications, Jagmohan, was not agreeable to changing the rules after the game had begun, he was shifted from the ministry.

Purchases of aircraft, whether for civilian or military use, have become controversial due to charges of corruption levelled in practically each case. Russi Mody observed, 'every time India buys an aircraft, 10 more millionaires are created.' The response of the then Civil Aviation Minister, C. M. Ibrahim, to this comment was a classic understatement, 'the observation was in bad taste' (*TOI*, 5 January 1997).

The 2G spectrum scam shows just how arbitrary and ad hoc the decision-making process truly is. But it is necessary to add a rider to this exposition. In all the cases mentioned here, private players benefitted at the cost of the exchequer.

UPA I and II

The government has announced its resolve to tackle graft but there is no evidence of any resolute action. The 2G spectrum scam, involving *potential loss* to the exchequer of about Rs 1.76 lakh crore or $40 billion, has exposed how deep and all pervasive is the involvement of the corporate sector in the mismanagement in the country. Rather than seriously examining what led to such an enormous potential loss, the Congress Party's 'man for all seasons' Telecom Minister Kapil

Sibal had the gumption to say that there was zero revenue loss in the 2G scam. Even the Supreme Court took umbrage at this flippant approach and asked the minister to behave with 'some sense of responsibility' and ordered the CBI to conduct the probe without coming under anyone's influence (*IE*, 22 January 2011). The Supreme Court Bench hearing the case asked the CBI to lay its hands on big corporate houses and government officials who may have had a role in the scam 'as mere summoning them for examining them may not be sufficient.' The court further observed, 'We have a large number of persons who think themselves to be above the law. Law must catch them. It should be done with greater expedition. Merely [because] they are in the list of Forbes or they are millionaires does not make any difference' (*Data India*, 13 February 2011). Subramanian Swami has rightly underlined that, 'The bitter truth thus is that India's corporate world's success stories are founded on fudged accounts and on undisclosed and unreported funding through black money held by corrupt politicians and notorious criminals' (Swami 2011: 7).

The opposition parties had agitated intensely for the setting up of a JPC on the 2G scam. The government was staunchly opposed to it and as a result, the entire winter session of Parliament in 2011 was wasted. Finally the government reluctantly conceded the demand. The working of the JPC has, however, once again raised important questions of its utility and effectiveness. The committee functioned in a highly partisan manner. In spite of persistent demands, it did not call any minister to tender evidence, though the role of the Prime Minister, Finance Minister P. Chidambaram and A. Raja, the then Telecommunications Minister, was suspect. In fact, Raja himself was keen to appear before the committee. And, as a prime accused, he could have been a star witness. But, obviously, the government did not want to be embarrassed with the prospect of Raja involving the Prime Minister and Chidambaram and even Pranab Mukherjee, the then Finance Minister and now the President of India, as the persons who had been kept in the loop fully in all the highly questionable decisions. Without giving a hearing to A. Raja, against all canons of natural justice, the draft JPC report came to the conclusion that Raja had misled the Prime Minister! A similar stand has been taken by the PM in the coal scam where in fact his responsibility is much more direct as he was also the Coal Minister during the relevant period. Manmohan Singh must be the most misled (or taken for a ride) Prime Minister since Independence, in spite of his decades of experience in administration at the highest levels. Manmohan Singh has emerged as the undisputed Teflon Prime Minister so far. His wall of silence on all highly controversial issues is frustrating the country. The 2G scam JPC will go down in history the same way as the Bofors JPC. Fifteen members of the JPC belonging to diverse political parties have written to the Speaker of Lok Sabha expressing their lack of confidence in the Chairman of the JPC, P. C. Chacko. The Congress Party, in turn, has demanded that the three prominent BJP members who were ministers during the NDA regime should be dropped from the JPC due to their conflict of interest. This demand has been made at a time when the committee is about to finalize its report! All these goings on have proved once again, if any further proof was required, that a JPC cannot be expected to be the instrument for fixing accountability in any politically sensitive case.

This is a unique case in which both the Public Accounts Committee (PAC) and the JPC are inquiring into the matter. Even though Prime Minister Manmohan Singh had written to the Chairman of PAC, Murli Manohar Joshi, that he was ready to appear before the committee, the chairman did not act on it. It was shocking to see Pranab Mukherjee, the then Minister for Finance, opposing the Prime Minister's offer to appear before PAC on the ground that constitutionally, the Prime Minister is answerable to the Lok Sabha and not to any committee. This is strange logic indeed. Reference may be made in this context to the observations of the Speaker in the Third Lok Sabha made on 22 August 1966, 'The most important thing that I have to bring to the notice of the House is that *the PAC is a House in miniature*. Its decisions should be respected and its dignity enhanced. There all parties work together in team spirit and no note of dissent is appended or allowed. They work in the interest of the nation and of the House on behalf of the House' (Kashyap 1996: 115). Against this background, Pranab Mukherjee's comment, who was then the senior-most Cabinet minister and who is now the President of India, was appalling. The Chairman of the JPC, P. C. Chacko, has already raised questions over the scope of PAC's inquiry. Such a parallel probe is unprecedented and it would not be a surprise if the two committees come to diametrically opposite conclusions.

The C&AG has also submitted reports pertaining to the favouritism and irregularities committed in three major infrastructure areas of coal, Delhi airport and power. The C&AG report with respect to coal block allocations is particularly damning. The private firms to which coal blocks were allotted on an ad hoc basis gained Rs 1.86 lakh crore; despite repeated advice from the Law Ministry, competitive bidding was delayed; and considerable time was wasted by the Coal Ministry after it was advised to proceed with auctioning. It must be noted that Prime Minister Manmohan Singh held additional charge of the Coal Ministry between 2004 and 2006 and was thus directly responsible for these lapses. As for the Delhi airport project, the C&AG has stated that land was given away to the private company at a token lease amount of Rs 100 per annum. Permission to charge a development fee was given only after signing of the contract. The C&AG has also made some critical comments on Reliance Power's mega power project.

A very unusual and unique feature of the working of the government surfaced when the 2G scandal broke. Prime Minister Manmohan Singh dissociated himself from certain decisions taken and advice given by the PMO! This would suggest, as has been suspected all along, that in reality the PMO was taking orders from some extra-constitutional centre of power. This brings into question the whole functioning of the government at the highest level.

C&AG reports and the study done by the National Institute of Rural Development show the large-scale misappropriation of funds in the Mahatma Gandhi Rural Employment Guarantee Scheme. The Supreme Court has said that the reports showed that there was massive misappropriation of 88 per cent of allocated funds in some districts in Odisha. The court has stated that if the Centre does not step in to take any decision to order an inquiry, 'we would step in'.

The *Indian Oil & Gas* magazine has detailed the scam involving billions of dollars in the import of LNG from Qatar by Petronet LNG Limited (PLL), a state sector company owned by four oil sector giants and presided over by the Petroleum Secretary. Looking at the number of scams floating around, presumably it would have to wait its turn in the queue. The magazine is blunt, 'Like the two-faced Roman god, PLL is the only organization in the country that can present at the same time a public and a private face. One must ask whether all the duplicity and double dealing at PLL can be ascribed to this inherent dichotomy in its DNA' (*Oil & Natural Gas*, 10 November 2011: 16).

Earlier, Bofors, the bank scam, the Satyam scam and others had underlined how deep the malaise was. Criminal cases pertaining to the previous telecom scam during P. V. Narasimha Rao's government in the mid-1990s, involving Sukh Ram, the then Minister of State for Telecommunications, were referred to earlier. But it is interesting to note that Sukh Ram became the favourite of both the Congress and the BJP for some time when the corruption cases against him were pending in courts. This shows how the two largest national political parties are not really serious about eradication of corruption. In the much-talked about fodder scam cases, the CBI had filed 53 cases against 430 accused. Of these, Lalu Prasad Yadav is an accused in five cases and they are still to be decided by the courts though 17 years have elapsed since they were registered. Only cases involving 'lesser mortals' have been decided so far. It is a similar story with the *Tehelka* scam involving Bangaru Laxman, the then President of BJP, Jaya Jetly and others. While Bangaru Laxman has been convicted to undergo imprisonment for four years, cases against the others are still pending. Bangaru Laxman's appeal is also pending in the court and in the meanwhile, he is out on bail. The only recent notable case for corruption was the conviction, for ten years in jail, in January 2013 of former Haryana Chief Minister, Om Prakash Chautala, and his MLA son in the 1999 teachers' recruitment scam. His appeals to the High Court and the Supreme Court will now take several more years.

Addressing an Interpol anti-corruption programme, A. P. Singh, the then Director of CBI said, US$500 billion (nearly Rs 30 lakh crore) had been stashed away illegally by Indians in tax heavens abroad, and that Indians were the biggest depositors in Swiss banks (*IE*,14, February 2012). But the central government remains unconcerned. In spite of terse comments from the Supreme Court urging the government to take energetic steps to investigate the accounts held by Indians in tax heavens abroad, the government has brazenly declined to reveal the names of foreign account holders. The government has also contested the Supreme Court directive to set up a special investigation team under the chairmanship of a retired judge of the Supreme Court with representatives from all concerned central government agencies such as the CBI, Enforcement Directorate, RAW and so on. The manner in which a superficial white paper on black money was placed in Parliament by the government on the very last day of the Budget session in 2012, thereby evading any discussion thereon, brings out the government's half-hearted approach to the problem. This clearly shows the reluctance of the government to deal decisively with the problem of black money and rampant tax evasion in the country, though the then President of India, Pratibha Patil, while addressing the joint session of Parliament on 21 February 2011, had assured that 'black money parked abroad will be brought back...My government will spare no effort in bringing back to India what belongs to it and bring the guilty to book' (*IE*, 22 February, 2011). All this has remained on paper.

Even after the one-man committee, comprising former C&AG V. K. Shunglu, indicted the then Lieutenant Governor, Tejinder Khanna, and Chief Minister, Sheila Dixit, in the Commonwealth games scam, no action has been taken and the matter has been brushed under the carpet. Even in the earlier Commonwealth Youth games held in Pune in 2008, the PAC of Maharashtra legislature has recommended that Suresh Kalmadi, Chairman of the Organizing Committee should be held responsible for the defalcation of Rs 33 crore and be criminally prosecuted (*Loksatta*, 18 April 2013). Looking at past experience, it is unlikely that any further action will be taken. Anil Ambani, when he was a Rajya Sabha member, was nominated to the Standing Committee on Finance. Suresh Kalmadi and A. Raja, who are both facing serious criminal charges and are out on bail, are members of prestigious committees of Parliament.

The efforts of Ashwani Kumar, the then Law Minister, and joint secretaries in the PMO and the Coal Ministry to prevail on the CBI to amend its investigation report before its submission in the Supreme Court scandalized the highest court. Clearly, this was meant to avoid focus on Prime Minister Manmohan Singh's role in the coal scam, not just as Coal Minister but also as the head of the government. Manmohan Singh's reluctance to ask Ashwani Kumar to step down from ministership till public pressure became unbearable, cast a serious reflection on the Prime Minister's sense of values and ethical standards. This sort of brazenness was never seen even in the worst days of Indira Gandhi and Rajiv Gandhi. This highlights that the definition of the honesty and integrity of a person itself needs to be revisited. A person should be honest not only so far as his personal dealings are concerned. He must be equally vigilant, strict and uncompromising with respect to the dealings of his colleagues in the ministry, and his subordinates. Looked at from this perspective, Manmohan Singh's avowed honesty and integrity has been irretrievably eroded.

The National Rural Employment Guarantee Act (NREGA), 2005, guarantees every rural household 100 days of employment of manual work in a year at a minimum wage within a radius of 5 kilometres. NREGA guidelines provide for a compulsory social audit. As compared to 100 days of guaranteed work in a year envisaged by the act, it was possible to provide only 38 days of work for each rural household in 2007–08 and 45 days of work in 2006–07. A survey conducted during May-June 2007 by Delhi-based Centre for Food Security to assess and evaluate NREGA's performance in Odisha covering 100 villages in six districts shows that:

- Out of Rs 733 crore spent under NREGA in the state during 2006–07, more than Rs 500 crore has been siphoned off and misappropriated;
- Less than 25 per cent of the funds reached the targeted population; and
- There are thousands of villages in the state where about 80–90 per cent of NREGA funds have been misappropriated.

In another study conducted by the National Institute of Rural Development (NIRD) in Odisha, it was found that a large chunk of money for NREGA, had gone into a black hole. The study found the presence of a large proportion of ghost workers, ghost man-days and ghost wages (Mishra, Das and Sahoo, 2009: 144–45). C&AG audit reports have come to similar conclusions. The issue has also been agitated in the Supreme Court through a PIL. The position in several other states will be no different.

The situation is so shocking that no sector has remained free from the virus of corruption. It was suspected for long that the number of students shown on the rosters of primary schools in Maharashtra was far inflated and the actual numbers were much lower. A survey of school attendance in standards I–VIII showed that more than 12 lakh students were bogus and crores of rupees of grants were being literally looted from the exchequer, year after year. Even after more than five years, no action has been taken by the state government in the matter (*Loksatta*, 6 October 2011).

Multiple scams involving natural resources such as land and mineral resources, plunder of environmentally fragile areas and rampant encroachments on public lands are only a few of the examples which readily come to mind. Zero tolerance for corruption has become the pet peroration of all those in power. But obviously their tolerance for corruption is limitless, for no action is taken in most of these cases. For the first time in recent years right thinking people in the country are asking whether India has become a 'banana republic'.

A Mockery of Secularism

The Indian Constitution is acclaimed for its very enlightened provisions pertaining to secularism, in spite of the trauma of the Partition on a religious basis and the unimaginable bitterness and distrust between Hindus and Muslims following savage massacres and human suffering. Reference may be made, in particular, to the following provisions: Article 14 (equality before law), Article 15 (prohibition of discrimination on grounds of religion, race, caste, sex or place of birth), Article 16 (equality of opportunity in matters of public employment), Article 19 (protection of certain rights regarding freedom of speech, etc.), Article 25 (freedom of conscience and free profession, practice and propagation of religion), Article 26 (freedom to manage religious affairs), Article 27 (freedom as to payment of taxes for promotion of any particular religion), Article 28 (freedom as to attendance at religious instruction or religious worship in certain educational institutions), Article 29 (protection of interests of minorities to conserve their language, script and culture), Article 30 (rights of minorities to establish and administer educational institutions) and Article 350A, which directs the state to provide facilities for instruction in the mother tongue at the primary stage of education. The report of the committee appointed by the Congress President to suggest amendments to the Constitution (Swaran Singh Committee) had recommended that 'the concepts of secularism and socialism should be clearly spelt out in the Constitution.' Accordingly, by the Forty-second Amendment Act, 1976, the words 'sovereign democratic republic' in the preamble to the Constitution were substituted by the words 'sovereign socialist secular democratic republic' to underline the socialist and secular character of the Constitution. Article 51A pertaining to fundamental duties, which was inserted by the same amendment act, *inter alia*, obliges every citizen of India to promote harmony and the spirit of common brotherhood amongst all the people of India transcending religious, linguistic and regional or sectional diversities, and to value and preserve the rich heritage of our composite culture. The Supreme Court has held that secularism is a part of the basic structure of the Constitution and Parliament has no powers to amend, curtail or restrict it in any way.

Like several other western concepts such as the rule of law, universal franchise, independence of the judiciary and so on, which were incorporated in the Indian Constitution, secularism too was a western concept, alien to Indian history. However, secularism as enunciated in the Indian Constitution does not have the same connotation as it does in the west. It does not mean being atheist, agnostic or irreligious. Perhaps it is for this reason that efforts made in the debates in the Constituent Assembly to make specific mention of the principle of secularism in the Constitution or to mention the word 'secular' in the Preamble had failed. In the Indian context what secularism means is that the state will not be theocratic and will give equal respect to all religions and treat all religions equally. So far as an individual is concerned, it lays down that there can be no discrimination on the basis of religion. More than anything else, these provisions, which formed part of fundamental rights, provided a reassurance to the minorities that their rights such as to practice and propagate their religion and administer their own educational institutions will be safe under the guardianship of the Supreme Court, which persuaded them to give up their demands for separate electorates. The Supreme Court highlighted in the case of *T. M. A. Pai Foundation v. State of Karnataka* that 'although the idea of secularism may have been borrowed in the Indian Constitution from the West, it has adopted its own unique brand of secularism based on particular history and exigency.' The main question is to what extent these precepts have taken roots and how far have they have been translated into reality.

At the outset it needs to be noted that secularism is the anti-thesis of communalism. The fact that India has not been able to firmly deal with communalism so far is proof of its failure in adhering to the constitutional mandate of secularism. Particularly disturbing are recent cases of mass violence perpetrated by the majority community on minorities—riots against Sikhs in 1984, riots in Mumbai after the demolition of the Babri Masjid in December 1992 and January 1993, riots against Muslims in Godhra and other places in Gujarat in 2002, and the attacks on Christians and churches in a number of states in 2008. More disturbing is the reluctance of the state to enforce the rule of law and to make effective use of the powers available to it under the provisions of various statutes.

The Mirage of Secularism

There is widespread disenchantment with the concept of secularism in all sections of society. At one end of the spectrum is anger in the majority community at the so-called pseudo-secularism practiced by a number of political parties. A large section of the majority community believes that these supposedly secular parties have a single point programme of appeasement of Muslims. Convincing proof of this was the passage of the Muslim Women (Protection of Rights on Divorce) Act, 1986, to set at naught the decision of the Supreme Court in the *Shah Bano* case (AIR 1985 SC 945). This clearly showed that the fundamentalist Muslim elements were able to prevail upon the government to undertake such a backward looking and retrograde legislation. Upendra Baxi in his article 'The Shah Bano Reversal: Coup against Constitution' emphasizes that the act violated every single major provision of the Constitution. He underlines that, 'If the Supreme Court acquiesces with this gesture of extraordinary defiance of the Constitution, it will cease to be both *Supreme* and a *Court*' (Baxi 1994: 93–94). Arun Shourie, one of the trenchant critics of the act has stated, 'The Bill was not considered by the Council of Ministers (it should have been the Cabinet) before it was introduced in the Lok Sabha. It was put to the Council after it had been introduced by A. K. Sen [Law Minister] on 25 February, and then it was, of course, presented as a *fait accomplice*...It was a political decision, the Prime Minister at last told the Congress Parliamentary Party on 28 February.' Shourie has also stated that the material collected by the government from a number of Muslim countries showed that 'one Muslim country after another had in fact modernised its family laws.' That is why the promised background paper setting out provisions of family laws as they prevailed in Islamic countries was not circulated. Shourie has further stated, 'The signal will not be lost on anyone. Certainly not in Punjab. Having expressed so much solicitude for the personal law of the Muslims, how will this government deny the demand for a separate "Sikh personal law" that the Akalis had put forward and which is duly listed in the official white paper on the Punjab agitation?' (Shourie 1993: 262–63).

According to Arif Mohammad Khan, the then Minister of State in MHA, who was a strong critic of the bill, 'nine Muslim countries already have laws that require the husband to provide maintenance to the wife he divorces' (Shourie 1987: 98). But this was not to be in India. This is an eloquent commentary on our secularism.

Another example is the opposition of these parties to enacting a uniform civil code, in spite of it being a part of the directive principles of state policy laid down by the Constitution over 60 years ago. The founding fathers of the Constitution included the provision for a uniform civil code (UCC) in the directive principles of state policy, instead of making it a fundamental right so as to give time for a consensus to develop on the subject. Jawaharlal Nehru wrote, 'It seems to me that a uniform civil code for the whole of India is essential. Yet I realise that it cannot be imposed on unwilling people. It should, therefore, be made optional to begin with, and individuals and groups may voluntarily accept it and come within its scope. The state should meanwhile carry on propaganda in its favour' (Gopal and Iyengar 2003: 39).

In reply to the debate on uniform civil code in the Constituent Assembly on 23 November 1948, B. R. Ambedkar stated, 'The only province the civil law has not been able to invade so far is marriage and succession...up to 1935, the North-West Frontier Province was not subject to the Shariat law. It followed the Hindu law in the matter of succession and in other matters, so much so that in 1939 that the central legislature had to come into the field and to abrogate the application of the Hindu law to the Muslims of the North-West Frontier Province and to apply the Shariat law to them. My hon'ble friends have forgotten, that, apart from the North-West Frontier Province, up till 1937 the rest of India, in various parts, such as the United Provinces, the Central Provinces and Bombay, the Muslims to a large extent were governed by the Hindu law in the matter of succession...In North Malabar, the Marumakkathayam Law applied to all—not only to Hindus but also the Muslims...*It is, therefore, no use making a categorical statement that the Muslim law has been immutable law which they have been following from ancient times. That law as such was not applicable in certain parts and it has been made applicable ten years ago'* (Kashyap 1998: 110–13).

Speaking in the Constituent Assembly on 23 November 1948, K. M. Munshi underlined: Nowhere in advanced Muslim countries has the personal law of each minority been recognised as so sacrosanct as to prevent the enactment of a civil code. Take for instance Turkey or Egypt. No minority in these countries is permitted to have such rights...When the Shariat Act was passed or when certain laws were passed in the central legislature in the old regime, the Khojas and Cutchi Memons were highly dissatisfied...We want to divorce religion from personal law, from what may be called social relations or from the rights of parties as regards inheritance or succession (Kashyap 1998: 105–07).

Unfortunately, with vote bank politics in sway, the prospects in this regard have receded. B. N. Tandon, who was Joint Secretary to Prime Minister Indira Gandhi, has written:

> Karan Singh [the then Minister for Family Planning] spoke very clearly in the PAC [Political Affairs Committee of the Cabinet]. He courageously stated that one of the directive principles of our Constitution is that we should have uniform civil code applicable to the whole country and yet even twenty-five years later we are hesitant in considering the issue. *Whenever there is any discussion of social reforms we always exclude the Muslim community from its ambit. This is not only improper, but is also not in the interest of the Muslims. It amounts to encouraging their feelings of separateness and backwardness.* His statement had quite an impact but the PM twisted the discussion to her purpose and in the end no decision was taken (Tandon 2006: 53).

As women's organizations and others have been urging, personal laws of most religions have one common feature, namely, their gender bias. The Supreme Court had observed in the *Shah Bano* case (*Mohd. Ahmed Khan v. Shah Bano Begum and Others*, AIR 1985 SC 945) that, 'Piecemeal attempts by courts...to bridge the gap between personal laws cannot take the place of a uniform civil code. Justice for all is a far more satisfactory way of dispensing justice than is justice from case to case.' In *Ms Jorden Diengdeh v. S.S. Chopra*, AIR 1985 SC 935, the court observed, 'We suggest that the time has come for the intervention of legislature in these matters to provide for a uniform code of marriage and divorce.' In yet another case, *Sarla Mudgal v. Union of India*, AIR 1995 SC 1531, the court reiterated, 'One wonders how long it will take for the government of the day to implement the mandate of the framers of the Constitution under Article 44... [which] is based on a concept that there is no necessary connection between religion and personal law in a civilized society.' In this case, the court directed the central government to file an affidavit as to why it had not taken any steps in the matter. It is not known if the direction was acted upon. Justice Ruma Pal, a Judge of the Supreme Court, stated that the goal of uniformity cannot be left to the ideas and interpretations of judges and concluded that 'ultimately the people of India themselves, through education, open debate, and responsible political action, will have to elect a government that will move Article 44 from a directive principle to fundamental right for all citizens of modern India' (Godbole 2006: 536–37). This suggestion was reiterated by the then CJI V. N. Khare, 'It is a matter of regret that Article 44 of the Constitution has not been given effect to. Parliament is still to step in for framing a common civil code in the country. A common civil code will help the cause of national integration by removing the contradictions based on ideologies' (*TOI*, 24 July 2003). Justice V. D. Tulzapurkar, the then Judge of the Supreme Court, asserted:

In the context of fighting the poison of communalism, the relevance of a uniform civil code cannot be disputed; in fact it will provide a juristic solution to the communal problem by striking at its root cause. Nay, it will foster secular forces so essential in achieving social justice and common nationality. Since our Constitution envisages one society with one singular citizenship, it is highly desirable that one single set of civil laws should govern all its citizens...A more glaring instance of an abject surrender to pressures exerted by fundamentalists, obscurantists and religious fanatics of the largest minority community in the country with electoral considerations in mind would be difficult to find. *Does not ritualistic invocation or incantation of the principle of secularism in the face of such behaviour sound hypocritical? When the political will to strike at fundamentalism is lacking, secularism will always remain an unattainable ideal* (Tulzapurkar 1987: 17–18).

There has been no serious effort to build a political consensus on the subject. Rather, this subject has become a taboo for political parties.

The Apex Court had also asked the government to undertake legislations for the compulsory registration of marriages and adoption of children but this too has not been possible due to the resistance of Muslims, though such legislations are on the statute books in a number of Muslim countries.

Unabated illegal migration from Bangladesh and its serious security and other implications have been neglected by the governments headed by the so-called secular parties at the Centre and in states like Assam, West Bengal and Bihar for the last six decades since Independence. By all accounts, illegal migrants from Bangladesh now exceed 20 million.

Continuance of subsidy for Haj pilgrims which amounted to as much as Rs 450 crore in 2008, when no such subsidy is being given to pilgrims of any other religion, is yet another grievance of Hindus.

The opposition of 'secular' political parties to enacting a strict law to deal with terrorism on the ground that it will create disaffection among Muslims has become another bone of contention. The P. V. Narasimha Rao government permitted TADA (Terrorist and Disruptive Activities Act) to lapse on the plea that it discriminated against Muslims. The repeal of POTA by the UPA government, as soon as it came to power, has further strengthened the perception that vote bank compulsions have prevailed over national security interests. The Centre has also withheld President's assent to the legislations proposed by some states to deal firmly with terrorism. The widespread impression that the UPA government and the state governments of its constituent parties are soft on terror, in which a number of Muslim organizations are involved, has not helped in dispelling the impression that secularism is at discount in the country. Pronouncements by several prominent leaders of the UPA in support of SIMI (Students Islamic Movement of India), which has been banned by the central government, has caused widespread consternation in the background of the alleged involvement of SIMI activists in a number of terrorist attacks in the country. In the same category is the recent decision of the Akhilesh Yadav government in UP to withdraw cases against some Muslims allegedly involved in acts of terrorism. Fortunately, the High Court has stayed the order.

Acquiescence by the government in setting up of Sharia courts, as a parallel system of justice, is considered as yet another evidence of appeasement of Muslims and has led to the matter being agitated in the Supreme Court through a PIL. The fatwa issued by Darul Uloom Deoband in the Imrana case—that she cannot go back to her husband after being raped by her father-in-law—was widely criticized but the then Chief Minister, 'Maulana' Mulayam Singh Yadav, backed it saying it was issued by learned people and they must have given it necessary thought! A cartoon by Unni shows a subordinate police officer telling his superior, 'Refer it to RBI, Sir. The matter concerns a vote bank' (*IE*, 1 July 2005). The then Prime Minister, V. P. Singh, declaring prophet Mohammad's birthday as a national holiday from the ramparts of the Red Fort in his Independence Day speech in 1990 was clearly an attempt to appease Muslims. In the same league was the UPA's plan in 2006 to divide government spending according to the share of religious groups, though this was unconstitutional. Ultimately, this move was given up due to public protests.

The government succumbing to the pressure of fundamentalist Muslims in not extending the visa and denying the request for a long-term visa to Taslima Nasreen, the progressive Bangladeshi writer, discussed later in this chapter, is perceived as yet another example of the sham secularism of the concerned political parties.

Perceptions of Minorities

While the majority community has this long (and unending) list of grievances regarding appeasement of Muslims, the Muslims are by no means satisfied with what they have had to face since Independence. Their most serious charge is that the successive Congress governments at the Centre had indirectly encouraged the Ram *janmabhoomi* agitation of the Hindu rightist parties—the Rajiv Gandhi government opening the lock of the temple in the Babri Mosque in which the idols of Ram Lalla were clandestinely kept by the Hindus, permitting them to commence construction of the plinth of the temple on the basis of their dubious claim that the title to the land in question was undisputed, and the Narasimha Rao government's failure to protect the Babri Masjid from demolition on 6 December 1992. They believe that the Congress Party, by these actions, wanted to please the Hindu vote bank.

A cross-section of liberal Muslims believes that while the government has pandered to the obscurantists and fundamentalists among them, it has not been adequately supportive of the progressive elements, and has in fact under-cut their efforts.

The perceptions of common Muslims about their plight, as elaborated by the Sachar Committee report, are indeed disturbing. The committee has stated:

Apparently, the social, cultural and public interactive spaces in India can be very daunting for the Indian Muslims...They carry a double burden of being labelled as 'anti-national' and as being 'appeased' at the same time. While Muslims need to prove on a daily basis that they are not 'anti-national' and 'terrorists', it is not recognised that the alleged 'appeasement' has not resulted in the desired level of socio-economic development of the community. The committee has pointed out that Muslim identity affects everyday living in a variety of ways that range from being unable to rent/buy a house to accessing good schools for their children. In general, Muslims complained to the committee that they are constantly looked upon with a great degree of suspicion not only by certain sections of society but also by public institutions and governance structures. This has a depressing effect on their psyche. Some women who interacted with the committee informed it of how in corporate offices hijab-wearing Muslim women were finding it increasingly difficult to find jobs. Inadequate representation of Muslims in government jobs, police and paramilitary forces is another major grievance of the Muslims. In most of the government departments and public sector undertakings, the share of Muslim workers does not exceed 5 per cent. Fearing for their security, Muslims are increasingly resorting to living in ghettos across the country. This is more pronounced in communally sensitive towns and cities. It was suggested to the Sachar committee that Muslims living together in concentrated pockets has made them easy targets for neglect by municipal and government authorities. From poor civic amenities in Muslim localities, non-representation in positions of political power and the bureaucracy, to police atrocities committed against them—the perception of being discriminated against is overpowering amongst a wide cross section of Muslims, particularly among the youth.

Though the Constitution casts a responsibility on the state to provide education to minorities in their mother tongue at the primary stage, Muslims have a legitimate grievance that there are very few Urdu-medium schools in Muslim localities. Lack of municipal and government primary schools has also forced them to send their children to madrasas.

The Sachar Committee found that Muslims face fairly high levels of poverty. Their conditions on the whole are only slightly better than those of Scheduled Castes (SCs) and Scheduled Tribes (STs). While there are variations in the conditions of Muslims across states, the situation of the community in urban areas seems to be particularly bad in relative terms in almost all states except Kerala, Assam, Tamil Nadu, Odisha, Himachal Pradesh and Punjab. Their relative position in rural areas is somewhat better but here again in most states poverty levels among Muslims are higher than all socio-religious communities, except SCs and STs.

It is not therefore surprising that several prominent Muslim leaders have been expounding the need for Muslims to form a new all-India political party of their own to agitate their grievances. Syed Ahmed Bukhari has charged that 'the Congress is no longer a secular party. He has threatened a mass campaign to agitate the grievances of Muslims' (*Tehelka*, 8 November 2008: 3). There are increasing demands for reservation for Muslims in government jobs and institutions of higher learning on the basis of religion. It is reported that the Ranganath Mishra Commission recommended that 15 per cent of government jobs as well as admissions to higher educational institutions should be reserved for minorities and of this 10 per cent should be earmarked for Muslims. There are also demands that the representation of Muslims in the legislatures should at least be equal to their proportion in the total population (13.4 per cent). These grievances and demands of Muslims are no different than those in the pre-Partition days. The provisions and safeguards embedded in the Constitution do not seem to have made any difference.

S. S. Jodhka has forcefully argued that 'it was for the first time that facts about the "development deficit" among the Indian Muslims were presented by the Sachar Committee with the support of such comprehensive data...Questions of cultural identity are indeed very critical, but they will have to be articulated through the language of citizenship and democratic rights. The Sachar committee report opens up this possibility' (Jodhka 2007: 2996–998). However, the two most important recommendations of the Sachar Committee to set up an equal opportunity commission and the compilation of a diversity index to target all backward communities with educational and other promotional efforts, seem to have fallen by the wayside.

Another religious minority, the Christians, is facing increasing opposition and violence primarily due to their attempts at conversion of people to Christianity. This has resulted in damage to several churches and injury to some priests and nuns. It is interesting to note that the Supreme Court has asked the Odisha government to be 'generous enough' and relook at its 'secular' policy which prevents the government from giving any compensation to any place of worship (IE, 23 October 2008). The Centre had to send advisories from the Ministry of Home Affairs to governments in Odisha, Karnataka and Kerala to take effective steps to quell violence against Christians and to maintain law and order in the states. However, these can carry any weight only if the Centre is able to take the next step of imposition of President's rule under Article 356, if the advice is not heeded by the states. Looking to the composition of the Lok Sabha and the Rajya Sabha, it is certain that the government will find it difficult to get support for any such action.

Demolition of the Babri Masjid and its Aftermath

The issues pertaining to secularism came to the fore prominently after the demolition of the Babri Masjid on 6 December 1992 and the country-wide communal riots that followed. The central government had failed to take appropriate steps to protect the Masjid, in spite of all information available to it that the Government of Utter Pradesh was not inclined to take any steps to do so. With the Masjid, the secular credentials of the P. V. Narasimha Rao government too were shattered completely.

To rehabilitate its image, the government introduced on 29 July 1993 two bills in Parliament for delinking religion from politics. The first related to an amendment to the Constitution to provide that the state shall have respect for all religions, and to confer powers to the Parliament to ban any association or body of individuals if it promotes or attempts to promote disharmony or feeling of enmity, hatred or ill-will between different classes of citizens on grounds of religion, race, place of birth, residence, language, caste or community. The bill further provided that making use of religion, including religious symbols, for the purpose of getting elected to Parliament or to state legislatures or promoting or attempting to promote a feeling of enmity, hatred or ill-will would be a ground for disqualification.

The second bill was to amend the Representation of the People Act (RPA) so as to provide that no association or body shall be registered by the Election Commission as a political party if the association or body bears a religious name, since such a religious name could be said to contain an appeal to vote for the political party on ground of religion which will be detrimental to the cause of secular democracy. A provision was also proposed under which a complaint could be made to the High Court within whose jurisdiction the main office of the political party is situated, for cancelling the registration of a political party where such political party bears a religious name or the memorandum or the rules and regulations of the political party no longer confirm to the proposed provisions. A time limit of 90 days was laid down within which political parties with religious names will be required to change such names and conform to the new law.

These bills were introduced without making any effort to build a national consensus on relevant issues. Clearly, the government did not want to share the credit for the proposed amendments with any other political parties. As was to be expected, both the bills met with stiff resistance not just from political parties in the opposition but also the media, intellectuals and a large cross-section of society. Finally, the move had to be shelved (Kashyap 1993: 51–63).

It is interesting to note that a similar attempt made while framing the Constitution had also failed in terms of any discernable impact. In the Constituent Assembly (Legislative), a resolution was moved on 3 April 1948 by Ananthasayanam Ayyangar to ban communal parties. Ayyangar underlined that the time had come to separate religion from politics. There was an almost unanimous acceptance of the resolution barring the single dissenting note by Ishaq Seth. Finally, the following resolution was passed:

> Whereas it is essential for the proper functioning of democracy and the growth of national unity and solidarity that communalism should be eliminated from Indian life, this assembly is of the opinion that no communal organisation which by its constitution or by the exercise of discretionary power vested in any of its officers and organs, admits to or excludes from its membership persons on grounds of religion, race and caste, or any of them should be permitted to engage in any activities other than those essential for the bonafide religious, cultural, social and educational needs of the community, and that all steps, legislative and administrative, necessary to prevent such activities should be taken (Kashyap 1993: 84–136).

There has been no follow-up action on the resolution though the situation has degenerated over the years due to the menace of fundamentalism increasing enormously in all religions.[5]

Court Pronouncements

The importance of the issues involved is underlined by the series of election petitions filed over the years in which candidates have solicited votes on the basis of religion. In one such case pertaining to election for the Santacruz Legislative Assembly constituency, for example, the Bombay High Court held that:

> the voluminous oral as well as documentary evidence leaves no room for doubt that the plank of Hindutva/Hinduism/Hindu was used...The campaign was on the basis of appealing for votes on the basis of first respondent's community and religion, i.e., the Hindu community and religion and that there was an attempt to create enmity and hatred between different classes of citizens on the basis of religion, community and caste particularly the Hindus and the Muslims.

When the matter went in appeal to the Supreme Court (*Abhiram Singh v. C. D. Commachen and Others*, 1996, 3 SCC 665), the three-judge Bench directed on 16 April 1996 that the case be placed before a larger Bench of five judges 'and, if possible, at an early date so that all questions arising in the present appeal could be decided authoritatively and expeditiously.' Unfortunately, the case is still pending.

In yet another case, *Ebrahim Sulaiman Sait v. M. C. Mohammed and another* (AIR 1980 SC 354), the court observed:

> Reading the speech as a whole it cannot be denied that its tone is communal, but in this country communal parties are allowed to function in politics. That being so, how an appeal to the voters, such as the one made in the speech in question should be viewed in the context of corrupt practices mentioned in the Act, has been explained by Gajendragadkar C. J., speaking for the court in *Kultar Singh v. Mukhtiar Singh*, "It is well known that there are several [political] parties in this country which subscribe to different political and economic ideologies, but their membership is confined to, or predominantly held by, members of particular communities or religions. So long as law does not prohibit the formation of such parties and in fact recognises them for the purpose of election and parliamentary life, it would be necessary to remember that an appeal made by such candidates of such parties for votes may, if successful, lead to their election and in an indirect way, may conceivably be influenced by considerations of religion, race, caste, community or language. This infirmity cannot perhaps be avoided so long as parties are allowed to function and are recognised, though their composition may be predominantly based on membership of particular communities or religion."

This helplessness of the highest court of the land must be noted.

Some election petitions have been dismissed by the Supreme Court on the tenuous distinction between the Hindu religion and Hindutva. Thus, in *Manohar Joshi v. Nitin Bhaurao Patil and another* (AIR 1996 SC 796), the Court held, 'The word "Hindutva" by itself does not invariably mean Hindu religion and it is the context and the manner of its use which is material for deciding the meaning of the word "Hindutva" in a particular text. It cannot be held that in the abstract the mere word "Hindutva" by itself invariably means Hindu religion.' In *Dr Ramesh Yeshwant Prabhoo v. Prabhakar Kashinath Kunte* (AIR 1996 SC 1113), the court held:

> No precise meaning can be ascribed to the terms 'Hindu', 'Hindutva' and 'Hinduism'; and no meaning in the abstract can confine it to the narrow limits of religion alone, excluding the content of Indian culture and heritage. *The term 'Hindutva' is related more to the way of life of the people in the sub-continent.* It is difficult to say that the term 'Hindutva' or 'Hinduism' *per se*, in the abstract, can be assumed to mean and be equated with narrow fundamentalist Hindu religious bigotry, or be construed to fall within the prohibition in sub-section (3) and/or (3A)of section 123 of the R. P. Act. Ordinarily 'Hindutva' is understood as a way of life or a state of mind and it is not to be equated with or understood as religious Hindu fundamentalism. *The word 'Hindutva' is used and understood as a synonym of 'Indianisation' i.e. development of uniform culture by obliterating the differences between all the cultures co-existing in the country.* Considering the terms 'Hinduism' or 'Hindutva' *per se* as depicting hostility, enmity or intolerance towards other religious faiths or professing communalism, proceeds from an improper appreciation and perception of the true meaning of these expressions.

Needless to say, this philosophical discourse is hardly relevant in the emotionally charged atmosphere during electioneering. Muslims and persons of other religious denominations of minorities are hardly likely to subscribe or take kindly to this interpretation. In fact, this interpretation is the anti-thesis of the two nation theory on which the Partition of the country had taken place. It will also evoke fears of obliterating the religious and cultural identities of the minorities in the country. Equally difficult to understand is the logic of the court in its assertion that, 'A mere statement that the first Hindu state will be established in Maharashtra is by itself not an appeal for votes on the ground of his religion but the expression, at best, of such a hope.' The fact that all these election petitions were based on the speeches made by the leaders of the Shiv Sena and BJP, whose political ideology is based on the furtherance of Hindu religion at any cost, also has an important bearing on the issues at hand. It is unfortunate that the tenets on which these judgments of the Supreme Court were based and which have such an important bearing on secularism have not been reviewed by a larger Constitution Bench so far.

Reference must be made to another important judgment of the Supreme Court in *S. R. Bommai v. Union of India* (AIR 1994 SC 2092). While dealing, *inter alia*, with the case of the dismissal of the three state governments of Madhya Pradesh, Himachal Pradesh and Rajasthan by the Centre in 1992, Justice Sawant and Justice Kuldip Singh, who wrote the judgment, stated:

> Secularism is one of the basic features of the Constitution. While freedom of religion is guaranteed to all persons in India, from the point of view of the state, religion, faith or belief of a person is immaterial. To the State, all are equal and are entitled to be treated equally. In matters of state, religion has no place. *No political party can simultaneously be a religious party. Politics and religion cannot be mixed. Any state government which pursues unsecular policies or unsecular course of action acts contrary to the Constitutional mandate and renders itself amenable to action under Article 356.*

There is no dissent or qualification or reservation by any of the other judges on this part of the judgment. Soli Sorabjee has rightly stated that 'the propositions are over-broadly stated' (*Journal Section* (1994) 3 SCC, p. 30). In the comprehensive article on the judgment, Justice H. R. Khanna, former Judge of the Supreme Court, wrote:

> The decision of the court in respect of the three states in question would have serious repercussions on the survival or coming into power of BJP in any state…It would also warrant the dismissal of all BJP governments if and when they come into power in any state…Yet ever since the commencement of the Constitution we have had political parties like Muslim League, Akali Dal and Hindu Mahasabha. Some of these parties like Akali Dal have formed state governments, yet no one has so far thought of dismissing such government because of the label of the party or its allegiance or affinity to some religion… No judgment of the Supreme Court, in the opinion of the writer, can and should ignore the ground realities of political life in the country. Life of law, it is said, is not logic, but experience and one may add, taking due cognisance of the political and social realities. Constitutional law cannot operate in vacuum or choose to reside in some higher region cut off from the world of existing political and social realities (Khanna 1994: 156-7).

The judgments of the Supreme Court thus give diametrically opposite signals so far as secularism is concerned. In a decision given in 2005, the court held that housing societies may exclude from membership people of different castes or communities, and frame their bylaws in such a way that membership is restricted to a particular caste or creed. As *The Lawyers Collective* editorially commented, 'The implications of this judgment are horrendous. The consequences for religious groups are even more frightening' (*The Lawyers Collective* 2005). It is well known that segregation in housing and educational institutions had a major influence on the thinking of religious groups and communities and has been responsible for their feelings of alienation. Social unrest and riots are, in no small measure, due to such segregation. And such segregation is not confined only to the lower strata of these communities. As news reports point out from time to time, even well-off Muslim families and public figures find it difficult to get suitable accommodation in metropolitan cities like Mumbai, Pune and Bengaluru. Shabana Azmi has claimed that she and her husband Javed Akhtar could not buy a flat in Mumbai because they were Muslims. She has stated that Saif Ali Khan had also faced similar prejudice. Arshad Warsi has also said that he, too, had the same problem (*Outlook*, 22 September 2008: 88). Television actor, Aamir Ali, filed a PIL in the Bombay High Court for being refused an apartment in Lokhandwala Complex 'just because he was a Muslim' (*IE*, 4 August 2007). In Pune, a housing society in a well-off locality refused permission to one of its members to sell his flat to a Muslim. During the 1993 riots in Mumbai, members of some communal parties were reported to have gone from one building to another to identify and target Muslim residents in the buildings. Shukla has pointed out how Muslim lawyers have been intimidated by advocates from the majority community in Lucknow for defending terror accused (Shukla 2008: 14–15).

Equally disturbing is the judgment of the Supreme Court with respect to the Bombay Prevention of Excommunication Act, 1949 which laid down that 'Notwithstanding anything contained in any law, custom or usage for the time being in force to the contrary, no excommunication of a member of any community shall be valid and shall be of any effect.' The act came to be challenged by the Head of the Daudi Bohra community. The Bombay High Court dismissed the petition but the Supreme Court (*Sardar Syedna Taher Saifuddin Saheb v. State of Bombay*, AIR 1962 SC 853) declared the said legislation as void, in spite of the fact that the Constitution has given freedom of conscience, faith and belief to every citizen (Dharmadhikari 1988). Chief Justice Sinha, in his minority judgment, held that, 'The Act is intended to do away with all that mischief of treating a human being as a "pariah" and of depriving him of his human dignity and of his right to follow the dictates of his own conscience. The act is thus aimed at fulfilment of the individual liberty of conscience guaranteed by Article 25 (1) of the Constitution and not in derogation of it.' Former Chief Justice of India, P. B. Gajendragadkar, too underlined that the judgment of the Bombay High Court which was acclaimed as a progressive judgment when it was delivered, unfortunately received a knock-out blow when the Supreme Court set it aside. He stated that if he had sat on the Bench to hear the case, as was originally intended, he would have strived to uphold the judgment of the Bombay High Court (Gajendragadkar 1982: 148). It is unfortunate that the judgment has remained unchallenged so far.

Propagation of One's Religion

The Constitution gives a fundamental right to profess, practice and *propagate* one's religion. During the discussion in the Constituent Assembly, some minorities had claimed that their religion obliged them to propagate their religion and this freedom must be available to them. Unfortunately, this was agreed to by the Constituent Assembly. But several other secular countries like Nepal do not give the right of propagation of one's religion. It needs to be examined whether a review of this provision is called for in light of the experience so far. Jawaharlal Nehru had stated in his circular letter to the Pradesh Congress Committees on 5 August 1954, 'Our Constitution is based on this secular perception and gives freedom to all religions, even freedom to proselytize. Personally, I do not appreciate attempts at mass proselytization. But that is a personal opinion of my own, and I have no business to thrust it on others. I can understand an individual changing his religion because of certain convictions. I do not understand attempts at mass conversions, which can have no business with individual or personal conviction and which have often behind them some political urge' (Jawaharlal Nehru Papers, quoted in *Muslim India* 2008: 12).

Way back in 1955, complaints were received in Rajgarh district in Madhya Pradesh that names of newly admitted children in schools were being changed to Christian names. Enquiries made in the matter showed that there was substance in the complaints. A Christian Missionary Activities Enquiry Committee was appointed by the state government in April 1954 to look into the allegations against activities of Christian missionaries. This matter was raised by the Pope with Prime Minister Nehru when he visited the Vatican in July 1955. On return, Nehru wrote to Ravi Shankar Shukla, Chief Minister, saying, 'I hope that you will do something to get rid of this general impression that Catholics are being persecuted in Madhya Pradesh' (Jawaharlal Nehru Memorial Fund 2001: 160–61). I have mentioned these details to show that religious conversions is a long standing problem which has been agitating the majority community. The fact that it was raised at the level of the Pope shows just how keen was the interest in missionary activities at the highest level in the Vatican.

Around 50 Catholic organizations from across Mumbai have reportedly written to the Maharashtra Chief Minister, Prithviraj Chavan, asking him to withdraw an Anti-Conversion Bill, which they fear will be introduced in the Legislative Assembly soon. They term the bill anti-minority and against the constitutional rights of a minority and urge that 'this anti-conversion Bill should be confined (sic) to the dustbin of history' (*Sunday Guardian*, 7 July 2013). Would these organizations be so agitated unless they are actively involved in the game of conversions?

Attempts at the conversion of SCs, STs and poorer sections of society by Christian missionaries have been one of the important factors for communal tensions and violence as evidenced in the recent cases in Karnataka, Odisha, Kerala and Madhya Pradesh. The distribution of population of each religion by caste categories is particularly striking so far as Christians are concerned as compared to the other religions. The Sachar Committee report shows that while 9 per cent of the Christians are SCs, 32.8 per cent are STs, 24.8 per cent are OBCs (other backward classes) and 33.3 per cent are 'others'. Thus, nearly 67 per cent of the Christian population is accounted for by SCs, STs and OBCs. For Hindus, the corresponding figure is 74 per cent. Among Muslims, the preponderant percentage is that of OBCs (39.2 per cent).[6] While large-scale conversions to Buddhism have also taken place, there has been no hostile reaction to it among Hindus in general and Hindu fundamentalists, in particular, as Buddhism is accepted as a stream of Hinduism. The time has come to seriously examine the wide-ranging implications of religious conversions of Hindus to other religions, particularly its impact on social cohesion and public order. More importantly, the very concept of secularism is being increasingly questioned by Hindus due to the unrestricted freedom given to religious organizations to carry out conversions with monetary and other inducements.

Bajaj talks about the disturbing demographic changes in the north-east, 'Large parts of Assam have turned predominantly Muslim and Nagaland, Mizoram and the whole of Manipur, except the valley districts, have become predominantly Christian. In these areas the changes are almost complete and the only issue of interest is whether the remnants of Hindus in these areas would continue to stay there or will their already negligible presence decline further' (Bajaj 2011: 60).

Constitutional issues pertaining to conversion were examined by the Supreme Court as far back as 1977 in the context of the enactments by Madhya Pradesh and Orissa (*Rev Stainislaus v. State of Madhya Pradesh and others; State of Orissa and others v. Mrs Yulitha Hyde and others etc.*, AIR 1977 SC 908). The court held:

> What Article 25 (1) grants is not the right to convert another person to one's own religion....It has to be remembered that Article 25 (1) guarantees 'freedom of conscience' to every citizen, and not merely to the followers of any particular religion and that, in turn, postulates that there is no fundamental right to convert another person to one's own religion because if a person purposely undertakes the conversion of another person to his religion, as distinguished from his effort to transmit or spread the tenets of his religion, that would impinge on the 'freedom of conscience' guaranteed to all the citizens of the country.

The court also held that if a thing 'disturbs the current of the life of the community, and does not merely affect an individual, it would amount to disturbance of the public order. Thus, if an attempt is made to raise communal passions, e.g., on the ground that some one has been "forcibly" converted to another religion, it would, in all probability, give rise to an apprehension of a breach of the public order, affecting the community at large...The two Acts [of Madhya Pradesh and Orissa] do not provide for the regulation of religion.' The court therefore upheld the validity of both the enactments prohibiting conversions by force, fraud, inducements, allurements etc.

In spite of this authoritative pronouncement, the central government has failed to take a clear stand on the matter and to lay down a policy on the subject. This has led to public perception that the government does not like to displease the religious minorities in general and Christians in particular. One saving grace is that Muslims have not been resorting to mass conversions in recent years, except for the large-scale migration from Bangladesh. Since Article 25 is a part of the basic structure of the constitution, the Parliament will not be competent to amend it to delete the word 'propagate' but, the government can issue suitable guidelines in the light of the judgment of the Supreme Court.[7] This will remove a major irritant and ensure that public order is not adversely affected. It will also restore the faith of the majority community in the concept of secularism.

Since considerable foreign funding is received by Christian missionaries, effective use could have been made of the Foreign Contributions (Regulation) Act (FCRA) to check the malpractices in conversions. Unfortunately, the original purpose and objectives with which FCRA was enacted have been totally lost sight of. Instead FCRA has become a tool for harassing NGOs and other bodies doing development work.

Making Elections More Representative

As brought out in the section on electoral reforms, one way to address the menace of vote bank politics, which has been primarily responsible for undermining secularism, is by laying down by law that a candidate must win at least 50 per cent plus one vote for being declared elected. The present first-past-the-post system results in a majority of legislators getting elected on a minority vote. The proposed change will make democracy more representative and force a candidate to seek the support of all cross-sections of the constituency and not appeal to voters only on the basis of caste, community, creed or religion. In April 2004, BJP leader L. K. Advani had publicly admitted, 'Babri hurt me and party; we will never support the VHP and the RSS in their demands for the takeover of Kashi and Mathura' (*IE*, 6 April 2004). In June 2013, with an eye on the impending 2014 Lok Sabha elections, the BJP declared its intention to come out with a 'vision document' for the empowerment of Muslims. This is a welcome development.

The Highly Disturbing Manifestation of Alienation

It is frightening to see that the disenchantment with secularism has led to both the Muslims and Hindus (and in the decade of the 1990s even the Sikhs) turning to terrorism. It is more disturbing that many of the persons involved in such acts are well-educated and highly motivated. This is a unique case of alienation of *all* religious communities in the country. Not long ago, all terrorist acts used to be routinely ascribed to Pakistan's ISI and terrorist organizations in Bangladesh. Thereafter it was found that terrorism was increasingly home-grown and Indian Muslims were largely responsible for it. Now even Hindus have joined the fray, with some Hindu religious leaders taking the initiative to support or organize acts of terror. The involvement of some serving and retired officers of the armed forces, which represent the best traditions of secularism in the country, shows the depth to which the poison of communal feelings and disenchantment with secularism has spread. It will be disastrous to overlook this phenomenon as a mere aberration. The long-term implications of this development for the unity, integrity and even survival of the country are horrendous and must not be lost sight of. BJP President Rajnath Singh has gone to the extent of saying that if the Hindu terrorism card is overplayed by the Congress and the UPA, it will lead to civil war in the country. It will be wrong to look at the issue as merely one of law and order. It is imperative that the root cause, namely, the feeling of alienation, injustice and discrimination be addressed with a sense of urgency.

Futile deliberations and outcome of the meeting of the National Integration Council (NIC) held in October 2008 shed some light on this. The background note circulated by the government for the meeting had nothing to say on critical issues except to hark back to the declaration of objectives adopted by the NIC as far back as 1968! This was the epitome of intellectual bankruptcy.

In the run-up to the next general elections due in 2014, the war of words on secularism has come in focus with Narendra Modi's criticism that 'whenever the Congress faces crisis—whether it is corruption, inflation, directives from the Supreme Court or the rape of a young girl—it wears the burqa of secularism and hides in a bunker instead of coming forward and answering the people.' Such free for all and rhetoric is likely to create more doubts in the minds of the people at large about the concept of secularism.

In a pluralistic society such as that in India, secularism was expected to be a unifying force to build bridges between religious communities. Instead, secularism itself has become the single-most divisive force, particularly with general elections due in 2014. The latest in this disturbing trend is the comment by the Congress Party that Indian Mujahideen (IM), the terrorist organization in India, was born as a reaction to the Godhra riots in 2002. This is stated to be based on what NIA has said in its charge sheet. Congress General Secretary Shakeel Ahmed said that the BJP's communal politics set off a 'chain reaction' on the issue of terror. 'If they [BJP] forsake their communal politics, outfits like the IM will cease to exist,' he said (*IE*, 22 July 2013). After getting enough mileage out of the statement, the Congress Party later distanced itself from it, after perhaps realizing that a charge could be made that the 1984 pogrom against the Sikhs in Delhi was responsible for the Sikh militancy and insurgency which plagued the country in the late 1980s and 1990s. Further, it was simplistic to suggest that fundamentalist Muslim outfits would cease to function if the BJP gave up its communal politics. Such charges and counter-charges are counter-productive and only weaken the voices of sanity. Public life and discourse is thus being increasingly divided on the basis of the real, perceived or motivated imputation of the label of secular versus Hindu nationalists.

Reference may be invited to the thoughtful and thought-provoking report of the Concerned Citizens Tribunal on the Gujarat riots in 2002, referred to earlier, in which it has been suggested that:

- The government should suitably amend electoral laws so as to disallow parties that espouse a particular religion, and which act or behave by word of mouth, print or any other manner with a view to securing power through a religious policy, to contest elections to Parliament, to the Assembly, to the municipal corporations [or] to panchayats.
- The government should also appoint high-powered commissions.
- The government should determine the extent of communalization within the administration (bureaucracy) and suggest various methods to remedy the situation so as to ensure a secular, independent administration.
- The government should take steps to determine the extent of communalization of education and educational institutions, and to suggest various steps to ensure that future generations are not in any way communalized before they come out of schools and colleges (Concerned Citizens Tribunal 2002: 169).

All efforts made so far to ban communal parties and organizations and to prohibit them from entering political life have been unsuccessful. B. N. Tandon wrote, 'PM [Indira Gandhi] has never been guided by any principles or rules. She has but one objective—to win the elections somehow. She is not averse to any alliance if it will help her win—she has tied up with the Muslim League in Kerala, the Shiv Sena in Bombay and the Akalis in Punjab at different times. But for public consumption she has always maintained that she is opposed to narrow communal parties. But this is not the reality' (Tandon 2003: 325).

As seen earlier, the scope of the efforts to contain communal parties was also restricted to laws relating to elections to Parliament and state legislatures.

While these are no doubt important objectives, they by themselves, are not enough. It is imperative to establish a mechanism to translate secularism from a precept into reality in the governance and public life of the country.

Creating a Commission on Secularism

Clearly, the time has come to create a new institution, namely, a Commission on Secularism (COS) for ensuring adherence to the constitutional mandate on secularism. I had propounded this idea while discussing the lessons of Partition in my book *The Holocaust of Indian Partition—An Inquest* (Godbole 2006: 543). To be effective, such a commission must be appointed by an amendment to the Constitution and should be presided over by a former Chief Justice of India, with five other members drawn from among eminent jurists, former judges of the Supreme Court, chief justices of high courts and other public figures of highest integrity and reputation. The selection of the chairman and members of the COS should be transparently apolitical. The selection committee may comprise of the Vice President of India, the Prime Minister, the Speaker, the Chief Justice of India, union Home Minister and leaders of the opposition in the Lok Sabha and the Rajya Sabha.

Such a commission will be able to take a holistic view on all matters pertaining to secularism and even intervene in matters coming up before high courts and the Supreme Court. Reference may be made in this context to the very laudable role played by the National Human Right Commission (NHRC) which intervened in cases pertaining to the Godhra pogrom before the Supreme Court and has become an important moral voice to reckon with. At the time when there are no national leaders of stature, with any moral authority or credibility left in the country, COS will be ideally suited to fill the vacuum.

COS will be best equipped to create public awareness on secularism. Its open hearings will provide an opportunity to all political parties, intellectuals, religious leaders, NGOs and concerned citizens to argue their points of view, orally or in writing, either in person or through an advocate, in a free and fair manner. Keeping in view the basic purpose of setting up the COS, it is proposed that the hearings before the commission should also be televised. It is only through such a public discourse that the values of secularism enshrined in the Constitution can be translated into reality.

The commission should have the responsibility to pronounce judgments on all declarations, actions and programmes of political parties, public institutions, state and central governments, electronic and print media and others, so far as their impact on secularism is concerned. The commission may take cognisance of such actions *suo motu* or on an application from any individual or organization. The decision of the commission should be binding on all concerned, unless it is set aside or modified by the Supreme Court. Thus, inevitably the powers and authority of COS will have to be much wider than those of NHRC, whose recommendations are not binding on the government. It may be relevant in this context to recall that the often violent agitations for ban on cow slaughter subsided when the matter went before the high courts and later the Supreme Court, irrespective of the merits of their decisions. Similarly, the highly emotive and explosive issues pertaining to implementation of secular policies need to be depoliticized by entrusting them to a constitutional commission such as the COS. It may be recalled that Turkey's ruling Justice and Development Party (AKP) faced a serious battle for survival in 2007 when the country's constitutional court reviewed a case to ban the party for its alleged anti-secular activities in violation of the Turkish Constitution.

The reports of all commissions and bodies set up by the government are required to be submitted by them to the government which in turn submits them to Parliament in due course of time. Often, there is considerable delay in the process and the government chooses the time politically most convenient and opportune for the purpose. Looking to the special position proposed to be accorded to the COS, it is suggested that the annual or any special reports of the commission may be submitted by the commission directly to Parliament and the government, and released simultaneously to the media and the public.

The question which remains is whether there will be statesmanship and political will to support this far-reaching and overdue political reform. In the politics of opportunism prevailing in the country, it will not be an easy task. It is only the pressure of public opinion which will force the political parties to act in the matter. A national campaign needs to be launched to prevail upon all political parties to initiate and support steps for a constitutional amendment for setting up a commission on secularism, after the Sixteenth Lok Sabha is constituted in 2014.

Illegal Migration from Bangladesh[8]

Insistence on excessive secrecy in all matters has been the hallmark of governance in India, irrespective of which political party is in power, whether at the Centre or in the states. It may be pertinent to recall what Justice K. K. Mathew, quoting Justice Polak, stated in a Supreme Court case (1979, 3 SCC), 'The secrecy system has become much less a means by which government protects national security than a means by which government safeguards its reputation, dissembles its purpose, buries its mistakes, manipulates its citizens, maximises its power and corrupts itself.' Illegal migration from Bangladesh is one issue which brings out how true these perceptive observations are. Due to the conspiracy of silence by almost all political parties in varying degrees, the issue, in spite of its serious social, political, economic, security and law and order implications has not been permitted to come on the national agenda. If at all, it is viewed as a regional problem affecting the northeast and a few states.

In analysing illegal migration from Bangladesh, it is necessary to take note of a few salient factors. The fact that there was considerable migration in Assam from erstwhile East Bengal when it was a part of India, is important but cannot be a justification for the continuance of the same trend after Independence. Illegal migration from East Pakistan and later Bangladesh must be seen in the radically changed context of the Partition of the country on the basis of the tenuous, totally mischievous and ill-conceived two-nation theory. Those in Bangladesh who are now advocating the specious concept of *lebensraum* or living space ought to have paused and pondered on it before clamouring for the creation of Pakistan. The fact that the Muslim League was making demands for other contiguous districts/parts of districts of Assam, Bengal and Bihar as a part of East Pakistan can also hardly be lost sight of. The process of Islamization being continued through illegal migration cannot be disassociated from this tragic history of the Partition of the country. The mischievous ploy adopted by sham 'secular' political parties in India to give a communal colour to the question, therefore, needs to be exposed as nothing less than anti-national.

There have been repeated allegations over the years that successive Congress governments in Assam had actively encouraged migration from Bangladesh. The record of the CPI(M) government in West Bengal has been no better. Some political parties have unabashedly stood in the way of deleting names of illegal migrants from voters' lists. Not too long ago, there was practically a revolt in the Assam Cabinet over the deletion of such names. Unfortunately even the BJP, the so-called fascist Hindu party, did not have the courage to take a principled stand on the concerned issues when it came to power at the Centre. This reluctance was amply evident from a number of significant pointers. **First**, though the Task Force on Border Management appointed by the NDA government, of which I was the chairman, had made a recommendation that its report should be published to make people aware of the critical issues pertaining to the management of international borders, the report was not made public. **Second**, the government failed to issue an ordinance to repeal the Illegal Migrants (Determination by Tribunals) (IMDT) Act, which was yet another major recommendation of the task force. In fact, the BJP, which was the main constituent of the government, had itself repeatedly advocated the repeal of the act when it was in opposition. Presumably this was only political rhetoric. It is true that the NDA government did not have a majority in the Rajya Sabha. But as was done in the case of enacting POTA, a joint session of both the Houses could have been called to approve the repeal of the IMDT Act. The security implications of IMDT Act were no less significant than in the case of POTA. But, perhaps, the BJP too was worried about the combined impact of enacting POTA and the repeal of the

IMDT Act on Muslims. How is the BJP different then from the Congress and the other sham 'secular' political parties? **Third**, the concentration of madrasas and mosques, set up with substantial foreign funding in border areas whose demographic composition has undergone a radical change, is well documented. The NDA government failed to take any action to have this proliferation brought under the close scrutiny of the concerned state and central agencies. No new law was required to be passed for the purpose. FCRA, which has been rampantly misused to harass NGOs, has remained a dead letter so far as foreign funding for spreading fundamentalist, religious and terrorist ideology is concerned. It is true that most of these foreign funds are received through hawala transactions but a close watch on such transactions through various agencies could have at least curtailed the flow to some extent. As recommended by the Task Force on Border Management, it could have been made mandatory that approval of district authorities would be necessary before establishing any places of worship or madrasas in the border belt of about 10 kilometres. The mainstreaming of madrasas and having state level boards to oversee their activities, at least in so far as border areas are concerned, is long overdue. But due to apprehensions about inviting the ire of Muslims, political parties are reluctant to even talk of such matters, leave aside taking any action on them. Needless to say, the process of the Arabization of Muslims is a factor which can be overlooked only at the peril of national security.

Major recommendations of the task force on the management of the Bangladesh border, which were accepted by the Group of Ministers (GoM) of the NDA government, have remained without any energetic and time-bound actions though over a decade has elapsed (Government of India 2001). The first was the adoption of the principle of 'one border one Force'. This was meant to make the concerned force, whether it be the Border Security Force (BSF), the Indo Tibetan Border Police (ITBP) or Assam Rifles, squarely responsible and accountable for its actions and inactions. Currently, since more than one force is operating in the same area, there is often a tendency to pass the buck from one to the other. The second related recommendation, which too had been accepted by GoM, was to lay down clear and unambiguous criteria for judging the performance of each force. This would enable, for example, making an assessment as to how effective the BSF has been in preventing illegal migration from across the border. The task force had recommended distinguishing between the border guarding forces which are to be used exclusively for deployment on the border and the other paramilitary and police forces, such as the CRPF, RPF and the CISF, which are to be used for internal security duties. The task force had recommended a clear-cut policy announcement that border guarding forces will not be withdrawn from the border, except in exceptional circumstances and within a defined period, of say five years, steps will be taken to adequately augment the strength of the state and central police forces for internal security duties. There is no evidence to show that such a time-bound action programme is being implemented by the Centre with any firm public commitment. Yet another important recommendation was to have a no-man's land all along the border which can be fully sanitized. Currently, the most unnatural, man-made border between India and Bangladesh, drawn by Radcliff, sitting in his office in just a few weeks, often runs through houses and divides them between the two countries. The cultivation of land is right up to the border with neighbours often tilling each other's land, whether they are Bangladeshi or Indian. In such a situation, it is impossible to stop illegal migration and border-crossing in any sense of the term.

Unfortunately, there is no political will to implement this recommendation. Yet another recommendation was that, due to the peculiar geographical features and reverine conditions, border fencing on several stretches of the Bangladesh border can hardly be effective in preventing illegal migration. While in some areas border fencing will be effective, in some others it is a futile and wasteful expenditure and to rely on such fencing will be foolhardy. It is not clear what steps are being taken to review the present policy and guard against such contingencies by other suitable measures. The task force had made a strong recommendation to substantially augment the water wing of the BSF to enable it to address the problem effectively. The GoM had concurred but there is no indication of concrete steps taken so far. These are only a few illustrative examples of how policies have continued to drift over the years, including during the NDA regime in Delhi. Looking to the pathological hatred of the constituents of the UPA government for its predecessor, it will be a surprise if any of the major decisions of the NDA government on this subject will be followed up vigorously.

A reference may be made to the efforts I had made in my capacity as union Home Secretary, way back in 1992, to bring this issue to the forefront and how they failed to make any headway. On 24 March 1992 I convened the first ever meeting of the chief secretaries from the concerned states and the Union Territory of Delhi to discuss a package of measures which could be adopted on an all-India basis to deal with the overwhelming problem of illegal migration. It came as a surprise to me that even at the official level there was reluctance on the part of some states, particularly West Bengal and Bihar, to deal with the problem firmly. In spite of this, I pursued the matter further and persuaded the union Home Minister to convene a meeting. Accordingly, a meeting of the chief ministers was held on 28 September 1992. The background note and the agenda prepared for the meeting were given wide publicity to create national awareness about the issues. The proposed programme of action included, among others, strengthening and modernizing BSF, constructing border roads and fencing, strengthening of the Prevention of Infiltration of Foreigners (PIF) scheme and the Mobile Task Force (MTF) scheme, issuing identity cards to bonafide residents in border areas, organizing a campaign from time to time for creating public awareness about the problem, keeping a close watch on and plugging the avenues which provide protection to illegal migrants and ensuring punitive action thereon, safeguards against easy access to certain unintended benefits to illegal migrants, safeguards against the admission of illegal migrants or their wards into educational institutions, safeguards against their acquisition of immovable property, safeguards against inclusion of their names in the voters' list, strict enforcement of protected area/restricted area orders, identifying villages prone to influx of illegal migrants, administrative and legal safeguards against employment of illegal migrants and enacting a central legislation for issuing identity cards.

The major features of the proposed legislation were also circulated to state governments for their comments. The background note emphasized that 'the threat posed by the illegal migrants to the economy and socio-cultural and political fabric of the country requires a "multi-pronged strategy". It is evident that the problem of illegal migration needs to be tackled by formulating an effective strategy jointly by the central and the state governments.' It can be seen that the comprehensive proposals placed before the chief ministers' meeting were unexceptional and should have been readily endorsed by them. But I was in for a surprise. The chief ministers of West Bengal and Bihar were opposed to any such action plan being adopted at the meeting. The draft of the press note endorsing the plan, which was proposed to be issued, did not meet with their approval. A great deal of persuasion was required on the part of the union Home Minister to make them agree to the issue of the press note. He had to repeatedly urge that if a consensus on the subject was not arrived at, it would convey a very wrong message to the country on this very vital subject and weaken whatever efforts were being made at the time to contain the problem. Finally, reluctantly, the press communiqué was agreed upon for release but it was clear that the programme of action adopted at the meeting was for public consumption and would remain on paper. Nothing has changed over the years since then and now the figure of illegal migrants from Bangladesh should be over 20 million.

As can be seen, this programme of action discussed back in 1992 included all the important elements that are crucial for tackling the problem of illegal migration. But, for want of political will, there has been no progress with respect to any one of them so far. Neither has there been the pressure of public opinion which could have forced the governments to take the necessary steps. This is borne out by yet another significant pointer. The urgency of instituting a scheme for issuing identity cards to all bonafide residents has been talked about ever since Independence. A pilot scheme for issuing such cards was first sanctioned by the central government in 1986 for selected areas in the states of Gujarat and Rajasthan. Significantly, the northeastern states were not considered vulnerable enough to be covered in the pilot scheme. The objectives of the pilot scheme were to register bonafide residents, collect reliable information regarding the status of the residents and to check the movement of visitors staying for over 30 days in the areas covered under the scheme. Subsequently, the states of Punjab and J&K also decided to implement the scheme in their border areas. The scheme was reviewed by the Committee of Secretaries in 1990 when it was decided to extend it to the border areas of all border states, in the first instance.

Accordingly, the scheme was sanctioned for the border areas in Assam, Mizoram and Tripura in March 1991. The fact that illegal migration has continued unabated in spite of this scheme shows that it has remained on paper. MHA has got at least two comprehensive studies done by reputed institutions to examine the feasibility and workability of the implementation of the scheme on an all-India basis. In spite of this, the central legislation for issuing identity cards has not made any headway. It must be underlined that the *Aadhar* card is not a substitute for this purpose. In fact, with the criterion of just the residence for issue of a *Aadhar* card, it will now be impossible to identify and take action against illegal migrants. The basic requirement for issuing *Aadhar* cards ought to have been the ascertainment of citizenship. It is amazing to see how this major lacuna has been lost sight of by MHA and other concerned ministries, before concurring with the proposal. Political parties have also not raised this point. It may also be relevant to note that the National Identity Authority of India Bill, 2010 to give statutory backing to *Aadhar* has been pending for the last three years due to lack of consensus among political parties on the subject. However, the scheme is being implemented uninterruptedly by spending thousands of crores of rupees on it each year. This is a travesty of parliamentary democracy. No political party objected to this nor has it insisted on the bill being passed expeditiously. If such a legislation had been in force, infructuous expenditure on schemes initiated by various authorities for issuing identity cards such as voters' identity cards by the Election Commission of India, permanent account number (PAN) by the income tax department and market participant and investor identification number (MAPIN) by SEBI (which has been held in abeyance pending further examination) could have been avoided.

Similarly, it is sad to see the neglect with respect to preparing a register of citizens. This scheme too has come up for discussion from time to time since Independence but there has been no political will to implement it. If action had been taken on both these issues, India would not have found itself as helpless and vulnerable as at present. This shows the lack of foresight and resolve on the part of the political leadership even in matters concerning national security.

A PIL praying for scrapping of the IMDT Act, which by any standards was a monstrosity and clearly undermined the interests of the country, could come up for final decision in the Supreme Court after a long delay of nearly five years. It is difficult to believe that such an ill-conceived and totally counter-productive legislation was a part of the Assam Accord which was supposed to address the problems faced by that state. This was yet another legislation which was passed by Parliament without any scrutiny or application of mind on the basis of a brute majority of the ruling political party and is an eloquent commentary on its capability to function as the highest law-making forum in the country. The fact that this law could remain on statute books for over two decades speaks volumes of the efficacy of the democratic processes and institutions in the country. The affidavits filed by the successive state and central governments too show how certain political parties have continued to woo Muslims blatantly at the cost of national interest.

In spite of repeated representations over the years, Congress governments failed to take action to have the IMDT (Illegal Migrants Determination by Tribunals) Act repealed. Finally, the matter was raised before the Supreme Court through a PIL (*Sarbananda Sonoval v. Union of India and another* [2005] 5 SCC 665) which led to the declaration of the IMDT Act as unconstitutional on 13 July 2005. The court's stinging observations are worth noting, 'The report of the Governor [of Assam], the affidavits and the other material on record show that millions of Bangladeshi nationals have crossed the international border and have occupied vast tracts of land. Their willingness to work at low wages has deprived Indian citizens and specifically people in Assam of employment opportunities and led to insurgency in Assam.' The court said that the presence of Bangladeshis in such large numbers 'has changed the demographic character of that region and the local people of Assam have been reduced to the status of minority in certain districts.' It added, 'this being the situation, there can be no manner of doubt that the state of Assam is facing external aggression and internal disturbance on account of large-scale immigration of Bangladeshi nationals...The impact is such that it not only affects the state of Assam, but also affects its sister states like Arunachal Pradesh, Meghalaya, Nagaland.' The court underlined that the foremost duty of the central government under Article 355 is to defend the borders of the country, prevent any trespass and make life of citizens safe and secure. The court directed that 'the provisions of the IMDT Act and the Rules made thereunder clearly negate the constitutional mandate contained in Article 355...[and] being wholly unconstitutional are struck down.' Even thereafter, the efforts of the UPA government to continue the special tribunals under the IMDT Act, rather than bringing all such cases under the Foreigners Act, have confirmed public perception that the 'secular' parties are prepared to compromise even national security in the interest of their vote bank politics. Finally, this matter too had to be taken to the Supreme Court in yet another PIL and the court declared these tribunals illegal. The final decision of the Apex Court scrapping the IMDT Act is a matter of some satisfaction but, looking to the lack of commitment by political parties to address the issue, one wonders whether this by itself will take us far.

It will be recalled that in 1997–98 the Shiv Sena-BJP coalition government in Maharashtra took up a programme to identify Bangladeshi nationals in Mumbai and to have them deported. All necessary legal procedures under the Foreigners Act were followed, cases were instituted in courts and, thereafter, with the orders of the courts, action to proceed with the deportation of the illegal migrants was taken. When the Maharashtra police escorted the foreigners to Kolkata on way to the Bangladesh border, they were attacked by hooligans and had to face demonstrations by left-leaning and so-called 'secular' political parties. The West Bengal police declined to give any help. There was a clamour in the 'secular' media against the Government of Maharashtra's move to identify and deport illegal migrants. Finally, the illegal migrants could not even be taken up to the Bangladesh border and they eventually returned to Mumbai to live happily ever after! This clearly shows that unless there is public awareness about the gravity of the issue, there is hardly any possibility of change in the present stance of political parties.

Another instance was of the circular re-issued by MHA, a few years after it was originally issued, making it obligatory on a person with whom a foreigner may be staying, to inform the police if the foreigner over-stayed beyond the visa period. These unexceptional instructions too had to be withdrawn due to clamour in the English media. And this at a time when several other countries have passed draconian laws to meet the threats posed to their national security. Though India has been a prime target of terrorist violence since 1990, there is total public apathy and disdain for matters concerning the security of the country.

It is a matter of regret that India has failed to raise the issue of illegal migration with the Government of Bangladesh in a serious and concerted manner over all these years. At one stage, it was believed that the settlement of the *Tin Bigha* question will create the proper climate for finding a solution to this long standing issue. This has proved futile. Thereafter, it was believed that the settlement of sharing of Ganga waters will provide the opportunity to bring up this issue for an amicable bilateral resolution. This too has proved to be a non-starter. In fact, during his visit to Dhaka for these negotiations, the then External Affairs Minister, I. K. Gujral, had stated that New Delhi had no plans to link water-sharing with any other outstanding issues between the two countries. On its part, the Government of Bangladesh has taken the extreme position that the problem of illegal migration is India's own creation and there is no migration from that country at all! Bangladesh Rifles (BDR), which is a counterpart of the BSF, has been most callous, unreasonable and uncooperative in its actions. There have been frequent instances of firing by BDR on the border. Against this background, it is difficult to believe that soon after the creation of Bangladesh an agreement was entered into by India and Bangladesh which envisaged close cooperation between the BSF and BDR, including joint operations by the two forces, joint border posts and so on. These are the new realities of the relationship between India and Bangladesh. But it will be impossible to find any long-term and lasting solution to the problem of illegal migration without active cooperation and help from the Bangladesh government.

Illegal migration from Bangladesh is no longer a regional problem and it cannot be ignored. The migrants have now spread into several states and in distant places such as Rajasthan, Delhi, Madhya Pradesh, Maharashtra and so on. They have become so much a part of the citizenry of the country that one of them was, in fact, appointed as a Special Executive Magistrate in Mumbai! They exert considerable influence on election results not only in several constituencies in Assam, West Bengal and Bihar but also in Delhi and some other states.

How to deal with millions of these illegal migrants is a question to which there are no easy answers, particularly if political parties in India consider protection of Bangladeshi migrant Muslims imperative for nursing their Muslim vote banks. Taking recourse to legal action under the Foreigners Act and putting up and pursuing cases against millions of illegal migrants in courts will be next to impossible. The easy way out, which is effectively being advocated by a number of political parties, is regularizing their stay even though this will encourage more and more Bangladeshis to infiltrate into India. And there will be reception committees of 'secular' political parties at the border to receive them with open arms! Sooner rather than later, pressures will build to give them *Aadhar* cards, if not Indian citizenship as well. A reference may be made in this context to the proliferation of slums in metropolitan cities such as Delhi and Mumbai and other large urban conglomerations. The regularization of hutments, time and again, has encouraged more people to flock to the cities and encroach on public and private lands with impunity. Since such slums are vote banks, whenever there is an election to the State Legislature and Parliament, the year for regularizing the hutments is brought forward. This whole process has given rise to a new mafia which has made millions of rupees by encroaching on vacant lands and public places with the active partnership of concerned public functionaries and selling the plots for construction of hutments. The same thing will happen once we publicly adopt the policy of regularizing the stay of illegal migrants. There is, therefore, no alternative to reversing the flow of illegal migrants and sending them back. But the question is whether India is prepared to adopt such a firm policy. If past experience is any guide, the unequivocal answer is No.

Illegal migration is due to both pull and push factors. Foremost among these are economic factors. Better employment opportunities in India act as a pull factor while poverty, subsistence living and ravages caused by floods and other natural calamities in Bangladesh act as push factors. This has to be accepted as a ground reality. In the coming years, these factors will undoubtedly intensify. It must also be accepted that there are several menial, agricultural and other jobs which Indian citizens are reluctant to do. The emoluments on which Bangladeshi migrants (and illegal migrants in particular) are prepared to work are also much less than what Indians want. Being unorganized, they can be exploited by their employers much more easily than Indian labour. All these factors must not be lost sight of in evolving a future policy. One way to deal with these ground realities is by instituting a scheme of work permits by which Bangladeshi migrants can be permitted to work in India for a specified period. The Task Force on Border Management had recommended adopting such a policy. The other step, to which a reference was made earlier, will be enacting a law prohibiting employment of a Bangladeshi, other than one who has a work permit. Such laws are in operation in a number of western countries and even in the Middle East. This suggestion was a part of the package proposed for the meeting of the chief ministers convened by the union Home Minister way back in 1992. Unfortunately, as in the case of several other suggestions, this too has remained without any action.

Knowledgeable observers of the scene have expressed fears that it will not be surprising if the future Chief Minister of Assam is an illegal migrant. The Indian Constitution does not bar a person of foreign origin from holding even the highest constitutional position in the country once he acquires citizenship. As things stand, anyone who enters India from Bangladesh, even illegally, becomes an Indian citizen in no time. And with national leaders like Ram Vilas Paswan who, after the elections to the Bihar Assembly in early 2005, was prepared for any compromise in the formation of a ministry if the Chief Minister was to be a Muslim, this day may not be far. In any case, most present incumbents of high political offices in the country are taking the same stand on illegal migration as a Chief Minister, or for that matter a Prime Minister drawn from the ranks of illegal migrants would take!

This discussion shows that it will be impossible to find a lasting solution to this gigantic problem unless pressure of public opinion is built to exert influence on political parties to address the underlying issues with urgency and a firm commitment. This will call for concerted action by civil society including various pressure groups, NGOs, the print and electronic media and intellectuals and influential persons who are fearless and committed enough to lend their names to this national cause. The present tendency to stigmatize anyone who speaks on this subject with some fervour and earnestness, as communal and a Hindu fascist has been largely responsible for the neglect of this subject. It is time that persons from all walks of life, primarily Indian Muslims, come forward to espouse this cause. This will make a huge difference to the perceptions and attitudes of political parties. The first step in this direction should be insisting on the central government bringing out a white paper on the subject for national debate and discussion.

Mounting Arrears in Courts

Universally, speedy justice is considered to be the hallmark of good governance. India fails this test now as it did at any point since Independence. In his letter dated 15 January 1980 to Indira Gandhi on her taking over as the Prime Minister, Justice P. N. Bhagwati lamented, 'I also wish to bring to your notice that the judicial system in our country is in a state of utter collapse...The Supreme Court is also reeling under the weight of arrears...The position is almost desperate and yet there does not seem to be any sense of urgency in the Court' (Shourie 1983: 304). Similar sentiments were expressed by CJI, P. Sathasivam, in August 2013, who lamented on the 'growing crisis' in the judiciary, manifested by ever-increasing pendency, consequent delays in the justice delivery system and a steady decline in the reputation of the judiciary as also of the legal profession (*IE*, 18 August 2013). This, once again, underscores the title of this book.

The Parliamentary Standing Committee (2001) expressed serious concerns about the long pendency of cases in various courts:

> The committee is particularly perturbed to note that cases are pending for over 50 years, 40 years, and 30 years in certain high courts. As per the data furnished by the government, M.P. High Court has a case pending since 1950, Patna High Court has a case pending since 1951, Rajasthan since 1956, Kolkata since 1955. The committee is equally disturbed to note that over 5 lakh cases are pending in the high courts for over 10 years. And the number of cases pending for 7–10 years are also as high as over 3 lakh...The High Courts have become the slowest layer in the judicial process...After the judgment of the Supreme Court in 1993, the government is bereft of a role in initiating the process of filling up of the vacancies. The maximum the government can do is to address letters to the chief minister of the state and the chief justices of the high courts, from time to time requesting them to make their recommendations for appointments of judges in the high courts to fill up vacancies expeditiously. There appears to be a widespread non-observance of any strict time frame at different levels in respect of filling up vacancies...The committee is of the view that the delays in judicial appointments is a matter of serious public concern. The committee is duty bound to point out that the failure to fill judicial vacancies promptly and punctually cannot be shielded or defended in the name of judicial independence (Parliament of India 2001: 7, 8,11,12).

Surprisingly, the union Law Minister, while speaking in the Rajya Sabha on 24 August 2001 observed that, 'the problem at the lower court level was not so grave. The figure of 2 crore [of arrears] was static. At least the figure is not increasing. The filing in 12,000 district courts all over the country and the disposal every year is practically the same.' A small consolation indeed.

As the Mid-Term Appraisal of the Tenth Five Year Plan has rightly stated, 'The process of delivery of justice to the common man is very long and tortuous. The long list of pending cases in courts, frequent adjournments, dilatory tactics by counsels and the extortive practice of charging the clients on per court hearing/ per diem basis and not on outcome basis are resulting in interminable litigation and unacceptable delays in adjudication' (Government of India 2005: 494).

With pendency of over 3 crore cases, decisions in court cases take not just years but decades. In fact, one is considered lucky if one gets a decision within one's lifetime. By comparison, the pendency of cases was just 1.64 lakh in 1957. The total pendency of cases in 1985 was 1.15 crore, comprising 1.49 lakh cases in the Supreme Court, 11.09 lakh in the high courts and 1.02 crore in the district and subordinate courts. By 1985, the disposal of cases was not keeping pace even with the institutions, leave aside reducing the pendency. The number of laws has increased 20 times since Independence. The World Bank has underlined that 'many of the institutions that support markets are publicly provided. The ability of the state to provide these institutions is therefore an important determinant of how well individuals behave in markets and how well markets function. Successful provision of such institutions is often referred to as good governance. The judicial system plays an important role in the development of the market economies' (The World Bank 2002: 120). Judged on this basis, India once again fails miserably.

One would have expected a high-level commission such as the NCRWC (2002) to go in-depth into the complex field of judicial administration in the country, particularly since a majority of its members were former judges of superior courts or jurists. NCRWC's report is, however, very disappointing on this score (Godbole 2002: 4008). Subhash C. Kashyap, who was a member of the NCRWC and Chairman of its Drafting and Editorial Committee, observed in his note of dissent, 'The chapter 7 of the report is titled "The Judiciary". This chapter particularly is seriously flawed and distorted. The much needed judicial reform issues have not even been touched or these got deleted in the final draft' (Government of India: 261, para viii).

After the onset of globalization, how the outside world looks upon a country has become more important than how those who live in it do. In the Gulshan Kumar murder case, the government was unable to get the accused, Nadeem, extradited from England because sufficient doubt was cast on whether, being a Muslim, he would be able to get justice in India! A similar plea was made on behalf of Abu Salem in a Portuguese court. However, since Salem was involved in a terrorist act, as opposed to Nadeem who was a suspect in a murder case, his plea was not upheld. The pressure from the United States on Portugal was also responsible for his eventual extradition. In commercial disputes, different considerations come into play. It is argued that unless such disputes get decided in the courts of law expeditiously, a country may not be considered an attractive destination for foreign investments. As was reported in *The Hindu* (3 October 2003), 'On September 13, 2003, a dramatic confrontation was reported. B. N. Kirpal, former Chief Justice of India, offered expert testimony for a Japanese company that its case should be heard in New York and not Delhi. On the other side was A. M. Ahmadi, another former CJI, who refuted Mr. Kirpal's depressing but accurate prediction that the case in India would take twenty years, to counter-predict that a case in Delhi would take one year. The former chief justices of India sparred with each other in a foreign jurisdiction to denigrate or defend India's justice system.'

Citing the above ICICI Bank case in the New York court, the Law Commission stressed the need to 'negate' the growing trend of judgments from US and UK courts generalizing that all cases take over 20 years for disposal in India. The Law Commission has proposed that a commercial division be set up in each High Court to deal exclusively with contracts, letters of credit, bank guarantees and such other business cases involving amounts in excess of Rs 5 crore.[9] Transparency International's Global Corruption Report (2007), which deals with the graft in judiciary in 32 countries, has attributed the bribes paid to the lower judicial officers in India for the huge backlog of cases. Nowhere else in the world perhaps is the pendency of cases as astronomical. However, the subject is not on the radar of policymakers in the real sense of the term, as can be seen from a recent random news item (*IE*, 30 May 2013) that a 95-year-old woman was awarded three-year rigorous imprisonment and a fine of Rs 20,000 by a court in Jaipur for encroaching on a plot of land belonging to the state government. This was for a crime committed by her at the age of 50 years! This in spite of the fact that the Supreme Court has recognized speedy trial of an accused as his fundamental right.

The subject of pendency of cases is discussed in a routine manner in the periodical meetings of chief ministers, law ministers, chief justices of high courts and other concerned ministers called by the Ministry of Law and addressed by the CJI, Prime Minister and at times even the President of India. But the actual impact thereof has been negligible.

Action has been taken to set up fast track courts, following the recommendation of the Eleventh Finance Commission a few years ago. But several states have been tardy in providing funds and taking expeditious follow up action. In the ultimate analysis, there is no alternative to increasing the number of judges to deal with the pending cases. The number of judges per million population in India is just 10.5, as compared with 41.6 in Australia, 75.2 in Canada, 50.9 in England and 107 in the US. As per the Justice Department's calculation, an additional 15,824 judges will be required if the pending cases in lower courts are to be cleared in one year...The additional number of judges which may be required to clear the backlog of cases in a period of seven years is say 1,400; in a period of five years 2,500; and in a period of three years 4,600. The committee has suggested that the aim should be to clear the arrears within three to four years, which is quite reasonable. As for the High Courts, the additional strength of judges to be added in high courts to liquidate total pendency of cases year-wise is: (i) in one year 974; (ii) in two years 488; and (iii) in three years 325 (Parliament of India 2001: 13, 15). Under the Centrally Sponsored Scheme for infrastructural development of the judiciary, the expenditure is to be shared between the Centre and the state on 50:50 basis. But the states are reluctant to bear the financial burden. This makes no sense. As compared to the huge expenditure incurred by the Centre and the states on a number of other schemes and programmes, the projected expenditure on increasing the number of courts and providing the requisite infrastructure will be negligible. But there is no political will to recognize this, let alone to act on it.

The other single biggest hurdle in reducing the pendency of cases is the opposition by the vested interests of advocates. The proposal to operate the courts in two shifts to enable more intensive use of the existing infrastructure has been opposed in some places by advocates. The amendments to the Civil Procedure Code intended to do away with dilatory procedures met with stiff opposition from advocates and led to a nationwide strike in 2000. As the *Economic Times* commented editorially, 'the lawyers themselves represent the problem [of judicial delays] and to allow them to pretend that they are the solution is a travesty...The civil cases drag on for 20 years on average, and at the current speed of disposal, it will take 324 years to clear the backlog of cases...The lawyers, of course, want to obstruct rather than advance justice' (*The ET*, 28 February 2000).

In an unusual protest, lawyers in the Madhya Pradesh High Court struck work on 13 July 2013 to protest against 'black sheep' who misuse their proximity to judges to guarantee favourable judgments for their clients. The High Court bar association claimed that it had identified 36 such lawyers as well as marked out 360 touts on the High Court premises. Most of these lawyers are either related to retired judges, worked as their juniors or were associated with them in some ways. In as many as 175 cases, clients wanted to change their advocates because the 'black sheep' had promised them guaranteed justice (*IE*, 14 July 2013). In all this, the most crucial stakeholder, namely, the common litigant, is a hapless and helpless bystander since he is not organized.

A number of committees, commissions and legal luminaries have suggested ways in which the arrears of court cases can be reduced. The Law Commission had also gone into this question. K. Subba Rao, former CJI, has, *inter alia*, suggested a number of steps, including village courts should be constituted with limited jurisdiction to dispose of small civil and criminal cases; there should be only one right to appeal to every aggrieved party on the decision of the original court; no person shall have a right to approach the Supreme Court by way of an appeal or petition in any matter—civil, criminal, or otherwise—but the court shall have discretionary power to entertain an appeal or petition against an order or judgment of a court, tribunal or authority. This will reduce the workload of the Supreme Court and enable it to entertain only matters of importance and decide them by the entire court (Rao 1973: 14). The Mid-Term Appraisal of the Tenth Five Year Plan cited earlier also suggested moving from a two appeal system to a single appeal system to give finality to judicial pronouncements. It also laid emphasis on improving the counsel-client relationship and suggested that the counsel fee payment system needs to be brought under some principled regulation to make the judicial process more client-friendly, creating an incentive for counsels to ensure early delivery of decisions. In sessions cases, this can be done by not allowing adjournments during sessions trial. In civil cases, the bar council or any other appropriate body should regulate the counsel remuneration system on an outcome basis (Government of India 2005: 494). The Approach Paper to the Eleventh Five Year Plan has rightly underlined that 'Quick and inexpensive dispensation of justice is an aspect of good governance which is of fundamental importance in a successful civil society...Fundamental reforms are needed to give justice two attributes: speed and affordability' (Government of India 2006: 7). Clearly, the wheel does not need to be reinvented. But there are no indications of any perceptible change in the situation in the foreseeable future.

Ninth Schedule: Fraud on the Constitution

Article 31B, which is the gross abuse of the power of amendment of the Constitution by Parliament and makes a mockery of the protection of fundamental rights guaranteed by the Constitution, reads as follows:

> Without prejudice to the generality of the provisions contained in Article 31A, none of the acts and regulations specified in the Ninth Schedule nor any of the provisions thereof shall be deemed to be void, or ever to have become void, on the ground that such act, regulation or provision is inconsistent with, or takes away or abridges any of the rights conferred by, any provisions of this Part, and notwithstanding any judgment, decree or order of any court or tribunal to the contrary, each of the said acts and regulations shall, subject to the power of any competent legislature to repeal or amend it, continue in force.

The acquiescence by the Supreme Court for years together in this grossly arbitrary provision, which was destructive of the rule of law, is difficult to fathom. The history of the Supreme Court can be divided into three phases: the phase of accommodation, co-terminus with the Jawaharlal Nehru era; the confrontation phase coinciding with the Indira Gandhi regime; and the phase of unchallenged supremacy thereafter.

The cumulative inclusion of 284 acts in the Ninth Schedule was the last straw! The acts included certain central and state enactments, the implementation of which had been held up by pending court cases. Hidayatullah has commented that 'then this process stopped because the Ninth Schedule threatened to become longer than the Constitution' (Hidayatullah 1983: 158). It is difficult to believe that this monstrosity commenced from 1951, the very first year following the adoption of the Constitution (Provisional Parliament Debates 1951: Cols. 8814–9089).

Baldev Singh has rightly pointed out that Articles 13 and 31B in Part III of the Constitution may appear to be paradoxical to any student of Indian constitutional law. The former forbids the state to make any law which takes away the rights of individuals and declares that any law in contravention of this clause shall, to the extent of contravention, be void. In contrast, Article 31B says that none of the acts and regulations specified in the Ninth Schedule nor any of the provisions thereof shall be deemed to be void, or ever to have become void, on the ground that such act, regulation or provision is inconsistent with, or takes away or abridges any of the rights conferred by any provisions of this Part (Singh 1995: 457–75).

Jawaharlal Nehru, while moving this unusual provision as a part of the very first amendment to the Constitution, stated in the Provisional Parliament, 'This Bill is not a very complicated one; nor is it a big one. Nevertheless, I need hardly point out that it is of intrinsic and great importance.' The Schedule, at the time of its incorporation in the Constitution, comprised only 13 acts, mostly agrarian. Nehru had said that 'every single measure included in this Schedule was carefully considered by our President and certified by him.' In his speech Nehru stated, 'Some Hon members have given notice of amendments to add other laws to the Ninth Schedule. I would beg of them not to press this matter. It is not with any great satisfaction or pleasure that we have produced this *long* schedule. We do not wish to add to it for two reasons. One is that the schedule consists of a particular type of legislation generally speaking and another type should not come in. Secondly, every single measure was carefully considered.' The amendment was not passed in a hurry. It was deliberated on in the select committee. The debate in the House lasted 6–7 days. The bill met with stiff opposition from the very thin ranks of the opposition parties in the House. B. R. Ambedkar, Minister of Law, supported the amendment on the basis of very weak logic, 'Prima facie it was an unusual procedure, but looked at from the point of view of principles on which those laws were made, to acquire estates and neither the principle of compensation nor the principle of discrimination should stand in the way of validity of it. Therefore, sentimentally there might be objection, but from the practical point of view there should not be any objection to declare such laws valid [because the Acts included in the schedule were not *ultra vires*].' Each one of these contentions is questionable. But finally the bill was passed with 238 *ayes* and 7 *nays*.

The 'device' of the Ninth Schedule, described as such in the Objects and Reasons to the Thirty-Ninth Amendment Act, was meant to meet the political urgency of abolition of zamindari but the medicine turned out to be worse than the disease. Its constitutional validity was upheld in *Sankari Prasad Singh v. Union of India* (1952/SCR 89) as well as *Sajjan Singh v. State of Rajasthan* (1965/SCR 933). However, one judge, Justice J. R. Mudholkar said, '*It is also a matter for consideration whether making a change in a basic feature of the Constitution can be regarded merely as an amendment or would it be, in effect rewriting a part of the Constitution; and if the latter, it would be within the purview of the article 368?*' which provides for an amendment to the Constitution (Noorani 2007: 731–32).

Initially, only tenancy laws and zamindari abolition laws were expected to be put in this Schedule but later other laws and even acts which had been struck down by courts as invalid were included. Highly controversial and draconian laws such as the maintenance of internal security act, national security act, prevention of publication of objectionable matter act, urban land (ceiling and regulation) act, amendment to RPA, insurance act, reservation laws of some states and so on were given protection against legal challenge by including them in the Ninth Schedule. Over the years, as many as 284 acts have been included in the Ninth Schedule. The government was also contemplating putting the Delhi Laws (Special Provisions) Act, 2006, pertaining to the sealing and demolition drive in the Ninth Schedule. It was only after the Supreme Court reacted sharply that the idea was dropped.

Justice Mehr Chand Mahajan has stated:

What seemed to some of us a dangerous precedent lay rather in the fact that the first amendment protected certain specified statutes passed by various state legislatures against attack for unconstitutionality before the court. Of course Indian Parliament has not gone—thanks to the Constitution itself—to the lengths to which the U.S. Congress had once proceeded when it had taken a case already before the court away from it! As the protected statutes mostly concerned existing rights in land which government was modifying and in some states even extinguishing, this provision seemed to some of us to be a sad failure on the part of the legislative draftsmen in clothing the intentions of the legislature in proper statutory form! (Mahajan 1963: 200).

However, as later experience showed, the initial intentions were quickly thrown overboard and this constitutional monstrosity became uglier and uglier as the years passed. It was as far back as 1972 that Justice J. C. Shah had stated, 'It is no secret that before the Constitution (Seventeenth Amendment) was moved in the Parliament, there was a clamour from the states to include in the Ninth Schedule a large number of Acts—literally hundreds of Acts...Enactment of

Article 31B and the Ninth Schedule constitutes a serious encroachment upon the rule of law' (Shah 1972: 52–53).

Justice Hidayatullah has stated:

Article 31 (C) which schedules certain acts of legislatures to protect them against the Constitution, is not a valid exercise of the power to amend the Constitution. Such a power is not an amendment of the Constitution but a 'frustration' of the Constitution. Next, that a Constitution cannot be amended retrospectively, except to correct a slip. Each Parliament speaks for itself, and while it is in office, the Constitution stands as made by it. A new Parliament can change the Constitution but cannot sit in the seat of the other Parliament and change the Constitution from a date when it was not in the saddle. We have attempted to change the Constitution from 26th January 1950, as if the Parliament making the change was sitting in the Constituent Assembly. In *Golaknath* case, I had summed this up by saying: Constitution is not a sonnet written on water. A Constitution continues unimpaired till it is changed, but it is changed only from the date when the change takes place and not earlier. In America, prohibition was once introduced and then later withdrawn; but both the articles are found in the Constitution. Our Parliament would have erased the earlier article as if it was never enacted...I had accepted the first amendment because it was acquiesced in for a long time and had become a part of our Constitution (Hidayatullah 1979: viii, 11).

It is surprising that in spite of the overwhelming view of a number of legal luminaries, the amendment has been held to be valid time and again by the Supreme Court. This was clearly the accommodation phase in the history of the Apex Court. In the *Shankari Prasad* case (AIR 1951 SC 458), Justice Patanjali Sastri, speaking on behalf of the court, held that article 31B and the Ninth Schedule would not affect the powers of courts to issue writs or entertain appeals. They will remain just the same and only a certain class of cases had been excluded from the purview of Part III and the courts. The court further said that the provisions were essentially amendments to the Constitution and Parliament alone had the power to do so. The constitutionality was again challenged in the *Sajjan Singh* case (AIR 1965 SC 845). In a majority judgment delivered by Gajendragadkar, C. J., reliance was placed on pith and substance and it was stated that the amendment was meant to further agrarian reforms and not meant to affect the powers of the court. However, as stated earlier, Mudholkar, J., in his minority judgment had already raised a question mark on the amendment. In the *Golak Nath* case (AIR 1967 SC 1643), Subba Rao, C. J., held that Parliament was incompetent to take away or abridge any of the fundamental rights and the previous amendments, namely, First, Fourth and Seventeenth amendments relating to the Ninth Schedule would have been unconstitutional and void but for the doctrine of prospective overruling. In the *Kesavanand Bharati* case (AIR 1973, SC 1461), again, the court was unanimous that the Ninth Schedule device was valid. The court felt it too late to question the validity of the Schedule. It further held that in view of the doctrine of basic structure propounded by it, laws added to the Ninth Schedule after this decision will be subject to the basic structure of the Constitution. In other words, the courts were granted power to test the validity of future laws in the Schedule. For example, in *I. R. Coelho v. State of Tamil Nadu and Others*, Civil Appeal Nos. 1344–45 of 1976, decided on 11 January 2007, the court held, 'A law that abrogates rights guaranteed by Part III of the Constitution, whether by amendment of any article of Part III or by insertion in the Ninth Schedule, if it violates the basic structure, such law will have to be invalidated in exercise of judicial review by the court. All amendments to the Constitution made on or after 1973 by which the Ninth Schedule is amended by inclusion of various laws therein shall have to be tested on the touchstone of the basic features of the Constitution.'

The entire issue came up before a nine-judge Constitution Bench of the Supreme Court in October-November 2006. It was interesting to see that apart from the Attorney General who appeared for the central government, senior advocates Soli Sorabjee, T. R. Andhyarujina and Ram Jethmalani (all for Tamil Nadu) defended the laws in the Schedule for protecting them from judicial scrutiny! (*IE*, 4 November 2006). It is important to note that this review arose out of a reference made by a five-judge Bench in 1999. Even on such an important matter, it took seven years for the reference to be listed before a nine-judge Bench. It is noteworthy that, even after a lapse of decades and so much past experience of how the Schedule was thoroughly misused by making a mockery of the tenet of judicial review which is a part of the basic structure of the Constitution, the central government's stand had not changed one bit. The affidavit filed by the central government argued that Article 31B was a protective umbrella which cured the *vice or defect of unconstitutionality* of the legislation on the ground of infringement of fundamental rights. The Centre also asserted that the Parliament had the power to include in the Ninth Schedule a law which was struck down on the ground of violation of fundamental rights!

By its decision dated 11 January 2007, the court laid down a dual test to examine the validity of a Ninth Schedule law: whether it violates any fundamental right and if so, whether it also violated the basic structure of the Constitution. If the answer to both the tests was affirmative, then only a law placed in the Ninth Schedule could be declared unconstitutional. This declaration would lead to a number of enactments being legally challenged. In the future, greater care will have to be taken by the government in sponsoring new legislations and proposing their inclusion in the Ninth Schedule since this process will not be automatic any longer. The judgment led to an angry outburst by M. Karunanidhi, Chief Minister of Tamil Nadu, who said that supporters of social justice were prepared 'to even shed blood' to protect the reservation quota. Reactions of several other political parties in Tamil Nadu were equally strong. This clearly showed immaturity on their part.

Clearly, the passing of the first amendment and creating the Ninth Schedule was a fraud on the Constitution (Baxi 1994: 89). Upendra Baxi has stated, 'In legal parlance, this expression describes that behaviour of a legislature which knowing fully well that it has no power to legislate on a subject matter yet proceeds to make a law in such a way that the transgression appears to be within its power.' Noorani called it an 'incongruity which degraded to worse' (Noorani 2007: 734). Let us hope recourse will not be taken to the Ninth Schedule at any time in the future.

Freedom of Expression and Insufferable Intolerance

The Indian Constitution is undoubtedly one of the most progressive documents which provides for freedom of expression as a fundamental right. Article 19 guarantees, *inter alia*, the right to freedom of speech and expression subject to reasonable restrictions in the interest of the sovereignty and integrity of India, the security of the state, friendly relations with foreign states, public order, decency or morality, or in relation to contempt of court, defamation or incitement to an offence. Hurting the sensibilities of any section cannot thus be a justification for curtailing the freedom of expression. But, the words public order, decency and morality have been grossly misinterpreted and misused for the purpose.

During the emergency, rigorous censorship was imposed not only on newspapers but also on the reporting of parliamentary proceedings and court judgments. This government's mindset of putting restrictions on freedom of expression has surfaced from time to time.

A prominent instance of this was the Defamation Bill which was introduced in Parliament by the Rajiv Gandhi government on 29 August 1988 (Kashyap 1998: 282–83). The bill was designed to curb press criticism of political figures and provided penalties for publishing material which injured an individual's reputation. For the first offence, the punishment was two years' imprisonment while for a repeat offence it could be up to five years. It allowed for defence on the ground that the accusations were true and in public interest but placed the onus of proof on the defendant. The bill was defended by the government as a consolidating law. The government argued that under our laws and the Constitution, the press had the same right of expression which ordinary citizens had and, therefore, it had to share the same responsibilities and had to impose upon itself the same restraint. The bill was passed by the Lok Sabha resulting in a mass walkout by opposition members. The passing of the bill evoked very loud protests from the press and the public. Ultimately, the government had to bow to the pressure and the bill was withdrawn.

India is clearly in the throes of a cultural emergency. Journalist and author, Suketu Mehta, has called it India's 'speech impediment'. Salman Rushdie said at the Jaipur literature festival, 'In India, it has become easy to attack cultural artefacts. People believe their identity is not defined by what they love, but by what you hate or are offended by. It is a spreading problem' (*IE*, 25 January 2013). He also rightly said, 'there are things in India that have got much worse, particularly in the area of free expression' (*IE*, 29 January 2013).

The most shocking instance of growing intolerance was the ghastly murder of social activist and intellectual, Narendra Dabholkar, in Pune on 20 August 2013. Dabholkar was leading, as his life's mission, a movement for enacting a law against superstition and banning of exploitative religious practices such as black magic. In spite of concerted efforts and peaceful agitations, the bill had been pending for 18 years and successive governments in Maharashtra were dragging their feet to pander to Hindu rightist groups and obscurantists. Dabholkar's murder has brought into sharp focus the extent to which those opposed to his progressive thoughts were prepared to go to silence his voice. Dabholkar's tragic death has awakened the Government of Maharashtra from its slumber and, to atone for its neglect of the cause espoused by Dabholkar, it issued, soon after Dabholkar's murder, an ordinance banning certain inhuman practices.

Increasingly, political parties, organizations and groups of people have started protesting against various forms of expression such as speech, writings, painting, dancing, social behaviour and so on. And action is taken by the state or the police to put curbs on different forms of expression with the ostensible intent of maintaining peace, rather than questioning the protestors. Over the years, it has been seen that the fundamental right of freedom of expression is increasingly under serious threat. Governments of all political parties in power at the Centre and in the states have been complicit in allowing this to occur. Any number of instances can be cited in support of this contention.

James Laine's book, *Shivaji—The Hindu King in Islamic India*, led to widespread agitations and violence in Maharashtra in 2004 due to derogatory references made by the author to Shivaji. The agitation led to an attack on the Bhandarkar Institute of Oriental Research in Pune, where Laine had worked when he was in India for research for the book and resulted in the destruction of precious documents and artefacts of historical and archaeological importance. It also assumed the colour of an anti-Brahmin agitation, an undercurrent which surfaces off and on in Maharashtra, in spite of its outward progressive image. All this led to the banning of Laine's book by the state government. Criminal cases were also launched against the author, the publisher and the so-called collaborators of the project who had assisted Laine in his research. While the remarks made by the author were offensive, the perennial question of whether banning a book is the best way to deal with such writing, surfaced once again. The atmosphere was so politically charged that any calm thinking or introspection was out of the question. Finally, the Bombay High Court quashed the ban order and also observed, 'Those who rule this country do not have the monopoly of wisdom and they can't decide what the sovereign people should know or not know.' Earlier, the Supreme Court had quashed the criminal proceedings (*IE*, 27 April 2007).

This is by no means a solitary case of its kind. Banning of books has been the favourite past-time of rulers in post-Independence India. Time and again the higher judiciary has had to step in to stem the tide of such arbitrary and politically motivated actions and uphold the fundamental right of freedom of expression and the right to know. But it is not just the government which bans books in India. A powerful industrialist also ensured that a book relating to his phenomenal rise and the manner in which he operated the levers of power, which was not very complimentary to him, was not available to readers in India!

The ugly face of Talibanization is also becoming evident time and again. A recent example of this was the threats given and hate messages sent to the first all-girls rock band, Pragaash (meaning from darkness to light), in Srinagar in J&K. The band was termed 'un-Islamic' by the grand Mufti Bashir-ud-din. This frightened the girls and the band was disbanded (*IE*, 6 February 2013). Cinema houses are not permitted to be operated in Kashmir valley. A literary festival proposed to be held in 2012 was cancelled due to the threats of protests. The latest in this series is the objection raised by Hurriyat hardliner Syed Ali Shah Geelani to the holding of a concert by Zubin Mehta in Srinagar in September 2013.

The Vice-Chancellor of Aligarh Muslim University has issued a diktat that if boys want to meet him, they will have to wear *sherwanis* and the girls will have to be dressed 'according to customs and traditions of the university' (*IE*, 28 April 2013). There were threats to a painting exhibition in Bengaluru over alleged vulgar depiction of Hindu deities.

Soli Sorabjee has lamented, 'One of the greatest dangers to our democracy is the virus of intolerance that has assumed menacing proportions. It is not confined to any particular class or community. The infection is widespread...The All-India Ulema Council has asked the Muslim community to boycott all Godrej products unless the company's Chairperson Adi Godrej apologises for hosting writer Salman Rushdie. A complaint has been filed by the Makkal Katchi against actress Shreya because of her skimpy outfit, which had offended the Hindu culture, whatever that means' (*IE*, 20 January 2008).

Bangladesh writer Taslima Nasreen's request for a long-term visa in India was rejected because of opposition from a section of fundamentalist Muslims. She was thrown out of Bangladesh in 1994. She tried to settle down in Europe but found it difficult to live in a place which has a totally different climate and culture than where she had grown up. She has written:

> I wanted to come to India. But India kept her doors firmly shut. Towards the end of 1999, I was given permission to visit India as a tourist...I eagerly chose India's state of West Bengal as my new home. But when I was physically attacked by Muslim fundamentalists, instead of taking action against them, the [state] government kept me under house arrest. Not only that, I was repeatedly asked to leave the state and, preferably, the country. When a group of Muslim fundamentalists organised a protest against my stay in India, I was thrown out of Bengal [which at the time was ruled by the Communists], the state that had been my home for years. Finally, the central government took charge and put me up in a safe house. But there was pressure from the Centre too for me to leave the country. Now, I am given permission to live in India, but only in Delhi. My enemies are just a handful of corrupt, ignorant Muslim fundamentalists but yet India cannot challenge them (Nasrin 2013: 46).

There must not be any other country in which an unreasonable minority is pampered so much. As the Indian Express commented, 'It is an ironic fact of India's democracy that questions of individual liberty and freedom of expression have never quite attained primacy. Examples abound of government resorting to censorship and bans and of political parties condoning and even colluding in the erosion of individual freedoms whenever moral police has loomed large or a vote bank is presumed to be under threat' (IE, 30 November 2007). In this background, it is difficult to believe that India gave asylum to 87 Korean prisoners of war in 1953.

It is a pity that a so-called progressive state like Maharashtra is in the forefront of moral policing. In 2005, the Congress-NCP government banned dance bars in Mumbai on the ground that 'dancing was derogatory to the dignity of women' and led to their exploitation. Fortunately, the Supreme Court slammed the Maharashtra government for its 'elitist' and 'discriminatory attitude' and upheld the right of women bar dancers to follow their profession. The state government has, however, indicated its intention of filing a revision petition and also exploring other alternatives to ensure that dance bars are not permitted to function in the state. The Maharashtra government seems to have made it a prestige issue. There were objections to the cheerleaders in IPL matches on the ground that they were provocatively dressed. In 2013, the BMC unanimously passed a resolution sponsored by a Shiv Sena corporator to ban lingerie-clad mannequins from shops on the ground that they led to sexual crimes! The provisions of the Indecent Representation of Women (Prohibition) Act have been invoked for the purpose. Some political outfits in Karnataka too have been active in moral policing and the state government has been a silent spectator. The same political parties and organizations have not, however, objected to the sexy, titillating 'item songs' in movies.

Ashis Nandy's ill-advised comment at the Jaipur literary festival rightly came in for adverse reaction. According to S. Anand, based on a YouTube video via ABP News, Nandy is reported to have said, 'It is a fact that most of the corrupt come from the OBCs, and the scheduled castes and now increasingly scheduled tribes. And as long as this is the case, [the] Indian Republic will survive. Also, I will give an example. One of the states with the least amount of corruption is the state of West Bengal, that is when the CPI(M) was there. And I want to propose to you, draw your attention to the fact, that in the last hundred years nobody from the opp...nobody from the OBCs, the backward classes, and the scheduled castes and the scheduled tribes have come anywhere near power in West Bengal. It is an absolutely clean state' (Anand 2013: 38–41). The statement created an uproar and there were demands for his arrest and prosecution under the Prevention of Atrocities Act. Later, Nandy said of his Jaipur utterances, 'It is not an accidental slip, it is a Freudian slip' and tried to explain his stand and how he was misunderstood. But, prima facie, Nandy's comments were highly casteist. It is his good fortune that the law, as interpreted by some, did not take its course! A Bench led by the then Chief Justice of India, Altamas Kabir, stayed Nandy's arrest in all criminal proceedings arising out of the statement. This case clearly brings out the need for restraint in relying on one's right to freedom of expression.

But not everyone is as lucky as Nandy. A number of movies, in regional languages and in Hindi (and even English), had to face the wrath of some sections of the people, even after the Censor Board of India had cleared them:

- *Ore Oru Gramathile* (once upon a time in a village), 1989—Tamil Nadu ban for 'anti-reservation theme'. Supreme Court lifted the ban.
- *Fanaa*, 2006—Banned in Gujarat for terrorist-linked theme.
- *The Da Vinci Code*, 2006—Banned in Andhra Pradesh, Goa, Tamil Nadu, Punjab, Nagaland and Mizoram.
- *Parzania*, 2007—Gujarat multiplex owners refused to screen the film based on the 2002 Gujarat riots.
- *Aarakshan*, 2011—Faced ban in Uttar Pradesh. The Mayawati government initially thought it was anti-Dalit.
- *Vishwaroopam*, 2013—Banned in Tamil Nadu. The ban lifted only after some scenes were removed (Joshi 2013: 42–44).

Other movies banned over the years include *Kissa Kursi Ka* (1970), *Kuttapathirikki* (1991), *Kamasutra: A Tale of Love Story* (1996), *Fire* (1996), *Water* (2005) and *Bandit Queen* (2005). The latest in this unending list is the movie *Madras Cafe* (2013), which is facing mob fury and stout opposition from LTTE supporters. Protests were also raised against the movie *Jodha Akbar* a few years ago. Anurag Kashyap, who has made several realistic movies said, 'My biggest grouse is that we can't make an actual political film in this country without camouflaging it...It's largely the political agencies (sic) that cause problems for a film maker.' Dibakar Banerjee, another well-known film-maker, said, 'The censor board is the least of our problems. We are more delayed by contentious elements in political lobby groups or the fear of proscription in some state. The bogey of destruction of public property and loss of life is always thrown at us' (*Express Aada, IE,* 17 May 2013). Shubhra Gupta stated, 'Watching it [*Kissa Kursee Ka*] now, you realise that "political" films did not have a dim future back then: What happened with *Kissa Kursi Ka* may have caused the permanent demise of films that tried telling a truly trenchant, stinging picture of real India. So craven are the times we live in, I can't think of a film like *Kissa Kursee Ka* being conceived of, let alone being made, any more' (Gupta 2013). But censorship does not stop here. Sometimes, film distributors take a hand in it, while at other times movie theatre associations become active. Kamal Haasan, actor and producer of *Vishwaroopam*, had to complain to the fair-trade regulator, the Competition Commission of India, with a request to intervene.

In the context of the *Vishwaroopam* controversy, Muslim groups in Tamil Nadu demanded that the Censor Board be reconstituted to reflect the sensitivities of the people. It is important to note that four southern states—Tamil Nadu, Andhra Pradesh, Kerala and Karnataka—have laws in place which empower them to stop exhibition of films certified by the Censor Board. It is time the constitutional implications of this are examined and, if necessary, a reference is made to the Supreme Court under Article 143 of the Constitution to seek its opinion on the subject.

Jamait-Ulama-Hind General Secretary Mahmood Madani had written to Prime Minister Manmohan Singh demanding that the posters of the movie *Race 2* be taken down because some of them, displayed in Kolkata, carry Koranic verses. The song *Ya hussain* was removed from the movie *David* over allegations that it hurt the religious sentiments of Muslims.

Cultural intolerance has also extended to theatre and literary writings. Salman Rushdie was prevented from going to the Jaipur and Kolkata literary events after fears were expressed that his presence might offend minorities. However, the worst case was that of eminent and world renowned artist M. F. Husain who finally left India in disgust. In a shocking case a group of young men and women belonging to the Kabir Kala Manch have been arrested by the Maharashtra police for singing songs of rebellion and supporting the Naxal cause. If one is not to be a leftist and empathize with such causes at a young age, how can one expect new thinking in the younger generation? On the one hand, the government makes an appeal to the Naxals to give up violence and join the mainstream of political life, and on the other in a case like the Kabir Kala Manch, the young participants have been put behind bars. This makes no sense. The police even objected to the young woman, who was eight months pregnant, getting bail. This is simply outrageous. Ironically, Anand Patwardhan, who has made a film featuring these militant songs, has got a national award. Patwardhan has rightly said, 'So it depends on which class and caste you belong to. These people have court cases against them, and I have a national award' (*The Sunday Guardian*, 19 May 2013). Equally shocking is the police questioning Prime Minister Rural Development Fellow Mahesh Raut and Harshali Potdar, working in Brahmapuri in Chandrapur district, for being sympathetic to the Naxal cause (*IE*, 23 June 2013).

The latest encroachment on the freedom of expression is the police action against the so-called objectionable writings in the social media. After Bal Thackeray died in November 2012, a young girl had rightly commented on Facebook about the shut-down of Mumbai and how it was uncalled for. It was shocking to see the police arresting the girl and her friend, who had supported her in her comment, obviously under pressure from local Shiv Sena leaders. Finally, the court had to come to their rescue. The court also directed that action should be taken against the concerned policemen and officers for harassing the girls. The court had to pull up the police again in July 2013 for not taking any action against the erring policemen.

Taking up a plea filed by a law student seeking directions to the authorities not to take action against anybody for posting allegedly objectionable comments, the Supreme Court directed that any such person will not be arrested by the police without permission of senior officers (*IE*, 17 May 2013). Even the *Comedy Central* news channel was banned for some time, as if Indians do not have the capacity to laugh at their own idiosyncrasies.

It may be recalled that even during the emergency when strict censorship was sought to be imposed on the press and on all forms of expression such as Parliament debates and even court judgments, the High Court of Bombay, in its landmark judgment in *Binod Rao v. M. R. Masani* (1976, 78 Bom. Law Reporter 125) delivered on 10 February 1976 had declared:

> It is not the function of the Censor acting under the Censorship Order to make all newspapers and periodicals trim their sails to one wind or to tow along in a single file or to speak in chorus with one voice. It is not for him to exercise his statutory powers to force public opinion into a single mould or to turn the press into an instrument for brainwashing the public. Under the Censorship Order the *Censor is appointed the nursemaid of democracy and not its gravedigger...* Merely because dissent, disapproval or criticism is expressed in strong language is no ground for banning its publication (Sorabjee 2001: 126).

It is a travesty that this precept which was courageously pronounced by the High Court, in spite of the rigours of the emergency, is not being heeded by the authorities even in normal times.

This narration raises the question whether the freedom of expression, as envisaged by the Constitution, can ever become a reality. Clearly, much will depend on public education and on creating awareness about the importance of the concept of freedom of expression. Unfortunately, this is largely considered an elitist concept. Guarding and promoting one's sectarian preserve is considered more important than ensuring another person's fundamental right to freedom of expression. Hardly ever are politicians, or for that matter intellectuals, prepared to take up such a cause and face the wrath of organized groups. It then becomes the fight of a single person against misguided community outfits and fundamentalists.

This brings me to the next, and even more important, point of the role of the police. It has to be admitted that the police is hardly ever sensitive or concerned about the protection of freedom of expression. Its primary and mostly the only concern is that of preventing breach of peace at any cost. As a result, even the slightest fear of agitation and disturbance to law and order is enough for the police to come down heavily in favour of agitators and law-breakers. In addition there is the ever-present spectre of political interference in the work of the police. In such circumstances, the police ceases to be a guardian of freedom of expression. This is in spite of the warning by the Supreme Court, in its order dated 30 March 1989 in the *Ore Oru Gramathile case* referred to earlier, that 'the state cannot plead its inability to handle the hostile audience problem. It is its obligatory duty to prevent it and protect the freedom of expression.' Unless sustained efforts are made to sensitize the police, administrators, vigilante groups, political executives and the public at large about the importance of safeguarding and protecting the freedom of expression, there is unlikely to be any change in the situation. Otherwise, as the time goes by, India will become an even more intolerant and unliveable society.

Notes

1. Article 311 (2) (c) reads as follows: 'Where the President or the Governor, as the case may be, is satisfied that in the interest of the security of the state it is not expedient to hold such inquiry.'
2. M/S Serajjuddin & Company was a firm of mine-owners operating in Orissa. After seven years of searches conducted at their premises by income tax and customs, there were newspaper reports in early 1963 that the firm's private papers and account books contained entries showing payments to some central and state ministers. This has been replayed again and again over the years as in hawala case in the 1990s and in Karnataka and Madhya Pradesh in 2012–13.

3. In a celebrated case, the Bombay High Court passed strictures against the state government authorities and said that the government must function as a trustee in such matters and observe strict standards of accountability and transparency.
4. Based on Godbole (2008: 79–82).
5. The primary membership of the Akali Dal is open only to one who belongs to the Sikh community.
6. Sachar Committee Report on Social, Economic and Educational Status of Muslim Community of India, 2008: Table 1.2.
7. The Madhya Pradesh Assembly passed the Madhya Pradesh Freedom of Religion (Amendment) Bill, 2013 in July 2013 to further tighten the provisions pertaining to conversion of persons from one religion to another (*IE*, 11 July 2013).
8. See Godbole 2006: v–xvi.
9. For a comprehensive discussion on the subject, see Godbole (2008: 1–17, 400–506).

5

IF THERE IS A POLITICAL WILL, THERE IS A WAY AHEAD

Liberty lies in the hearts of men and women; When it dies there, no constitution, no law, no court can do much to help it. While it lies there it needs no constitution, no law, no court to save it
Judge Learned Hand

Public Order and Security

Maintaining public order and security is the primary responsibility of the government and it cannot be neglected at any cost. However, in recent years both these have emerged as areas of concern. Even in matters pertaining to law and order and national security, politics comes first. Naxalism and Naxal violence is recognized as the most important threat to national security. There have been dozens of instances in the recent past where personnel from the paramilitary force have been killed by Naxalites by using land mines. There have also been a series of instances where revenue and police officers have been abducted and the government has conceded to the demands of releasing Naxalites arrested and kept in jail. There is no national policy as yet to deal with Naxalite violence. Naxalism has spread its tentacles far and wide. Practically one-third of the country is now known as the red corridor extending from the Nepal border in the north to Andhra Pradesh in the south. During 2008–12, 2,571 civilians and 1,089 security personnel were killed by Naxalites. An attack by Naxalites on a convoy of Congress Party workers and leaders in Baster district in Chhattisgarh on 25 May 2013 led to the killing of over 29 persons including prominent Congress Party leaders and security personnel. The attack also injured over 40 persons, including V. C. Shukla, former central minister, and led to the kidnapping of some others. Just three years earlier, Maoists had massacred 76 security personnel in Tadmetla on 6 April 2010. This was followed by a massacre in Chingawaram in Dantewada district on 17 May 2010 in which 31 persons, including 15 security personnel, were killed in a passenger bus. This was followed by a massacre in Dhauri in Narayanpur district on 29 June 2010 in which 27 CRPF men were killed. The growing strength and menace of the Naxalite movement seems unstoppable.

Prime Minister Manmohan Singh has declared that Naxalite violence has become the biggest threat to national security. It is well recognized that Naxalism cannot be treated as a mere law and order problem and that its causes lie much deeper in agrarian unrest, tardy implementation of land reforms, neglect of the problems of small and marginal farmers, grievances of project affected persons and so on. The worst part is that we, as a nation, have come to accept Naxalite violence as a given and there is no political will to deal with it decisively.

The expert group on Naxalism appointed by the Planning Commission identified 10 factors that appear to show significant variations between Naxalite affected and developed districts. They indicate the circumstances underlying rural unrest and the emergence of Naxalism to a significant extent. These factors are: high share of a SC/ST population; low levels of literacy; high level of infant mortality; low level of urbanization; high share of forest cover; high share of agricultural labour; low per capita food grain production; low level of road length per 100 sq km; high share of rural households which have no bank accounts; and high share of rural households without specified assets. The expert group rightly highlighted that there are several pockets in forest areas where there is a total vacuum in administration and that vacuum has been filled up by Naxalites (Government of India 2008: 20). There are no indications that Naxalite violence is likely to be contained in the foreseeable future. Unfortunately, no viable national strategy and time-bound action plan have as yet emerged with reference to which the performance of the states and other agencies can be assessed. We still seem to be groping in the dark and in the meanwhile hundreds of paramilitary personnel and civilians continue to lose their lives every few months due to Naxalite violence. The Centre has clearly failed to provide leadership on this important question.

Note also needs to be taken of the alienation of the people in the north-eastern region of the country due to the gross abuse of the Armed Forces Special Powers Act (AFSPA). The committee under the chairmanship of Justice B. P. Jeevan Reddy, a retired judge of the Supreme Court came to the conclusion that AFSPA should be repealed. The committee was of the view that it would be more appropriate to insert appropriate provisions, as may be necessary, into the Unlawful Activities (Prevention) Act, 1967. The judicial commission appointed by the Supreme Court and headed by Justice Santosh Hegde, a former judge of the Supreme Court, stated that the continuation of AFSPA is a 'mockery of the law' as it has been abused and is largely ineffective in tackling insurgency. The commission found that all the six sample cases of encounters considered by it were 'not genuine encounters' and that 'maximum force' was used (IE, 16 July 2013: 9). SARC too has recommended that AFSPA should be repealed. The government has not been able to take a decision in the matter due to the strong opposition of the armed forces and the Ministry of Defence. But this decision should not be postponed any longer. No part of the country can be governed for decades by using AFSPA. It is a negation of democratic governance. The alternative of strengthening the armed police in the states to take over the responsibility of containing insurgency must be seriously pursued.

Attention must be invited in this context to the provisions of the Fifth Schedule of the Constitution regarding provisions as to the administration and control of Scheduled Areas and Scheduled Tribes. Article 244(1) is rarely given its due importance though it is of great value to the lives of millions of tribals who live in remote and hilly tracts in the country. This article requires the President, in conjunction with the governors of the concerned states, to play a proactive role in ensuring good governance in the tribal areas notified under the Fifth Schedule to the Constitution. Continuing non-compliance of this article and its associated safeguards has created a near vacuum in governance as far as the tribals are concerned. As a result, the tribals are forced to lead marginal lives, are deprived of their constitutional rights, especially the right to live with dignity and confidence. The problems that confront them today are directly attributable to the absence of governance in the areas that constitute their habitat.

Notwithstanding anything in the Constitution, Clause 5(1) of Fifth Schedule requires all laws applicable to the rest of the country to be adapted to suit the interests of the tribals before they are extended to tribal areas. *Clearly, the Constitution has recognised that the tribals must not be assimilated in the general population hastily and arbitrarily and their special needs must be taken into account, before any laws are extended to these areas.* The Governor is empowered to decide the manner in which any law is to be made applicable to Scheduled Areas. Thus, certain laws may not apply, or apply in a modified form. The administration in these areas is to be kept at arms length. Even though more than six decades have passed since Independence, successive governments have done precious little to improve the situation. The governors who were expected to play a pivotal role have remained dysfunctional. The reason for this is obvious. Independent, democratic India is far too busy appeasing powerful corporates to worry about voiceless tribals.

There are several proposals for inclusion of predominantly tribal villages, left out of the Fifth Schedule by oversight or otherwise. Many of these proposals have been gathering dust in the corridors of the Ministry of Tribal Affairs for decades. These need to be revived, resuscitated and processed. There are other Fifth Schedule villages wantonly removed by district officials in different states, either out of ignorance, or by oversight, or out of deliberate design. The effect of this is depriving tribals of their land rights while benefitting non-tribal land-grabbers.

Clause 3 of the Fifth Schedule requires the President, through the office of the Governor of each state, to obtain periodical reports on the administration of the tribal areas and exercise a close oversight on the working of the political executive. Though the Constitution has incorporated these far-reaching provisions, in reality the process of such oversight has been reduced to a meaningless ritual, as a result of lack of sensitivity on the part of the political elite about the concerns of the tribals. This clause needs to be invoked to ensure that the governors of the concerned states take an interest in the administration of the tribal areas and help the President in exercising the necessary oversight on matters that are central to the lives of the tribals and ensure that the rights of the tribals are restored and fully protected.

The Commissioner for Scheduled Castes and Scheduled Tribes can become an effective institution in helping the political executive, Parliament and the President in playing their respective roles in safeguarding the interests of the tribals, provided the commission is fully empowered and its role is given due importance.

Under the Fifth Schedule, the executive power of the union extends to giving directions to states regarding the administration of tribal areas. It sets out detailed provisions as to how these areas are to be administered by setting up tribal advisory councils.

The Sixth Schedule provides for the administration of tribal areas in the states of Assam, Meghalaya, Tripura and Mizoram. The tribal councils have either not been constituted or, if constituted, are not consulted in all matters pertaining to the development of these areas. Royalty accruing from mining and deforestation of these areas has not been shared with the local communities. Even their languages and culture have been over-ridden. No effort has been made to publish textbooks for primary and secondary education in tribal languages. The medium of instruction continues to be the regional language of the area. It is not, therefore, surprising that there is so much suppressed anger, alienation and discontent in tribal areas.

B. D. Sharma and S. R. Sankaran, two eminent commentators on tribal welfare, in their excellent essays appended as Annexures 1 and 2 respectively (pp. 1–26) with the report of the Planning Commission's Expert Group on Development and Causes of Discontent, referred to earlier, analyse the real causes for tribal unrest and the rise of Naxalism and discuss the reforms in the structural and policy framework which are imperative if a real dent is to be made on the Naxal problem and tribals are to be given their due (Government of India 2008: 1–26). These two essays ought to be made compulsory reading for anyone working on these complex issues. I would suggest that a white paper on implementing the Fifth and the Sixth Schedules and the points underlined in these two essays be published by the government for wider debate and discussion so as to evolve a monitorable action plan on the subject.

In a welcome move, in August 2013 the central government appointed a high level committee, under the chairmanship of Virginius Xaxa, to investigate the socioeconomic status of tribals. The committee has been asked to look into issues concerning the tribal population, including identifying the regions where the tribals live and the 'visible changes' that have occurred in the wake of 'involuntary displacement' as well as 'enforced migration', comparing their assets and incomes to other social groups, identifying causes of disparity and assessing if there are adequate structures for implementing protective legislations (*IE*, 20 August 2013). One can only hope that the report, when received, will not meet the same fate as the Sachar Committee and Ranganath Mishra Commission reports on minorities, which have effectively been consigned to the archives.

At the same time, reference must be made to the other side of the story which has been presented by Patricia Mukhim, the editor of *The Shillong Times*:

> It is ridiculous to waive income tax from a tribal elite that is increasingly becoming as affluent as any of the non-tribal population in the metros of this country. But what is worse is that this has other implications. Everything they earn or get or extort through fair means or foul is 'white' money. This makes it attractive for others who have to carry the tax burden to use a tribal: (a) to avoid paying income tax and thereby earn more profits; (b) to do *benami* business in the name of a tribal; (c) to convert black money to white through several innovative methods such as setting up educational institutions or some such venture with the larger and more amorphous purpose of doing it 'in tribal interest'...I have realised, albeit belatedly, that the Land Ceiling Act has no takers...Look at how rich our politicians and bureaucrats are. They now do not send their children to school and college in India because these are not good enough. They send their kids to study in the UK, USA, Australia (Mukhim 2013: 14).

It is not therefore surprising that in elections in the small states in the north-east, there are so many multimillionaire candidates. The Constitution provides that the provision of income tax exemption should be reviewed every ten years but with an abundance of vested interests, this has remained on paper.

Equally disturbing is the large spread of terrorism in urban areas. To begin with, such violence was routinely ascribed to forces from across the border, that is Pakistan and more recently Bangladesh. But in recent times far rightist Hindu ideological groups are asserting themselves in perpetrating terrorist violence. These are indeed highly disturbing developments and have not received the attention that they deserve. Equally disconcerting has been the response of state governments in recent years to deal with terrorist violence. This is seen from the opposition from the major states to the setting up of the National Counter Terrorism Centre (NCTC) in the name of federalism. It is true that the Centre, irrespective of which political party was in power, grossly misused the powers entrusted to central investigating agencies such as the CBI and Enforcement Directorate. But to take a position that the powers of the Centre have to be restricted in dealing with terrorism is clearly short-sighted. Ways must be found to establish greater coordination between the Centre and the states in dealing with terrorist violence. The Centre must be given primacy in these efforts. The structure of NCTC needs further thought. Its proposed location in the IB needs to be reconsidered. But the manner in which major states have ganged up against the Centre on the subject is disturbing. Good governance will be possible only in an environment of peace and tranquillity.

Reference must be made to the restrictions reportedly placed on the IB in relaying terror intelligence alerts. News report said that this was a direct fallout of the Ishrat Jahan case. They further stated that MHA had made it 'mandatory' for IB to seek 'written approval from the Home Minister before issuing a terror related advisory or alert to the state police' (*Sunday Guardian*, 28 July 2013). If true, it betrays total lack of knowledge on the part of policymakers about how intelligence is collected or disseminated. It also exhibits our panicky reaction to incidents like the Ishrat Jahan encounter case. Intelligence, especially terror-related information, does not emerge in any predictable fashion.

When any state legislation is likely to impinge on a central legislation, the approval for such a legislation is withheld by the Governor till the Government of India approves it. This salutary constitutional provision has been grossly misused by the central government for its narrow political ends. With respect to the right to information, the view taken by the governors in states had not been uniform. While in some states this was considered to be a subject in the State List, in Madhya Pradesh the Governor took the view that this came in the Concurrent List and therefore the bill passed by the State Legislature had to be approved by the Centre. The central government sat over this proposal for months. It became a non-issue only after the Centre decided to bring in its own law on the subject. The position regarding the law to deal with organized crime is even more shocking. Such a law was originally passed by the Maharashtra legislature and was thereafter adopted in Karnataka, Andhra Pradesh and Delhi, but when the Gujarat legislature passed a similar bill, the Governor referred it to the Centre and that is where it continues to languish for years together. If dealing with organized crime, which often has close links with terrorist crime and also international linkages, is to be treated as a political tool, all that one can say is that god alone can save this country. It is this kind of a partisan attitude from the central government which has created a trust deficit in the states leading to suspicions regarding the bonafides of the Centre on every issue such as NIA, NCTC and reorganizing RPF and rationalizing its crime investigation responsibilities.

We seem to be losing the fight against terrorism which has been so highly debilitating and has brought into focus the weaknesses of the Centre's (and the states') authority and the limitations on its power. Under the Constitution, 'public order and police' are in the State List. At the time when the Constitution was framed, the founding fathers could not have visualized that organized crime and terrorism, with its international ramifications, would pose such serious threats. As a result, the Centre, which is otherwise so strong, has not been given any powers to deal with such horrendous crimes. As stated earlier, the states are suspicious of the Centre, as always, due to their experience of its high-handedness. They have therefore been stoutly opposing proposals for giving powers to the Centre to deal with terrorism, organized crime, serious communal violence, or enacting a separate law for the CBI.

In the meanwhile terrorist violence has been spreading with bomb blasts occurring in several parts of the country. In spite of this background, a decision was taken by the Government of Uttar Pradesh to withdraw cases against 19 persons who were involved in terrorist attacks. Charge sheets had already been filed in all these cases. By this action, since the accused are Muslims, the ruling Samajwadi Party is hoping to garner more minority votes in the 2014 Lok Sabha polls. This is the extent to which the politics is strangling the country. Fortunately, the High Court has stayed the withdrawal and has referred the matter to a larger Bench. If you sow the wind, you are bound to reap a whirlwind in which the lives of innocent, common persons will be lost.

There is also an urgent need to create a national police agency to deal with multi-state crimes. The Estimates Committee of Parliament had made such a recommendation way back in 1991. For example, the cricket betting and match fixing scandal which has burst on the scene and engulfed the Indian Premier League (IPL) (derisively referred to as the Indian *Papi* League, Indian Police League, Indian Plague League and the Indian Pathetic League) is spread over a number of states. Police in Maharashtra and Delhi are simultaneously engaged in unearthing it and, as is to be expected, games of one-up manship are being played to take credit. The Centre has no powers to create a special agency to investigate the offence unless the Supreme Court intervenes. This is totally untenable. Unless a larger role is assigned to the Centre to deal with such crimes, the situation is likely to deteriorate.

It may be recalled that the Constitution (Forty-second Amendment) Act, 1976 added a new Article 257A to the Constitution empowering the central government to send armed forces or other forces of the union for dealing with a grave situation of law and order in any state. Such a force was to act in accordance with the directions of the central government and not be subject to the control of the state government. The new article also empowered Parliament to specify, by law, the powers, functions and liabilities of the members of any such force deployed in a state. However, with widespread anger against the excesses committed during the emergency and the trampling of the states by the Centre, this article was repealed when the Janata government came to power by the Constitution (Forty-forth Amendment) Act, 1978, with effect from 20 June 1979. It was a typical case of throwing the baby out with the bath water!

In the 1990s MHA had proposed the setting up of a federal agency to deal with grave offences, which have inter-state and nation-wide ramifications. This was opposed by the states on the plea that it infringed on their constitutional right to maintain law and order. As discussed later in this chapter, not just the states but also the CBI was opposed to the creation of such a new agency. The Group of Ministers on Reforming the National Security System, under the chairmanship of L. K. Advani, the then Deputy Prime Minister and Home Minister, recommended that 'considering the worrisome internal security scenario in the country, the states may be approached again, at the *appropriate* time, to agree to this proposal, since it may become increasingly difficult for the state governments to handle such crimes on their own.' This was in February 2001 (Government of India 2001: 45). The appropriate time has still not come and there has been no progress since then.

Attention may be invited to another important recommendation of this group. It took note of constitutional provisions and found that the union government's ability to deal with situations caused by grave threats to internal security had eroded over the years. The group felt that 'it would be both appropriate and timely if the provisions contained in Article 355 [duty of the union to protect states against external aggression and internal disturbance] are made use of proactively. To do so, supporting legislation will have to be enacted, *inter alia*, to cover the following:

- *Suo motu* deployment of central forces, if the situation prevailing in the states so demands; the legislation will spell out situations in which such deployment may take place, as also its consequences.
- Defining powers, jurisdiction, privileges and liabilities of the members of central forces, while deployed in states, in accordance with Entry 2-A of the Union List [deployment of any armed forces of the union or any other force subject to the control of the union or any contingent or unit thereof in any state in aid of the civil power, powers, jurisdiction, privileges and liabilities of the members of such forces while on such deployment].
- Specifying situations construed as failure/break-down of constitutional machinery in a state, in which the central government can intervene to advise or direct, as the case may be, a state government and violations of these advisories/directions would invite action under Articles 365 [effect of failure to comply with, or to give effect to, directions given by the union]/352 [proclamation of Emergency].

Based on this, the group of ministers recommended that action may be taken with regard to the proposed legislation under Article 355 [duty of the union to protect states against external aggression and internal disturbances]:

- The matter be taken to the inter-state council and a small group of members of the council be constituted to examine the issue in all its dimensions.
- The matter be discussed with the leadership of all political parties to generate consensus.
- Simultaneously, a comprehensive reference may be made to the Law Commission on the question of strengthening Articles 352 [proclamation of Emergency] and 359 [suspension of the enforcement of the rights conferred in Part III during Emergencies], without compromising the spirit of democracy and federalism which guides the Constitution (Government of India 2001: 43–44).

It is noteworthy to see the extent to which the NDA government, which was in power at the Centre at the time, was prepared to go to strengthen the Centre. It may be recalled that earlier the BJP, which was responsible for the destruction of the Babri Masjid in December 1992, had stoutly opposed the deployment of central forces in Ayodhya and had in fact threatened a mass agitation if the Centre took any unilateral action. As a result, the demolition of the Babri Masjid could not be avoided though nearly 20,000 central forces were mobilized from all over the country and *stationed* within less than 10 kilometres of Ayodhya, as the state government *refused to deploy* these forces to guard the monument. Looking to the stance of the BJP and the state government, the then Prime Minister Narasimha Rao developed cold feet (Godbole 1996: 332–418). It is also important to note how far the NDA was prepared to go even in equipping the Centre with powers akin to the much maligned emergency in 1975–77 during Indira Gandhi's time. Be that as it may, looking to the highly worrisome internal security situation in the country, the fact that the NDA had put forth these proposals is important and needs to be built upon by UPA to create a larger national consensus on these critical issues.

The central government has prepared The Communal Violence (Prevention, Control and Rehabilitation of Victims) Bill, 2005 to deal with communal violence in the country. One of the important provisions of the proposed bill is the special powers of the union government to deal with communal violence in certain cases. In terms of Clause 55, the central government has been given powers to give directions to state governments in case of communal disturbances and to issue notifications declaring any area within a state as communally disturbed and to deploy armed forces wherever necessary. Where it is decided to deploy armed forces, an authority known as Unified Command may be constituted by the central government or state government for the purpose of coordinating and monitoring such deployment. Every notification declaring any area within a state as a communally disturbed area by the union government has to be laid before each House of Parliament (Government of India 2007: 242–44). The bill has been pending since 2005 and is unlikely to be passed due to the opposition of the states. As seen during the anti-Sikh riots in Delhi in 1984, the record of the central government in controlling communal violence is no better than that of the states. However, looking to the experience of Maharashtra during the Shiv Sena-BJP rule during the communal riots in December 1992 and January 1993 and the Godhra riots in Gujarat in 2002, over-riding powers in the matter need to be given to the Centre, as a counter-check in the system, subject to some important modifications to avoid the over-reach of centre.

In the meanwhile, the Constitution should at least be amended to shift the subjects of police and public order to the Concurrent List to enable both the Centre and the states to operate in the field. This will enable the Centre, for example, not just to station central forces anywhere in the country but also to *deploy* them, as may be necessary. Giving a larger role to the Centre will help in taking strong action against terrorism, organized crime and the outbreak of serious communal violence. The statesmanship of the leaders of political parties will be tested on this subject. I hope all political parties will rise above their narrow political interests and support an amendment to the Constitution in this regard.

Looking at the potential for misuse of intelligence agencies, namely, IB, RAW and NTRO by the central government, it is imperative that the working of these organizations is governed by a statute, and their funds are audited by C&AG.

As I had recommended in my book *India's Parliamentary Democracy on Trial*, a new joint standing committee on security and intelligence must be created to enable Parliament to oversee the activities of these institutions, as is being done in some other democracies (Godbole 2011: 339–40). Similar action needs to be taken with respect to state intelligence agencies.

The Widening Arc of Corruption

The government's position on tackling corruption is ambivalent, irrespective of which political party is in power. The slogan of zero tolerance for corruption has become empty and meaningless rhetoric like the often repeated other slogans— the law will take its course and howsoever high you may be, the law is above you. The reality is quite the contrary. The Law Commission in its 166th report (1999) observed, 'The Prevention of Corruption Act has totally failed in checking corruption. In spite of the fact that India is rated as one of the most corrupt countries in the world, the number of prosecutions and more so the number of convictions are ridiculously low.' International data on the number of persons convicted for bribery show that most countries have a much higher rate of conviction than India. Thus the conviction rate per 100,000 inhabitants in India was ridiculously low at 0.07 each in 1998 and 1999. The corresponding figures for China were 0.71 and 0.69, for Malaysia 1.04 and 2.82 and for the Republic of Korea 1.73 and 3.13 respectively (Government of India 2007: 110).

The pronouncements of various prime ministers and the ruling elite, from time to time, have hardly inspired confidence in the government's commitment to eradicating corruption. Indira Gandhi dismissed corruption as an international phenomenon. Harshad Mehta, prime accused in the bank scam, claimed to have personally given a suitcase stacked with currency notes worth Rs 1 crore to Prime Minister Narasimha Rao. Chandra Shekhar had the gumption to say that the time of the Lok Sabha should not be wasted in discussing corruption (*Loksatta*, 27 September 1997). He said, 'honesty is not everything. If a constable takes Rs 5 as a bribe, the entire country could not be ranked among the seventh most corrupt nations in the world. There is nothing wrong if he takes a few rupees to run his family' (*IE*, 26 December 1996). The then Prime Minister Inder Kumar Gujral, signifying the government's helplessness in the matter, declared from the ramparts of the Red Fort that a *satyagraha* should be launched by the people to tackle corruption! (*MT*, 15 September 1997). V. P. Singh, on demitting the office of Prime Minister, said that the crown of the prime ministership does not lie in Delhi, but in the treasure chest of a powerful industrial house [presumably Ambanis] in Mumbai. Balasaheb Thackeray, the then self-professed 'remote control' of the Shiv Sena-BJP government in Maharashtra, publicly stated that it would be impossible to run the government if action was to be taken against corrupt elements (*MT*, 5 January 1999). As a pragmatic communist, Jyoti Basu, the then Chief Minister of West Bengal, speaking in London, called for a five-year moratorium on corruption in India!! (*TOI*, 29 September 1991). At least three prime ministers—Indira Gandhi, Rajiv Gandhi and Narasimha Rao—were involved in corruption scandals. Unfortunately, none of them could be brought to book. Prime Minister Manmohan Singh, though personally honest, has presided over a ministry of mega scams such as 2G, coal gate, Commonwealth Games and purchase of helicopters for VVIPs, to name just a few. The convenient excuse which he has put forth that he was 'misled' in each one of these cases is far from convincing and speaks volumes about his capabilities or lack thereof. A Bihar minister openly asked how ministers can manage their affairs if they are not paid a 10 per cent cut on all contracts. A central minister ridiculed a question asked by a journalist by scoffing that no self-respecting minister will take a bribe of such a small amount! The then Prime Minister, V. P. Singh, rightly observed, 'It seems status defines criminality. Above a certain level of economic or political clout, crime does not exist' (*TOI*, 10 September 1998). Even 15 years later, the situation has not changed. B. R. Lall, an IPS officer who worked with the CBI for long, had, just before his death, written in an article that the agency's investigating officers 'are not supposed to cross the path of the elite...The rule of law does not apply to those who frame laws and who enforce them...Even honest investigating officers keep weighing the political and administrative consequences rather than the merits of a case before taking any action' (Lall 2012: 12–15). It is therefore not surprising that the CBI has a high conviction rate in cases against junior officers and a low conviction rate in cases against the politically powerful and high and mighty.

Every day, our newspapers are full of corruption cases and the sums involved are mind-boggling. A member of the Railway Board was arrested by the CBI for giving a bribe of Rs 90 lakh to the nephew of the then Railway Minister Pawan Kumar Bansal (*IE*, 4 May 2013). This was stated to be the first instalment out of the total bribe of Rs 10 crore which was agreed upon. If so much money has to be paid for getting a coveted posting, one can well imagine how much money the incumbent will be able to make during his tenure. It is not surprising that the Congress Party decided to brazen out the episode rather than taking the ethical and honourable course of asking Railway Minister Bansal to resign till public pressure became unbearable.

It is interesting to note that the UPA released in 2013 a 79-page report card of its accomplishments in every sector in the previous year, along with the progress that the country had made in the nine years of UPA rule. In so far as governance and corruption are concerned, all that the report card says is: (i) Amendments being sought to the Prevention of Corruption Act, and (ii) a host of anti-corruption and transparency legislations lined up, including the Lok Pal Bill (*IE*, 23 May 2013).

Markandey Katju, a former judge of the Supreme Court and now Chairman of the Press Council of India, has propounded the thesis that corruption will continue till India's industrialization is complete (Katju 2012: 11). Katju has asserted that:

> corruption is the normal feature of the transitional period when a society (such as India's) is passing from a feudal, agricultural stage to a modern industrial stage. Second, it is only when the transition is over and the country becomes a fully industrial society, like that in North America or Europe, that things will get relatively stabilised, and corruption will be considerably reduced. This, in my opinion, will take about 15 to 20 years more in India...I am not trying to justify corruption. I am only presenting a scientific analysis to show that corruption is inevitable in a transitional society like India.

I have given this lengthy quote as it comes from a former judge of the highest court in India who had himself expressed his acute anguish at the intolerable corruption from the Bench by saying, 'everyone wants to loot the country; the only panacea to rid the country of corrupt elements was to hang a few of them on the lamp post. The law does not permit us to do it but otherwise we would prefer to hang people like you to the lamp post' (*IE*, 8 March 2007). Against this background, his recent pontification is difficult to understand. There is no connection, whatsoever, between the stage of industrialization of a country and the prevalence of corruption. With advances in information technology and the increasing importance of the services sector, the process and the nature of industrialization in the conventional sense of the term has undergone a qualitative change. The argument put forth by Katju implies that the nation should accept corruption as an inevitable transitional phenomenon. Howsoever professedly scientific his exposition may be, it is revolting to common persons who are victims of rampant corruption. Further, Katju's arguments militate against the widely accepted concept of good governance. The menace of corruption can be curtailed only by adopting a comprehensive strategy as expounded later in this chapter.

Adopt an Inquisitorial System as in Europe[1]

The record of investigating agencies such as the CBI (popularly known as the Congress Bureau of Investigation or the Congress *Bachao* Bureau of Investigation), the Directorate of Enforcement, Revenue Intelligence and others is dismal. These agencies have been misused by whichever government is in power at the Centre. The most recent scandal pertains to Law Minister Ashwani Kumar and the Prime Minister's Office calling the senior investigating officers of the CBI to 'familiarize themselves' with the investigation in the coal scam and to take a hand in amending the investigation report to suit the government. Even the efforts of the Supreme Court in the hawala and other cases to ensure independence and autonomy of the institutions have failed. More troubling is the stand taken by CBI Director, Ranjit Sinha, that he was a part of the government and there was therefore nothing wrong in showing the investigation report to Law Minister Ashwani Kumar. With such a mindset, any talk about granting independence and autonomy to the CBI is futile. Sinha should have politely but firmly told the minister that the investigation report could not be shown to him, as the case was being monitored by the Supreme Court. But Sinha was prepared to go along. This is one more case where a senior officer preferred to crawl when he was asked to bend. The role of law officers in the government, who are expected to assist the court in arriving at the truth, is also highly questionable. Instead of attending the meeting called by the Law Minister the Attorney General and the Additional Solicitor General should have advised the minister not to convene the meeting.

There is often a clamour for handing over complicated and sensitive cases to the CBI but mostly the results are highly disappointing. There is a new demand these days that the investigations should be placed under the supervision of the Supreme Court. The latest case of this type is the Augusta Westland scam involving the purchase of VVIP helicopters. Obviously, this course of action will not be feasible except in a few politically sensitive or high profile cases. What should be done in the other cases is a million dollar question. Unless an answer is found, eradicating corruption will remain a quest in the wilderness. I have been advocating for some time that, to begin with, in important cases we should adopt the inquisitorial system followed in Europe from the thirteenth century onwards, as opposed to the accusatorial system prevalent in India, by putting police investigations under a judicial magistrate. In the inquisitorial system, the judge is expected to take the initiative and find out for himself by examining all relevant persons including the accused, what really happened, that is, what the truth was and then act according to the law. In the accusatorial system, the judge acts only as an umpire between the two contesting parties. Adopting the inquisitorial system will free the investigation from political and other extraneous influences. Judicial magistrates will work under the supervision of senior judicial officers and ultimately under the High Court. This will mean creating more posts of judicial magistrates but this extra expenditure will be well worth it if one looks at the dividend of establishing the rule of law. Having a high level panel for the selection of the incumbent for the post of Director CBI, as is being advocated as a part of the Lok Pal Bill, by itself will not be enough. What is equally important is ensuring an impartial investigation, free of any outside influence and interference, and making the Director CBI, ineligible for holding any public office after demitting charge of the post.

Create an Independent Directorate of Prosecution

It is equally necessary to create an independent Directorate of Prosecution. In the hawala case it was suggested to the Supreme Court that an institution of an independent public prosecutor should be created on the lines of that in the United States. Unfortunately, the court felt that the time had not yet come to give such a directive and that the government itself should take adequate steps in the matter instead. As experience has shown, with vested interests holding sway, it is unlikely that the government will mend its ways. Since UPA II came to power in 2009, four senior law officers at the level of Solicitor General and Additional Solicitor General have resigned due to differences with the government regarding handling of cases. It has been seen that appointments of public prosecutors are highly politicized. In the Bofors case, for example, public prosecutors failed to pursue public interest vigorously. In the 2G scam case, it was alleged that the public prosecutor representing the CBI had weakened the government case by sharing the government's thinking and strategy with one of the prime accused. At times, advocates representing the CBI have been found to be wanting. Matters have reached a stage where it is not advisable to delay remedial action any further. I would suggest that an independent Directorate of Prosecution (DP) be established urgently under the CVC. It should be his statutory responsibility to ensure vigorous and fair prosecution of all major government cases. I have deliberately recommended placing the DP under the CVC and not the Ministry of

Law since the experience of that ministry does not inspire confidence, particularly in politically sensitive cases such as Bofors, the 2G scam, coal gate and so on.

Ensure Independence of the CBI

The rapid deterioration in the working of the CBI has been studied and commented upon by a number of committees. These include, among others, the L. P. Singh Committee, the Shah Commission of Inquiry in police excesses during the emergency, the National Police Commission under the chairmanship of Dharma Vira and the Estimates Committee of Parliament.

The question of a separate legislation for the CBI was raised for the first time in Parliament on 29 April 1970 when, in reply to a question, the then union Home Minister Y. B. Chavan told Parliament, 'Certain central legislation is contemplated and is being examined in consultation with the Law Ministry and other relevant advisors.'

The Estimates Committee of Parliament (1991–92), *inter alia*, recommended that the government should bring forward a legislation defining the charter of CBI. It was also recommended that the CBI be given statutory status and well defined legal powers, and the Constitution should be amended for this purpose. It was also suggested that the question of creating a National Police Agency, as distinct from the CBI, be addressed promptly and with utmost seriousness. I was union Home Secretary when this recommendation was received. The committee was pressing for early comments of the Home Ministry. In view of the importance of the subject, an issues paper was prepared by the ministry for discussion in the Committee of Secretaries and it was sent to all the concerned ministries for their comments. The Ministry of Personnel was so upset with this initiative taken by MHA that the matter was represented by the then Minister of State for Personnel, Margaret Alva, to Prime Minister Narasimha Rao. He did not want the recommendations of the Estimates Committee to be pursued and asked Alva to inform the Home Minister accordingly. That was the end of the matter! (Godbole 1996: 320–22).

The Nineteenth report of the Parliamentary Standing Committee on Personnel, Public Grievances and Law and Justice, submitted to the Rajya Sabha on 10 May 2007, drew attention to earlier reports in which it was recommended that a separate law should be passed for CBI 'in tune with the requirements of the time to ensure credibility and impartiality.' Each of the committees, referred to earlier, has commented on the fundamental flaw in the working of the CBI, namely, excessive political interference.

In the recent past, the stand taken by the CBI in the Supreme Court in cases relating to Mayawati and Mulayam Singh Yadav in the disproportionate assets cases clearly showed it was 'his master's voice'. As stated earlier, in the coal gate scam investigation, which is being monitored by the Supreme Court, union Law Minister Ashwani Kumar had the temerity to call the Director of CBI and his officers for a discussion and go through the findings of investigation and the submissions proposed to be made to the court. It would have been unthinkable in normal times but the officers of the PMO and the Coal Ministry too were present during the said discussion and had the gumption to ensure that the Prime Minister's and the Coal Minister's (Manmohan Singh's) interests were properly safeguarded. Even after the political uproar in Parliament, in the media and in society at large, the Prime Minister categorically announced that Ashwani Kumar would not be asked to resign. This is not surprising considering that Kumar's indiscretion (to put it mildly) was meant to save the Prime Minister's skin. It was only when the pressure of public opinion became unbearable that Ashwani Kumar was asked to step down! This brazenness and stone-walling highlights how serious the problem of ensuring the independence and autonomy of the CBI is. Manmohan Singh seems to be so much indebted to Ashwani Kumar that he has now been appointed as special envoy for Japan with a Cabinet rank.

The Supreme Court, in its hearing of the coal gate case on 8 May 2013, castigated the government once again by saying that the CBI has become 'a caged parrot, speaking in its master's voice. It is a sordid saga that it is one parrot with many masters.' The amendments made by the joint secretaries in the PMO and the Coal Ministry and the Law Minister effectively changed 'the heart of the coal report', the court observed. The court said that the CBI should know how to stand up to all pulls and pressures. Against this background, it was shocking that Salman Khurshid, External Affairs Minister and himself a former Law Minister, behaved like a hair-splitting advocate and said, 'You should not be unfair to Ashwani...There's a thin line between interfering and remaining informed"!(*IE*, 19 May 2013). How clever can one get? It was a pitiable attempt to try to fool all the people all the time. The CBI admitted that it was an 'aberration' on its part to have shown the investigation report to the government. The court directed that the government come out with a law to insulate the CBI by 10 July 2013, which was to be the next date of hearing of the case. The government decided that a committee of retired judges be appointed to supervise the working of the CBI on a day to day basis. This does not make sense. Most important, the manner in which retired judges will be selected has not been made clear. The Supreme Court had suggested in the hawala case that the responsibility of supervising the CBI should be entrusted to CVC. The court had directed, 'The CVC shall be responsible for the efficient functioning of the CBI...The CVC shall be entrusted with the responsibility of superintendence over the CBI's functioning. The CBI shall report to the CVC about cases taken up for investigation...' (*Hawala judgment.*: 689). This will certainly be preferable as the CVC, being a statutory authority, will be accountable for his actions. In the alternative, the responsibility could be entrusted to the proposed Lok Pal, which the government has been resisting all along. The intention of the government clearly seems to be to keep the ultimate control of the CBI with itself and make only cosmetic changes.

Essentially, the CBI has always been used by the government as its exploitative arm to fix its political opponents and to serve its political ends from time to time. This issue has come up again in the context of the debate on the Lok Pal Bill. Demands have been made by the proponents of the bill that the CBI be placed under the Lok Pal and that the government should have no control over it in so far as the cases referred to it by the Lok Pal are concerned. But it is necessary to remember that handling anti-corruption cases is only one part of the charter of the CBI. It also deals with a whole gamut of criminal cases, including those related to terrorism. An answer therefore needs to be found which will address the ills of the CBI as a whole. A step in this direction will be giving a statutory status to the CBI by enacting a separate law for the purpose. This proposal has languished since 1970 due to strong opposition by states whose experience of the CBI has been far from happy. Unless the states are assured that the CBI will not be the handmaiden of the ruling party at the Centre, it will not be possible to obtain their cooperation. For this purpose, the objects and reason of the new law should categorically state that it is meant to give autonomy and independence to the CBI and the provisions of the act are meant to subserve this purpose. This can be ensured in the new legislation by creating, at the top, a governing board which will comprise of the representatives of the Centre and the states. Under the terms of appointment, the Director of the CBI must be made ineligible for holding any public office after retirement, as is the case with Chairman, Union Public Service Commission (UPSC) and C&AG. The problem is not confined to the CBI. It pertains to all important and sensitive police organizations. It must be underlined that the NDA had appointed seven IPS officers as governors. The UPA has done even better by appointing eight of them, including appointing them as members of the UPSC and the National Human Rights Commission. The modalities for the transfers, promotion and other service matters of the staff of the CBI should be the same as those of the central police organizations (CPOs), as per the directions of the Supreme Court, discussed later. This will require setting up of selection committees of officers to consider all such matters without any political or extraneous influences. The CVC should have the overall responsibility of overseeing the working of the CBI. He should be asked to submit an annual report on the working of the CBI to Parliament.

Make Indulging in Corruption Prohibitively Costly

The directive, known as 'single directive', which had come down from the British days, required the CBI to take government permission not only before filing charge sheets against public servants, but also before registering a case against any government official above the rank of a Joint Secretary. The Supreme Court had struck down the single directive. According to T. S. R. Subramanian, former Cabinet Secretary, 'the withdrawal of the single directive wreaked further havoc. It has opened the floodgates for frivolous enquiries and witch-hunts...Withdrawal of protection to upright officers has been the net result of the roll back of the single directive' (Subramanian 2004: 325). The directive was revived again in the CVC Act. The government has strongly defended its policy in the Supreme Court and has told the court that this authority could not be taken away even in a court-ordered or court-monitored investigation such as the coal blocks allotment case. The government refused to make any exception to the rule mandating the CBI to approach it for sanction to investigate officers at the level of Joint Secretary and above, as provided in Section 6A of the Delhi Special Police Establishment Act. The government went so far as to tell the court that the 'court is not at liberty to negate this provision even in exercise of powers under Articles 32 and 142' and that this requirement could not be waived 'under any circumstances' (*IE*, 18 July 2013). The Supreme Court has decided to join issues with the government and has declared that in a court-monitored investigation, the CBI can go ahead with the probe and no permission from the government is required (*IE*, 2 August 2013).

This stand needs to be examined from several angles. To begin with, it may be best to refer to what Prime Minister Jawaharlal Nehru has written, 'It is obviously necessary to protect public servants, but it is also necessary to protect the public from them' (Jawaharlal Nehru Memorial Fund 1998: 174). The morale of senior officers is likely to be adversely affected if there are no checks and balances in the system and the decision is left entirely to the CBI to decide whether to proceed against any officer. In taking a decision on the matter, the functioning and reputation of the CBI cannot be overlooked. Its high-handedness has been seen in several cases. There have also been instances of the CBI taking action to settle past scores. There is another equally, or even more, important aspect of the close nexus between politicians and senior civil servants which has come to light in all major cases of corruption. In some of these cases, such as Bofors, the government blatantly shielded the officers who had helped it in taking certain decisions. If the officers are not protected, they may not like to take the risk in taking arbitrary and opaque decisions. If this axis of evil is to be abolished, the powers which currently vest in the government, on whether to permit the CBI to investigate senior officers, must be done away with. At the same time, two precautions are necessary. First is to make CBI a statutory authority which will make it much more accountable to the courts and the people at large than it is at present. Second, it must be laid down that the CBI will have to take prior approval of the CVC before starting investigations and filing charge sheets against senior officers.

One of the reasons why corruption has spread its tentacles so far and wide is because it is considered a low risk, high gain activity. Another reason is that corrupt persons seem to be treated with respect and enjoy a certain status in society. It is time both of these are removed.

It is often noticed in cases of large value purchases that laying down technical parameters and financial evaluation of bids is done in accordance with prescribed procedures. And then money is demanded for making the correct decision! To deal with such a complex web is by no means easy. The war against corruption will have to be waged on many fronts. A mere setting up of the Lok Pal will not be enough, unless a comprehensive strategy is adopted to make indulging in corrupt practices a very costly endeavour for the incumbent. This will require concerted action on the following 26 points, among others:

1. Adopt a national policy on eradication of corruption which can be implemented simultaneously by all states, the Centre and their agencies;
2. Enact a separate law for the CBI guaranteeing its freedom and autonomy;
3. Amend the Prevention of Corruption Act, as recommended by SARC, to expand the definition of corruption to include gross perversion of the Constitution and democratic institutions amounting to wilful violation of oath of office; abuse of authority unduly favouring or harming someone; obstruction of justice; and squandering public money (Government of India 2007: 178);
4. Amend the Prevention of Corruption Act, as recommended by SARC, to include in its purview private sector providers of public utility services;
5. Bring under the Prevention of Corruption Act non-governmental agencies, which receive substantial funding, as recommended by SARC. Norms should be laid down that any institution or body that receives more than 50 per cent of its annual operating costs, or a sum equal to or greater than Rs 1 crore during any of the preceding three years shall be deemed to have obtained 'substantial funding' for that period;
6. Enact the Lok Pal Act by revisiting relevant issues;
7. Enact a model law on an all-India basis for Lok Ayuktas on the lines of recommendations of the conference of Lok Ayuktas;
8. Give constitutional status to the Lok Pal and Lok Ayuktas;
9. Do away with Section 19 of the Prevention of Corruption Act which provides that no court can take cognisance of a case against a public servant unless prior sanction of the authority competent to remove the accused from office has been obtained. Anumeha Jha points out that, 'about 66 per cent of the requests for sanction of prosecution of public servants on charges of corruption were pending with the central government at the end of 2010. Criminal prosecution was sanctioned in only six per cent of the

cases, while 94 per cent were let off the hook by serving (sic) departmental penalties. Also as many as 9,927 corruption cases investigated by the CBI were pending with the courts as 2010 ended' (Jha 2011: 35–36). In Maharashtra, the CBI could obtain conviction in hardly 25 per cent cases. From 2008 to June 2013, as many as 2,426 government servants were caught red-handed by the CBI while accepting bribes. Of these, only 550 were convicted by the courts (*Loksatta*, 19 July 2013). The requirement of prior government sanction has invariably led to controversy, particularly where prosecution of powerful politicians such as J. Jayalalitha, Mayawati, A. R. Antulay, Lalu Prasad Yadav or Mulayam Singh Yadav was concerned. For example, the sanction for the prosecution of Jayalalitha, the then Chief Minister of Tamil Nadu, granted by Governor Chenna Reddy was strongly criticized by Atal Bihari Vajpayee, leader of BJP in the Lok Sabha and Andhra Pradesh Chief Minister N. T. Rama Rao (*BS*, 4 April 1995). The decision of T. V. Rajeshwar, Governor of UP, to reject the CBI's request to prosecute Mayawati in the Taj Corridor case was highly questionable. This requirement has also led to inordinate delays in sanction of prosecution, thereby defeating the ends of justice. The Maharashtra Chief Minister, Prithviraj Chavan, withheld permission for anti-corruption enquiries against six ministers—five belonging to the NCP and one to Congress. The Maharashtra Cabinet refused permission to prosecute Minister for Medical Education, Vijaykumar Gavit, in an anti-corruption case, fearing that if permission is given in one case, other ministers facing similar enquiries too will have to be proceeded against. In such an exasperating situation, no alternative other than approaching the court in a writ petition is left. The government now proposes to extend this protection to retired officers and amending the law to provide that prior approval of the government will be required in every case involving a retired government officer of the rank of Joint Secretary and above. For reasons discussed earlier, it must be made clear in the proposed CBI legislation that it will have full freedom to prosecute anyone, irrespective of his position in the government, whether as minister or a senior civil servant, whether serving or retired, but it will have to obtain the approval of the CVC for the purpose;

10. Enhance the punishment for offences of corruption substantially;
11. Shift the burden of proof in such cases on the accused;
12. Curtail discretionary powers at all levels drastically. Wherever use of discretion is considered inevitable, guidelines may be prescribed for its use and such guidelines should be made public;
13. Set up as many special courts as may be necessary to ensure that each corruption case is disposed off within a year at the most. The decisions

of the courts in cases such as that of Sukh Ram, former union Minister of State for Communications, Bangaru Laxman, former President of the BJP and Ravinder Paul Singh Sidhu, former Chairman of the Punjab Public Service Commission, delivered after over 11 years of filing of cases will bear out the importance of this suggestion. This will no doubt require large expenditure but it will be well worth it. It was heartening to read that the Supreme Court had asked the government to set up, within eight weeks, 22 additional CBI courts for trying corruption cases (*IE*, 31 January 2013);

14. Energetic steps should be taken for the effective implementation of the Benami Act which has gathered dust for long enough, as the rules thereunder have not been notified. Steps have now been taken by the government to introduce a bill in Parliament for enacting a new comprehensive law on the subject. This needs to be expedited;

15. Steps should be taken to confiscate the property acquired by a corrupt public servant in his own name or in the name of his dependents from income which is beyond his known sources. Back in 1996 the Supreme Court had pointed out the inadequacy of the anti-corruption measures in the case of *Delhi Development Authority v. Skipper Construction Co. (P) Ltd.*, (1996, 4 SCC 622): '...a law providing for forfeiture of properties acquired by holders of "public office" (including the offices/posts in the public sector corporations) by indulging in corrupt and illegal acts and deals, is a crying necessity in the present state of our society. The law must extend not only to—as does SAFEMA [Smugglers and Foreign Exchange Manipulators (Forfeiture of Property) Act, 1976]—properties acquired in the name of the holder of such office but also to properties held in the names of his spouse, children or other relatives and associates. Once it is proved that the holder of such office has indulged in corrupt acts, all such properties should be attached forthwith. The law should place the burden of proving that the attached properties were not acquired with the aid of monies/properties received in the course of corrupt deals, upon the holder of that property as does SAFEMA whose validity has already been upheld by this court in the aforesaid decision of the larger Constitution Bench. *Such a law has become an absolute necessity, if the canker of corruption is not to prove the death-knell of this nation.* According to several perceptive observers, it has already reached near-fatal dimensions. *It is for Parliament to act in this matter, if they really mean business.*' The Law Commission of India took this suggestion seriously and suggested the enactment of a special law and drafted the Corrupt Public Servants (Forfeiture of Property) Bill in its 166th report and sent it to the government in 1999. There has been no action so far. It is gratifying to note that the states of

Bihar and Odisha have, in recent years, confiscated properties of some of their public servants and have converted them into schools and public offices. In this way, it should be possible to send a strong message to law-breakers that the government is serious on the subject;

16. Vigilance wings in various offices and the anti-corruption directorate in each state should be put under the Lok Ayukta;

17. Action should be taken to sanction prosecution and/or initiating a departmental inquiry in every case involving corruption, within a period of three months at the most.

18. The Santhanam Committee on Prevention of Corruption (1963) observed that the constitutional protection given to government servants by Article 311, which limits the doctrine of pleasure, was first given only by the Government of India Act, 1935. The committee also noted that judicial interpretation of Article 311 had resulted in making disciplinary proceedings highly involved (Government of India 1963: 113). The National Police Commission had recommended that sub-clause (c) of the proviso to Article 311 (2) may be amended to read as under:

> (c) Where the President or the Governor, as the case may be, is satisfied that in the interest of security of the state or the maintenance of integrity in public services in the state it is not expedient to hold such inquiry (Government of India 1980: 27).

This recommendation was made in 1980 but it is still gathering dust. I would suggest that Articles 311 of the Constitution should be amended to take away the protection provided therein to a public servant, if he is charged with corruption. However, the Group of Ministers seems to have decided against amending Article 311 (*The Statesman*, 31 July 2011). This decision needs to be reviewed;

19. The proposed enactment by the central government for protecting whistle-blowers covers only central government employees. Similar enactments need to be passed by all states for their employees.

20. Bribe-givers need to be held as responsible as bribe takers to make a real dent on the menace of corruption. The law should be amended to prosecute them as well;

21. Articles 105 and 194 of the Constitution should be amended to make it clear that the privilege mentioned therein will not be available to MPs and MLAs respectively in cases involving corruption. The suggestion made by the Supreme Court in the *Jharkhand Mukti Morcha* case to this effect, as also the recommendation of the NCRWC in this behalf have remained unimplemented so far;

22. Section 7 of the Prevention of Corruption Act should be amended, as recommended by SARC, to provide for a special offence of 'collusive bribery'. An offence could be classified as collusive bribery if the outcome or intended outcome of the transaction leads to a loss to state, public or private interest. It is suggested that in all such cases if it is established that the interest of the state or public has suffered because of an act of a public servant, then the court shall presume that the public servant and the beneficiary of the decision committed an offence of 'collusive bribery'. The punishment for all such cases of collusive bribery should be double that of other cases of bribery (Government of India 2007: 178);

23. A law should be enacted for protecting whistleblowers on the lines proposed by the Law Commission in its 179th report: Whistle-blowers exposing false claims, fraud or corruption should be protected by ensuring confidentiality and anonymity; protection from victimization in career, and other administrative measures to prevent bodily harm and harassment. The legislation should also cover corporate whistle-blowers unearthing fraud or serious damage to public interest by wilful acts of commission and omission. Acts of harassment or victimization of or retaliation against a whistle-blower should be criminal offences with substantial penalty and sentence;

24. The exemption given to the CBI from the Right to Information Act should be withdrawn. While information pertaining to cases which are under investigation could be withheld from the public, there is every justification to make available to the people information about closed or decided cases by releasing the relevant CBI papers. For example, the CBI is reported to have withdrawn a 12-year-old case, presumably registered during the NDA regime, against Congress President Sonia Gandhi's former Personal Secretary Vincent George, citing 'insufficient evidence' in its closure report. According to the CBI, George and his family's assets showed a quantum increase after 1990. His properties included houses and shops in South Delhi, a house in Bengaluru, a plot of land in Chennai, land in Kerala and a farmland on the outskirts of Delhi. He was found to have over Rs 1.5 crore in bank accounts (IE, 7 June 2013). People should have a right to know how the decision to close the case was arrived at. This will create confidence among the people about the proper working of the CBI and go a long way towards enhancing its credibility.

25. Standing committees of Parliament and state legislatures must be established to monitor the performance of the government in the matter of containing corruption, and most importantly;

26. Pressure of public opinion needs to be created for greater political and administrative will to deal with the menace of corruption effectively and expeditiously.

Electoral Reforms

The subject of electoral reforms has figured in the government's discussion with leaders of political parties on several occasions. Jayaprakash Narayan had put forth electoral reforms as one of the demands in his 'charter of demands' in 1975, prior to the declaration of emergency. Accordingly, Indira Gandhi had held talks with opposition leaders on 22 and 29 April 1975 (Kashyap 1997: 31). However, the Election Laws (Amendment) Bill introduced on 4 August 1975 and passed the next day was *only* intended to validate Indira Gandhi's election! The bill was passed within an hour in the Rajya Sabha the very next day, and received the President's assent on the same day! Only the V. P. Singh government took any real initiative to bring the subject of election reforms to the fore in 1990 by preparing a draft bill for the purpose (Government of India 1990). However, since the government was short-lived, nothing came out of these efforts. Even the special session of Parliament called during the term of the P. V. Narasimha Rao government failed to arrive at any consensus on outstanding issues relating to electoral reforms. While replying to the debate reviewing the state of the nation in Parliament, the then Prime Minister I. K. Gujral had made a number of specific promises. One of these pertained to electoral reforms. He said, 'The Bill is ready and we shall put it before an all-party committee' (*TOI*, 2 September 1997). Like his other promises, this too remained in thin air. We cannot even say it remained on paper! The Atal Bihari Vajpayee-led NDA government had also made an announcement that a comprehensive bill for electoral reforms will be placed before Parliament, but this never materialized. The UPA, being more mature in handling such matters, has neither made any commitment on the subject nor has it taken any action during its long regime of ten years. All that the Congress did in August 2013 was to send its suggestions on electoral reforms to the Law Commission (*IE*, 18 August 2013). Does this not mean that we cannot expect any forward movement on electoral reforms from our elected governments, irrespective of which political party/coalition is in power?

We can only look to the Supreme Court to usher in electoral reforms, particularly on sensitive issues. The Supreme Court has become the 'court of first resort' for addressing diverse public concerns which have been neglected by elected governments and the court's mostly forward-looking, progressive decisions have given the lead for new policies. In keeping with this trend, the Supreme Court has been responsible for some of the most significant electoral reforms. One of these pertained to the empowerment of voters by laying down that each candidate must declare his financial assets and liabilities and criminal background, if any, in an affidavit, along with his nomination papers. Though all political parties had ganged up against this decision and had insisted that the government should promulgate an ordinance to nullify the judgment, the Supreme Court reiterated its position on the subject and insisted on the Election Commission implementing its directive speedily.

The criminalization of politics is a matter of serious concern. Nearly 40 per cent of the MPs have criminal cases pending against them. Most of these involve serious offences. Because of the amendment made to the RPA, even though some of them have been convicted by courts, they continued to serve as MPs pending decisions on their appeals in higher courts. Several are ministers in the states and at the Centre. The Supreme Court, by its decision dated 10 July 2013, struck down Section 8(4) of the RPA, 1951, which protected the convicted MPs and MLAs from disqualification, if they appealed before a higher court within three months, on the ground of pendency of appeal. The court ruled that Parliament lacked legislative competence to enact this provision since it was in direct conflict with Articles 101(3)(a) and 190(3)(a) of the Constitution, which prohibit Parliament from deferring the date from which the disqualification will come into effect. The court has, however, softened the effect of its judgment by ruling that 'sitting members of Parliament and state legislatures who have already been convicted for any of the specified offences and who have filed appeals or revisions which are pending, should not be affected by the declaration of unconstitutionality of section 8(4) now made by us in this judgment.' Soli Sorabjee, a leading constitutional expert, while welcoming the judgment rightly questioned this part of the judgment and has argued that 'criminals do not deserve any sympathetic protection from the court by invocation in effect of the doctrine of prospective over-ruling. Law breakers should not be permitted at all to function as law makers. The court should have gone the whole hog' (Sorabjee 2013: 9). A number of political parties have questioned the judgment on various other points. Some experts believe that some operative parts of the judgment need to be further clarified by the court. Therefore, it will not be surprising if a revision petition is filed in the court or a request is made for referring the issues to a larger constitution Bench. Whatever it is, the pronouncement by the court needs to be wholeheartedly welcomed, as otherwise political parties will never allow the legislation to be passed on these lines. However, the government is planning to amend the RPA and bring in a constitutional amendment to nullify the Supreme Court order. As it appears, a long legal battle appears inevitable.

Another important pronouncement made by the Supreme Court on 10 July 2013 was also long overdue. The court ruled that a person who is in 'lawful custody', including under trials as well as those in police or judicial custody, cannot contest elections to the Lok Sabha or state assemblies. The Bench held that a person who cannot vote because he is jailed is not an 'elector' under the RPA, and therefore, he is disqualified from contesting elections. As I had pointed out in one of my earlier book, Pappu Yadav, who was convicted for murder and was undergoing a sentence in Purnia jail, contested the Lok Sabha elections in 1999 as an independent candidate and was elected with a lead of over 2 lakh votes, with 66.3 per cent votes, the highest in the state of Bihar. Pappu Kalani, a noted criminal undergoing sentence in Yeravada jail, was elected as an independent candidate to the Maharashtra Assembly in 1999 (Godbole 2003: 94). I have given just two examples to show how serious is the rot in the system. But the government has already initiated steps to amend the RPA to nullify the judgment of the Supreme Court.

The electoral scene in India has changed decisively during the last few years due to the supremacy of money and muscle power. More than 30 per cent of the MLAs and MPs are now millionaires. One cannot hope to get elected without spending huge sums of money. Gopinath Munde, Deputy Leader of Opposition in the Lok Sabha, publicly admitted that while he spent only Rs 29,000 on his first elections, he had to spend Rs 8 crore on his elections as a MP in 2009, when the ceiling on expenditure by a candidate for Parliament election was only Rs 25 lakh. There is a clamour that action must be taken against him by the Election Commission, but there must be scores of other MPs who have also incurred huge expenditures on their elections. The only mistake Munde made was to speak about it publicly while making a point about the urgency of electoral reforms. The Aam Aadmi Party, the latest party to enter the election fray, is reported to have selected some millionaires as its party candidates. We cannot blame them, if they have to make an effective showing in the forthcoming elections.

There is no inner party democracy and political parties have hardly any accountability. 'First families' or hereditary leadership has taken firm roots in all political parties, except the BJP and the left-leaning parties. 'Paid news' has been responsible for misleading voters regarding the true merits of candidates. Yet another disturbing feature is the disenchantment of the voters as reflected in low turnouts, particularly in urban areas and in metropolitan cities.

UPA I's common minimum programme (CMP) contained an important promise which has been lost sight of, not just by the people at large, but also the government itself. It stated that, 'As part of its commitment to electoral reforms, the UPA will initiate steps to introduce state funding of elections at the earliest.' Use of money power has become a major impediment in ensuring free and fair elections and a level playing field for all candidates. Political parties raising funds clandestinely has been one of the main causes of generation of black money in the country. It has also led to criminalization of politics and crony capitalism on a large scale. It is often argued that state funding of elections can address these concerns. The discussion on state funding of elections has so far been confined to giving assistance to individual candidates and for various reasons this is clearly neither feasible nor advisable. But, the Congress Party, in its submissions to the Law Commission in August 2013, once again suggested partial state funding of candidates. Prem Shankar Jha has suggested that the scheme should fund political parties and not the candidates. He has written:

> The most important requirement is that it should meet all of the financial needs of the parties, and not just a part of it. If it does not do that, the parties' dependence on criminal elements to finance them will continue. Second, the money in the fund should not be distributed in any form (such as TV time) to individual candidates but must go to the parties to which they belong. Third, the share of each party must be proportional to its share of votes in the last election. Fourth, the money should go only to recognised political parties. The Election Commission will have to establish a criterion for recognition. This is usually a minimum share of the vote. Fifth, there will have to be separate war chests for the central and state Assembly elections. Lastly, every paisa of expenditure will need to be audited. The Election Commission will have to be expanded and equipped to carry out this task (Jha 2004: 30).

However, this scheme too is not without its drawbacks. Political parties will still continue to raise money by donations from industries, builders and so on. This will be particularly true of political parties which are not eligible to get state funding. Candidates will also continue to spend their own money, in addition to what they get from their parties. It is thus doubtful if state funding will serve any useful purpose.

Coalition governments have been afflicted by serious issues regarding the responsibilities of coalition partners. Often, in the name of compulsions of coalition politics or 'coalition *dharma*' (which in reality is '*adharma*'), a phrase popularized by the then Prime Minister Atal Bihari Vajpayee, tenets of good governance and moral principles have been compromised. Against this background, any talk of India being the world's largest and most vibrant democracy sounds like hollow rhetoric.

The field of electoral reforms is vast and has a long and chequered history. In fact, it is a history of inaction, irrespective of which political party has been in power. Due to the constraints of time and space, I deal with only some important electoral reforms which will make a significant difference to the functioning of democracy in India:[2]

1. Elections to the state assemblies should be held along with those for the Lok Sabha. This will be much more convenient from every point of view and also save considerable expenditure. Four states had their Assembly elections along with the Lok Sabha elections in 2004. There is nothing to indicate that the mandate was affected in any way.
2. Voting ought to be made compulsory for every citizen by including it as a fundamental duty in Article 51A of the Constitution. The experience

of a number of countries which have taken this step shows that voting percentages have gone up substantially.

3. Simultaneous with these, providing for negative voting may be provided by adding the option of 'none of the above' at the end of the list of candidates in the electronic voting machine. Negative voting will be a strong signal to political parties to rethink about selection of candidates and to mend their ways.

4. It must be laid down that the Prime Minister and the Chief Minister of a state must have a popular mandate and must be an elected member of the Lok Sabha and Vidhan Sabha respectively. Such a proposal was contained in the Constitution (Thirty-second Amendment) Bill, 1973 which was introduced in the Lok Sabha on 16 May 1973. The bill was referred to a joint committee of the two Houses. In spite of several extensions, the joint committee failed to submit its report and as a result the bill lapsed on the dissolution of the Fifth Lok Sabha. (Kashyap, 1997: 104). This was clear proof of the lack of political will on the subject. But the issue is important enough and needs to be pursued.

5. The Constitution should be amended to provide for a 33 per cent quota for women in the Lok Sabha and state assemblies. This will be the surest way of empowering women. However, these efforts have been stalled since 1996. It is imperative to create a political consensus on the subject without any further delay.

6. A statutory limit must be put on the number of MLAs/MPs who may be given the perks and status of ministers. It is ridiculous that a small state like Meghalaya has five chief ministers—one regular Chief Minister, and four others who have been given the perks and facilities of the Chief Minister! Similar improprieties have been committed in several other states. This mockery of democracy and loot of the exchequer must end.

7. With a multi-religious, multi-lingual, multi-racial and multi-cultural society in India, it is imperative that a candidate declared elected should be able to represent such a diverse constituency in the real sense of the term. Currently, candidates are selected by political parties on the basis of the composition of the constituency and the selected candidate generally belongs to the majority component therein. The candidate also generally appeals to and relies on the members of his own caste and community. Minorities find very little space in their electioneering. This must change if democracy has to empower all sections of the population. At present, it is seen that the winning candidate often hardly gets 15–20 per cent of the votes cast in the election. This is a travesty of representative democracy. It is therefore necessary to specify that, in order to be declared a winner, a candidate must get a minimum of 50 per cent+1 votes. If no one emerges

successful in the first round, there should be a re-run between the two candidates winning the highest votes. This reform is long overdue, particularly keeping in view the fractured polity in the country.

8. A central law must be enacted to lay down all matters pertaining to political parties. These will include, among others, qualification for membership, commitment to secularism, promoting and practicing a clean public life, obligation not to give tickets to those with criminal backgrounds, adequate representation to women, minorities and other weaker sections, raising of funds and their audits, ensuring inner party democracy, holding regular and timely elections at all levels in a transparent manner and so on. The CIC's decision in 2013 to make the RTI Act applicable to selected national parties must be welcomed from this point of view even though it has met with stiff opposition from some parties. The Supreme Court has also suggested that the Parliament should enact a law to govern the working of political parties.

9. Looking to the inevitability of coalition governments in the foreseeable future, some salutary guidelines need to be agreed upon for their smooth functioning. It should be laid down that a coalition entered into before the elections on the basis of a common minimum programme should be given preference by the President/Governor for invitation to form the government over a coalition put together after election results are announced. Further, if a coalition partner in such a pre-election coalition walks out of the government for any reasons, it should be imperative for it to seek a fresh mandate from the electorate and till that time its members will cease to be members of the House. This will be the best way to impart stability to coalition arrangements.

10. A person should be disqualified for contesting an election if charges pertaining to serious offence(s) are framed by a magistrate against him after hearing evidence produced by the police. A striking example of this is that of Mohammed Shahabuddin, RJD MP from Siwan, against whom 52 cases are registered (*HT*, 9 May 2007). Atiq Ahmed, MP from UP, was on the run for nine months before he was arrested by Delhi police. Ahmed was wanted in nine cases, including that of murder in UP and was carrying a reward of Rs 20,000 (*IE*, 2 February 2008). Arun Gavali, a MLA in Maharashtra, has been charged under the dreaded Maharashtra Organized Crime Control Act (MOCCA). Another MLA from Maharashtra, Anil Gote, has been similarly charged under MOCCA (*Sakal*, 30 April 2008).

11. A sitting MLA/MP should be disqualified from holding public office if charges are framed against him in a court. If such a person already holds a public office, it should be incumbent on him to resign from the public office immediately. In Bihar, during the 12-year regime of Lalu Prasad

Yadav and his wife Rabri Devi as chief ministers, 11 ministers had to go to jail (*Sakal*, 22 July 2002). The Minister for Minority Affairs in the union Cabinet, Rahman Khan, has been booked under the Prevention of Corruption Act, the Wakf Act and the IPC, following an order by the Lok Ayukta court in Bijapur district. He has also been found guilty of defrauding the Amaranth Cooperative Bank in Karnataka by RBI and the Karnataka Registrar of Cooperative Societies (*The Sunday Guardian*, 4 and 11 November 2012). The Supreme Court has admitted a PIL on the question of whether the President should refuse to administer the oath of office as minister to a person with a criminal background. With widespread criminalization of politics and where almost all parties give tickets to persons with criminal backgrounds and later make them ministers, this is a highly sensitive political issue which no political party wants to address. The Supreme Court has asked the Centre and the states to respond to the following questions before the matter is placed before a Constitution Bench: Whether a minister charged with a serious offence by a court of law should resign; whether a charge sheeted person can be appointed as a minister; whether the President/Governor could advise PM/CM to drop such ministers; whether presumption of innocence till pronounced guilty by a court of law is applicable to a person when he is being appointed as minister; whether laying down of parameters in this regard would amount to interference by the judiciary in the parliamentary domain (*TOI*, 20 February 2007). Several of these questions will not be relevant in mature democracies in the western world and the fact that they have to be posed by the Apex Court is an eloquent commentary on the state of public life and its deterioration in India over the years. Interestingly, it is for the first time that the last question—whether any decision by the court will be considered interference by the judiciary in the parliamentary domain—has been framed by the court for consideration. The outcome of this case will have considerable significance and impact on the political life of the country.

12. It may be recalled that during ten months in 1967–68, there were as many as 438 defections. Of these, 210 became members of the council of ministers. There were wholesale defections in Andhra Pradesh, J&K, Karnataka, Haryana and Sikkim (Vivekanandan 1995: 296). This virus has been contained to some extent by the anti-defection law. A proposal to disqualify a political defector from his continued membership of the legislature was first contained in the Constitution (Thirty-second Amendment) Bill, 1973 which was introduced in the Lok Sabha on 16 May 1973. The bill was referred to a joint committee of the two Houses. In spite of several extensions, the joint committee failed to submit its

report and as a result the bill lapsed on the dissolution of the Fifth Lok Sabha (Kashyap, 1997: 104). This was clear proof of the lack of political will on the subject. Finally, it was only in 1985 that a Constitution amendment could be effected. But the law now needs to be amended in the light of experience gained so far to make a clear distinction between dissent and defection to ensure that dissenting voices in a political party are not suppressed. Also, the power to hear anti-defection cases should be entrusted to the Election Commission of India. The President/Governor should be empowered to act on the basis of EC's recommendations.

13. The NDA government did a major disservice to the country by amending the RPA and doing away with the domiciliary requirement for contesting elections to the Rajya Sabha. This made a mockery of the principle of federalism, irrespective of what the Supreme Court has held. Further, it has negated the nomenclature of the Rajya Sabha as the House of States. It needs to be laid down that a person will have to be ordinarily resident in the state if he wishes to contest an election to the Rajya Sabha from that state.

14. Promising distribution of freebies in election manifestoes to lure voters has reached absurd proportions and is making a mockery of free and fair elections. The list of freebies is endless—colour television sets, pressure cookers, LPG stoves and gas connections, mobile phones, laptops, bicycles and so on. After the last Assembly elections in Tamil Nadu, the cost of the freebies to the exchequer was Rs 2,400 crore. Since no political party is interested in addressing the issue, the matter was raised in a PIL before the Supreme Court. The court directed that the EC should take up the task of forming guidelines under the Model Code of Conduct, for election manifestos in consultation with political parties. However, the observations of the court, 'distribution of largesse such as TVs and laptops to eligible and deserving persons was directly related to the directive principles of state policy', (*IE*, 6 July 2013), if true, are likely to be misunderstood and used by political parties to justify their present practices. At the same time, the court itself seems to have felt that giving such allurements during elections makes a mockery of ensuring a level playing field for all candidates and free and fair elections.

15. The menace of 'paid news' needs to be put down firmly if the sanctity of elections is to be safeguarded. For this purpose, exemplary punishments must be provided to all those who indulge in this foul game, namely, the candidates, media houses, printers, publishers, broadcasters, consultants and so on. Candidates against whom such charges are proved must be debarred from contesting any election for a period of six years. Strict action also needs to be taken against media houses.

In a country wedded to democracy, ensuring free and fair elections and a level playing field for all candidates is supremely important. But no political party in India has a real commitment to this cause. Based on this criterion of good governance too, India's record leaves a great deal to be desired.

Right to Property

One of the fall-outs of the socialist pattern of society, which was adopted at Jawaharlal Nehru's bidding, was doing away with the right to property as a fundamental right.[3] 'During the Nehru Phase which may be said to have closed in 1964, as many as 17 constitutional amendments were enacted. Of these, four affected fundamental rights, with three seeking to amend property provisions' (Kashyap 1990: 66). The Government of India wanting to pursue land reforms was understandable but in that guise to abolish the right to property as a fundamental right was totally unjustified. In most cases of acquisition of land, it is seen that the land belongs to common people. Giving them reasonable compensation is the right thing to do. Speaking on the right to property, Nehru had described the land question as being a 'dynamic, moving, changing and revolutionary' one. But in the case of *State of Madras v. Shrimati Champakam Dorairajan*, the Supreme Court said, 'The chapter on fundamental rights is sacrosanct and not liable to be abridged by any legislative or executive act or order except to the extent provided in the particular Article in Part III. The directive principles of state policy have to conform to and run subsidiary to the chapter on fundamental rights' (Kashyap 1990: 67). This position of the Supreme Court underwent a change later.

To clarify the position and to give effect to what was believed to be the real intention of the framers of the Constitution, new Articles 31A and 31B and the Ninth Schedule were inserted in the Constitution by the First Amendment.

The Constitution (Forty-second Amendment) Bill, 1976, *inter alia*, spelt out expressly the high ideals of socialism, secularism and integrity of the nation. It is interesting to note that when the Bill was being debated in Parliament, one of the criticisms voiced in both the Houses was that inclusion of the word 'socialist' in the preamble to the Constitution would, by itself, hardly serve any purpose, especially when the right to property was still being retained. Many members were also very critical of the fact that the bill had not provided for the deletion of the right to property from among the fundamental rights listed in Part III of the Constitution. They maintained that right to property was inconsistent with the concept of socialism which was now being inscribed in the Preamble and demanded that it [right to property] should be altogether dropped from the Constitution (Kashyap, 1997: 91–92, 97). When the motion *for the consideration* of the bill was put to vote, the House divided, *Ayes* 346, *Noes* 2 and the motion was declared adopted. When the *motion for passing* of the bill was put to vote, the

House divided, *Ayes* 366, *Noes* 4 and the bill was declared as passed. This shows the populist mindset which prevailed in all political parties.

N. A. Palkhivala, eminent constitutional expert, has stated that the right to property is often derided as the 'least defensible' right in a socialist democracy and is considered a dirty word. But he has highlighted that there is no democracy anywhere in the world where as a matter of constitutional law or practice the right to property is not recognized and respected. It appears in the Magna Carta (1215) and the French Declaration of the Rights of Man (1789). It is recognized in the constitutions of the US, Australia, Japan, West Germany, Canada, Nigeria and so on. The Universal Declaration of Human Rights (1948) also recognizes the right to private property. India is a signatory to that Declaration. The framers of the Indian Constitution attached sufficient importance to property to incorporate it in the chapter on fundamental rights. Suggestions by some members of the Assembly to remove this right from the chapter on fundamental rights and to put it in a separate part were not accepted. Palkhivala has rightly made a strong plea for its reinstatement as a fundamental right (Palhivala 1974: 34–40).

During the course of marathon arguments on the *Kesavananda Bharati* case in the Supreme Court, Nani Palkhivala described the Twenty-fifth Amendment to the Constitution as a 'monumental outrage'. By this amendment, Article 31C [saving laws giving effect to certain directive principles] was inserted in the Constitution which, said Palkhivala, 'is a vast octopus, a new monster that can entangle and devour property in all forms, in addition to land' (Kamath 2007: 180).

M. Hidayatullah, former CJI, was always of the view that it was a mistake to put property rights in the chapter on fundamental rights and to enforce those rights as such (Hidayatullah 1979: vii). He felt that property rights should have been protected in a different way. Similar views were expressed by several other judges.

H. M. Seervai has emphasized that several other fundamental rights such as right to freedom of religion will be adversely affected if the right to property was not a guaranteed fundamental right and if the obligation to pay compensation for private property acquired for a public purpose was not provided for (Seervai 1978: 150, 154).

Atul M. Setalvad has stated that while there was no unanimity on what the 'basic features' of the Constitution were, it is clear that fundamental right to property is not one of them. Setalvad has emphasized that today:

> the citizen of India has no right whatever to hold property and his property can be taken away by the legislature without any restraint. It is also curious that whilst, when the Seventeenth Amendment was introduced, an exception was carved out to Article 31A to the effect that the state could not acquire land

within the limits of the land ceiling law then in force without paying full market value for such land. Even this restraint was overlooked when the Supreme Court pronounced unequivocally that no person in India had a protected right to hold property. The right to hold property is universally recognised, and many other fundamental rights which are not curtailed so far cannot be effectively enjoyed without this right.

There is thus complete agreement between eminent constitutional experts such as H. M. Seervai, Nani Palkhivala and Atul M. Setalvad on this point.

Article 26 gives the right to every religious denomination to own and acquire movable and immovable property. However, after the right to property was removed as a fundamental right and retained only as a legal right under Article 300A for all individuals and institutions, except for minority institutions whose right to hold and acquire property remained as a fundamental right. The main question thus is whether right to property should be a fundamental right or just a legal right.

Atul Setalvad has said, 'one can only hope, now that socialism is out of fashion throughout the world, that the Supreme Court of India will reconsider its previous rulings on the subject...And the very flexibility introduced in *Kesavananda*, while undesirable in principle, gives the opportunity for a future Bench to alter the position of, say, the right to property' (Setalvad 2001: 78–79).

The government should undertake an amendment to the Constitution to make the right to property a fundamental right. This is particularly important since foreign investors are given guarantees, and covenants and undertakings are entered into to protect their investments against take-overs, expropriations, nationalization etc., without reasonable and market-related compensation, and even to provide for mutually acceptable arbitration mechanisms. There is no reason why a domestic property holder should be treated any differently. An opportunity should also be taken to delete the word 'socialist' from the Preamble to the Constitution, as it has lost all relevance. But since the Preamble is a part of the basic structure of the Constitution, this hypocrisy will have to continue.

Menace of Lobbying

In the name of globalization, we are copying some of the worst practices of western capitalism and the Wall Street. One of these is the close nexus between business, industry, the corporate world and the government. The emergence of lobbying firms is an off-shoot of this new culture of governance. Lobbyists have played a prominent role in all major purchases in defence, civil aviation, petroleum and natural gas, fertilizers and so on. To this rapidly growing list has been added telecommunications, which is expanding at a fast rate. The most recent case of the 2G scam was brought to light by the Niira Radia tapes in which even appointments of preferred ministers in given ministries were sought to be influenced by vested interests. Equally shocking was the stand taken by Ratan Tata in the Supreme Court that his right to privacy needed to be protected by prohibiting the publication of the contents of the Niira Radia tapes! This is further underlined by the observations of the Supreme Court cited in the following paragraph. The CBI is reported to have confirmed criminality in the Radia tapes and has told the Supreme Court that it will be willing to start a probe. The court agreed that there were several 'uncomfortable' issues and 'lurking dangers' in the conversations and promised to order a 'thorough' investigation. The court rightly asked why the income tax department had not prepared transcripts of the tapes until it was ordered by the court. The court was incensed that if it had not ordered the preparing of transcripts, all this would never have seen the light of the day. Why did the income tax department not do it on its own? the court asked (*IE*, 1 August 2013). In its further hearing, the Supreme Court once again pulled up the CBI for not taking action on the Radia tapes, saying they revealed 'serious issues' that were 'much more than 2G', including the presence of middlemen 'virtually in every government field'. The tapes purported conversations with politicians, industrialists and journalists. 'It was such a serious matter but entire attention was paid only to the 2G case while all other issues were sidelined,' said the Bench (*IE*, 8 August 2013). The CBI has now told the Supreme Court that based on the Radia tapes, it would like to probe into corporates, ex-judges and politicians and has alleged 'criminality or irregularity' involving Tatas, Ambanis, Unitech, ex-Chief Minister Koda and the DMK (*IE*, 10 August 2013). This is yet another instance of the nexus between the bureaucracy, corporates, politicians and criminals, which I have discussed separately. Equally shocking is the stand taken by the central government in the Supreme Court against the publication of these tapes (*IE*, 28 August 2013). It was bad enough when the state was undeservedly safeguarding its secrets. Now it wants to safeguard the secrets of the private sector even when they adversely affect the rule of law and national security. Clearly, there is something deeply rotten in the system of governance in India.

But this was not the first case of high profile lobbying. Public memory is phenomenally short. To set the record straight, Prime Minister Atal Bihari Vajpayee had shifted minister Jagmohan from the Telecommunication Ministry to the Ministry of Urban Development. The outgoing minister was found to be totally inflexible by industry in dealing with the problems of operators. Jagmohan had stuck to his stand that licence fee payment was a contractual obligation and the change-over to a revenue sharing system could not be justified. Attorney General Soli Sorabjee had conveniently advised that the existing operators could be allowed to migrate to the revenue share regime and that 'public revenue is not synonymous with public interest' (*TOI*, 24 June 1999). The opposition parties had charged that the government had given in to the telecom lobby. In a statement, the CPM politburo said that powerful telecom companies owed the government Rs 4,500 crore for cellular and basic phone licence fees and other back payments. They accused Prime Minister Vajpayee of 'tarnishing his image by resorting to this blatant act of favouritism' and demanded the President's intervention. The Congress Party said that the caretaker government had no authority to take any far-reaching policy decisions. Ajit Jogi said it appeared that Jagmohan was removed from the Telecommunications Ministry to help cellular companies. He maintained that there were reports that a lobby of owners of cellular companies, considered close to the Prime Minister and his son-in-law, had been working overtime to ensure Jagmohan's exit from this key ministry. Janata Dal leader S. Jaipal Reddy said Jagmohan's shifting was fraught with major policy ramifications. The PMO was obviously under pressure from certain industrial houses (*TOI*, 10 June 1999). It is a interesting that S. Jaipal Reddy too was shifted from the Ministry of Petroleum and Natural Gas during the UPA II regime due to alleged pressure from a powerful business house.

It is time that relevant issues pertaining to lobbying are addressed fully and the parameters within which lobbying can be permitted are delineated by passing a legislation for the purpose. The objective must be bringing in public accountability and transparency in this field. Data on lobbyists and their work must be compiled systematically. This information must be in the public domain and should be easily available on payment of a reasonable fee.

Professional Bodies

The shady affairs of a number of professional bodies such as the Indian Medical Council and the Technical Education Council have come to light in recent years. The government has given autonomy to these bodies under the respective legislations and it was expected that these and similar other professional bodies would conduct their affairs diligently, transparently and responsibly. Unfortunately, this has not been possible for a variety of reasons. They have often failed in taking prompt and exemplary action against deviant members. People feel helpless in getting their grievances redressed. This is all the more important in view of the increasing sphere of influence and the rapidly expanding activities of the non-governmental sector. The commercialization of higher education is a case in point.

The game of cricket in India has always been a money-spinner. With the introduction of the Indian Premier League (IPL) and the media hype, it is not just the players but all those associated with the game, including bookies and fixers, who have become millionaires. Match-fixing scandals had erupted even before the IPL and were mostly brushed under the carpet by sports bodies.

In spite of persistent demands, the report of the committee appointed under the chairmanship of Y. V. Chandrachud, former CJI, in 1997 was never made public by the BCCI. No one knew what remedial actions, if any, were taken on the report by the BCCI to avoid recurrence of such cases in the future.

Clearly, the question of the autonomy of these institutions needs a fresh look. But this should not mean a larger role for the government, as that would be equally corrosive. To begin with, at least two steps need to be taken. The first is to bring these institutions within the purview of the Right to Information Act. This will be an effective way of keeping their activities under public surveillance and ensuring transparency and accountability in their functioning. This will also instil a sense of social responsibility in them, which is long overdue. The second is appointing an independent ombudsman for a group of professional bodies. This will make them accountable in a real sense. The ombudsman should be a serving or a retired Chief Justice of a High Court or a Supreme Court judge.

Public-Private Partnership Projects

The rapidly expanding list of public-private partnership (PPP) projects is another area of concern. Due to the constraints of financial resources, the states and the Centre are taking increasing recourse to funding and executing projects in partnership with the private sector. Most large infrastructure projects are now being executed on this basis. While in some cases, projects are transferred to the government immediately on completion, in other cases the executing agency operates the project and on completion of the specified term, transfers it to the government. Public contribution is raised by a levy or a toll on the users of the facility. Unfortunately, the manner in and the terms on which contracts are awarded for PPP projects is often opaque, thereby undermining public interest. As a result, recovery of toll is much in excess of the investment on the project and reasonable returns thereon. In some cases, it is seen that the contractor has been given excessive concessions. In recent years, the collection of airport charges and tolls for roads has become highly controversial. There is justifiable public anger and frustration at the whole process. As a last resort, PILs have been filed in some cases. As in most other cases in which information is sought, the response of the government has generally been far from forthcoming.

Looking to the growing importance of PPP projects and the need to increase their public acceptability, it is necessary that the C&AG audit is extended to such projects. The same should hold good where contracts are awarded for oil exploration and extraction or leases given for captive coal mines. The recent case of the Krishna Godavari (KG) basin D6 has become highly controversial due to the alleged gross overestimation of reserves, gold plating of capital cost of the project and the efforts of the lessee to recover the exorbitant cost by stepping up the gas price. Public confidence in such projects can be ensured only by subjecting them to a detailed C&AG audit. It appears that the KG D6 audit has been stalled due to the insistence of the lessee that the C&AG do only the financial audit and not the performance or propriety audit. Reliance Industries has also made a bizarre proposal and demanded that the C&AG, which is a constitutional authority, should sign a confidentiality agreement with it and undertake 'not to publish or otherwise disclose the confidential information to any person in any manner whatsoever' etc. (*The Sunday Guardian*, 10 March 2013). Agreeing to such preposterous conditions and escape routes will be against public interest, keeping in view the observation of the Supreme Court that in such projects the role of the government, which is the owner, cannot be permitted to be compromised. This is important since the cost of the project is to be finally recovered from consumers. Any gold plating of the project as has been the case in several projects including Enron and the Krishna Godavari basin D6 gas project militate against public interest. A value for money audit will ensure that the consumers are not made to pay unnecessarily.

The saga of special economic zones (SEZs) has been similarly controversial. These zones are a big drain on the national exchequer. Several SEZs had effectively become real estate development projects and the sponsors of these projects had made huge profits. The resultant public protests led to the disbanding of some SEZs and returning the land to those from whom it was acquired.

Yet another safeguard which is necessary is bringing such projects in the purview of the Right to Information Act. Public scrutiny of such projects will go a long way in ensuring their accountability and transparency.

Notes

1. The judge or the magistrate takes upon himself the duty to ascertain the facts through witnesses after giving an opportunity to persons concerned who may be affected by the determination of facts.
2. For detailed discussion, see Godbole (2011: 242–75).
3. The phrase 'commanding heights' of the economy used extensively during the height of frenzy about socialism in Indira Gandhi's regime was first used by Lenin to describe his New Economic Policy in 1922. The 'fellow travellers' could not even coin their own phrase!

6

THE STRENGTH OF A DEMOCRACY
LIES IN ITS INSTITUTIONS

> Not even all the darkness of the night can
> extinguish a candle which has been lit
> Chinese proverb

Ensuring the Integrity of Institutions

Sanjoy Bagchi has written, 'China lacks the political institutions that can perform their tasks, while India, which has them, has allowed many of them to atrophy through neglect or get corrupted till they have all but ceased to function' (Bagchi 2011: 166).

A democracy can only be as strong as its institutions. A vibrant and effective democracy needs to be underpinned by strong institutional support. Unfortunately, there has been a serious and long-term undermining of institutions crucial for India's governance. These include governors, C&AG, public service commissions, Lok Ayuktas, election commissioners at the state and central levels, higher civil services, police, and regulatory bodies. Each of these institutions has been deliberately undermined and weakened over the years.

The most abrasive instance of this kind is the working of the National Advisory Council (NAC) under the chairmanship of Sonia Gandhi comprising a charmed circle of NGOs and social activists. It has functioned like a super Cabinet, laying down policies and questioning government decisions. It is an outstanding example of wielding authority without accountability, which should be an anathema to democracy.

Governors

Jawaharlal Nehru treated governorships as sinecures for accommodating elderly politicians or loyal civil servants who were to be put to pasture and could not be usefully utilized elsewhere. G. K. Reddy has invited attention to the fact that Pandit Pant had Giri transferred abruptly from Uttar Pradesh when he found him rather unaccommodating and inconvenient. The then Maharashtra Chief

Minister, Morarji Desai, prided himself in not forwarding any file of consequence to the Governor even for routine approval. Pattabhi Sitaramayya complained bitterly that he generally read in newspapers of the orders and notifications issued in his name (Bhagyalaxmi 1992: 9). Former West Bengal Governor Dharma Vira believed that governors 'generally' functioned 'objectively', but that they have been guided by the wishes of the powers-that-be at the Centre. How, he asked, can governors act independently when they 'hold office at the pleasure of the ministry in power at the Centre?' (Granville 1999: 607). Over the years, these offices have been largely politicized but it may be recalled that a Committee of Governors under the chairmanship of Bhagawan Sahai had clearly stated in 1971 that the Governor was an independent head of state drawing his authority from the Constitution. He was not concerned with and was above political parties and was not subordinate in any way to the Government of India. However, the central government has observed this precept more in breach. At least two governors were involved in the hawala scandal and had to resign. B. K. Nehru, who had the distinction of serving as Governor in Assam, J&K, and Gujarat has, in his book *Nice Guys Finish Second*, shown how the office of Governor has been politicized and devalued and how he was transferred from J&K, like a civil servant,[1] for failing to abide by the diktat of Indira Gandhi to sack Chief Minister Farooq Abdullah and install Gul Shah. Nehru has stated:

> the inducement for defecting had then to be substantial. The standard rate was two lakh rupees in cash and a ministership; this latter would, of course, provide the defector with a substantially larger cash return even though his career in office might be short. *The funds were provided by my friend Tirath Ram Amla, a staunch and tried Congress worker, and were supplied to him in cash from Congress Party money in Delhi, transported in the mail pouches of the Intelligence Bureau.* The use of official machinery for party purposes had by then become so commonplace that it did not call for any eyebrows to be even slightly raised (Nehru 1997: 620–21, 626–27). I have used italics at suitable places to bring out the emphasis.

B. K. Nehru has emphasized that:

> the concept of what a Governor was and what he was supposed to do has changed completely. The erosion of the original concept commenced fairly early after Independence. It started with Governors being 'transferred' from State to State during their five-year tenure of office, a practice totally alien to the letter and spirit of the Constitution. The Governor's position now is very clearly that he is not an independent official, that he is under the orders of the central government and, more often than not, he is an agent or an active member of the party in power at the Centre...Homi Talyarkhan, then Governor of Sikkim,

proudly announced to me that he had taken action in Sikkim which would ensure that the Congress Party would always remain in power in that State. He hoped that I was doing the same in J&K (Nehru 1997: 618).

The salient guidelines suggested by the Sarkaria Commission on Centre-State Relations (1988), NCRWC (2002) and the Punchhi Commission (2010) regarding the selection and appointment of governors have been blatantly disregarded by successive governments at the Centre. It was recommended by these commissions that a person who is active in politics should not be appointed as Governor. It was also suggested that governors should not enter active politics after demitting office.

But, the reality is quite the opposite. During the NDA regime, several prominent loyal BJP workers were appointed as governors including K. R. Malkani (Pondicherry), S. S. Bhandari (Gujarat), Bhai Mahavir (Madhya Pradesh), Vishnukant Shashtri (Uttar Pradesh), Suraj Bhan (Himachal Pradesh) and Kedarnath Sahani (Sikkim). The Congress had followed the practice of rewarding its party leadership in this manner from Independence itself. At least two governors, Ram Naresh Yadav (MP) and Aziz Qureshi (Uttarakhand), publicly declared their gratitude to Congress President Sonia Gandhi for their appointments. Ram Naresh Yadav called on Sonia Gandhi for advice (?) before writing to the Chief Minister to reconvene the Assembly session to discuss the no-confidence motion against the government (*IE*, 29 July 2013). Apart from the highly questionable propriety of such an action, it is its brazenness which is so striking. H. R. Bharadwaj, Governor of Karnataka, went to the extent of declaring that he is a Congressman first. The offices of governors and ministers have become inter-changeable (Sushil Kumar Shinde, Jagmohan, S. M. Krishna). Governors are looked upon as representing the central government and not the President of India. Most governors are blatantly partisan in their dealings with state governments. They are often perceived as instruments of the ruling party at the Centre. P. Venkatasubbaiah, Romesh Bhandari and Buta Singh, the then governors of Karnataka, UP and Bihar respectively, had to resign following strictures by the Supreme Court for doing New Delhi's bidding. Another Governor, Bhanu Pratap Singh, had to be dismissed. A C&AG report notes how Devanand Konwar, the then Governor of Bihar, had taken 53 flights to various cities in 2011–12, with nothing on official records to show why. The then Education Minister in Bihar, P. K. Shahi, said that he was ashamed to admit that vice chancellors were being appointed on payment. Indeed, a joke that suggested that appointments to offices of vice chancellors and college principals were available on equated monthly instalments (EMIs) went viral in the state. In an unprecedented move, the then Deputy Chief Minister Sushil Kumar Modi and many of his Cabinet colleagues demanded a CBI inquiry into allegations against the Governor (*Outlook*, 25 March 2013). The Supreme Court has pronounced that the appointments made by Konwar as Chancellor were not only 'illegal' but also 'contemptuous'. The court noted that the decision of making these appointments, by way of three notifications, was made without an effective consultation with the state government and in 'contemptuous disregard' of the orders passed by the Patna High Court. 'What is most shocking is that the Chancellor selected two Vice Chancellors and one Pro-Vice Chancellor despite the fact that they were facing prosecutions under the IPC, SC/ST Act and the Prevention of Corruption Act...against some other persons, there were charges of wrongful withdrawal of TA, DA,' the Bench noted (*IE*, 20 August 2013). Konwar was merely transferred to another state as Governor and has not been asked to resign. N. D. Tiwari, Governor of Andhra Pradesh, had to resign after serious allegations surfaced about his sexual exploits. The long list of governors who have had to resign due to allegations includes Prabhat Kumar, Romesh Bhandari, Sheila Kaul, Motilal Vohra, Bhanu Pratap Singh, Chenna Reddi, Jagmohan, Baliram Bhagat and Krishna Pal Singh.

As highlighted in Chapter 3, the partisan attitude of governors is often evident in matters pertaining to the imposition of President's rule under Article 356 of the Constitution. It was only after the decision of the Supreme Court in the *Bommai* case that this blatant misuse of office was curtailed with the declaration by the court that even the President's discretion and decision can be reviewed by the court. In cases of such partisan decisions, inevitably, there is a demand for the recall or transfer of the Governor, hardly befitting the high constitutional office.

The nadir was reached in 1990, when the V. P. Singh government took the decision to ask for resignations from all governors appointed by Rajiv Gandhi. Some governors resisted this move, while some others protested. B. G. Deshmukh, who was then the Principal Secretary to the Prime Minister, has written, Romesh Bhandari, Lieutenant Governor of Delhi, declined to resign and 'dared the Prime Minister to sack him. I suggested the usual bureaucratic *via media* of giving Bhandari an inconvenient posting and he was thus appointed Lieutenant Governor of Andaman and Nicobar Islands. Since he had political ambitions and did not want to be away from Delhi, he resigned and we got him out of the Prime Minister's way' (Deshmukh 2004: 253). Equating governors with civil servants was thus complete!

Lok Ayukta

The office of the Lok Ayukta has similarly been deliberately weakened in a number of states. In states such as Odisha, Punjab and Haryana, the post of the Lok Ayukta was peremptorily abolished by issue of an ordinance to stop him from holding inquiries against some ministers. The posts were revived later when the government changed. In Gujarat, the post of the Lok Ayukta remained vacant for a number of years due to the differences between the Chief Minister and the leader of opposition regarding the person to be appointed. Finally, the Governor went ahead and appointed a person recommended by the leader of opposition and the Chief Justice of the High Court! This decision was challenged by the state government but has been inexplicably upheld by the High Court and the Supreme Court. As it is said, at times, the judgment of the Supreme Court is final only because there is no appeal over that decision! But, the position of the new Lok Ayukta became so untenable with the non-cooperation of the state government that he tendered his resignation.

Higher Judiciary

I have drawn attention in Chapter 3 to the harrowing experience of the emergency declared by Indira Gandhi in 1975. Whatever the outward claims of its achievements, this period was marked by the undermining and weakening of all major institutions—Parliament, higher judiciary, higher civil services, media and sensitive security organizations such as R&AW and IB, CBI, the Directorate of Enforcement.[2] The precept of 'either you are with us or you are against us' can be a death knell for the independence and autonomy of institutions. While the Parliament, judiciary and media have recovered the lost ground, the other institutions have been permanently weakened and demoralized. The Supreme Court would defend itself against such attacks on its autonomy in the future by pronouncing a number of decisions such as taking to itself the power of appointing judges of high courts and the Supreme Court and expanding the scope of public interest litigations. However, the other institutions at the receiving end, such as higher civil services and the police, are left at the mercy of the political executive. The country is paying a heavy price for it.

Efforts have continued over the years to reduce the distance between the judiciary and the other organs of the state. To give a few instances: M. C. Chagla, the then Chief Justice of Bombay High Court, joined the Congress, became an MP, then a minister and later Ambassador to the US. K. C. Hegde, a Supreme Court judge, joined the BJP to become a MP and later Speaker of Lok Sabha. CJI Ranganath Mishra became a Congress MP. CJI M. Hidayatullah became the Vice President of India.

Cabinet Secretary

This post of the highest civil servant in the country was expected to be the linchpin of the whole administrative apparatus. The first Administrative Reforms Commission stated, 'A Cabinet Secretary is not only the principal adviser to the

Prime Minister and the Cabinet but also the head of the civil services and a co-ordinating authority amongst various ministries. In addition, he is a useful link between the political apparatus of the government and its bureaucratic machinery.' But, over the years, this institution has been devalued beyond recognition. As shown in Chapter 1, the expansion and empowerment of the PMO and its hegemonic powers has undercut the Cabinet secretariat.

Changing the Cabinet Secretary with a change in government would have been totally unthinkable in the British system which we have consciously adopted. However, India has done the unthinkable. At least two Cabinet secretaries were put on the shelf and appointed as Secretary of the Inter-State Council by the V. P. Singh government and the UPA I government to appoint their favourites to the post. Rajiv Gandhi too shifted P. K. Kaul, Cabinet Secretary, abruptly but was at least gracious enough to appoint him as Ambassador to the US. Prime Minister Manmohan Singh superceded nearly ten secretaries to the government and 'supposedly' appointed 'a person of his choice' as Cabinet Secretary. B. G. Deshmukh, former Cabinet Secretary and Principal Secretary to the Prime Minister, has written:

> The Cabinet Secretary has to maintain a delicate balance between the political executive and the permanent bureaucracy. As chief advisor to the Cabinet and the Prime Minister, he has to tackle delicate quasi-political issues with impartiality between the opposition parties and the ruling party. Unfortunately, two of my immediate successors [presumably T. N. Seshan and V. C. Pande] fell prey to this (sic) temptation and caused immense damage to the institution of Cabinet Secretary...P. K. Kaul had become Cabinet Secretary in early 1985, superseding some officers, among them K. V. Ramanathan from an earlier batch. It was widely discussed then that this was due to the intervention of influential Uttar Pradesh ministers, especially Arun Nehru. Apparently, Rajiv Gandhi had started distancing himself from Arun Nehru and perhaps wanted to remove a Cabinet Secretary who was the latter's choice...I suggested Roma Majumdar as my successor [as Cabinet Secretary]...Rajiv Gandhi's reaction was simple and firm. He said, '*I want a Cabinet Secretary personally loyal to me as we are having general elections within a year*. I therefore want Seshan to be your successor' (Deshmukh 2004: 142, 204, 206).

The best way to demoralize the permanent civil service is to permit extensions to officers after their retirement, which blocks the promotion prospects of other officers, particularly where the topmost post in the civil service is concerned. However, in recent years, practically every Cabinet Secretary has been given an extension. This is particularly reprehensible in the case of the Cabinet Secretary who then loses his freedom to advise the Prime Minister freely and objectively.

Another factor which has led to the undermining of the post of Cabinet Secretary is that some of the incumbents have taken up assignments in the garb of consultants and appointment to the boards of directors of major companies. The cooling off rule, by which a person is not allowed to take up private employment for a period of two years from the date of retirement, with anyone with whom he might have dealt with in an official capacity, is circumvented by posing as a consultant.

Election Commission

The Election Commission of India has also not escaped from the attempts of the government to interfere in and influence its functioning. B. G. Deshmukh has stated, 'To take care of a rather difficult Chief Election Commissioner, Peri Shastri, the government suddenly appointed two Additional Election Commissioners who had the full confidence of the government' (Deshmukh 2004: 213). Their appointment was set aside by the Supreme Court later. More brazen was the manner in which one of the Election Commissioners, known to be close to the Gandhi-Nehru family and 10 Janpath, was appointed. Fortunately, he could not do much damage.

Narendra Modi, Chief Minister of Gujarat, had the temerity to heckle the CEC as 'anti-Hindu' but he did not have the grace to apologise even after he won the elections. Lalu Yadav irresponsibly charged that the EC had an upper caste bias. The Left parties had also heckled the EC at the time of the West Bengal Assembly elections. They wanted, among other things, that the EC's expenditure should be monitored. As IE had commented editorially:

> More important is the question whether the Left's anger against the EC is a reflection that India's third largest political group [as it then was], after the Congress and the BJP, hasn't quite come to terms with the concept of institutional checks and balances. Whether what the Left has done in Bengal in terms of politically co-opting institutions is the model it wants for India? If Left wants to rule India [no such hopes at any time in the near future], as it surely does, it must know India does not want that (IE, 31 August 2006).

The UPA, with a view to under-cutting the EC, has been toying with the idea of converting the Model Code of Conduct for political parties into law. This may look innocuous but it will have major implications for the functioning of the EC as all cases of violations of the code will then have to go before the courts, and not the EC. As T. S. Krishnamurthy, former CEC, has emphasized, 'the superiority of the Model Code of Conduct, as it obtains, is that its enforcement power is with the EC as it is able to swiftly swing into action and take appropriate measures to create impact for the voters to feel that an unbiased body has taken a stern and severe action as a result of which no one is at a disadvantage' (Krishnamurthy 2012: 10). If the code is to be made into a law, the legal powers to enforce it must be retained with the EC, if the election process is to continue to be credible.

The tendency of some central ministers such as Salman Khurshid to question the authority of the Election Commission are causing anxiety among a large cross-section of the people. In February 2012, during the elections to the State Legislature in UP, the Election Commission had to seek the President of India's immediate and decisive intervention about Khurshid's deliberate violation of the Model Code of Conduct. In his letter to the President, S. Y. Quraishi, the then CEC, stated, 'We have found the tone and tenor of the union minister [Khurshid] dismissive and utterly contemptuous about the commission's lawful direction to him [about his public announcements of reservation for backward Muslims], besides the fact that his action is damaging the level playing field in the election' (IE, 12 February 2012). The disturbing fact was that Khurshid was defiant and unremorseful, in spite of being spoken to by the Congress Party and the Prime Minister. And Khurshid's was not an isolated case. Some other central ministers also followed suit. Khurshid's defiant attitude was rewarded later by his elevation to the prestigious post of Minister for External Affairs, giving a strong signal of where the government stood so far as institutional integrity was concerned.

The state election commissions have been similarly devalued. These statutory offices have been given the responsibility to coordinate and supervise the elections to Parliament and state legislatures under the supervision of the Election Commission of India, and to conduct on its own authority elections to local bodies. For this purpose, they have been given the rank and status of high court judges. But often the effort of state governments is to deny them this stature. The then Election Commissioner of Maharashtra, Nand Lal, declined to appear before a committee of the State Legislature on the ground that being a statutory authority, his decisions could not be questioned by it. Taking umbrage at this 'affront', the state Assembly hauled him for the contempt of the legislature on 27 March 2008 and created history by sentencing him to two days of imprisonment. He was admitted to the Arthur Road jail in Mumbai like a common criminal. The Congress-NCP government was a party to this atrocious decision. So were the opposition parties since the Committee on Privileges, on which opposition parties were represented, had given a unanimous report holding that Nand Lal had committed a breach of privilege. However, after Nand Lal was convicted, the leader of opposition in the legislative council, Pandurang Phundkar, said, 'The state government is strangling democracy through the act' (IE, 29 March 2008). Hypocrisy must have some limit. Nand Lal had publicly charged that the then Chief Minister, Vilasrao Deshmukh, had vindictively taken this action against him as, in spite of considerable political pressure, he had refused to de-reserve the Latur Lok Sabha constituency. Nand Lal was released from prison the next day after he challenged his conviction in the High Court. In the process, public esteem of the office of the State Election Commissioner was permanently damaged.

The State Election Commissioner of West Bengal, Mira Pande, is facing stiff and unreasonable opposition from the Trinamool Congress government over several issues pertaining to the holding of village panchayat elections. The ridiculous extent to which this confrontation has gone can be seen from the fact that during the legal battle with the government, Advocate General Bimal Chatterjee, is reported to have said that the poll panel was behaving like a 'beautiful lady throwing tantrums' (*IE*, 11 July 2013).

C&AG

The office of the C&AG was politicized by the NDA government when the incumbents to the post, T. N. Chaturvedi, was first nominated to the Rajya Sabha and later elevated to the post of Governor. The government was often put on the mat by the then C&AG, Vinod Rai. His audit reports on the 2G scam, coal gate and Commonwealth Games, in particular, shook the government. The C&AG was also poised to audit Reliance's KG D6 project. The ruling party made snide remarks about Vinod Rai's 'political ambitions' and he was publicly warned not to exceed his constitutional mandate. Rai's tenure ended at the end of June 2013. Deliberate and inspired news items were circulated about the government's intention to make C&AG a multi-member body. The appointment of the new C&AG was not free from controversy and a PIL was filed in the Supreme Court challenging his appointment. The court declined to entertain it and asked the applicants to approach the Delhi High Court.

It may be recalled that Ambedkar had stated in the Constituent Assembly that the C&AG was perhaps the most important office under the Constitution as it was expected to keep a close watch on the functioning of the government and its expenditure. We have travelled a long distance since then. The Congress Party was reportedly examining the option of moving a privilege motion against the then C&AG! (*IE*, 16 January 2011). Referring to the Telecom Minister Kapil Sibal's remarks rubbishing the C&AG report on 2G spectrum allocation, Murli Manohar Joshi, Chairman of PAC, wrote a letter to the Speaker questioning how parliamentary propriety and democratic practices had been undermined by Sibal's actions. He requested prompt action by the Speaker 'to stop such constitutional impropriety'.

Increasingly, C&AG reports are used or abused depending on who is at the receiving end. It may be recalled that when the C&AG gave its highly critical report on purchase of coffins by the army and the opposition parties led by the Congress were gunning for Defence Minister, George Fernandes, the then Law Minister, Arun Jaitley, had contemptuously stated in a press conference that he had more faith in the army generals than the C&AG! It was shocking to see Prime Minister Manmohan Singh himself questioning the activist stance of C&AG Vinod Rai. It was, however, gratifying that Rai held his ground against the Prime Minister. If important constitutional offices are sought to be weakened and their credibility lowered in this manner, there will be no hope of ever winning the war against corruption and maladministration.

State Public Service Commissions

These constitutional authorities have come into disrepute in several states due to the politicization of the institutions and questionable selection of incumbents. Former Chairman of the Punjab Public Service Commission, Ravinder Paul Singh Sidhu, who was involved in a major corruption scandal in 2002, was recently convicted by the court to undergo rigorous imprisonment. The then Chairman of the Bihar Public Service Commission, Ram Ashray Yadav, was suspended after inquiry by the Supreme Court on a reference by the President of India (*TOI*, 24 January 1997). The Maharashtra Public Service Commission (MPSC) has also come in for adverse attention more than once. The appointment of Shashikant Karnik as Chairman, MPSC, by the Shiv Sena-BJP government after his controversial term as Vice Chancellor of Bombay University was widely questioned. One of the members, Sayalee Joshi, was arrested and later removed from the membership of the commission. When a reference was made in her case to the Supreme Court, the court observed:

> There is no doubt that the PSC has clearly fallen from grace and the exalted status it enjoys under the Constitution. That one scam after another should erupt in respect of such a constitutional body is a very disturbing aspect. If constitutional institutions fail in their duties or stray from the straight and narrow path, it would be a great blow to democracy, a system of governance that we have given to ourselves, and the great vision that our constitutional framers had about the future of the country (Baruah 2009: editorial).

Some of the other PSCs which have come to similar adverse notice include Assam, Karnataka and Haryana, to name only a few. One of the five members appointed to the Haryana Public Service Commission is an accused facing trial in two cases of murder and attempt to murder. The other members are also reported to be politically well-connected. Incidentally, after the Punjab and Haryana High Court directed in August 2011 that the two states frame transparent guidelines for making such appointments, the Hooda government in Haryana approached the Supreme Court and got a favourable judgment against these High Court guidelines (*IE*, 28 July 2013). The prime cause of this sad and alarming state of affairs is the politicization of the organizations, appointment of the chairman and members of the commission purely on a political basis with total disregard for the qualifications prescribed for such appointments, rampant corruption and so on. This shows that merely giving constitutional status to an organization is no guarantee that it will be permitted to function properly.

Demoralization of Intelligence Agencies

I have referred to the gross misuse of the IB, CBI and other police agencies during the emergency earlier, to which attention was invited by the Shah Commission of inquiry. The Parliamentary Committee on Privileges had also held the then Director, CBI, responsible for harassing officers who had collected information regarding the affairs of Maruti Udyog, to reply to a Parliament question and he, along with Indira Gandhi, had been sentenced to prison terms. The gross misuse of the CBI by successive governments has come in for harsh comments by the high courts and the Supreme Court.

The one-up-manship of the CBI in the Ishrat Jahan fake encounter case and the public controversy over the alleged role of a senior officer of the IB is the latest example of the politicization of sensitive security institutions. The interrogation report of David C. Headley prepared by the NIA in 2010, claims that Ishrat Jahan was a Lashkar-e-Taiba operative. Headley is reported to have told NIA officers that the 'Ishrat Jahan module was one of Muzzammil's botched up operations.' This flies in the face of the claim consistently made by the CBI that Ishrat Jahan was not a part of any terror network (*Sunday Guardian*, 23 June 2013). In a further news report it came to light that in the letter purportedly written by the legal attaché of the US embassy in Delhi mention was made about Ishrat having been a suicide bomber (*IE*, 29 August 2013). The Home Ministry's affidavit filed in the Gujarat High Court in August 2009 also called Ishrat a terrorist. The affidavit also mentioned the statement that was issued by Lashkar-e-Taiba on Ishrat's death (*Sunday Guardian*, 7 July 2013). However, the Home Ministry has now taken a stand that the statement made by Headley to the FBI was confidential and could not be divulged. These contradictory positions taken by the Home Ministry raise serious suspicions that politics is being played in the matter. V. G. Vaidya, former Director, IB, has stated:

> Investigating under the scrutiny of the high court, one can understand CBI's anxiety to provide a foolproof case...It proceeded to interrogate the officer of the IB to establish what it perceived was his complicity and excessive involvement leading to the alleged fake encounter that killed Ishrat along with some others. CBI's actions received (or inspired!!) media publicity pitting the two vital security outfits of the country against each other (*Rediff.com*).

The CBI should have started its investigation by concentrating first on whether Ishrat Jahan and her companions were terrorists. But this crucial issue seems to have been relegated to the back-burner. The CBI should have familiarized itself with the standard operating procedures for senior field officers of the IB, which require them to remain in touch with the Chief Minister, Home Minister and senior police and other officers of the state government, irrespective of the political colour of the state government. It is also necessary to remember that the IB has no police powers and is not empowered to arrest anyone. But the way the controversy suddenly sprung up in 2013 about an encounter which took place nine years ago in 2004, certainly raises many inconvenient questions. The Supreme Court appropriately called the CBI the government's parrot, which sings whatever tune the government wants it to. Some Congress leaders have described the IB as a chicken. If the purpose is to run down the institutions in public esteem that purpose has certainly been served.

National Disaster Management Agency

The latest in the long list of institutions which have become play-things in the hands of the government is the National Disaster Management Authority (NDMA). It is a 'shining' example of the spoils system, which is often recommended for adoption in India by some 'well-meaning' persons. The head of the authority is now a former MLA from Andhra Pradesh, a post earlier held by the former Chief of the Armed Forces of the country! With false notions of prestige and position, all heads of divisions have been given the status of ministers of state, while the head of the organization has a Cabinet rank! In recent man-made and natural disasters, neglect of this vital institution cost the country dearly in terms of loss of precious lives, property and infrastructure. As was to be expected, the C&AG raised a number of valid points on the functioning of NDMA. With such a record in such diverse fields, how can India lay any claim for good governance in the country?

Every Office Has a Price

The office of Speaker of the Lok Sabha has been devalued and compromised more than once by appointing incumbents as governors or central ministers— Ananthasayanam and Hukam Singh as governors of Bihar and Rajasthan respectively, and G. S. Dhillon, Balram Jakhar and Shivraj Patil as central ministers, to name a few. The same was true in the case of at least two Chief Election Commissioners. One of them was appointed as a Governor (R. K. Trivedi) and the other (M. S. Gill), first as a Rajya Sabha member and later (hold your breath!) a Minister of State in the central council of ministers consisting of some 70 ministers. Some retired Supreme Court judges and chief justices too have been similarly appointed as governors. The government clearly wants to show that the holder of every constitutional office has a price and can be influenced by offering him a suitable post. How can the independence and authority of such offices be safeguarded in such a situation?

The Farce of Consultation

The appointment of P. J. Thomas, against whom a criminal case has been pending, as Chief Vigilance Commissioner, disregarding the objection of the leader of opposition, was unjustifiable but was defended by the government for absurd reasons. In its affidavit, the government averred, 'Thomas was "fully eligible" for the post and the "question of his suitability" and integrity was strictly in the domain of the appointing authority, and was outside the purview of the Supreme Court in a judicial proceeding.' It further stressed that the law did not require consensus on the appointment. The appointment was set aside by the Supreme Court by drawing a distinction between judicial review and merit review. While doing so, the court enunciated the important concept of institutional integrity and held that the appointment, at the helm of the country's highest integrity institution, of a person against whom a charge of corruption was pending, undermined the effectiveness and integrity of the institution. The same brazen attitude was evident on the part of the government in appointing two members, Cyriac Joseph, a former judge of the Supreme Court and the then NIA chief S. C. Sinha, to NHRC in 2013 despite objections raised by the leaders of opposition in the Lok Sabha and the Rajya Sabha.

It must be appreciated that the basic intention of broad-basing the selection committee and laying down the procedure of consulting the leader(s) of opposition is to ensure that appointments to crucial posts are made in a manner which will increase their credibility and acceptability. Routinely overruling the objections and carrying the decision on the basis of a majority, does not make sense since the government will always have a majority in the selection panel.

Is There a Way Out?

Clearly, the demolition of institutions has become a one-point programme for the government. Against this background, it is necessary to lay down some clear guidelines with respect to such important constitutional and statutory offices. **First,** making appointments to such posts should not be the prerogative of the government alone. The selection panel for appointments should consist of the Vice President, Prime Minister, the Chief Justice of the Supreme Court, leaders of opposition in the Lok Sabha and the Rajya Sabha and the concerned minister.

Second, it should be laid down that each decision must be unanimous to ensure that consultations do not become a mere formality. **Third**, the appointment must be for a fixed term of five years. **Fourth**, if there are any serious complaints against the incumbent, he should be asked to resign by the President of India, but only after a full inquiry by a panel of Supreme Court judges. **Fifth**, it must also be laid down that the holder of office will not be eligible for any appointment under the central or any state government and he will also not be eligible to contest any election for a period of five years after demitting office. These precautions will ensure requisite independence of these posts and enhance their credibility, apart from increasing public confidence in these offices.

Administrative Reforms

Strides by Some Countries

The state and its functions are being reviewed all over the world. What functions the state must perform is a question that is being widely debated, though perceptions differ from country to country. As a part of these endeavours, exercises were undertaken for downsizing governments in a number of countries and the results achieved thereby are indeed impressive. In the UK, government activities were reviewed to identify those which might work better if they were 'hived off' and run by bodies outside the departmental framework, albeit subject to overall ministerial guidance. The 'Next Steps' report proposed two fundamental changes, the implementation of which has continued to shape the structure of the bureaucracy:

- There should be a split between the service delivery and the making of policy. As a consequence, there should be real devolution of power to executive agencies in the area of service delivery, which will cover approximately 95 per cent of civil service activity.
- There should be the end of the fiction that the minister is responsible for everything done by officials in his or her name.

After an initial shaky start, the recommendations of the report began to be acted upon in 1988–89. Government departments were required to review their activities and to consider five possibilities: abolition, privatization, contracting out, creating an agency and preserving the status quo.[3]

As a result, large parts of the civil service have been hived off and have been given agency status. As of May 2002, there were 127 UK agencies, of which 92 reported to Whitehall departments and 76 per cent of the civil servants worked in Next Steps agencies. In 1998 it was calculated that there were 304 executive agencies, 563 advisory agencies, 69 tribunals and 137 boards of visitors to penal establishments. Understandably, the administrative landscape has become more complex. The doctrine of 'New Public Management' includes 'hands-on professional management in the public sector; standards of performance; output controls; the break-up of large bureaucratic structures; greater public sector competition; and greater discipline in resource use. These developments pose new challenges for public law relating to accountability, susceptibility to judicial review, and the appropriate procedural and substantive norms to be applied to such bodies' (Craig 2003: 92–95).

Sauvik Chakravarti has talked about how the New Public Management or NPM has resulted in radically changing processes of government in Anglo-Saxon nations world-wide. The first basic principle is to separate the role of the state as a 'provider' of any service from that of a 'producer'. This separation can be done in three ways: privatization which results in complete separation, 'contractorization', which yields impermanent separation, and hiving-off to an 'agency' which is incomplete separation. Chakravarti aptly concludes, 'While Whitehall has been effectively de-Humphreyfied [recall Yes Minister], we [in India] remain with the successors of colonial *burra saabs*. And their political masters' (Chakravarti 1997).

Another feature of these reforms is the thrust on the privatization of public sector undertakings. For this purpose, investments have also been made in sick units to make them profitable and to attract private sector bidders for their takeovers. By contrast, India continues to invest in bottomless pits like Scooter India, and starting new public sector units in the constituencies of central ministers, Sonia Gandhi and Rahul Gandhi.

The US Government Performance And Results Act (GPRA) of 1993 provides for establishing strategic planning and performance measurements in the federal government to keep a check on the waste and inefficiency in federal programmes which undermine the confidence of the American people in the government. The act provides for arriving at an outcome measure, output measure, performance goal, performance indicator, programme activity and programme evaluation. Donald F. Kettl, in his statement before the Senate and House of Representatives' committees, cited ten reasons why GPRA can help Congress solve the problems that must be solved:

- We must tackle both the performance and budget deficits.
- Performance measurement is the keystone to reducing both deficits.
- Performance measurement provides Congress with critical information about agencies' strategic decisions.
- Strategic plans provide a road map to achieving success.
- Performance measurement connects plans with results.
- Performance measurement can improve the authorization process.

- Performance measurement can improve the appropriations process.
- Performance measurement is no magic bullet—but it helps Congress do what has to be done.
- Performance measurement can transform the President's budget submission to Congress.
- Performance measurement can vastly improve congressional policymaking.

In conclusion, Kettl states that GPRA should not be viewed as an end in itself. It provides, rather, a tool to help members of Congress do what they have to do, and do it in ways that no other existing tool allows (Kettl: 1-11).

Reference may be made to the 'unique' report, 'Enhancing Accountability for Performance in the British Columbia Public Sector' prepared jointly by the Auditor General's office and the Deputy Ministers' Council to improve accountability and performance management. 'I know of no other jurisdiction in Canada where such a relationship exists,' noted Auditor General George I. Morfitt. The report emphasizes that accountability for results is critical, not only for legislators in assessing government performance, but for the government itself in managing its programmes and services on behalf of the public. Accountability—the obligation to account for responsibilities conferred—is a concept fundamental to a democratic system. The accountability framework evolved by the report covers, 'who is accountable to whom and for what; what information should be reported; how much information should be reported; what the quality of information should be; how the information should be verified; how accountability information should be provided; when accountability information should be provided; and what Legislative Assembly should do with the information it receives' (Auditor General of British Columbia with Deputy Ministers' Council 1995).

There is an information overload in India at all levels. The report of the task force on good governance appointed by the Government of Andhra Pradesh, under the chairmanship of this author underlined:

It is generally believed that information is power. But, it is rarely recognised that too much of information can become a drag on the system. This is particularly important in the age of information technology...The other corollary in this regard is equally important. Information should not be unnecessarily permitted to be transmitted to levels where it is unlikely to be used meaningfully (Government of Andhra Pradesh 2000: 19).

The need for collection of information is never examined carefully. Neither is the received information verified, collated and put to use in a timely manner. Looked at from this perspective, it can be seen how important the exercise undertaken by a small state in Canada is. There is so much to learn from what is being done elsewhere in the world, if only we keep our eyes and ears open. And if there is a political will to do anything.

In June 2013, the UK government renewed the Prime Minister's aspiration of the government being the most open and transparent in the world by inviting the public to comment on UK's draft National Action Plan on transparency, open data and open policymaking.[4] The government, in collaboration with civil society organizations, published a draft of the UK's second Open Government Partnership (OGP) National Action Plan for public consultations. The draft plan, 'From Open Data to Open Government', sets out the UK's commitments to:

- improve accountability
- increase citizen participation
- release more open data
- build international partnerships to achieve greater transparency worldwide.

In October, the UK will submit the final plan to the international Open Government Partnership (OGP) , of which the UK is currently lead co-chair. OGP brings together 59 national governments and civil society organizations.

Transparency and open data have been at the heart of the UK government's reforming agenda. Under the UK presidency, all G8 countries adopted an Open Data Charter. This set out five strategic principles, including an expectation that governments will publish data openly by default, alongside principles to increase the quality, quantity and re-use of the data released. G8 members also identified 14 high-value areas from which they will release data to unlock its economic potential, support innovation and provide greater accountability.

Drewry and Butcher have shown that in the US, a Code of Ethics asks civil servants 'to put loyalty to the highest moral principles and country above loyalty to persons, party or government department'. In addition, the 1978 Civil Service Reform Act protects officials who leak information which they believe reveals 'mismanagement, a gross waste of public funds, an abuse of authority, or a substantial and specific danger to public health and safety' (Gavin and Butcher 1988: 177).

India Is a Different Story

There is one common thread among the Marxists and globalizing capitalists. And it is that the state should wither away. As can be seen, in neither of the two systems is this true. In the communist system the party and the bureaucracy become all powerful. In the capitalist system while the captains of capitalism would like to have a free run, experience all over the world has shown that this can be disastrous. Recent catastrophic events both in the US and in Europe have shown that it is suicidal if checks and counter-checks are not established. The recent 'Occupy Wall Street' movement with its 'we are the 99%' chant has shown how powerful public reaction can be. Therefore, to assume that in India liberalization, globalization and economic reforms will imply contracting the role of the bureaucracy will be unjustified. In fact, an emphasis on public expenditures on social sectors such as food security, rural development, primary and secondary education and healthcare will mean a substantial expansion of the bureaucracy. Looked at from this point of view, it is necessary to take a fresh look at some of the common misconceptions such as the one that revenue expenditure which is largely in terms of salary bills is necessarily unproductive. It is also necessary to do away with the current distinction between Plan and non-Plan expenditure since in such a categorization it is assumed that non-Plan expenditure is necessarily unproductive and therefore needs to be curtailed.

Administrative reforms are a permanent item on the agenda for governance reforms. According to one estimate, over 600 committees and commissions have gone into the question of administrative reforms in the states and at the Centre since Independence. The last one in this chain is the Second Administrative Reforms Commission (SARC) which submitted its 15-volume report to the Centre. Some of these reports make for very good reading. A number of these reports are thought provoking and well-conceived. It is also understood that a number of these reports have been examined and a series of recommendations have been accepted by the government. For example, the department of personnel and training stated in its annual report 2010–11 that the SARC report on 'Ethics in Governance' 'contains 134 recommendations, out of which 85 recommendations have been accepted, 24 recommendations were not accepted, 3 recommendations were deferred and 18 recommendations referred to other fora' (Government of India, Annual Report 2010-11: 154–55).

But such a bland statement does not make anyone any wiser as there is no evidence of any change in the working of government departments.

Way back in 1997, during the golden jubilee celebrations of India's Independence, the then Speaker of the Lok Sabha, P. A. Sangma questioned the need for the Centre to have ministries of agriculture, rural development and sports and youth affairs. There is, in fact, no reason why the Government of India should maintain large ministries in subjects which are in the State List. But ministries are looked upon as berths for politicians and officials. Unfortunately, no politician is prepared to bell the cat!

It is often argued that as globalization proceeds, the government will contract and become increasingly redundant for a common person. But in reality this is far from true. In fact, as stated earlier, with increasing social sector spending by the government and proliferation of regulatory institutions, the spread of the government will increase rapidly. There is also a common misperception that with increased computerization, corruption will decline. A study undertaken in Andhra Pradesh shows that this is not necessarily true. Money still has to be paid by way of facilitation and good will! For example, the computerization of registration offices has improved the working of these offices but the question of how to reduce and simplify the voluminous paper work still remains (Caselly 2004: 1151–1156).

Unfortunately, in India, this subject has not been taken seriously either by the Centre or by the states. Creating jobs in the government sector is looked upon as a primary objective by the political party in power. The Fifth Pay Commission placed major emphasis on downsizing the government. The substantial pay increases proposed by the commission were based on the assumption that government staff will be broadly curtailed by 30 per cent. But, as brought out earlier, conveniently the government acted only on the recommendations pertaining to the revision of pay and pension and completely sidelined the downsizing of the government. In this background the Sixth Pay Commission did not make any such radical recommendations regarding the downsizing of the government. But the fact remains that this subject can be neglected only at the peril of the government and the people at large.

Rampant politicization of the civil services continues to be a serious problem. Transfer bazaars are a common bane of the system. Officers and lower staff openly flaunt their connections to political masters, whether MLAs, MPs or ministers. In a number of scams, the names of officers are as prominently involved as those of politicians and ministers. The All India Services (AIS), which were rightly known as the steel frame of India, have lost their élan. In fact, one needs to question whether we require such all-India services. The protection provided to these services under the Constitution has remained on paper. Powers of transfers and even suspension of AIS officers have been blatantly misused by the states, and the Centre has been a mere passive onlooker. The very latest such case was that of A. Khemka, IAS officer of the Haryana cadre, who was repeatedly transferred during the last few months for having crossed the path of Robert Vadra, the powerful son-in-law of Sonia Gandhi, and cancelling his scandalous land deal.[5] The higher judiciary has not been helpful in providing relief in such cases.

As stated earlier, important recommendations made by the Law Commission in its 166th report pertaining to the enactment of a law for forfeiture of property of corrupt public servants and a bill prepared by the commission for the purpose have been pending consideration of the government since February 1999. Both the NDA and the UPA I and II have been in power since then.

As also referred to earlier, the Law Commission, in its 57th and 130th reports recommended enacting a legislation prohibiting benami transactions and acquiring properties held benami. A law titled 'The Benami Transactions (Prohibition)

Act', 1988, precludes the person who acquired the property in the name of another person from claiming it as his own. Section 3 of the act prohibits benami transactions, while Section 4 prohibits the acquirer from recovering the property from the benamidar. Unfortunately, in the last 25 years since the enactment of the law, rules have not been prescribed by the government for the purposes of sub-section (1) of Section 5, with the result that the government has not been in a position to confiscate properties acquired by real owners in the names of their benamidars. Interestingly, during this period, several governments—the United Front, V. P. Singh and Chandra Shekhar governments, Congress, NDA and UPA—belonging to almost all political parties have come to power but there was no political commitment on the part of any of them to take action on this point!

Laws providing for protection of whistle-blowers have been on statute books of the US, Australia, UK and New Zealand for quite some time. The earliest, the Whistle-blowers Protection Act, was passed in the US in 1986. Deshmukh has brought out that it started with the False Claims Act proposed by Abraham Lincoln in 1862 (strengthened in 1986). This was followed by the Whistle-blowers Protection Act of 1989 (amended in 1994) and the Sarbanes-Oxley Act of 2002, which came about after the mega corporate scandals in companies like Enron and WorldCom. *This act makes it mandatory for a company board to put in place whistle-blower policies*...Comparing the two cases of whistle-blowers in India and Australia, Aditi Datta wrote in *The Hindu* on 3 February 2004:

> Both cases are classic examples of whistle-blowing. Both men were insiders who, coming to know of corruption and malpractices in their organisations, brought it to light—something that the others in their departments did not dare. Their circumstances too were similar...The point of divergence comes only when we look at the treatment meted out to whistle-blowers and the consequences that followed. In India, Satyendra Dubey was murdered. Just two days later, in Australia, Andrew Wilkins was presented with the 'Whistle-blower of the Year' award (Deshmukh 2012: 24).

Other countries which have taken similar steps include South Africa, Australia (Public Interest Disclosure Act, 1994), the UK (Public Interest Disclosure Act, 1998) and New Zealand (the Protected Disclosure Act, 2000).[6] In India, unfortunately, in spite of directions by the Supreme Court, the central government is still dragging its feet on the subject.

Even some small steps can go a long way in making administration citizen-friendly and responsive to citizens. Illustratively, these could include cutting down a citizen's interface with government; reducing the discretionary powers of ministers and officers, and wherever use of discretion is inevitable, to lay down clear guidelines for the manner in which it is to be used, and more importantly, publicizing the guidelines; carrying out periodical exit surveys of persons visiting government offices to identify the areas of work which are prone to corruption, procedures which could be simplified, paperwork reduced, etc.; and to attend to the manifestations of the 'broken window syndrome' to improve the image, efficiency and look of the offices. But, even a beginning has not been made on any of these points. The Fifth Pay Commission observed, 'Currently, government employees in the central government have certain duties and responsibilities under the conduct rules. These have to be completely re-written so as to be in accord with modern notions of accountability.' This was way back in 1997. No action has been taken thereon so far. The Official Secrets Act continues to hold sway, even though it has been repealed or modified to reduce its rigour in a number of other democracies. Another step of modifying the format of the oath of office and secrecy so as to cast an obligation on the ministers and officers not to withhold information from people in the name of secrecy has also not been taken as yet.

Widespread corruption in development schemes and programmes throughout the length and breadth of the country has been the single most important contributory factor in the alienation of the people. Routing payments to beneficiaries through their bank accounts is not an answer to the problem, as seen from the agricultural loan write-off scheme. More effective will be a social audit of the schemes by respected persons in the locality with no political leanings who can objectively and transparently look at the expenditures and their outcomes. This will be even more effective than the voucher audit of C&AG, in so far as social sector schemes are concerned. Unfortunately, no political party while in power has taken this step which has the potential of revolutionizing the local administration.

Often the government is the monopoly supplier of goods and services. This was particularly so till several activities were thrown open by the government to the private sector. Telecommunications is an outstanding example of the arrogant attitude of government employees in the sector. It was shocking to read the statement of the telephone department in Nagpur in a writ petition in the High Court against poor services provided by it. The department stated in its affidavit that it had not given a guarantee of good service to consumers at any time and if they were dissatisfied with its service, they were free to surrender their telephones! (*Loksatta*, 8 April 1997). Since there were no private telephone service providers at the time, a poor customer had no option but to put up with such antics of government departments. The situation has changed radically for the better since then wherever competition has come in. It is gratifying that SARC has taken note of this phenomenon and has suggested that steps should be taken to promote competition, 'Every department/ministry may undertake an immediate exercise to identify areas where the existing "monopoly of functions" can be tempered with competition. A similar exercise may be done at the level of state governments and local bodies' (Government of India 2007: 188).

Early action needs to be taken on this recommendation.

Emphasis on globalization and economic reforms has also led to some very questionable initiatives in so far as public services are concerned. One such initiative was permitting government servants to go on deputation to private sector companies for a period of up to five years and then to return to government service thereafter. Permitting government servants to go on deputation in this manner to large builders and industrialists such as Tatas, Birlas and Ambanis can create an unholy nexus between government functionaries and these companies. It is necessary to underline that blindly copying such practices from Japan and western countries, which do not suit the ethos of this country, unnecessarily brings the process of economic reforms into controversy.

It is important to note that the states have an important role to play in ushering in administrative reforms since all development schemes and programmes are implemented by them. If administration at the cutting edge level is to improve and bring some relief to a common person, states' commitment to administrative reforms is imperative. Merely passing some enactments or issuing executive instructions by central government for its staff is not enough. But the biggest challenge is how to enthuse the states in the matter. No political party is interested in undertaking administrative reforms, though by now all political parties have been in power in the Centre and in the states at some time or the other. This makes for depressing reading but such is life.

Police Reforms

A reference must be made to the structure of police organizations and the manner of their functioning in the country. The police are still governed by the ancient Police Act of 1861. The provisions of the act were meant to subserve the interests and objectives of British rulers and are grossly inadequate in dealing with the current ground realities such as gross violations of human rights, encounter killings, custodial deaths, tendency of the police to take law into its own hands, gross political interference in the working of the police and its resultant politicization. The rule of law has become a dead letter and no one believes the usual peroration of the rulers that the 'law will take its own course'.

A number of committees and commissions have gone into the working of the police and made some valuable suggestions. Foremost among these is the National Police Commission under the chairmanship of Dharma Vira which submitted its 8-volume reports during 1978–81. Indira Gandhi, after she came back to power in 1980, had in fact directed that the commission should be wound up, even before completing its deliberations by 31 May 1981, though the commission was in the process of examining some major matters such as terrorism, intelligence, state criminal investigation departments, criminal justice system and railway police (Government of India 1981: 32). She also withdrew the police commission reports from the central ministries. As a result, though several years had elapsed, neither the Centre nor the state government were inclined to take any follow-up action on these reports. Finally, it was only during the United Front Government that MHA wrote to state governments to take action on the reports but there was no progress. As a last resort, PILs were filed in high courts and the Supreme Court to force the state governments and the Centre to take follow-up action. Of these, the PIL filed by Prakash Singh and others (WP (civil) No. 310 of 1996) was admitted on 30 July 1996. The petition was strongly opposed by some large states and the Centre. In the decision given a decade later, on 22 September 2006, the court issued a series of directions for the reorganization of police departments to reduce political interference in their work, to ensure minimum tenure to officers and so on. The court further directed that till an appropriate legislation was enacted, its guidelines would be in force. The judgment was to be implemented before 31 December 2006.

As many as 12 chief ministers, cutting across party lines, alleged that the Supreme Court's directions were an infringement on the powers of the states, undermined the federal structure and eroded the authority of the legislature. Some chief ministers also wrote to the Prime Minister expressing their unhappiness and requested that the Centre should either file a review petition or call a meeting of chief ministers. Later, the review petition filed by some states was dismissed by the court.

The thrust of the directions of the court was: The selection of the Director General of Police (DGP) should be made from a panel of three names recommended by a committee which would include the Chairman of the Union Public Service Commission; the DGP and other senior functionaries should have a minimum tenure of two years; all service matters of officers and staff should be entrusted to committees of officers and there should be no political or other extraneous influence in their deliberations; field officers at crucial levels should also have a tenure of two years; there should be a separate committee to look into public grievances against the police; there should be a State Security Commission to oversee the working of the police in the state; and the leader of the opposition should be made a member of this commission. In short, the directions were meant to keep political interference away from police transfers and other service matters and to provide for a tenure of two years for important posts.

Since most states continued to drag their feet, a very unusual step was taken by the court to appoint a committee under Justice K. T. Thomas, a retired judge of the Supreme Court to pursue the matter with the states and to ascertain why the court's orders were not being implemented. The Thomas Committee expressed its 'dismay over the total indifference to the issue of reforms in the functioning of police being exhibited by the states.' The court did not take cognisance of the contempt petitions filed for non-implementation of court orders. Even the orders of the highest court have not been respected where political vested interests of states are concerned. The Model Police Act drafted by the Soli Sorabjee Committee, at the behest of the central government in 2006, has also not been enacted by the states and the Centre (in respect of union territories), though 14 states have passed new police acts. However, most of them do not incorporate the directions of the Supreme Court.

There can be two opinions on the demand for autonomy for the police. It is by no means clear that autonomy will be the answer to the ills afflicting the police. The Government of Kerala appointed a committee under the chairmanship of Justice K. T. Thomas to examine the extent to which the autonomy granted to Kerala police had served its purpose. The committee's report is not particularly reassuring. Perhaps it is more important to see how community participation can be improved in the functioning of the police. Restricting political and other interference in the working of the police should go a long way in mending matters. To give just one instance, the then Mumbai Police Commissioner (CP) used to touch the feet of Bal Thackeray, who was the 'remote control' during the Shiv-Sena BJP regime in Maharashtra in the 1990s. Once, while doing so, his cap fell down. Even Bal Thackeray was so horrified at the obsequious behaviour that he kicked him, shouting in Marathi, 'Can you not keep the sanctity of the uniform?' This juicy news was leaked by Thackeray's police guards. That CP was popularly known as 'Police *Shakha Pramukh*', in keeping with the nomenclature in the Shiv Sena. But Maharashtra was not alone in such feudalistic behaviour. A personal security officer of the then Uttar Pradesh Chief Minister Mayawati was caught on camera as he bent down to wipe her dusty shoes with his handkerchief.

In the self-proclaimed progressive state of Maharashtra, Home Minister R. R. Patil took over the powers to transfer and promote even subordinate police officers from the DGP, thereby making him a figurehead. It was only after persistent protests by senior officers and the public at large that these orders were reversed. The Maharashtra Transfer of Officers Act, which was passed at the insistence of Anna Hazare, came handy for the government in the exercise of powers by Minister Patil. Anna Hazare had gone on a fast and insisted on the state government enacting a law for regulating transfers of government servants. When I was consulted about the draft bill, I cautioned Hazare not to agree to it as it would increase the powers of ministers and the Chief Minister in transfer matters. But Hazare was too gullible and did not bother to consider the implications carefully. The Chief Minister of Maharashtra, Prithviraj Chavan, has once again publicly declared that it will not be possible to act on the directions of the Supreme Court to divest the ministers of the powers of transfers of police personnel (*IE*, 29 August 2013).

It is tragic that a surfeit of laws has led to frustrating the rule of law in the country. The police has been over-stretched in ensuring the implementation of all kinds of laws. It is time that the responsibility for implementing some laws aimed at social reforms is taken out of the purview of the police and entrusted to the concerned administrative departments such as social welfare and its subordinate offices. It must be made mandatory that when a bill is introduced in Parliament/ State Legislature, along with the statements of objects and reasons and delegated legislation, an assessment of the staff required for its implementation is also presented and the requisite funds provided for. Certain actions such as gambling, prostitution and consumption of alcoholic drinks also need to be decriminalized. Thus, for example, a distinction needs to be made between 'fixing a match' and 'betting', which is no different from a lottery, which is legal. It is futile to enact a new law against betting. Instead, it may be better to impose a tax on betting to garner more revenue.

All these issues need to be considered *de novo* and the states persuaded to implement the inevitable reforms. But who will bell the cat? Unfortunately, the word of the Centre does not count with the states any longer in matters pertaining to the All India Services. The last card soliciting the intervention of the Supreme Court too has been tried, but in vain. There is a severe drought of statesmanship all over the country. I hope this does not mean that there is no way out of this *cul-de-sac*. This highlights once again the imperatives and urgency of recognizing good governance as a fundamental right. Once this is done, police reforms will inevitably have to form a part of the strategy for translating the concept into reality.

Parliamentary Democracy—More Negatives Than Positives[7]

Over six decades have elapsed since the parliamentary system was adopted by India. This is long enough time to assess the working of these institutions.[8] At the outset it must be noted that India is one of the very few developing countries in which parliamentary democracy has taken firm roots. Timely and free and fair elections, and peaceful transfer of power on each occasion, in keeping with the mandate of the people, can be cited as some of its most noteworthy achievements. Except for the aberration of the emergency in 1975–77, and in spite of several weaknesses in electoral laws, no one has ever seriously entertained the thought of jettisoning the parliamentary system. This speaks volumes of its intrinsic strength and public acceptance.

While there is large scope for improving the functioning of Parliament,[9] its positive contribution to strengthening democratic forces in the country and instilling some semblance of accountability and transparency in governance must be recognized. This has been more so in the recent years which have seen the emergence of coalition politics, both at the Centre and in the states. The fact that the government is reluctant to face the Parliament is convincing proof of its effectiveness. Every major scam has attracted close attention in Parliament and debates in Parliament, howsoever polarised they may have been, have been instrumental in creating strong public opinion and awareness about the concerned issues. There are also issues on which MPs have joined hands across the spectrum of political parties and this has put the government on the defensive. Without such a vocal and at times strident opposition, the government could not have been made accountable.

These endeavours have been actively assisted by in-depth analyses and bold stand taken by constitutional bodies such as the judiciary, C&AG, the Election Commission of India and the newly established statutory bodies such as the state and central Information Commissions. It is to the credit of the system that these bodies have been permitted to function without political interference. Equally important is the role of the media. Any discussion on the contribution of Parliament will be incomplete without a reference to the role played by these bodies.

Parliament's role in fostering the unity and integrity of the country must be given due recognition. Several issues which fall in the State List are often taken up for discussion in Parliament, thereby creating pressure of public opinion on the government. These include, for example, law and order situations, Naxal violence, the Singur agitation, farmers' suicides, the Adarsh Housing Society scam in Mumbai and the Godhra riots. Parliament has thus rightly emerged as the highest forum for debating issues which are of nation-wide concern.

The stonewalling of Parliament, however, has become a matter of serious concern. This was amply evident when the UPA government unreasonably refused the opposition parties' demand for setting up of a JPC to enquire into the 2G spectrum scam. As a result, one whole session of Parliament was wasted. There have also been some recent disturbing developments like the government giving in to highly unreasonable demands in Parliament as was evident in the controversy surrounding some cartoons of Nehru and Ambedkar in textbooks published by the National Council for Education Research and Training (NCERT) or in raising the amount under MPLADS from Rs 2 crore to Rs 5 crore per annum. In the same category are the hefty increases in pay and allowances sanctioned by the MPs to themselves from time to time.

Let us now turn to the functioning of Parliament which leaves a great deal to be desired. Though 60 years have elapsed since the setting up of Parliament, it has not been subjected to an independent scrutiny by stakeholders. Such a study would have brought to light several deficiencies and weaknesses in its functioning. I briefly touch upon some of them in the following discussion.

The foremost concern is regarding the short duration of sessions. In the early years following Independence, Parliament met for over 120–130 days in a year. This period has come down steeply over the years and now Parliament meets for hardly 50–60 days in a year. As a result, business has to be rushed through the Houses, thereby leaving not just members of opposition parties but also the ruling parties dissatisfied at having been deprived of the opportunity to raise many issues of concern. The primary reason for the curtailment of Parliament sessions is the reluctance and diffidence of the government to face Parliament and the onslaught not just of the opposition but also its own members on several points. A related unsavoury feature in recent years has been the government's tendency to curtail Parliament sessions to suit its own political ends. This was amply clear when the government was planning to issue an ordinance on the office of profit. Abrupt curtailment of the session led to the disturbing development of the central Budget having to be passed without any scrutiny by parliamentary committees. It is imperative that the discretionary powers of the government regarding the convening and continuance of Parliament sessions are curtailed. The only way this can be done is by laying down by legislation the minimum number of days for which the Parliament must meet and a broad timetable for the purpose. Under such a legislation the power to advise the President of India on convening Parliament sessions should vest in the Speaker, as opposed to the government as at present. It can be laid down that the Speaker should hold consultations with the leaders of all political parties before tendering his advise to the President. This single step will go a long way in strengthening parliamentary democracy in the country.

Traditionally the Question Hour was considered sacrosanct as it provides an opportunity for MPs to cross-examine the government closely and to hold it accountable. It is for this purpose that the Question Hour is considered inviolable. No other business, howsoever urgent it may be, is permitted to intrude in the Question Hour, unless the House passes a resolution to suspend it in exceptional and rare situations. However, recent years have seen much dilution in the importance of the Question Hour and serious doubts are being expressed about its very need. Often it is noticed that the members who had tabled the question remain absent. Or there are hardly any supplementaries raised by members. On rare occasions, the entire list of questions has been exhausted in less than an hour which is earmarked for Question Hour. This important instrument for ensuring the government's accountability to Parliament has thus been blunted. Unless efforts are made to revive the importance of Question Hour, parliamentary democracy will be a serious loser.

Parliament sessions are presently marked by unsavoury and undisciplined behaviour of members. There is often a clamour for raising issues which MPs consider important but the government is in no mood to concede these demands due to the pressures of government business. This results in chaotic scenes day after day, marked by frequent adjournments and walkouts. In the process over 20 per cent of the time in each session is lost without transacting any business. A solution must be found to ensure more productive use of Parliament's time. One way of doing this is to equitably divide the total time of each session between the government and opposition parties. It could also be laid down that after division of time, if business in the House is disrupted and the House has to be adjourned the time lost will be deducted from the share of the concerned parties responsible for it and added to the share of the other side. This will be an incentive for political parties to help transact business in an orderly manner and to make use of the available time most productively.

In the ultimate analysis it can only be the pressure of public opinion that can help in the orderly functioning of Parliament. Towards this end a number of steps could be taken. One, to prepare a report card of each member of his work in the House such as number of starred and unstarred questions asked by the member, short duration discussions proposed, participation in debates on various subjects and sponsoring of private members' legislation. If a member has disrupted the business of the House by his conduct or has taken recourse to walking out of the House or defying the Speaker's instructions, such matters should also be brought out in the member's report card. An important aspect of the report card will be the extent of absenteeism of the member from the House. It is often noticed that the House is deserted after Question Hour and hardly any members are present in the House when there are serious discussions and debates taking place. It has also been noticed that often members do not remain present in the House when the starred questions tabled by them are due to be taken up. At times this is ascribed to the pressure brought by persons whose interests are likely to be adversely affected by the discussion. Thus, it can be a win-win situation for a member in that he can get paid for asking a question and later for remaining absent when the question is due to come up for a reply. These practices can be curtailed only by adopting the principle of 'no work no pay'. If a member remains absent during the discussion, he should be made to forego the emoluments for the day. Successive Speakers have made attempts to obtain the concurrence of leaders of political parties to adopt the rule of 'no work no pay' but all these efforts have been unsuccessful so far. This is a sad commentary on the mindset of our law-givers.

It is a matter of shame that on several occasions, the general Budget has been passed by Parliament without any discussion. Even otherwise the demands for grants of only a few major ministries are taken up for discussion in the House and all others are passed without discussion. To some extent the situation has now improved since the Budget demands are referred to parliamentary committees for scrutiny. However, most reports of the committees are perfunctory and do not make any impact on the working of the government. This is partly due to the fact that there is no independent scrutiny of Budget proposals for want of requisite expertise. To fill this void steps have been taken in some western democracies to create a separate Budget Office for Parliament which is suitably staffed by experts in concerned disciplines. It is time such an office is set up in the Indian Parliament as well.

It is an open secret that the misbehaviour of members is often orchestrated by political parties. It is reported that leaders of concerned parties chalk out a strategy for the conduct of their members during the day and individual members hardly have any option but to abide by the dictates of the party. If Parliament's business has to be improved, ways will have to be found to hold political parties responsible for the misbehaviour of their members. Here again, it is only the pressure of public opinion which can make a difference to the situation. This purpose can be served if the Lok Sabha and the Rajya Sabha secretariats bring out a report card of the conduct of each political party at the end of each session. Such report cards will inevitably get wide publicity leading to adverse comments by the public and media, wherever called for.

Making laws is one of the most important functions of Parliament. Unfortunately, at present it receives the least attention of law makers. Bills are often passed at the speed of lightning and within a short span of 10–15 minutes as many as 8–10 bills are passed without any discussion. Since there is no provision for a 'sunset clause' by which an act becomes extinct or can come up for review at the end of a specified period, any half-baked legislation passed in this manner remains on the statute book for years. It is often argued that since bills are scrutinized by the concerned parliamentary committees, there is nothing wrong with the present system of passing bills in this manner. However, this argument does not hold water for various reasons. **First,** not all bills are referred to parliamentary committees for scrutiny. For one reason or another, the government brings some bills before Parliament without submitting them to a committee. **Second,** even if a bill is scrutinized by a committee it cannot be presumed that it needs no further modifications or refinements. **Third,** the deliberations of parliamentary committees are not open to the media and it is not known what stand individual members or their parties take on the subject. In such a situation, to presume that the committees are the best judge on the given subject and represent the opinion of the House can hardly be sustained. In fact every report of a committee must come before the House for discussion, after it is made public and all stakeholders are given an opportunity to comment thereon. Examining a bill by a committee should be only a step in the process of deliberations on the bill and cannot be a substitute for a discussion on the bill in the full House.

Ideally, the work of the committees itself needs to be improved in various ways. One of these is to make the deliberations of the committee open to the public and the media. The specious and untenable argument which is currently put forth against this suggestion is that this will lead to members of the committees playing to the galleries, as happens in the House, and the members will tend to take party lines on the subject. But experience shows that most of the time deliberations in the committees are on party lines and follow the policies prescribed by the concerned parties. It is also necessary that the committees be provided with assistance from experts and knowledgeable persons in the field. This will make the committees' work much more productive and meaningful. Therefore, the entire committee system needs to be revamped if deliberations in the committees are to be considered a substitute for discussion in the House. If the suggestion made earlier that Parliament must meet for at least 130 days in a year is implemented, there will be enough time for detailed discussions on legislative measures.

Conflict of interest has emerged as a major concern in recent years. Parliament has now become a club of millionaires and, as can be expected, has inevitably a number of vested interests. Another recent phenomenon is of several prominent persons in industry and business becoming Members of Parliament. If Parliament is to be a truly representative body, obviously one cannot object to industrialists and business tycoons becoming MPs. But it must be ensured that vested interests are not permitted to bend the policies of the government. In recent years it has been seen that MPs representing particular interests and lobbies have been made members of the concerned subject committees, thereby providing them an opportunity to influence the working of the concerned ministries. Strict rules need to be framed to safeguard against these eventualities. For this purpose 'registers of interests' need to be maintained by both the Lok Sabha and the Rajya Sabha secretariats. It must be made mandatory for members to furnish information pertaining to themselves and their dependants on their holdings of shares in companies, directorships of companies etc. Such registers are maintained by parliamentary bodies in a number of western democracies but the response to this suggestion in India has been lukewarm so far. In fact information contained in these registers ought to be in the public domain and people should be able to access this information by paying a reasonable fee. The functioning of every MP must be adjudged on the basis of his interests and he should not be permitted to ask questions, participate in discussions or seen to bring direct or indirect pressure on the government to subserve his interests.

The arbitrary and frequent revisions of pay and allowances of MPs has become a matter of concern. No one grudges a reasonable increase in the emoluments of MPs from time to time but the modality for the purpose is equally important. Ideally, the question of revision of emoluments of MPs should be referred to an independent commission of experts as in the case of pay commissions for government employees. The report of such a commission should be made public and stakeholders should have an opportunity to comment on it. After such a scrutiny, the report along with the government's proposals for pay revisions can be placed before Parliament for its consideration. Presently these issues are considered only by a committee of MPs and thereafter the proposals are rushed through the House, most often without any discussion. This is clearly a case of conflict of interest. India is perhaps the only democracy in the world in which emoluments of MPs are decided in such an arbitrary manner. Somnath Chatterjee, during his tenure as Speaker, made concerted efforts to have a committee of experts appointed for pay revisions but the proposal was turned down by leaders of political parties. The government also seems to be reluctant to force the issue.

Several precepts and practices pertaining to Parliament hark back to the British era. In fact a great deal of the Constitution itself is based on the Government of India Act of 1935. One such practice pertains to an address by the President. In the initial years, the President addressed each session of Parliament. Fortunately, wiser counsels prevailed later and now the President addresses only the first session of the year. The President's address is primarily a patchwork of paragraphs submitted by individual ministries and makes for a very dull and drab speech. This has been the situation year after year. Nearly 20 hours of Parliament's time in each House are spent on discussing the President's address and the reply to the discussion by the government. This valuable time can be saved by doing away with the President's address. This is a long overdue reform and the only explanation for its non-implementation is lethargy of successive governments and lack of political will.

At the time when the Constitution was framed its founding fathers had not realized that they had reduced the powers of Parliament in some very important areas. The Constitution does not require that international treaties, agreements and covenants be approved by Parliament. Over the last few years the ambit of these international commitments has increased substantially and it is no longer confined to foreign policy issues. Thus, trade, aid, environment, human rights and other commitments bind the actions of the government in diverse ways. It is necessary that there is broad national consensus on these matters to strengthen the hands of the government in their implementation. And such a commitment can come only with the approval of the highest national forum. It is therefore imperative to amend the Constitution to lay down that all international treaties, agreements and covenants will have to be approved by Parliament before they become effective.

Yet another area which has been kept out of the purview of Parliament is the oversight of intelligence and crime investigative agencies such as the CBI and the Directorate of Enforcement. Intelligence agencies, namely IB and RA&W, are presently scrupulously kept out of the purview of Parliament and the executive guards its turf in the matter vigilantly. However, this is not in keeping with the trends and practices in a number of western democracies such as the United Kingdom, United States, Australia and New Zealand. Unfettered powers of the government pertaining to these powerful institutions can no longer be left unsupervised by Parliament. The manner in which the oversight of these institutions is to be carried out can be carefully spelt out as has been done in these countries. Thus, Parliament should not have the power to go into specific cases of surveillance and enquiries. Its role should be confined to discussions on broad policy matters and the overall image, efficiency and contribution of these institutions.

Centre-state relations are becoming increasingly complex and sensitive. The states have a feeling that, under one pretext or another, the Centre is making inroads into areas which are in the domain of the states. There are increasing complaints that there is lack of dialogue between the Centre and the states on crucial matters such as the NCTC, setting up of the Lok Pal, empowerment of Lok Ayuktas, Naxalism and RPF's jurisdiction. This lack of trust between the Centre and the states is becoming increasingly evident in the states' opposition to central initiatives in a number of crucial areas. In this context the role of the Rajya Sabha, which by its name signifies that it is the Chamber of the States, assumes importance. The Constitution had visualized the Rajya Sabha as a chamber representing the states and that its approval would be necessary in matters affecting the interests of the states. Thus, for example, creating any new all-India service requires specific approval of the Rajya Sabha. If a law is to be passed by Parliament on a subject in the State List, approval of the Rajya Sabha is imperative. The Rajya Sabha is thus an integral part of the federal structure adopted by the Constitution. Unfortunately, in matters of electing members to the Rajya Sabha this principle has been compromised with the blessing of the Supreme Court. Till recently, a person could not contest an election to the Rajya Sabha unless he was a resident of that state. This led to a number of prominent central leaders and ministers filing blatantly false affidavits claiming that they were residents of the concerned states. The NDA government has to be faulted for bringing forth an amendment doing away with this requirement of residence for contesting elections to the Rajya Sabha. This was challenged in a PIL before the Supreme Court but surprisingly the Supreme Court held that the legislation was *intra virus* and that anyone could contest from anywhere in the country. According to the Supreme Court, requirement of residence was not a part of the test of federalism. This meant literally turning the argument on its head but since this is the decision of the highest court there is nothing that can be done except to amend the law on the subject. But such are the vested interests of all political parties in accommodating their favourites in the Rajya Sabha through the back door that it is unlikely that this legislation will ever be repealed. Given this situation, one needs to question whether there is a need for a Second Chamber which is just a replication of the lower House. Increasingly there is nothing to distinguish the Rajya Sabha from the Lok Sabha in terms of its composition, conduct of business, indiscipline, shouting brigades and walk-outs. It can no longer claim to be a House of Elders in which issues are debated objectively, dispassionately and in depth. It is therefore time to seriously consider abolishing the Rajya Sabha and the Second Chambers (legislative councils) in states in which they are in existence. This suggestion is fully justified in light of the experience gained so far. In fact, Jawaharlal Nehru and Mahatma Gandhi were not in favour of the Second Chamber. But it was retained in the Constitution as a compromise. However, Ambedkar clarified in the Constituent Assembly that if at any stage the Second Chamber was found to be inconvenient or unnecessary, it could always be abolished. That time has come now.

The Anti-Defection Act was passed with considerable fanfare during the Rajiv Gandhi regime. The experience of the working of this legislation needs to be closely reviewed to take some major corrective actions. It can be seriously questioned whether the law has led to any reduction in defections. For example, this law has had no impact in Karnataka. The powers to decide cases of defection have been given to presiding officers and this has clearly been counter-productive. Often political considerations have weighed with the presiding officers in taking decisions. At times decisions have been inordinately delayed to suit the convenience of the ruling political party. In several cases decisions given by the presiding officers have been set aside by the Supreme Court. Looking to the importance of the subject, it needs to be seriously considered if powers to decide defection cases should be entrusted to the Election Commission of India. The President/Governor can be authorized to take decisions on the recommendation of the Election Commission. Any appeal over such decisions would lie with the Supreme Court.

The second most important amendment which is necessary pertains to the definition of the word 'defection'. At present, any member voting against the party line comes within the ambit of defection. As a result, there is hardly any freedom left to the members to express their views on any subject in the House, if it is not in keeping with the party line. This has resulted in making the whole system moribund. It is interesting to note that in England, which is considered to be the mother of modern democracy, ruling party members are free to express their views on any subject and even to vote against the government's proposal. This was amply evident recently when the bill for restructuring the House of Lords had to be deferred by the ruling party due to the intense opposition in Parliament, including from its own members. The same was the case with respect to important legislations such as on issuing national identity cards and surveillance practices in the country. In yet another recent instance, the government's proposal of intervening in Syria in August 2013 met with stiff resistance from both sides of the House and the government had to beat a hasty retreat.

If individual members are not permitted to exercise their judgement on issues coming up in the House it can become a travesty of democracy. Defeat of the government on any legislation need not necessarily be considered warranting resignation by the government, unless it is on an important budgetary matter or on highly important national issues. In fact, no whip should be issued by political parties to its members on any subject, except in exceptional circumstances. Such an amendment to the Anti-Defection Act will bring about a qualitative change in the functioning of Parliament and improve the credibility and acceptance of the institution.

A JPC is an important instrument for holding the government accountable for its actions and inactions. Unfortunately, in India this instrument has been blunted for various reasons. A number of JPC reports have been ineffective in addressing the issues and holding the government accountable. The most prominent of these is the Bofors case. It was wrong on the part of the opposition parties to have boycotted the JPC, thereby making it easier for the government to whitewash the entire affair. Equally disappointing was the report of the JPC on the bank scam. The deliberations of the JPC on the 2G scam seem to be heading in the same direction. It will indeed be unfortunate if, in case after case, the instrument of the JPC is blunted and loses its credibility. Ways must be found to adopt the best practices from other countries in such parliamentary enquiries. It is seen that in England even the Prime Minister is called to give evidence before committees and is cross-examined closely, wherever necessary. We have much to learn from these instances.

The Constitution had envisaged that a separate law would be passed to deal with matters pertaining to Parliament staff. Australia and New Zealand have enacted such laws which ensure independence of Parliament from the executive and at the same time prevent arbitrary actions. Though six decades have elapsed since the setting up of Parliament, such a law has not been enacted in India so far. In the name of independence and autonomy, Parliament's presiding officers have often indulged in arbitrary actions. It is in larger interests that the existing situation is not permitted to continue any longer. A legislation can provide the requisite checks and balances in the system, without compromising the autonomy and independence of Parliament.

It is important to ensure that the public image of Parliament is not allowed to be sullied by the misbehaviour of a few MPs. Thus, for example, acceptance of cash by a few MPs in 2008 for asking questions in Parliament had become a scandal. Fortunately, Parliament took prompt action by expelling the concerned MPs. But criminal cases against them are still languishing. In fact, the Supreme Court has rapped Delhi Police and asked why no custodial interrogation had been conducted in the case. The court observed, 'We are not happy at all with the probe done by the Delhi Police. This is not the way to prove the offence of such serious nature' (*Data India*, 17 June to 23 July 2011).

A great deal of what has been stated here is equally applicable to the functioning of state legislatures. In fact, in several states their functioning is worse than that of Parliament. The duration of sessions has been curtailed considerably and often a legislature's sessions are held only for the purpose of getting the budget and supplementary demands passed and for transaction of other urgent government business such as conversion of ordinances into laws. Reference must also be made to the partisan manner in which the constitutional provision of nominating persons having special knowledge or practical experience with respect to matters such as literature, science, art, the cooperative movement and social service, to legislative councils has been grossly misused in Maharashtra. P. C. Alexander, the then Governor of Maharashtra, nominated 12 active politicians to the upper house of State Legislature in February 2002, without raising any questions. It was seen that 90 out of the 99 persons nominated by the Governor of Maharashtra to the upper house in the 48 years till 2008 were politicians (*MT*, 16 March 2008). It is pertinent to note in this context that President Shankar Dayal Sharma had rejected the Prime Minister's advise that certain persons be nominated to the Rajya Sabha because they did not fulfil the qualifications prescribed by Article 80(3): special knowledge or practical experience in respect of certain matters (Noorani 2000: 267).

Finally, it must be stated that parliamentary democracy in India has failed on another important test of encouraging grassroots democracy. Indian democracy is more a 'hereditary and dynastic democracy' in which ruling families have perpetuated their hold on parliamentary institutions for years. There are now 'first families' at all levels, not just at the national level. Prime Minister Manmohan Singh is a former member of the Indian Economic Service and Vice President, Hamid Ansari and Lok Sabha Speaker, Meira Kumar, are former members of the Indian Foreign Service!

Disenchantment with the functioning of parliamentary democracy in India is largely due to the deficiencies which can be easily remedied if there is a political will for the purpose.

Lok Pal And Lok Ayuktas

There has been considerable public upheaval in recent months on the controversy surrounding the establishment of a Lok Pal at the Centre. The establishment of the Lok Pal has been pending for about 48 years. The bill for the creation of a Lok Pal has gone through a dozen attempts. Its various versions have been considered by several parliamentary committees. In the last such effort, the Rajya Sabha referred the Lok Pal Bill to its select committee whose report was received in April 2013 and is under the consideration of the government. It is not yet clear when the revised bill is likely to be brought before the Rajya Sabha by the government. Serious questions still remain regarding the likely efficacy or effectiveness of the Lok Pal. Most of the political parties, though outwardly supporting the setting up of the Lok Pal are opposed to making it an effective instrument of policy. This is amply evident from the stand taken by several political parties in Parliament on the creation of a Lok Pal and the half-hearted attitude evident in their stand on Lok Ayuktas.

International Experience

The Santhanam Committee on Prevention of Corruption (1963) studied the arrangements made in some other countries like Sweden and Denmark where the institution of an ombudsman exists. The ombudsman is responsible for examining all complaints of maladministration or unfair administrative action, whether it is due to corrupt motives, or spite, or mere laziness, or inefficiency. The Santhanam Committee noted the fact that in New Zealand, an act had been passed to set up an office known as the office of the parliamentary commissioner for a similar purpose. In France, the institution of administrative courts is intended to provide a cheap and quick remedy for redressal of grievances against administrative decisions. In Soviet Russia, the procurator-general, his regional and area assistants serve as a link between the citizen and the administration for the purpose of redress of grievances. The committee, however, did not copy any of these institutions to any extent. It only accepted the idea of broadening the scope of the present machinery to include investigations into public complaints made through specific responsible agencies and recommended that a directorate should be created in the CVC to deal with general complaints of citizens (Government of India 1963: 206, 208). However, the government did not accept this recommendation and decided that the CVC should deal only with the prevention of corruption and maintaining integrity in public life. The question of setting up a proper grievance redressal mechanism has thus eluded this country for over 50 years!

In its judgment in the *Centre for Public Interest Litigation and another v. Union of India and another* (writ petition(c) No. 348 of 2010), given on 3 March 2011, the Supreme Court stated that in Australia, US, UK and Canada there exists a concept of integrity institutions. In Hong Kong, there is an independent commission against corruption. In Western Australia, there exists a statutory corruption commission. In Queensland, there is a misconduct commission. In New South Wales, there is a police integrity commission. All these come within the category of integrity institutions. The court expressed the view that the CVC was also an integrity institution.

Donald C. Rowat has illustrated how extensive the use of the institution of the ombudsman has been and how significant the variations among the countries are (Rowat 1965). He has underlined how the lack of full and accurate information about the actual working of the ombudsman has led to considerable misinterpretations. For example, the ombudsman seldom holds oral hearings, and when he or some other official designated by him does so, the minutes are released but the hearings themselves are never open to the public. The names of complainants and officials involved are not ordinarily released. In transplanting the institution to India, it is important that these features are borne in mind.

Lok Pal

First Administrative Reforms Commission

The need for an authority to deal with cases of corruption in the ranks of the government was under discussion for a number of years since Independence. The Administrative Reforms Committee (ARC) noted in its interim report that strong views were expressed on the subject in parliamentary discussions on the Prevention of Corruption (Second Amendment) Bill, 1952, the Criminal Law Amendment Bill, 1952, the Commission of Inquiry Bill, 1952 and the Prevention of Corruption (Amendment) Bill, 1955. On 3 April 1963, when the demands for the grants of the Law Ministry were being debated, the need for setting up an institution of the ombudsman type in India was strongly stressed. The Rajasthan Administrative Reforms Commission, in its report submitted in September 1963, recommended the appointment of an ombudsman for the state. Jawaharlal Nehru, speaking at the All India Congress Committee in Jaipur on 3 November 1963, said that the system of the ombudsman fascinated him, for the ombudsman had overall authority to deal with charges even against the Prime Minister and commanded the respect and confidence of all. However, he felt that in a big country like India, the introduction of such a system was beset with difficulties. The subsequent discussions on the subject have shown how perceptive this observation was.

In October 1966 the first ARC recommended setting up of a Lok Pal to look into complaints against administrative acts of ministers and secretaries to the government at the Centre and in the states. The commission felt that at the level at which ministers and secretaries functioned, it might often be difficult to decide where the role of one functionary ended and that of the other began. The line of demarcation between the responsibilities and influence of the minister and secretary was thin; in any case much depended on their personal equation and personality and it was most likely that in many a case determining the responsibilities of both of them was involved. The Lok Ayukta, to be appointed in each state and one at the Centre, were to look into the administrative acts of other authorities (Government of India 1966). The commission took note of the increasing sphere of government activities; justice through courts under the modern system of judiciary was generally both expensive and dilatory, whereas an individual wished to seek, and appreciated, quick and cheap justice; the growing encroachment of the state on citizens' rights; and vast area of administrative discretion in which facilities for redressal of grievances were not available.

As for the institutions established for the purpose in Scandinavian countries, New Zealand and the United Kingdom, the commission noted that the ombudsman was virtually a parliamentary institution though he was not, and could not be, a MP. He was independent of the judiciary, the executive and the legislature. Military departments were also within his jurisdiction. His position was analogous to that of the highest or high judicial functionaries in the country. He was left comparatively free to choose his own methods and agencies of investigation. The investigations were of an informal character. The expenditure of his office was subject to parliamentary control.

The ARC, *inter alia*, stated that:

- The experience of comparatively small countries like Sweden, Norway, Denmark and New Zealand, having small areas and containing small population, cannot be necessarily a precedent for India with such a vast area and population. An ombudsman on the analogy of those countries would require a very large staff and it would not be possible to maintain the private and informal character of investigation which has been a prominent feature of the institution in those countries.
- Norway, Sweden, Denmark, New Zealand and the U.K. have centralised administrations whereas India is a federation based on a division of functions between the states and the Centre in terms of central, state and concurrent lists. This would raise the problem of separate jurisdiction of the ombudsman and so many authorities which he would have to deal [with]. In Canada, where there is a federal government and a number of provincial governments, it was realised that if an ombudsman were created under the federal law, he would not have jurisdiction over the provinces and the provinces would have to establish their own ombudsman.

The ARC highlighted that public opinion had been agitated for a long time over the prevalence of corruption in the administration. The commission suggested that this institution should deal with such cases as well, but where the cases are such as might involve criminal charges or misconduct cognizable by a court, the case should be brought to the notice of the Prime Minister, or the Chief Minister, as the case may be. The commission felt that *the present system of vigilance commissions wherever operative will then become redundant and would have to be abolished on the setting up of the institution.*

The main features of the institutions of Lok Pal and Lok Ayukta, as delineated by the commission, were:

1. They should be demonstrably independent and impartial.
2. Their investigations and proceedings should be conducted in private and should be informal in character.
3. Their appointment should, as far as possible, be non-political.
4. Their status should compare with the highest judicial functionaries in the country.
5. They should deal with matters in the discretionary field involving acts of injustice, corruption or favouritism.
6. Their proceedings should not be subject to judicial interference and they should have the maximum latitude and powers in obtaining information relevant to their duties.
7. They should not look forward to any benefits or pecuniary advantage from the executive government.
8. In addition to making investigations on the basis of complaints received by him, the Lok Pal may also *suo motu* investigate administrative acts of injustice, maladministration, favouritism to any person, accrual of personal benefit or gain to the administrative authority responsible for the act, etc.
9. Any decision taken more than 12 months before the date of the complaint will not be looked into.

The commission also appended with its recommendations a draft bill on the subject. The commission underlined that for the Lok Pal to be fully effective and for him to acquire power, without conflict with other functionaries under the Constitution, it would be necessary to give a constitutional status to his office, powers, functions, etc. The commission however felt that it was not necessary for the government to wait for this to materialize before setting up the office. The constitutional amendment and any consequential modification of the relevant statute could follow. In the meantime, the commission suggested that the government can ensure that the Lok Pal and Lok Ayukta are appointed and took preparatory action to set up his office etc.

While the approach of the ARC was sound and a number of recommendations salutary, some important points arise which must be taken into account whenever it is 'propitious' to proceed further in the matter. **First,** in the current context of Centre-state relations and the concerns of the states regarding federalism, it is unlikely that they will agree to their Chief Minister, ministers and secretaries being covered by the Lok Pal Act. They will insist that this matter should be left to be dealt with by the states. **Second,** it is most important that the Lok Pal and Lok Ayukta are given constitutional status. But, the central government seems to be dragging its feet on the matter. There is no reason why a Constitution amendment bill cannot be introduced at the same time as the bill for establishing a Lok Pal. **Third,** the Centre seems to have given up the proposal to have a central enactment for the Lok Ayukta, which has also been the demand of the conference of Lok Ayuktas for quite some time. Serious efforts need to be made at the political level to persuade the states to agree to a central legislation. Hopefully, this will be feasible after the Lok Sabha elections in 2014. **Fourth**, the suggestion of the commission to abolish the CVC is not only not feasible or advisable but it will also be retrograde. There is no reason to believe that the role of CVC will be subsumed by the Lok Pal. **Fifth**, the suggestion of the ARC that the enquiries by the Lok Pal should be private and informal is also difficult to agree to. Much water has flown since the time the report of the ARC was submitted in 1966. Now, that the RTI Act has taken firm roots, all enquiries before Lok Pal must be by open hearing as in the courts of law. **Sixth**, the commission has suggested that the appointment of Lok Pal should, as far as possible, be non-political. In fact, the selection of Lok Pal will have to be by a transparent procedure and the selection must not only be non-political but must be seen to be such. **Seventh,** the limit of 12 months suggested by the ARC for taking cognizance of the complaints should be increased to ten years. **Eighth**, the Prime Minister and chief ministers are excluded from the purview of the Lok Pal. For reasons discussed separately, this will not be advisable. The Prime Minister and chief ministers must be brought under the purview of the Lok Pal and Lok Ayukta respectively. **Ninth**, MLAs and MPs are also left out of Lok Pal's jurisdiction. This too is not justified. In short, the scheme of ARC is somewhat out-of-date and needs to be suitably amplified to suit the requirements of present times.

Second Administrative Reforms Commission

The Second Administrative Reforms Commission (SARC) recommended that the Lok Pal should be created by amending the Constitution, with his role and jurisdiction being embodied in it. It suggested that the jurisdiction of Lok Pal should extend to all ministers of the union (except the Prime Minister), all state chief ministers, all persons holding public office equivalent in rank to a union minister and MPs. It further recommended that in case an inquiry against a public functionary establishes the involvement of any other public official along with the public functionary, the Lok Pal should have the power to hold an inquiry against such public servant(s) also. The commission recommended that the Prime Minister should be kept out of the jurisdiction of the Lok Pal. The Lok Pal should consist of a serving or retired judge of the Supreme Court as the chairperson, an eminent jurist as a member, and the CVC as an ex-officio member. The selection panel is to comprise of the Vice President of India, the Prime Minister, the leader of opposition, the Speaker and the CJI. It is suggested that the chairperson and member of Lok Pal should be appointed only for one term of three years and they should not hold any office under government thereafter, except being the CJI. The commission suggested that the Lok Pal should also be entrusted with the task of undertaking a national campaign for raising the standards of ethics in public life (Government of India 2007: 183–84).

It can be seen that SARC's report raises some important questions. **First,** in view of the recent debate on federalism, it is unlikely that the states will agree to chief ministers being brought under the jurisdiction of the Lok Pal. And it is not necessary to do so either. All state ministers, including the Chief Minister, should be under the jurisdiction of Lok Ayukta. **Second,** there is no reason why the Prime Minister should be kept out of the purview of Lok Pal. As I have stated elsewhere, at least three previous prime ministers (Indira Gandhi, Rajiv Gandhi and Narasimha Rao) were embroiled in serious corruption scandals. Recent controversies involving the present Prime Minister Manmohan Singh underline that the Prime Minister must also be held accountable for his actions and inactions. **Third,** all senior officers of and above the rank of joint secretaries and equivalent must also be brought under the Lok Pal. Otherwise, the war against corruption will be meaningless. **Fourth,** there is no need to bring in the CVC as an ex-officio member. This office is already over-loaded. Further, since the CVC is involved in decision-making processes in major corruption cases, there will be a conflict of interest if he is also to be the Lok Pal. Instead, one or more full time members may be appointed. **Fifth,** considering the complexities of the issues and the need for familiarization, the proposed term of three years is too short. Instead, a five-year term would be advisable. **Sixth,** the Lok Pal should not be involved in any campaign for raising ethical standards in public life. This cannot be the responsibility of a constitutional office.

Changing Profiles of Lok Pal Bills

Over the years, the ambit of Lok Pal, as visualized in various bills, has undergone considerable changes. The first two bills (1968 and 1971) proposed two separate institutions of Lok Pal and Lok Ayukta. The first was to deal with ministers and secretaries in the government, and the second with the other staff. The scheme of the Lok Pal under the 1977 bill was materially different. First, the bill did not talk about the Lok Ayukta. Instead, it provided for the appointment of special Lok Pals for the expeditious disposal of cases. Second, it included the Prime Minister in the ambit of Lok Pal. Third, while the two earlier bills covered both allegations of misconduct and grievances, the 1977 bill excluded grievances from its purview. Fourth, the 1977 bill did not apply to government officers. It covered only ministers and MPs. Fifth, the bill excluded consultations with the leader of the opposition for appointing the Lok Pal, as presumably, the Janata government, which had brought forward the bill, did not want to have anything to do with the Congress (Indira) at that time (Rajya Sabha Secretariat 1996: 22–25).

The 1985 bill, introduced by the Rajiv Gandhi government, was again radically different in that the Prime Minister and MPs were excluded from its purview. Second, the scope of complaints was restricted to relevant provisions of the Prevention of Corruption Act and the Indian Penal Code. Third, the Lok Pal was given power to stay any criminal investigation with respect to the same allegations. Fourth, prosecution on allegations held unproven or false by the Lok Pal was barred.

The bill introduced by the National Front government in 1989 had its own distinguishing features. First, the Prime Minister was once again brought in the purview of the Lok Pal. Second, if any allegations against the Prime Minister were substantiated either wholly or partly, the report of the Lok Pal was to go to the Speaker for being laid before the House within 90 days of its receipt. In contrast, under the 1985 bill, the report of the Lok Pal in such cases was to be sent to the Prime Minister and he was enjoined to place it without delay before the council of ministers. Third, the 1985 bill empowered the President to appoint as Lok Pal a person who is or has been or is qualified to be a judge of the Supreme Court. This last category would have included any advocate with ten years of practice. The 1989 bill restricted the qualifications to only two categories, namely, serving and retired judges of the Supreme Court. Fourth, unlike the previous bills, the 1989 bill proposed that the Lok Pal should comprise the chairman and two members.

Thus, the emphasis was more on prevention of corruption rather than on redressal of grievances. While in the 1968 and 1971 bills, the emphasis was on 'complaints' and 'grievances' of maladministration, in the 1977, 1985 and 1989 bills, the emphasis shifted to 'allegations of corruption'.

The 1998 Lok Pal Bill envisaged that the Lok Pal would be a three-member body with all the three persons drawn from the judiciary; the selection panel was to consist of the Vice President of India as Chairman, Prime Minister, Speaker, Home Minister, and leaders of opposition in the Lok Sabha and the Rajya Sabha; the Prime Minister and other ministers and MPs were to be brought in the purview of Lok Pal; Lok Pal was to deal with complaints punishable under the Prevention of Corruption Act, 1988; the Lok Pal was to have a term of three years and he was to be made ineligible for reappointment; he was also to be ineligible for holding any office of profit; and each inquiry was to be completed within six months, and each inquiry to be made by the three members sitting jointly.

The bill was considered by the department-related standing committee (Parliament of India 1999). Particular reference may be made to the discussion therein on bringing MPs under the Lok Pal. The committee members expressed diverse views on the subject:

- In view of Supreme Court judgment bringing MPs within the definition of public servants under the Prevention of Corruption Act, there was no need for bringing the MPs within the jurisdiction of Lok Pal as it would be tantamount to double jeopardy;
- MPs should not be subjected to the disciplinary authority of an agency outside the jurisdiction of the House in consonance with the views of the ethics committee which is a permanent institution of the House;
- Subjecting MPs to an outside disciplinary authority would affect the supremacy of Parliament;
- There was need for establishing the institution of Lok Pal as corruption had increased manifold in high places after Independence and there had been a general perception that persons holding high offices were not being punished; and
- By establishing the institution of Lok Pal the supremacy of Parliament would not be eroded as it would be a creation of Parliament. The supremacy of Parliament would in effect be reiterated with the establishment of Lok Pal.

The committee requested that the government examine all these aspects before proceeding further with the bill. Among the amendments suggested by the committee, reference may be made to its suggestion that apart from mentioning ineligibility to hold office of profit under the central or state government, the chairperson and members should also be made ineligible for the gubernatorial posts and diplomatic assignments, administrators of union territories etc. after ceasing to hold the office. In other words, they should be debarred from holding any office in the Government of India. The committee also expressed reservations about the provision in the bill that MPs should not be permitted to sit or vote as members of either House till they furnished declaration of assets and liabilities. The committee felt that the constitutional validity of this needed to be examined by the government and the opinion of the Attorney General may also be obtained. The committee also suggested that punishment may be imposed on an applicant only if the complaint was found to be frivolous and had been filed with a mala fide intention.

The Lok Pal and Lok Ayukta Bill, 2013, introduced in Parliament by the UPA II government, is qualitatively different from the bills introduced by successive governments in the past and shows that the government did not have a mind of its own and permitted itself to be unreasonably pressurized by the Anna Hazare team. The government appeared to have been unduly influenced by the orchestrated public demonstrations and excessive media hype. It was clearly not able to take a principled stand on a number of issues. The bill is also unworkable for various reasons discussed hereafter.

The Lok Pal legislation is a minefield of critical issues and the Lok Pal and Lok Ayukta Bill, 2013, has come a long way from the original concept of the Lok Pal as was conceived by the first ARC in 1966. A few important aspects need further inspection.

The position on whether the Prime Minister should be brought in the purview of the Lok Pal has undergone a change from time to time. But looking to the deplorable record of at least three previous prime ministers cited earlier, the Prime Minister must be brought in the purview of the Lok Pal. It may be recalled that the concept of Lok Pal had 'fascinated' Jawaharlal Nehru precisely for the reason that the Lok Pal would even be able to look into allegations against the Prime Minister.

It seems that MPs are opposed to being brought under the Lok Pal. Since they are public servants, there is every justification in bringing them under Lok Pal but it remains to be seen how this will finally be dealt with when the bill is passed by Parliament. It may be recalled that in some of the earlier bills, MPs were kept out of the purview of the Lok Pal. A reference may be made to a recent case involving serious criminal charges involving some MPs. On 22 July 2008, during the debate on the motion of confidence in the council of ministers, three MPs came to the well of the Lok Sabha with two bags, took out bundles of currency notes from the bags and placed them on the table of the House. The MPs alleged that they had been offered money in connection with voting on the motion of confidence. The Speaker appointed a committee to investigate the matter fully. The committee's report which was laid on the table of the Lok Sabha on 15 December 2008 makes for very sad and disturbing reading in that the committee failed to examine the two Rajya Sabha members, Amar Singh and Ahmed Patel, who were also allegedly involved in the episode on the specious plea that the rules did not permit it. The committee merely recommended that the procedure for requiring the appearance of a member of one House before the other House or committee thereof, as recommended by the Committee of Privileges (second Lok Sabha) in its sixth report in 1958, needs to be reviewed to bring it at par with the position as is obtaining now in the Parliament of United Kingdom by which 'a general leave is granted to any member requested to attend as a witness before a Lords Committee or its sub-committee or a Commons Committee or its sub-committee, if he thinks fit'. The committee felt that it was time a similar procedure is adopted in the Lok Sabha and the Rajya Sabha by amending the rules of procedure of the two Houses. There is no reason why such a change could not have been asked for and made while the committee was deliberating on this highly sensitive issue. The committee after spending tax payers' money for several months merely recommended that 'this matter may be probed further by an appropriate investigating agency' (Lok Sabha Secretariat 2008: 57). This could have been done by the Speaker as soon as the matter was raised in the House. In fact, it was not necessary for the police to wait for a formal reference from the Lok Sabha as the alleged offence had taken place outside the premises of the Lok Sabha. Even after a considerable lapse of time, the police investigation is still dragging on. The Delhi High Court has expressed its unhappiness at the tardy investigation. Against this background, there is no reason why such cases should not be brought in the purview of the Lok Pal. Only matters pertaining to the conduct of business in Parliament may appropriately be said to fall within the purview of the presiding officers and committees of Parliament. All other matters should legitimately come within the jurisdiction of the Lok Pal.

The question of whether the CBI should be placed under the Lok Pal has also become a contentious issue. The CBI should not be placed under the Lok Pal. For reasons stated previously, it will be best to place the CBI under the CVC, rather than the Lok Pal. In Chapter 5, I have suggested arrangements to safeguard the independence and autonomy of the CBI.

A demand has been made that matters pertaining to disciplinary action with respect to higher judiciary also need to be brought in the purview of the Lok Pal. I do not agree with this approach. It must not be forgotten that the institution of Lok Pal must function within the framework of the Constitution and must not be a substitute for existing constitutional institutions, as seems to be the efforts of Hazare and his followers. Separate institutional arrangements need to be evolved for dealing with improprieties, deviant behaviour and complaints against members of the higher judiciary. It will not be advisable to place these matters under the Lok Pal.

At the instance of the Anna Hazare team, the government agreed to bring all its employees, including class C and D employees, in the purview of Lok Pal. This will divert the attention of the Lok Pal to the base of the pyramid rather than the higher echelons of administration. To cope with this huge workload, the Lok Pal will require its own large bureaucracy spread over the whole country. This will be totally counter-productive and militate against the original objective that the Lok Pal be created to deal with corruption and maladministration at the level of the ministers and secretaries in the government, and later expanded to include elected representatives.

According to the original concept incorporated in the bill, there was to be only one Lok Pal. With the unwieldy jurisdiction of the Lok Pal as envisaged in the 2013 bill, the number of Lok Pals has been increased to eight. In years to come, there will be demands to increase the number further and to establish benches of Lok Pals in various parts of the country. Such a top-heavy anti-corruption organization will clearly be counter-productive. Further, providing for inquiry by persons of the status of Supreme Court judges into complaints against Class C and D employees will certainly be overkill.

For the first time in a statutory body like Lok Pal, which will hopefully be converted later into a constitutional body, reservation for SCs, STs and minorities is proposed. This is inadvisable since there are no such provisions for other constitutional and statutory bodies, though this aspect is borne in mind by appointing authorities in making appointments to these bodies.

Under political pressure, the government decided to exclude the armed forces from the purview of the Lok Pal. There seems no justification to do so, considering the large-scale corruption in the armed forces. Such short-term compromises have already been the bane of good governance for a long time.

The feature of the ombudsman scheme in a number of countries, which requires the names of the complainant and the person complained against to be kept secret, will go against the widely held precept of 'naming and shaming'. In recent years, even the CVC has put the names of officers against whom vigilance inquiries are in progress on his website.

In India, complainants will not be satisfied if there is no oral inquiry or the complainant is not given a chance to put across his point of view. The same position will hold true with respect to some other aspects of the functioning of Lok Pal.

It is unfortunate that the question of giving constitutional status to the Lok Pal (and the Lok Ayukta) has fallen by the wayside in the midst of the controversy surrounding other provisions of the bill. Let us hope that this important issue will not be lost sight of and a Constitution amendment bill will be moved along with the final Lok Pal Bill.

Lok Ayukta

SARC recommended that the Constitution should be amended to incorporate a provision making it obligatory on the part of state governments to establish the institution of Lok Ayukta and stipulate the general principles about its structure, power and functions. According to the commission, a Lok Ayukta should be a multi-member body consisting of a judicial member as chairperson, an eminent jurist, an eminent administrator and the head of the State Vigilance commission as an ex-officio member. The chairperson should be a retired Supreme Court judge or a retired Chief Justice of a High Court. The selection panel for the chairperson and members should comprise of the Chief Minister, Chief Justice of the High Court and the leader of opposition in the Legislative Assembly. There need not be an *upa* (deputy) Lok Ayukta.

SARC also suggested that the jurisdiction of the Lok Ayuktas should extend only to cases involving corruption. They should not look into general public grievances. The Lok Ayuktas should deal with cases of corruption against ministers and MLAs. The commission recommended that the chairperson and members of Lok Ayukta should be appointed strictly for one term only and they should not hold any public office under the government thereafter. It is important to note that SARC suggested that the Lok Ayukta should have its own machinery for investigations. Initially, it may take officers on deputation from the state government, but over a period of five years, it should take steps to recruit its own cadre and train them properly. The commission also suggested that all cases of corruption should be referred to the Lok Pal and Lok Ayukta and these should not be referred to any commission of inquiry (Government of India: 184–85).

As in the case of Lok Pal, SARC's recommendations with respect to the Lok Ayukta raise a number of questions. **First,** the suggestion to appoint the head of the State Vigilance Commission as an ex-officio member of the Lok Ayukta is not advisable. **Second,** as presently constituted, Lok Ayuktas are also responsible for looking into grievances of people, and not just corruption cases. It may be advisable to continue the present position as mere corruption cases may not provide enough work to such a high power body in all states. **Third,** for greater impact the jurisdiction of Lok Ayukta should also extend to senior civil servants both in the field and in the secretariat. **Fourth,** the recommendation to confine the appointment to only one term is well taken but that term should be of five years and not three years. **Fifth,** the proposed selection panel for the chairperson and members is unexceptional but, looking to the experience of Gujarat, it must be clearly laid down that the decision must be unanimous. **Sixth,** the recommendation that a commission of inquiry should not be appointed to look into any corruption cases and all such cases should be referred to the Lok Ayukta, is salutary and would strengthen the institution of the Lok Ayukta.

It must be underlined that the experience of the working of the Lok Ayuktas in the states presents a disheartening picture. Though these offices have been created in nearly 20 states and in some cases over 25 years ago, their impact is practically nil, except in a few states such as Karnataka and Madhya Pradesh. Several former Lok Ayuktas themselves have expressed their disenchantment with the institution and some (such as former Lok Ayuktas of Rajasthan and Madhya Pradesh) have publicly expressed the view that it is a waste of public money to continue these institutions, and that these should be wound up. Justice Shamim, former Lok Ayukta of Delhi, complained that though the government spent almost Rs 1.25 crore on the institution annually, he received less than five actionable complaints every year. It is necessary that the reasons for this are analysed carefully. Such an analysis will show that the main lacuna is that there is no uniformity in the provisions of these state enactments. The All India Conference of Lok Ayuktas has repeatedly suggested that there should be an all-India enactment and constitutional status be given to the Lok Ayukta by amending the Constitution. The conference also suggested that some important powers be given to the Lok Ayuktas for their effective functioning. These include grant of power to take *suo motu* action, powers of carrying out raids and seizures, placing dedicated police units at their disposal, prompt action by the state government on the recommendations of the Lok Ayuktas, financial autonomy, treating the expenditure on the institution as a 'charged expenditure', and so on. These points have been reiterated by several Lok Ayuktas in their articles in the volume published in 1995 (Norman and Singh 1995). These are unexceptional. Unfortunately, most of these powers have not been granted to Lok Ayuktas.

The experience of the functioning of the Lok Ayukta in Maharashtra is no better. Though over a decade has elapsed, a series of suggestions made in my *Report of the One Man Committee on Good Governance* (July 2001) have been lying unattended in the state government. These include:

- entrusting the Lok Ayukta with the overall responsibilities of overseeing vigilance work in the state;
- putting the Director General (anti-corruption) under the overall charge of the Lok Ayukta;
- sanctioning a special investigation team of police officers for being placed at the disposal of the Lok Ayukta as in Karnataka and Madhya Pradesh;
- entrusting the responsibility to the Lok Ayukta to release his reports to the general public as soon as they are presented to the government, from time to time;
- giving financial autonomy to the Lok Ayukta and making the expenditure of the office of Lok Ayukta 'charged' expenditure;
- treating the recommendation of the Lok Ayukta to sanction prosecution in a case as mandatory;
- deleting Section 10(2) of the Maharashtra Lok Ayukta Act which requires that the name of the applicant and the officer complained against be kept confidential;
- continuing enquiries against public servants even after they have demitted office;
- acting on the recommendations of the All India Conference of Lok Ayuktas such as enlarging the jurisdiction of Lok Ayuktas, giving them special powers etc; and
- bringing in the electricity and transport undertakings of the state government under the purview of the Lok Ayukta.

One of the suggestions made by the Conference of Lok Ayuktas over two decades ago was that constitutional status should be given to the Lok Ayuktas and state enactments should be on an uniform basis. Currently, the provisions of Lok Ayukta enactments differ a great deal from state to state. It is necessary to emphasize that in Punjab, Haryana and Odisha, the posts of Lok Ayuktas were abolished peremptorily when enquiries were started by the Lok Ayuktas against politically powerful ministers or in sensitive matters.

As stated earlier, in Gujarat, the post of Lok Ayukta was vacant for over seven years due to the divergence of opinion between the Chief Minister and the leader of opposition on the incumbent to be appointed as Lok Ayukta. Finally, the Governor appointed a person who was not recommended by the Chief

Minister but had been found acceptable to the Chief Justice of the High Court and the leader of opposition, as the new Lok Ayukta. Surprisingly, this action of the Governor was upheld by the High Court as also the Supreme Court. Thus, Gujarat had a Lok Ayukta who was not acceptable to the state government. It is not surprising that he has since tendered his resignation. To make appointments to constitutional positions in this manner reduces the credibility of the post and brings it down in public esteem.

All this goes to show the importance of having an all-India enactment on the subject and giving it a constitutional status. But in the name of federalism some states like West Bengal have insisted that the provisions pertaining to the model enactment on Lok Ayukta, contained in the Lok Pal and Lok Ayukta Bill 2013, should be deleted. The select committee of the Rajya Sabha has also made a similar recommendation. To do so will be a retrograde step but the central government does not seem to have any alternative than to concede this demand, if the Lok Pal Bill has to be passed by Parliament. This is largely because of the failure of the central government to hold intensive discussions with state governments to bring them on board before introducing the bill. The same is true of the proposal to give constitutional status to Lok Ayuktas. The ostensible reasons put forth by some states that the Centre should not encroach on their powers is clearly misconceived and meant to stall action which has been long overdue. The Centre succumbing to such pressure shows a lack of political will, and once again underlines the ambivalence of the Centre in dealing with issues crucial for eradication of corruption.

Ombudsman for Local Bodies

The SARC deserves to be complimented for recommending the setting up of an ombudsman for local bodies in a group of districts to investigate cases against the functionaries of the local bodies. It is suggested that the ombudsman should be empowered to investigate cases of corruption or maladministration by functionaries of local bodies. In Chapter 1, I have referred to the serious problem of maladministration of urban local bodies. It is time an independent, credible and apolitical body such as an ombudsman is appointed for large municipal corporations or for a group of urban local bodies, depending on their size and complexities, to remedy the situation. The Constitution needs to be amended to make it obligatory on the states to appoint such ombudsmen. Such a step will be more effective than taking recourse to a PIL and will be widely welcomed.

Ombudsman for Professional Bodies

It is imperative that the functioning of various autonomous and independent bodies in all sectors are brought under the purview of ombudsmen. This will be the most effective grievance redressal mechanism and will act as a valve in relieving pressures of discontent. Transparent functioning of ombudsmen and their passing self-contained 'speaking orders' will go a long way in empowering citizens.

To Conclude

It is necessary to remember that the Lok Pal or the Lok Ayukta is not a magic wand, as is being made out to be. It is also not the only remedy for the ills of corruption and maladministration. It can only be one of the instruments in a larger strategy for dealing with the menace outlined in this book.

As K. C. Wheare has rightly said, 'The success of ombudsman is likely to be greatest in the sort of political and constitutional community which needs him least. It is essentially the sort of institution which can only be effective where habits of constitutionalism are well established and are believed in. It is more likely to make good government better than bad government good.'[10]

Declare Good Governance a Fundamental Right

Looking at the state of affairs discussed in this book, the importance of good governance can hardly be over-emphasized. My colleague E. A. S. Sarma and I had filed a writ petition in the Supreme Court in 2004 praying that just as the court had recognized certain rights such as the right to privacy, right to information and freedom of press as fundamental rights, it should also recognize good governance as a fundamental right of every citizen (Godbole and Sarma 2004: 46-48). It was underlined that good governance is recognized as a prime objective in several leading democracies in the world. The countries which are in the forefront in these efforts include Australia, New Zealand, Singapore, the United States and the United Kingdom. We had pleaded that once this is done, a number of statutory and institutional changes will inevitably have to be undertaken by the government. We had further pleaded that higher civil services should be recognized by the court as the main instrument for translating the right to good governance into reality and towards this end had suggested a series of steps for improving the functioning of the civil services. It was emphasized that the basic features of the Constitution identified by the Supreme Court will remain on paper if the ills afflicting the civil services, which have been responsible for what NCRWC has called 'pervasive disenchantment' with the governance of the country, remain unattended. The prayers in the petition included, among others, directions by the court that good governance and permanent and politically neutral civil services are intrinsic to the scheme of the Constitution and part of its basic structure; officials, before starting their careers, in addition to taking the oath of loyalty to the Constitution, should also swear to abide by the basic principles of good governance and to give unequivocal commitment to the basic tenets of the Constitution. Towards this end, government servants' conduct rules should be completely rewritten so as to be in accord with modern notions of accountability, and so on. We had hoped that the admission and hearing of the petition will help generate country-wide debate and discussion on the issues and lead to building up of the pressure of public opinion on the subject. Unfortunately, the Supreme Court refused to admit the PIL. Maybe its time had not yet come!

The plight of higher civil services continues to agitate discerning people all over the country. Some 84 persons who had retired from the highest positions in various central and All India Services have filed another PIL in the Supreme Court. The most important difference between the two PILs is that while our PIL asked for protection to the higher civil services in the context of good governance, the latter PIL deals only with the service conditions and their protection. It is hoped the latest PIL will meet with a better fate than ours did since the issues involved are crucial for the governance of the country.

Compile Indices of Good Governance and Opacity

A welcome and reassuring recent development is the recognition that good governance can be politically rewarding. The much-talked about concept of anti-incumbency in elections has been overturned in a number of states which had shown significant progress in development. These included Bihar, Delhi, Gujarat, Madhya Pradesh and Odisha. It is heartening to see the states vying with each other in projecting their rates of growth, the initiatives taken for good governance and so on. Some of the initiatives taken by Bihar and Odisha have been referred to earlier. Clearly, they have stolen a march over even some of the advanced states. It is gratifying to note that good governance has emerged as a major issue in the Lok Sabha elections in 2014. Narendra Modi, Chief Minister of Gujarat, is staking his claim as a possible prime ministerial candidate for the BJP on the ground that Gujarat is the best governed state in the country.

Often times comparisons between states appear to be politically biased. Thus, the performance of Gujarat is often run down, primarily because it is headed by Narendra Modi of Godhra communal holocaust ill-repute. There are also dissenting voices regarding the exceptional performance of the Nitish Kumar government in Bihar. Looking at the importance of good governance for the country, comparisons among states and for that matter the evaluation of the Centre, need to be put on an objective and scientific basis by compiling an annual index of good governance.

Translating the concept of good governance into reality is not an easy task. Unless there is political and administrative commitment of the highest order, it is more likely that important objectives of good governance will be lost sight of or deliberately overlooked. It is also necessary that continuous pressure of public opinion is maintained on those in authority who are answerable for good governance. Towards this end it is imperative that an index of good governance is compiled and published annually. Wide consultations will have to be held with civil society groups and stakeholders regarding the elements which should be incorporated in the index. Such an index can be a talking point for the states and the Centre to canvass their case as a destination for domestic and foreign investments. It will also enable inter-state comparisons on the performance of different states. At some stage in the future, if good governance is recognized as a fundamental right of every citizen, as was urged in my PIL referred to earlier, these efforts will be further strengthened. Recent elections to state legislatures and the Lok Sabha have shown that good governance can help the ruling political party/ alliance in getting re-elected, thereby nullifying the myth of the anti-incumbency factor. Good governance can also become good politics.

The index can include the rate of growth of state domestic product, reduction in poverty, implementation performance of important social sector schemes, infant mortality, proportion of female child births to male child births, malnutrition, school drop-out rates, custodial deaths, communal violence, industrial peace, crime against weaker sections, cases of human rights violations and outcomes of fast track courts. There should be wide-ranging discussion on the components of the index so as to make it as acceptable, comprehensive and comparable as possible.

One of the important components of good governance is the transparency in the working of the government. This can be highlighted by compiling an annual opacity index which will show how open, accountable and predictable the decision-making in government is.

To Sum Up

Just as war is too serious a matter to be left only to the generals, governance is too serious a matter to be left only to politicians and bureaucrats. All stakeholders from all walks of life must become active participants in keeping a close watch over it. Only when a million, and in the case of India a billion, eyes and ears are so deployed can some change for the better be expected.

Notes

1. When Principal Secretary to Prime Minister rang up B. K. Nehru to hurry up with his departure from Srinagar, Nehru had shouted back at him to say that his departure date had been fixed and he was not a bloody *chaprasi* [peon] to be turned out at a moment's notice. Dharma Vira, Governor of West Bengal, had used exactly

the same words to the Cabinet Secretary of his time about his not being a 'bloody *chaprasi*' (see, Nehru 1997: 639).

2. For example, while participating in a Parliament debate on supersession of judges and appointing the CJI, Union Steel Minister M. Kumaramangalam, who was a close advisor to Prime Minister Indira Gandhi, brazenly stated, 'The executive, while exercising its discretion, can and ought to see that the person to be appointed as the CJI must be one who would create conditions which would avoid any confrontation between the Supreme Court on one side and the executive and the legislature on the other. He must be one who would acknowledge the supremacy of Parliament, and give leadership to the court, and above all, would be able to respond to the changing winds' (see, Hegde 1973: 42). There could not have been a clearer enunciation of the concept of a 'committed judiciary'.

3. This, in essence, is the same as the zero base budgeting undertaken by the Government of Maharashtra in the late 1980s, referred to earlier, which was given up as soon as Sharad Pawar became Chief Minister in 1989.

4. UK opens up its plans for transparency and open data for open government partnerships (OGP), https://www. gov.uk/govt/news, dated 27 June 2013.

5. The last few decades have seen the rise of powerful sons-in-law near the seats of power—Robert Vadra, son-in-law of Sonia Gandhi, Ranjan Bhattacharya of Atal Bihari Vajpaye, Gurunath Maiyappan of N. Srinivasan, BCCI President, Sadanand Sule of Sharad Pawar, Anil Kumar of late Y. S. Rajasekhara Reddy, and Chandrababu Naidu of N. T. Rama Rao, to name a few (see, *Outlook* 2013: 42 –45).

6. Sharon Watkins, a former Arther Anderson accountant, joined Enron in 1993 and worked for the man who later became Chief Finance Officer, Andy Fastow. As a result of her memos to Chief Executive Officer Kenneth Lay urging the company to change the accounting practices and restate the earnings, she became known to the world as the Enron whistle-blower. In her memo she said, 'It sure looks to the layman on the street that we are hiding losses in a related company and will compensate the company with Enron stock in the future. I am incredibly nervous that we will implode in a wave of accounting scandals.' She testified before the House and the Senate hearings investigating Enron business practices in February 2002 and was named, along with others, as one of *Time* magazine's 2002 Persons of the Year (see, Swartz with Watkins 2003).

7. (Godbole 2012: 73–85).

8. This section is largely based on the writer's book (Godbole 2011).

9. The word Parliament includes state legislatures.

10. Sir Kenneth Clinton Wheare was an Australian academic who spent most of his career at Oxford University in England. He was an expert on the history of the constitutions of the British Commonwealth.

ABBREVIATIONS

AA	Asian Age
AFSPA	Armed Forces Special Powers Act
AIR	All India Reporter
AIS	All India Service
ARC	Administrative Reforms Commission
BBC.	British Broadcasting Corporation
BCCI	Board for Control of Cricket in India
BDR	Bangladesh Rifles
BJP	Bharatiya Janata Party
BMC	Brihan Mumbai Municipal Corporation
BS	Business Standard
BSF	Border Security Force
BSP	Bahujan Samaj Party
CAA	Civil Aviation Authority
C&AG	Comptroller and Auditor General
CBDT	Central Board of Direct Taxes
CBI	Central Bureau of Investigation
CEC	Chief Election Commissioner
CJI	Chief Justice of India
CIC	Chief Information Commission
CII	Confederation of Indian Industry
CISF	Central Industial Security Force
CMP	Common Minimum Programme
COS	Commission on Secularism
CP	Commissioner of Police
CPI	Communist Party of India
CPM	Communist Party (Marxist)
CPO	Central Police Organization
CrPC	Criminal Procedure Code
CRPF	Central Reserve Police Force
CVC	Central/Chief Vigilance Commissioner
DGCA	Directorate General of Civil Aviation
DOT	Department of Telecommunications
DP	Directorate of Prosecution

DPC	Dabhol Power Company
EC	Election Commission
EPW	Economic and Political Weekly
ERC	Energy Review Committee
ERC	Electricity Regulatory Commission
ET	Economic Times
FCRA	Foreign Contribution (Regulation) Act
FE	Financial Express
FIR	First Information Report
GDP	Gross Domestic Product
GOI	Government of India
GOM	Group of Ministers
GOM	Government of Maharashtra
GPRA	Government Performance and Results Act
HDR	Human Development Report
HT	Hindustan Times
IB	Intelligence Bureau
ICAO	International Civil Aviation Organization
ICS	Indian Civil Service
IE	Indian Express
IGP	Inspector General of Police
IIC	India International Centre
IM	Indian Mujahideen
IMDT	Illegal Migrants (Determination by Tribunals) Act
IP	Indian Police
IPCL	Indian Petrochemicals Corporation Limited
ISI	Inter-Services Intelligence
ITAT	Income Tax Appellate Tribunal
ITBP	Indo Tibetan Border Police
JMM	Jharkhand Mukti Morcha
JD (U)	Janata Dal (United)
JPC	Joint Parliamentary Committee
J&K	Jammu and Kashmir
LIC	Life Insurance Corporation of India
MMBTU	Million Metre British Thermal Units
MHA	Ministry of Home Affairs
MISA	Maintenance of Internal Security Act
MLA	Member of Legislative Assembly
MLC	Member of Legislative Council
MOCCA	Maharashtra Organized Crime Control Act
MPLADS	Members of Parliament Local Area Development Scheme

MSCMD	Million Standard Cubic Metres a Day
MSEB	Maharashtra State Electricity Board
MTF	Mobile Task Force
NAC	National Advisory Council
NCP	Nationalist Congress Party
NCRWC	National Commission to Review the Working of the Constitution
NCTC	National Counter Terrorism Centre
NDA	National Democratic Alliance
NDMA	National Disaster Management Agency
NGO	Non-Government Organization
NIC	National Integration Council
NHRC	National Human Rights Commission
NIA	National Investigation Agency
NIRD	National Institute of Rural Development
NREGA	National Rural Employment Guarantee Act
NTRO	National Technical Research Organization
OBC	Other Backward Caste
OECD	Organization for Economic Cooperation and Development
OSA	Official Secrets Act
OUP	Oxford University Press
PAC	Political Affairs Committee/ Public Accounts Committee
PIL	Public Interest Litigation
PMO	Prime Minister's Office
POTA	Prevention of Terrorism Act
PPA	Power Purchase Agreement
PPP	Public Private Partnership
PSC	Public Service Commission
PSU	Public Sector Undertaking
RAW	Research and Analysis Wing
RBI	Reserve Bank of India
RJD	Rashtriya Janata Dal
RIL	Reliance Industries Limited
RPA	Representation of People Act
RPF	Railway Protection Force
RSS	Rashtriya Swayamsevak Sangh
RTI	Right to Information
SARC	Second Administrative Reforms Commission
SC	Scheduled Caste
SEB	State Electricity Board
SEBI	Securities and Exchange Board of India
SEZ	Special Economic Zone

SIMI	Students Islamic Movement of India
ST	Scheduled Tribe
TADA	Terrorist and Disruptive Activities Act
TOI	Times Of India
TOP	Transfer Of Power
TRAI	Telecom Regulatory Authority of India
UNDP	United Nations Development Programme
UNIDO	United Nations Industrial Development Organization
UPA	United Progressive Alliance
UPSC	Union Public Service Commission
UTI	Unit Trust of India
VHP	Vishwa Hindu Parishad
VIP	Very Important Person

BIBLIOGRAPHY

Books and Reports

Ahrens Joachim, Rolf Caspers, Janine Weingarth, ed., *Good Governance in the 21st Century*, Edward Elgar Publishing Limited, U.K., 2011.

Auditor General of British Columbia with Deputy Ministers' Council, *Enhancing Accountability for Performance in the British Columbia Public Sector*, June 1995.

Basu Debashis, *Face Value—Creation and Destruction of Shareholder Value in India*, Ken Source Business Books, Mumbai, 2003.

Baxi Upendra, *The Crisis in the Indian Legal System*, Vikas Publishing House, New Delhi, 1982.

Baxi Upendra, *Liberty and Corruption: The Antulay Case and Beyond*, Eastern Book Company, Lucknow, 1989.

Baxi Upendra, *Inhuman Wrongs and Human Rights: Unconventional Essays*, Har-Anand Publications, New Delhi, 1994.

Bhagyalaxmi J., ed., *Capital Witness: Selected Writings of G. K. Reddy*, Allied Publishers, New Delhi, 1992.

Chandrachud Y. V., *The Basics of Indian Constitution: Its Search for Social Change and the Role of Judges*, Publications Division, Information and Broadcasting Ministry, New Delhi, 1989.

Chopra Pran, ed., *The Supreme Court versus The Constitution—A Challenge to Federalism*, Sage Publications, New Delhi, 2006.

Chopra S. K., ed., *Towards Good Governance*, Konark Publishers/India International Centre, Delhi, 1997.

Concerned Citizens Tribunal—Gujarat 2002, *Crime Against Humanity, An Inquiry into the Carnage in Gujarat: Findings and recommendations*, 21 November 2002.

Craig P. G., *Administrative Law*, fifth edition, Thomson, Sweet and Maxwell, London, 2003.

Desai A. R., ed., *Violations of Democratic Rights in India*, vol. I, Popular Prakashan, Bombay, 1986.

Deshmukh B. G., *A Cabinet Secretary Looks Back: From Poona to the Prime Minister's Office*, HarperCollins Publishers India, New Delhi, 2004.

Deshmukh Vikas, *Towards Better Corporate Governance—Completing the Unfinished Agenda*, Pune International Centre, Pune, 2012.

Dhagamwar Vasudha, *Criminal Justice or Chaos*, Har-Anand Publications, New Delhi, 1997.

Dhaka Rajvir S., *RTI and Good Governance*, Concept Publishing, New Delhi, 2010.

Dhar P. N., *Indira Gandhi, the 'Emergency' and Indian Democracy*, OUP, New Delhi, 2002.

Drewry Gavin and Butcher Tony, *The Civil Service Today*, Basil Blackwell, U.K., 1988, p. 177.

Gajendragadkar Justice P. B., *To the Best of My Memory*, Bharatiya Vidya Bhavan, Bombay, 1982.

Gera Nalini, *Ram Jethmalani: The Authorised Biography*, Viking, New Delhi, 2002.

Gill S. S., *The Dynasty—A Political Biography of the Premier Ruling Family of Modern India*, HarperCollins, India, 1996.

Godbole Madhav, *Unfinished Innings—Recollections and Reflections of a Civil Servant*, Orient Longman, New Delhi, 1996.

Godbole Madhav, *Public Accountability and Transparency: The Imperatives of Good Governance*, Orient Longman, New Delhi, 2003.

Godbole Madhav, Sarma E. A. S., *A Quest for Good Governance*, Advocacy Perspectives, Working Paper Series No. 20, National Centre for Advocacy Studies, Pune, May 2004.

Godbole Madhav, *The Holocaust of Indian Partition—An Inquest*, Rupa & Co., New Delhi, 2006.

Godbole Madhav, *The Judiciary and Governance in India*, Rupa & Co., New Delhi, 2008.

Godbole Madhav, *India's Parliamentary Democracy on Trial*, Rupa & Co., New Delhi, 2011.

Goel S. L., *Right to Information and Good Governance*, Deep and Deep Publications, New Delhi, 2007.

Gopal S. and Iyengar Uma, ed., *The Essential Writings of Jawaharlal Nehru*, vol. II, OUP, New Delhi, 2003.

Government of Andhra Pradesh, *Report of the Task Force on Good Governance*, Hyderabad, 2000.

Government of India, Cabinet Secretariat, Paul H. Appleby, *Public Administration in India: Report of a Survey*, New Delhi, May, 1953.

Government of India, Cabinet Secretariat, Paul H. Appleby, *Re-examination of India's Administrative System with Special Reference to Administration of Government's Industrial and Commercial Enterprises*, New Delhi, 1959.

Government of India, Ministry of Law, *Law Commission of India: Twenty-Fourth Report (The Commissions of Inquiry Act, 1952)*, December 1962.

Government of India, *Report of the Railway Accidents Committee*, 1962.

Government of India, Ministry of Home Affairs, *Report of the Committee on Prevention of Corruption*, 1963.

Government of India, Ministry of Home Affairs, *Interim Report of the Administrative Reforms Commission on Problems of Redress of Citizens' Grievances*, New Delhi, 1966.

Government of India, *Report of the Railways Accidents Inquiry Committee*, 1968.

Government of India, Ministry of Home Affairs, *Shah Commission of Inquiry, Interim Report I*, March 1978.

Government of India, Ministry of Home Affairs, *Shah Commission of Inquiry, Interim Report II*, April 1978.

Government of India, Ministry of Home Affairs, *Shah Commission of Inquiry, Interim and Final Report*, August 1978.

Government of India, Ministry of Home Affairs, *P. Jaganmohan Reddy Commission of Inquiry Regarding Shri Bansi Lal*, 23 June 1978.

Government of India, Ministry of Home Affairs, *Report of the Commission of Inquiry on Maruti Affairs*, 31 May 1979.

Government of India, Ministry of Home Affairs, *The Justice Grover Commission of Inquiry, Second and Final Report*, 1979.

Government of India, Ministry of Home Affairs, *Second Report of the National Police Commission*, 1979.

Government of India, Ministry of Home Affairs, *Third Report of the National Police Commission*, January 1980.

Government of India, Ministry of Home Affairs, *Eighth and Concluding Report of the National Police Commission*, May 1981.

Government Of India, *Summary of Recommendations of the Commission on Centre-State Relations*, New Delhi, 1986.

Government of India, Ministry of Home Affairs, *Report of the Commission on Centre-State Relations*, Part I, 1988.

Government of India, Ministry of Law and Justice, Legislative Department, *Report of the Committee on Electoral Reforms (Goswami Committee)*, May 1990.

Government of India, Ministry of Home Affairs, *Vohra Committee Report*, New Delhi, October 1993.

Government of India, *National Human Development Report, 2001*, New Delhi.

Government of India, *Report of the National Commission to Review the Working of the Constitution*, 2001.

Government of India, Cabinet Secretariat, *Recommendations of the Group of Ministers on Reforming the National Security System*, February 2001.

Government of India, Ministry of Home Affairs, *Report of the Committee on Reforms of Criminal Justice System*, vol. I, March 2003.

Government of India, Planning Commission, *Mid-Term Appraisal of Tenth Five Year Plan 2002-07*, 2005.

Government of India, *Report of the National Commission for Enterprises in the Unorganised Sector*, New Delhi, 2005.

Government of India, Planning Commission, *Towards Faster and More inclusive Growth: An Approach to the 11th Five Year Plan*, New Delhi, June 2006.

Government of India, Second Administrative Reforms Commission, *Right to Information: Master Key to Good Governance*, First Report, June 2006.

Government of India, Second Administrative Reforms Commission, Fourth Report, *Ethics in Governance*, 2007.

Government of India, Second Administrative Reforms Commission, Fifth Report, *Public Order*, New Delhi, 2007.

Government of India, Planning Commission, *Report of the Expert Group on Development and Causes of Discontent, Unrest and Extremism*, vols. I and II, 2008.

Government of India, *Sachar Committee Report on Social, Economic and Educational Status of Muslim Community of India*, New Delhi,2008.

Government of India, Ministry of Personnel and Administrative Reforms, Second Administrative Reforms Commission, *Organisational Structure of Government of India*, Thirteenth Report, New Delhi, April 2009.

Government of India, Department of Personnel and Training, *Annual Report 2010-11*.

Government of Maharashtra, Report of the Lentin Commission of Inquiry, Bombay, 1987.

Government of Maharashtra, *Report of the Srikrishna Commission Appointed for Inquiry into the Riots at Mumbai during December 1992 and January 1993*, August 1998.

Government of Maharashtra, *Memorandum of Action To Be Taken by Government on the Report of the Commission of Inquiry Appointed for Making Enquiries into the Incidents of Communal Riots Which Occurred in the Police Commissionerate of Mumbai During December 1992 and January 1993 and Serial Bomb Blasts Which Occurred on 12th March 1993*, 1998.

Government of Maharashtra, *Report of the Energy Review Committee*, Part I, April 10, 2001.

Granville Austin, *Working a Democratic Constitution: The Indian Experience*, OUP, New Delhi, 1999.

Hegde K. S., *Crisis in Indian Judiciary*, Sindhu Publications, Bombay, 1973.

Hidayatullah M., *A Judge's Miscellany*, Second Series, N. M. Tripathi, Bombay, 1979.

Hidayatullah M., *Right to Property and the Indian Constitution*, Arnold Heinemann, Calcutta, 1983.

India Today, 6 April 2009, quoted in Government of India, Ministry of Personnel and Administrative Reforms, Second Administrative Reforms Commission, *Organisational Structure of Government of India*, Thirteenth Report, New Delhi, April 2009.

Indian Law Institute, *Annual Survey of Indian Law*, 1994, reprint.

Jain J. K., The Judiciary: Courts in Crisis, in Jain C. K., ed., *Constitution of India— In Precept and Practice*, CBS Publishers and Distributors, New Delhi, 1992.

Jawaharlal Nehru Memorial Fund, *Selected Works of Jawaharlal Nehru*, second series, vol. 15, New Delhi, 1993.

Jawaharlal Nehru Memorial Fund, *Selected Works of Jawaharlal Nehru*, vol. 16, New Delhi, 1994.

Jawaharlal Nehru Memorial Fund, *Selected Works of Jawaharlal Nehru*, second series, vol. 19, New Delhi, 1996, pp. 453-466.

Jawaharlal Nehru Memorial Fund, *Selected Works of Jawaharlal Nehru*, vol. 23, New Delhi, 1998.

Jawaharlal Nehru Memorial Fund, *Selected Works of Jawaharlal Nehru*, Second Series, vol. 29, New Delhi, 2001.

Jawaharlal Nehru Memorial Fund, *Selected Works of Jawaharlal Nehru*, vol. 30, New Delhi, 2002.

Jawaharlal Nehru Memorial Fund, *Selected Works of Jawaharlal Nehru*, second series, vol. 31, New Delhi, 2002.

Jawaharlal Nehru Memorial Fund, *Selected Works of Jawaharlal Nehru*, second series, vol. 32, New Delhi, 2003.

Jayakar Pupul, *Indira Gandhi—A Biography*, Vikings, New Delhi, 1988.

Kamath M. V., *Nani A Palkhivala—A Life*, Hay House, India, 2007.

Kapoor Suneera, ed., Thoughts and Vision of Jawaharlal Nehru, Anamika Publishers and Distributors, New Delhi, 2005.

Kashyap Subhash C., *The Political System and Institution Building Under Jawaharlal Nehru*, National Publishing House, New Delhi, 1990.

Kashyap Subhash C., *Reforming the Constitution*, UBS Publishers Distributors Limited, New Delhi, 1992.

Kashyap Subhash C., *Delinking Religion and Politics*, Vimot Publishers, New Delhi, 1993.

Kashyap Subhash C., *History of the Parliament of India*, vol. III, Shipra Publications, Delhi, 1996.

Kashyap Subhash C., *History of the Parliament of India*, vol. IV, Shipra Publications, Delhi, 1997.

Kashyap Subhash C., ed., *100 Best Parliamentary Speeches 1947-1997*, HarperCollins Publishers India, New Delhi, 1998.

Kashyap Subhash C., *History of the Parliament of India*, vol. V, Shipra Publications, Delhi, 1998.

Kashyap Subhash C., *Blueprint of Political Reforms*, Shipra Publications, Delhi, 2003.

Kettl Donald F., *Implementation of the Government Performance and Results Act of 1993*, Congressional Testimony, The Brookings Institution, Washington D.C.

Khanna H. R., *Neither Roses Nor Thorns*, Eastern Book Company, Lucknow, 1986.

Klitgaard Robert, Cleaning up and invigorating the civil service, *Public Administration and Development*, vol. 17, John Wiley & Sons, USA, 1997.

Kripalani J. B., *My Times: An Autobiography*, Rupa & Co., New Delhi, 2004.

Lall B. R., *Free the CBI—Power Games in Bhopal and Other Cases*, Manas Publications, New Delhi, 2011.

Laxminath A., *Basic Structure and Constitutional Amendments—Limitations and Justiciability*, Deep & Deep Publications, New Delhi, 2002.

Lewis Norman and Singh S. S., ed., *Ombudsmen: India and the World Community*, Indian Institute of Public Administration and British Council Division of the British High Commission, New Delhi, 1995.

Limaye Madhu, *Cabinet Government in India*, Radiant Publishers, Delhi, 1989.

Limaye Madhu, *Janata Party Experiment: An Insider's Account of Opposition Politics 1977-1980*, vol. II, B.R. Publishing Corporation, Delhi, 1994.

Lok Sabha Secretariat, *Constituent Assembly Debates*, volume I, New Delhi, 1985.

Lok Sabha Secretariat, *Report of the Joint Committee to Enquire Into Bofors Contract*, Eighth Lok Sabha, April 1988.

Lok Sabha Secretariat, *Report of Joint Committee to Enquire into Irregularities in Securities and Banking Transactions*, vol. I, New Delhi, December 1993.

Lok Sabha Secretariat, Extracts From The Fourth Report Of The Committee Of Privileges, Lok Sabha, Regarding Codification of Parliamentary Privileges, *Privileges Digest*, vol. XL, December 1995.

Lok Sabha secretariat, *The Journal of Parliamentary Information*, vol. XLII, No. 2, June 1996.

Lok Sabha Secretariat, *Report of the Committee to Inquire into the Complaint by Some Members Regarding Alleged Offer of Money to Them in Connection with Voting on the Motion of Confidence (Fourteenth Lok Sabha)*, New Delhi, December 2008.

Lok Sabha Secretariat, *The Constitution (One Hundred and Eighth Amendment) Bill, 2008*.

Malhotra Inder, *India: Trapped in Uncertainty*, UBS Publishers, New Delhi, 1991.

Malik P. L., *The Commissions of Inquiry Act, 1952*, Eastern Book Company, Lucknow, 1995.

Mahajan Justice Mehr Chand, *Looking Back*, Asia Publishing House, Bombay, 1963.

Mimi Swartz with Sharon Watkins, *Power Failure—The Inside Story of the Collapse of Enron*, Doubleday, NY, 2003.

Mishra Sudhansu Sekher, Das S. K., Sahoo Rajan Kumar, ed., *Right to Information (RTI) and Rural Development in India*, New Century Publications, New Delhi, 2009.

Mukherjee Rudrangshu, ed., *Great Speeches of Modern India*, Random House, New Delhi, 2007.

Mullik B. N., *My Years With Nehru 1948-1964*, Allied Publishers, New Delhi, 1972.

Mullik B. N., *My Years With Nehru—The Chinese Betrayal*, Allied Publishers, New Delhi, 1971.

Mullik B. N., *My Years With Nehru—Kashmir*, Allied Publishers, New Delhi, 1971.

Murthy R. C., *The Fall of Angels*, HarperCollins, India, New Delhi, 1995.

Narasimha Rao P. V., *Ayodhya 6 December 1992*, Penguin India, *2006*.

Nehru B. K., *Nice Guys Finish Second*, Viking, New Delhi, 1997.

Nicholas Mansergh (editor-in-chief), The Transfer of Power 1942-7 (TOP), Her Majesty's Stationary Office, London, Vol. IX.

Noorani A. G., *Ministers' Misconduct*, Vikas Publishing House, Delhi, 1973.

Noorani A. G., *Constitutional Questions in India—The President, Parliament and the States*, OUP, New Delhi, 2000.

Palhivala N. A., *Our Constitution: Defaced and Defiled*, Macmillan, Delhi, 1974.

Palkhivala N. A., *We, The Nation: The Lost Decade*, UBS Publishers, New Delhi, 1994.

Parliament of India, Rajya Sabha, Department-Related Parliamentary Standing Committee of the Ministry of Home Affairs, *12th Report on the Lokpal Bill, 1998*, February 1999.

Parliament of India, Rajya Sabha, *85th Report of Department-Related Parliamentary Committee on Home Affairs on Law's Delays: Arrears in Courts*, December 2001.

Prayas, *A Good Beginning but Challenges Galore—A Survey Based Study of Resources, Transparency, and Public Participation in Electricity Regulatory Commissions in India*, Prayas Energy Group, Pune, 2003.

Provisional Parliament Debates, *The Constitution (First Amendment) Bill, 1951*, 16-18 May 1951, cols. 8814-9089.

Rajya Sabha Secretariat, *Lokpal in India*, New Delhi, 1996.

Rowat Donald C., ed., *The Ombudsman: Citizen's Defender*, George Allen & Unwin, London, 1965.

SarDesai D. R. and Anand Mohan, ed., *The Legacy of Nehru: A Centennial Assessment*, Promilla & Co. Publishers, New Delhi, 1992.

Seervai H. M., *The Emergency, Future Safeguards and the Habeas Corpus Case: A Criticism*, N. M. Tripathi Private Limited, Bombay, 1978.

Shah Justice J. C., *The Rule of Law and the Indian Constitution*, N. M. Tripathi, Bombay, 1972.

Sharma Mool Chand, *Justice P. N. Bhagwati: Court, Constitution and Human Rights*, Universal Book Traders, Delhi, 1995.

Shourie Arun, *Institutions in the Janata Phase*, Popular Prakashan, Bombay, 1980.

Shourie Arun, *Mrs. Gandhi's Second Term*, Vikas Publishing House, New Delhi, 1983.

Shourie Arun, *Religion in Politics*, Roli Books International, New Delhi, 1987.

Shourie Arun, *Indian Controversies—Essays on Religion in Politics*, ASA Publications, New Delhi, 1993.

Shourie Arun, *Governance and the Sclerosis That Has Set In*, Rupa & Co., New Delhi, 2004.

Subba Rao K., *Social Justice and Law*, Institute of Constitutional and Parliamentary Studies, New Delhi, 1974.

Subba Rao K. et al, *Judiciary and Social Change*, Christian Literature Society, Ecumenical Christian Centre, Bengaluru, 1973.

Subramanian T. S. R., *Journeys Through Babudom and Netaland—Governance in India*, Rupa & Co., New Delhi, 2004.

Subramanian Swami, *2G Spectrum Scam*, Har-Anand Publications, New Delhi, 2011.

Swartz Mimi with Watkins Sharon, *Power Failure—The Inside Story of the Collapse of Enron*, Doubleday, NY, 2003.

Tandon B. N., *PMO Diary I: Prelude to the Emergency*, Konark Publishers, New Delhi, 2003.

Tandon B. N., *PMO Diary II, The Emergency*, Konark Publishers, New Delhi, 2006.

Tiwari Ramesh Kumar, *Human Rights—Bonded Labour in India*, Foundation Books, Delhi, 2011.

Transparency International, *Global Corruption Report 2003*, Profile Books Limited, London, 2003.

UNDP, *Tackling Corruption, Transforming Laws: Accelerating Human Development in Asia and the Pacific*, Macmillan, Delhi, 2008.

Vibhute K. I., ed., *Criminal Justice*, Eastern Book Company, Lucknow, 2004.

Visvanathan Shiv and Sethi Harsh, ed., *Foul Play—Chronicles of Corruption 1947-97*, Banyan Books, New Delhi, 1998.

Vivekanandan B., ed., *Echoes in Parliament—Madhu Dandavate's Speeches in Parliament (1971-1990)*, Allied Publishers, New Delhi, 1995.

World Bank, *World Development Report 2002: Building Institutions for Markets*, New York: OUP.

Zail Singh, *Memoirs of Zail Singh, The Seventh President of India*, Har-Anand Publications Private Limited, New Delhi, 1997.

Articles

Alam Srinivas, Telescams cheaper by the dozen, *gfiles*, 10 January 2012.

Anand S., The Nandy Bully, *Outlook*, 1 February 2013.

Antony M. J., Mushrooming Illegalities, *Business Standard*, 6 April 2005.

Apartheid, by any other name, *The Lawyers Collective*, April 2005.

Arundhati Roy, Corporate money has no nationality. They just run India, *Outlook*, 22 April 2013.

Bagchi Sanjoy, The China Syndrome, *Dialogue Quarterly*, New Delhi, January-March 2011.

Bajaj J. K, Religious Demography of the North-Eastern States of India: Trends to Look for in the Census 2011, *Dialogue Quarterly*, vo. 12, No.3, January-March 2011.

Baruah T. L., What Ails Public Service Commissions, editorial, *The Assam Tribune*, Guwahati, 14 January 2009.

Bhandare Murlidhar C., MP's immunity: Amend the statute, *TOI*, 30 April 1998.

Chakravarti Sauvik, NPM: The hollow state, *The Economic Times*, 13 August 1997.

Chaudhuri Kalyan and Krishnaswamy Chetan, Pressing for Free Trade—Major Urges India to accelerate Reforms, *Frontline*, 7 February 1997.

Dalrymple William, What Happened to India's Economic Miracle?, *The New Statesman*, July 2013.

Deshmukh Vikas, *Towards Better Corporate Governance—Completing the Unfinished Agenda*, Pune International Centre, Pune, 2012.

Dharmadhikari, Justice C. S., Criminal Justice System and Tribes in India, *AIR (Jour)* 1988.

Don't delay further, editorial, *The Economic Times*, 28 February 2000.

Editorial, Blind Justice: The Law Is Not A Family Business, *Economic Times*, 30 July 2003.

Editorial, Taslima as litmus test, *IE*, 30 November 2007.

Gadgil Madhav, Opinion, The Goa Dossier: Ghats of Perdition—Lopsided development can kill a fragile mountain ecosystem, *Outlook*, 10 June 2013.

Godbole Madhav, The Sham War on Corruption, The Hindu, 30 September 1997, in Godbole Madhav, *The Changing Times, A Commentary on Current Affairs*, Orient Longman, New Delhi, 2000.

Godbole Madhav, Serving the Master, Indian Express, 25 August 1995, in Madhav Godbole, *The Changing Times: A Commentary on Current Affairs*, New Delhi, Orient Longman, 2000.

Godbole Madhav, Report of Constitution Review Commission—Some Reflections, *Economic and Political Weekly*, 28 September 2002.

Godbole Madhav, *Electricity Regulatory Commissions in India: The Jury Is Still Out*, The Tenth Dr. D. T. Lakdawala Memorial Lecture, Dr. D. T. Lakdawala Memorial Trust, Gujarat Institute of Development Research, Ahmedabad, May 2002.

Godbole Madhav, Criminal Justice System in India—Bane of Human Rights, in K. I. Vibhute, ed., *Criminal Justice*, Eastern Book Company, Lucknow, 2004.

Godbole Madhav, Foreward for Kumar B. B. ed., *Illegal Migration from Bangladesh*, Astha Bharati, Delhi and Concept Publishing Company, New Delhi, 2006.

Godbole Madhav, Sarma E. A. S., Aftershocks of Dabhol Power Project, *Economic and Political Weekly*, 26 August 2006.

Godbole Madhav, Ayodhya and India's Mahabharat: Constitutional Issues and Proprieties, *Economic and Political Weekly*, 27 May 2006.

Godbole Madhav, Judicial Activism and Good Governance in India, *South Asian Journal*, October-December 2010, Lahore, Pakistan.

Godbole Madhav, Ignominy of Being a Civil Servant, *Dialogue Quarterly*, vol. 13, No. 2, New Delhi, October-December 2011.

Godbole Madhav, Parliamentary Democracy—More Negatives than Positives, *Dialogue Quarterly*, July-September 2012.

Gupta Shubhra, Power Games—Why the banned film *Kissa Kursi Ka* still speaks to us in these craven times, *eye*, *Indian Express*, 28 April-4 May 2013.

Jacques Martin, Why China Does Not See Itself As A Model, *The Globalist*, 6 June 2013.

Jawaharlal Nehru Papers, Nehru Memorial Museum and Library, New Delhi, quoted in *Muslim India*, August 2008.

Jha Anumeha, Changing the Mindset of the Bureaucracy—Facilitating Easier access to Information, *Common Cause*, vol. xxx, No.1, January-March 2011.

Jha Prem Shankar, The Public War chest, *Outlook*, 14 June 2004.

Jodhka Surinder S., Perceptions and Receptions: Sachar Committee and the Secular Left, *EPW*, 21 July 2007.

Jonathan Caselly, Public Sector Reform and Corruption: CARD Facade in Andhra Pradesh, *Economic and Political Weekly*, 13 March 2004.

Joshi Namrata, The Broken Image, *Outlook*, 11 February 2013.

Kalyan Chaudhuri and Chetan Krishnaswamy, Pressing for freer trade—Major urges India to accelerate reforms, *Frontline*, 7 February 1997.

Khanna, Justice H. R., Supreme Court Judgment on Article 356, *AIR (Jour)* 1994.

Krishnamurthy T. S., Don't break the code, *IE*, 23 February 2012.

Lakshaminath A., The Power of the Supreme Court to Transfer Criminal Cases—A Critical Appraisal of A. R. Antulay v. R. S. Nayak, *AIR (Jour)*, 1991.

Lall B. R., The King Can Do No Wrong, *gfiles*, vol. 5, Issue 10, January 2012.

Lele Uma, Maggie Klousia-Marquis and Sambuddha Goswami, Good Governance for Food, Water and Energy Security, SciVersa, ScienceDirect, Stockholm, Sweden, *www.sciencedirect.com*,2013.

Manohar Justice Sujata, Human Rights and the Judiciary, *Dialogue Quarterly*, vol. 14, No. 4, April-June 2013.

Markandey Katju, India, in transition and corrupt, *The Indian Express*, 8 August 2012.

Mukhim Patricia, Time to pay income tax, *Dialogue Quarterly*, vol. 14, No. 3, January-March 2013.

Mustafa Seema, Off Limits, Return of the ghost of Bofors, *The Sunday Guardian*, 9 January 2011.

Nariman Fali S., Fifty Years of the Supreme Court: A Balance Sheet of Performance, *The Indian Advocate*, vol. 29, 1999-2000.

Nasrin Taslima, India has no courage, *Outlook*, 15 July 2013.

Noorani A. G., Ninth Schedule and the Supreme Court, *Economic and Political Weekly*, 3 March 2007.

Noorani A. G., "Objection, Milord", *Outlook*, 8 September 2008,

Oil & Natural Gas, vol. 18, No. 15, 10 November 2011, New Delhi.

Pai Panandiker D. H., Can reforms wait any longer? *Hindustan Times*, 6 January 1997.

Public Affairs Centre, *Public Eye*, Bengaluru, January-March 2001.

Post SC judgment in JMM case: Is bribery legal now? Perspective, *ET*, 28 April 1998.

Rao T. N. R., A Wellhead of Blunders, *Outlook*, 15 July 2013.

Ruma Pal, Primary Education and the Law, *IIC Quarterly*, August 2006.

Sarma E. A. S., *Economic Development and Energy Planning: The Myths and the Reality*, Girish Sant Memorial Annual Lecture, 2013, Prayas, Pune, 2013.

Sarma E. A. S., The KG basin price hike socialises costs and privatises profits, *Business Standard*, New Delhi, 3 June 2013.

Sarma E. A. S., Natural Gas Price Hike—Subsidising Producers' Profits?, *EPW*, 13 July 2013.

Setalvad Atul M., India's Higher Judiciary: Some Significant Failures, in Venkat Iyer, ed., *Constitutional Perspectives—Essays in Honour and Memory of H.M. Seervai*, Universal Law Publishing Company, Delhi, 2001.

Sethi Surya P., Making a mockery of domestic gas pricing, *The Hindu*, 18 January 2013.

Shahina K. K., The underfed and the unscrupulous, "agenda, Infochange News & Features, Centre for Communication and Development studies, Pune, Issue 24, 2012.

Shukla Srawan, Criminal Intimidation, *Tehelka*, 6 September 2008.

Singh Baldev, Ninth Schedule to Constitution of India: A Study, *Journal of Indian Law Institute*, Vol. 37, 1995.

Singh Shiv Raj, Jawaharlal Nehru and Public Administration, in Kapoor Suneera, ed., *Thoughts and Vision of Jawaharlal Nehru*, Anamika Publishers and Distributors, New Delhi, 2005.

Slums hold key to Delhi throne, *gfiles*, July 2013.

Sorabjee Soli J., Freedom of Expression and the Indian Constitution, in Venkat Iyer, ed. *Constitutional Perspectives—Essays in Honour and Memory of H. M. Seervai*, Universal Law Publishing Company, Delhi, 2001.

Sorabjee Soli J., With Utmost Respect, Mr. Speaker, *IE*, 2 May 2007.

Sorabjee Soli J., An Overdue Cleansing Has Begun, *IE*, 12 July 2013.

Somnath Chatterjee, 'Activism of any institution has to be first directed to the due discharge of its own duties', excerpt from the Dr. Kailash Nath Katju Memorial Lecture on Separation of Powers under the Constitution and Judicial Activism, New Delhi, 26 April 2007, *Indian Express*, 28 April 2007.

Sorabjee Soli J., Indian Democracy: Reality or Myth? We Have Pledges to Fulfil, First V. M. Tarkunde Memorial Lecture, *Radical Humanist*, New Delhi, 2006.

Srinivas Alam, Telescams cheaper by the dozen, *gfiles*, vol. 5, issue 10, January 2012.

Subrahmanyam K., Politicised Civil Services, *Common Cause*, vol. XXI No.1.

Subrahmanyam K., Blocked channels, *ET*, 27 December 1994.

Subramaniam Duella Chitra, Opinion, *Outlook*, 7 May 2012.
Thatcher Margaret, The political economy of freedom, speech at the Rajiv Gandhi jubilee memorial lecture on 21 August 1995, , *ET*, 26 August 1995.
Tulzapurkar Justice, V. D. Uniform Civil Code, *AIR (Jour)*, 1987.
Vineet Narain & Others vs. Union of India & Another, 1997 (7) *SCALE*.
Vineeta Rai, Administration & Governance—2nd A.R.C. Perspective, *Dialogue Quarterly*, vol. 13, No.2, New Delhi, October-December 2011.
Virendra Kapoor, No Holds Barred, *The Sunday Guardian*, 28 April 2013.

Newspapers and Periodicals

Asian Age
Assam Tribune
Business Standard
Covert
Dialogue Quarterly
Data India
Economic and Political Weekly
Economic Times
Financial Express
Frontline
gfiles
Hindustan Times
Indian Advocate
Indian Express
Loksatta
Maharashtra Times
Muslim India
OtherSide
Outlook
Newsweek
Radical Humanist
Sakal
Statesman
Sunday
Sunday Guardian
Tehelka
Times of India
The Radical Humanist